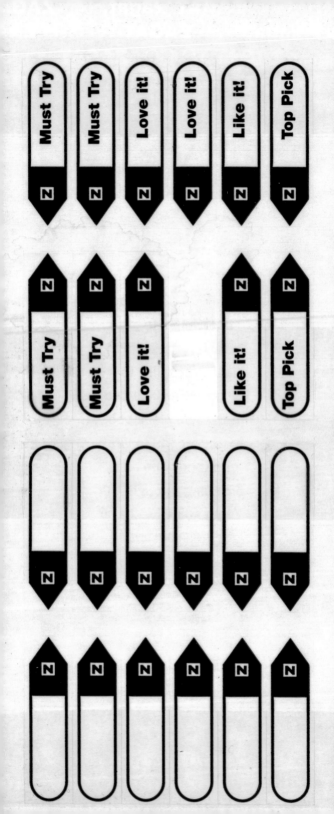

ZAGAT®

London
Restaurants
2009

LOCAL EDITORS AND COORDINATORS
Sholto Douglas-Home and Susan Kessler
STAFF EDITOR
Troy Segal

Published and distributed by
Zagat Survey, LLC
4 Columbus Circle
New York, NY 10019
T: 212.977.6000
E: london@zagat.com
www.zagat.com

ACKNOWLEDGMENTS

We thank Deborah Bennett, Karen Bonham, Claire Coleman, Ricki Conway, Alex, Louis and Tallula Douglas-Home, Rosanne Johnston, Larry Kessler, Le Cordon Bleu (London), Pamela and Michael Lester, Leuka 2000, Margaret Levin, Anne Semmes, Alexandra Spezzotti, Peter Vogl, Susan Weingarten and Jeffrey Weingarten, as well as the following members of our staff: Caitlin Eichelberger (assistant editor), Amy Cao (editorial assistant), Brian Albert, Sean Beachell, Maryanne Bertollo, Sandy Cheng, Reni Chin, Larry Cohn, Deirdre Donovan, Alison Flick, Jeff Freier, Justin Hartung, Roy Jacob, Natalie Lebert, Mike Liao, Dave Makulec, Andre Pilette, Kimberly Rosado, Becky Ruthenburg, Donna Marino Wilkins, Liz Borod Wright, Sharon Yates, Anna Zappia and Kyle Zolner.

Contents

Ratings & Symbols

Zagat Top Spot	Name	Symbols		Cuisine	Zagat Ratings			
					FOOD	DECOR	SERVICE	COST

Area, Address & Contact*

Ⓩ **Tim & Nina's** ◑ *British* ▽ 23 | 5 | 9 | £9

Covent Garden | Exeter St., WC2 (Covent Garden) | 020-7123 4567 | www.zagat.com

Review, surveyor comments in quotes

Open seven days a week, 24 hours a day (some say that's "168 hours too many"), this "chaotic" Covent Garden dive serving "cheap, no-nonsense" fish 'n' chips is "ideal" for a "quick grease fix"; no one's impressed by the "tired, tatty decor" or "patchy service", but judging from its "perpetual queues", the "no-frills" food and prices are "spot-on."

Ratings

Food, Decor and **Service** are rated on the Zagat 0 to 30 scale.

0	–	9	poor to fair
10	–	15	fair to good
16	–	19	good to very good
20	–	25	very good to excellent
26	–	30	extraordinary to perfection
	▽		low response	less reliable

Cost

Reflects our surveyors' average estimate of the price of a dinner with one drink and service and is a benchmark only. Lunch is usually 25% less. For **newcomers** or survey **write-ins** listed without ratings, the price range is indicated as follows:

I	£20 and below
M	£21 to £35
E	£36 to £50
VE	£51 or more

Symbols

Ⓩ	Zagat Top Spot (highest ratings, popularity and importance)
◑	serves after 11 PM
Ⓢ	closed on Sunday
Ⓜ	closed on Monday
⊄	no credit cards accepted

Maps

Index maps show restaurants with the highest Food ratings (excluding private clubs) in those areas.

---

* From outside the U.K., dial international code (e.g. 011 from the U.S.) +44, then omit first zero of the listed number.

About This Survey

Here are the results of our **2009 London Restaurants Survey,** covering 1,173 eateries in the city as well as favourites outside the M25. Like all of our guides, this one is based on the collective opinions of thousands of local consumers who have been there before you. Ratings have been updated throughout. We have retained a prior year's review for some places that have had no significant factual or ratings changes.

WHO PARTICIPATED: Input from 5,309 frequent diners forms the basis for the ratings and reviews in this guide (their comments are shown in quotation marks within the reviews). Of these surveyors, 38% are women, 62% men; the breakdown by age is 9% in their 20s; 27%, 30s; 22%, 40s; 20%, 50s; and 22%, 60s or above. Collectively they bring roughly 696,000 annual meals worth of experience to this Survey. We sincerely thank each of these participants – this book is really "theirs."

HELPFUL LISTS: Whether you're looking for a celebratory meal, a hot scene or a bargain bite, our top lists and indexes can help you find exactly the right place. See Most Popular (page 7), Key Newcomers (page 9), Top Ratings (pages 10–16), Best Buys (page 17) and Set-Price Bargains (page 18). We've also provided 35 handy indexes.

OUR EDITORS: Special thanks go to our local editors and coordinators: Susan Kessler, cookbook author and consultant for numerous lifestyle publications in the U.K. and U.S., and Sholto Douglas-Home, a London restaurant critic for the past two decades.

ABOUT ZAGAT: This marks our 29th year reporting on the shared experiences of consumers like you. What started in 1979 as a hobby involving 200 of our friends has come a long way. Today we have over 325,000 surveyors and now cover airlines, bars, clubs, dining, entertaining, golf, hotels, lounges, movies, music, resorts, shopping, spas, theatre and tourist attractions worldwide.

VOTE AND COMMENT: We invite you to join any of our upcoming surveys at **ZAGAT.com.** There you can rate and review establishments year-round without charge. In fact, in exchange for participating you will receive a free copy of the resulting guide when published.

AVAILABILITY: Zagat guides are available in all major bookshops as well as on **ZAGAT.com, ZAGAT.mobi** (for web-enabled mobile phones) and **ZAGAT TO GO** (for smartphones). All of these products allow you to reserve at thousands of places with just one click.

FEEDBACK: There is always room for improvement, thus we invite your comments and suggestions about any aspect of our performance. Just contact us at **london@zagat.com.**

New York, NY
10 September, 2008

Nina and Tim Zagat

What's New

Whatever economic storm clouds are on the horizon, Londoners show no signs of ending their love affair with restaurants. Most surveyors (82%) report eating out as much as or even more than they did two years ago, taking 77% of those meals for leisure – vs. business – purposes. In return, restaurateurs are responding with a robust array of offerings.

ASKING FOR SECONDS: One sign of the rosy scene is the flood of chef-owners opening second venues fast on the heels of their original venture; in fact, South Bank's **Bincho Yakitori** had been in business only 10 months before its Soho sibling was born. Other fledglings spreading their wings include the Cheyne Walk Brasserie crew with **Waterloo Brasserie,** Acorn House with **Water House** and Salt Yard with **Dehesa.** These informal eateries fit the temper of the times, since over two-thirds of surveyors say the sort of place they typically patronise is a bistro/brasserie (36%) or other casual venue (33%).

HUMMING HOTELS: If money were no object, however, 43% would prefer an haute cuisine establishment – a taste that might be satisfied at one of the new hotel-based destinations around town. Whilst the biggest news is the arrival of **Alain Ducasse at The Dorchester,** the Grosvenor House's spacious **BORD'EAUX** also aims at Francophiles, and The Lanesborough goes Italian with **Apsleys.** Others opt for Modern European: The Langham hotel has spared little expense creating **The Landau,** and the Westbury's £20 million refurb includes the airy, art deco-themed **Artisan.**

BRIGHT LIGHTS, BIG CITY: The City boasts its fair share of masters of the universe, so it's no surprise that many of the year's notable debuts have been in, or close by, the financial centre: the bohemian **Brickhouse** in Brick Lane, the earthy **Hix Oyster & Chop House** by Smithfield Market, the sumptuous **Kenza** near Liverpool Street and the sophisticated **Northbank** near Millennium Bridge.

CHAIN GANGS: Slowly but surely, the stigma of chain eateries is fading. Eclectic newcomers like **Napket,** purveyor of self-styled snob food (think Parma ham finger focaccia), and **Daylesford Cafe** are attracting a well-heeled clientele to their multiple locations. Their secret? High-quality, fashionable foodstuffs – Daylesford's are organic – and trendy environs – e.g. the communal tables with iPod stations at Napket.

PAYING FOR QUALITY: Although the average cost of a meal has risen 3.7% to £40.55 (about $80) in the last year – causing 76% of surveyors to report spending more than in 2006 – few penny-pinch when it comes to conscientious eating. Some 73% are willing to shell out extra for sustainably raised or procured products – as they do at **Whole Foods Market,** the U.S. grocer whose Kensington premises have been packed with punters partaking of its natural and organic comestibles since it opened.

London
10 September, 2008

Sholto Douglas-Home

subscribe to ZAGAT.com

Most Popular

These places are plotted on the map at the back of the book.

1. Wagamama | *Japanese*
2. Ivy, The | *British/European*
3. J. Sheekey | *Seafood*
4. Nobu London | *Japanese*
5. Wolseley, The | *European*
6. Gordon Ramsay/68 Royal | *French*
7. Hakkasan | *Chinese*
8. Gordon Ramsay/Claridge's | *European*
9. Le Gavroche | *French*
10. Square, The | *French*
11. Zuma | *Japanese*
12. Rules | *British/Chophouse*
13. Yauatcha* | *Chinese*
14. Zafferano | *Italian*
15. Pétrus | *French*
16. L'Atelier Joël Robuchon | *French*
17. Le Caprice | *British/European*
18. Gaucho Grill | *Argent./Chop.*
19. Locanda Locatelli | *Italian*
20. River Café | *Italian*
21. Nobu Berkeley St | *Japanese*
22. Pizza Express | *Pizza*
23. Busaba Eathai | *Thai*
24. Chez Bruce* | *British*
25. maze | *French*
26. Amaya | *Indian*
27. Scott's* | *Seafood*
28. Tamarind | *Indian*
29. Fat Duck | *European*
30. Capital Rest. | *French*
31. Asia de Cuba | *Asian/Cuban*
32. Wilton's | *British/Seafood*
33. St. John | *British*
34. Ledbury, The | *French*
35. Alain Ducasse | *French*
36. Arbutus | *European*
37. Cinnamon Club | *Indian*
38. Royal China* | *Chinese*
39. Boxwood Café | *British*
40. Pied à Terre* | *French*

It's obvious that many of the above restaurants are among the London area's most expensive, but if popularity were calibrated to price, we suspect that a number of other restaurants would join their ranks. Thus, we have added a list of 80 Best Buys on page 17.

* Indicates a tie with restaurant above

KEY NEWCOMERS

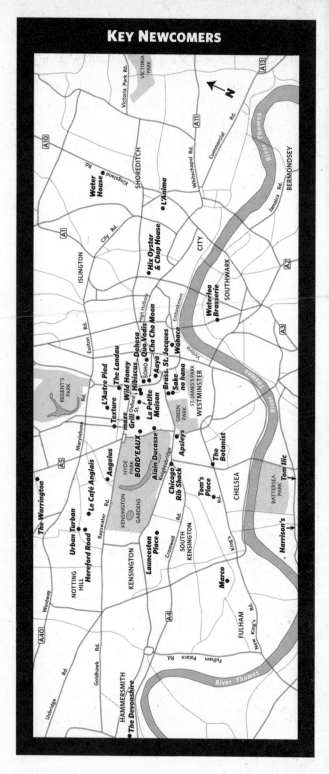

subscribe to ZAGAT.com

Key Newcomers

Our editors' take on the year's top arrivals. See page 233 for a full list.

Aaya | *Japanese*	La Petite Maison | *Mediterranean*
Alain Ducasse | *French*	Launceston Place | *British*
Angelus | *French*	L'Autre Pied | *European*
Apsleys | *Italian*	Le Café Anglais | *French*
BORD'EAUX | *French*	Marco | *British/French*
Botanist, The | *European*	maze Grill | *Chophouse*
Brasserie St. Jacques | *French*	Quo Vadis | *British*
Cha Cha Moon | *Chinese*	Sake no hana | *Japanese*
Chicago Rib Shack | *BBQ*	Texture | *European*
Dehesa | *Italian/Spanish*	Tom Ilic | *European*
Devonshire, The | *British*	Tom's Place | *British/Seafood*
Harrison's | *Eclectic*	Urban Turban | *Indian*
Hereford Road | *British*	Wahaca | *Mexican*
Hibiscus | *French*	Warrington, The | *British*
Hix Oyster/Chop House | *British*	Water House | *European*
Landau, The | *European*	Waterloo Brasserie | *French*
L'Anima | *Italian*	Wild Honey | *British*

The future will see a stream of intriguing newcomers in the capital. At publication time, big-name chefs bringing their talents to London include **Hélène Darroze**'s much-heralded arrival at The Connaught, and Lyon-based toque Jean-Christophe Ansanay-Alex taking over the former Lundum's space in South Ken with **Ambassade de L'Ile.** As ever, the Gordon Ramsay empire continues to make news, with protégée chef Angela Hartnett resurfacing at **Murano** in Zen Central's old digs; Ms. Hartnett is also scheduled to take the helm of a new Ramsay project near Regent's Park, **York & Albany,** which will include a gastro-pub, deli, events space and bedrooms. Meanwhile, Marcus Wareing – who was ending his association with the Ramsay fold at press time – will unveil his new venture in the former Pétrus space.

The pace of openings continues with the Edwardian-themed **Bob Bob Ricard** in Soho; the debut of **Devonshire Terrace,** an NYC-type brasserie for City types to chomp on; and an offshoot of an actual Manhattan eatery, **Megu,** arriving in Mayfair. A former head chef at Moro will go solo in Soho with **Boca de Lupo**; a high-end Chinese, **Min Jiang,** is set to take over the 10th floor of the Royal Garden Hotel with a terrific view across Hyde Park; and fashion store maven Joseph Ettedgui is one of the new owners planning to revive the late, great **Mirabelle** in Mayfair.

Top Food Ratings

Excludes places with low votes.

29 Gordon Ramsay/68 Royal | *French*
Chez Bruce | *British*

28 La Trompette | *Euro./French*
River Café | *Italian*
Ledbury, The | *French*
Pétrus | *French*
Gravetye Manor | *British*
New Tayyabs* | *Pakistani*

27 Le Manoir/Quat' | *French*
Jin Kichi | *Japanese*
Square, The | *French*
Fat Duck | *European*
Le Gavroche | *French*
St. John | *British*
L'Atelier Joël Robuchon | *French*
Pied à Terre | *French*
Rasoi Vineet Bhatia | *Indian*
Waterside Inn | *French*
Nobu London | *Japanese*
Hunan | *Chinese*

Zuma | *Japanese*

26 Assaggi | *Italian*
Alain Ducasse | *French*
Oslo Court | *French*
Club Gascon | *French*
J. Sheekey | *Seafood*
Capital Rest. | *French*
Defune* | *Japanese*
Roussillon | *French*
Greenhouse, The | *French*
Le Vacherin | *French*
Nobu Berkeley St | *Japanese*
Morgan M | *French*
Ubon* | *Japanese*
Umu | *Japanese*
Amaya | *Indian*
Sweetings | *British/Seafood*
Michael Moore | *Eclectic*
Gordon Ramsay/Claridge's | *European*
Richard Corrigan | *British/Irish*

BY CUISINE

AMERICAN

21 Sophie's Steak
Lucky 7
19 Christopher's
18 Automat
Bodeans

ASIAN

24 Park, The
22 e&o
Bam-Bou
Eight Over Eight
21 Asia de Cuba

BRITISH (MODERN)

29 Chez Bruce
28 Gravetye Manor
27 St. John
26 Richard Corrigan
Clarke's

BRITISH (TRAD.)

26 Sweetings
25 Goring Dining Rm.
Wilton's
24 Bentley's
Rhodes 24

CHINESE

27 Hunan
26 Yauatcha
25 Hakkasan
24 Royal China Club
Mandarin Kitchen

CHOPHOUSES

24 Hawksmoor
23 Rules
22 Rib Room
Gaucho Grill
Butlers Wharf

ECLECTIC

26 Michael Moore
25 Mosimann's (club)
23 Books for Cooks
22 Providores, The
21 Bacchus

EUROPEAN (MODERN)

28 La Trompette
27 Fat Duck
26 Gordon Ramsay/Claridge's
25 Foliage
Glasshouse, The

FISH 'N' CHIPS

26 Sweetings
24 North Sea
23 Golden Hind
22 Two Brothers Fish
20 Seashell

FRENCH (BISTRO)

26 Le Vacherin
23 Comptoir Gascon
Galvin Bistrot
Racine
Le Café du Marché

FRENCH (CLASSIC)

27 Le Gavroche
Waterside Inn
26 Oslo Court
25 Foliage
L'Oranger

FRENCH (NEW)

29 Gordon Ramsay/68 Royal
28 Ledbury, The
Pétrus
27 Le Manoir/Quat'
Square, The

INDIAN

27 Rasoi Vineet Bhatia
26 Amaya
25 Star of India
Tamarind
Vama

ITALIAN

28 River Café
26 Assaggi
25 Zafferano
La Genova
Locanda Locatelli

JAPANESE

27 Jin Kichi
Nobu London
Zuma
26 Defune
Nobu Berkeley St

LEBANESE

23 Al Sultan
Al Waha
22 Fairuz
Ishbilia
Maroush

MEDITERRANEAN

25 La Petite Maison
Moro
Fifteen
23 Eagle, The
21 Nicole's

PIZZA

23 Il Bordello
22 Osteria Basilico
21 Oliveto
20 Basilico
Delfino

SEAFOOD

26 J. Sheekey
Sweetings
25 Wilton's
24 Bentley's
Scott's

SPANISH

25 Fino
Cambio de Tercio
Barrafina
24 Tapas Brindisa
22 Eyre Brothers

THAI

24 Nahm
Patara
22 Busaba Eathai
21 Mango Tree
20 Blue Elephant

VEGETARIAN

26 Roussillon
Morgan M
25 Gate, The
24 Food for Thought
Rasa

BY SPECIAL FEATURE

BREAKFAST

24 Cinnamon Club
23 St. John Bread/Wine
22 Tom's Kitchen
Wolseley, The
21 Cecconi's

BRUNCH

24 Le Caprice
22 Providores, The
Villandry
Tom's Kitchen
21 Lucky 7

BUSINESS LUNCH

27 Square, The
   Le Gavroche
26 Greenhouse, The
24 Rhodes 24
22 St. Alban

CHEESE BOARDS

29 Gordon Ramsay/68 Royal
   Chez Bruce
28 Pétrus
26 Greenhouse
25 Tom Aikens

CHILD-FRIENDLY

27 Zuma
21 Oliveto
21 La Famiglia
20 Le Café Anglais
18 Tom's Place

COMMUNAL TABLES

25 La Fromagerie
   Ottolenghi
24 Food for Thought
23 Baker & Spice
22 Providores, The

EXPERIMENTAL

27 Fat Duck
   St. John
   Rasoi Vineet Bhatia
24 Dinings
23 Books for Cooks

GASTROPUBS

25 Anchor & Hope
24 Great Queen St.
23 Eagle, The
   Greyhound, The
22 Narrow, The

HOTEL DINING

28 Pétrus
      (The Berkeley)
   Gravetye Manor
27 Le Manoir/Quat'
   Waterside Inn
   Nobu London
      (Metropolitan Hotel)

IN-STORE EATING

23 Books for Cooks
21 Fifth Floor
   Nicole's
   1707 Wine Bar
20 St. James's

LATE NIGHT

26 J. Sheekey
   Nobu Berkeley St
   Amaya
   Yauatcha
25 Hakkasan

MEET FOR A DRINK

27 L'Atelier Joël Robuchon
   Zuma
26 Nobu Berkeley St
25 Roka
   maze

NEWCOMERS (RATED)

26 Alain Ducasse
25 La Petite Maison
24 Hereford Road
   Hibiscus
23 Wild Honey

OLDE ENGLAND

26 Sweetings (1889)
25 Wilton's (1742)
23 Rules (1798)
22 Hind's Head (1690)
21 Quality Chop House (1875)

OUTDOOR

28 River Café
   Ledbury, The
25 L'Oranger
22 Narrow, The
20 Le Pont de la Tour

PEOPLE-WATCHING

27 Zuma
25 La Petite Maison
22 Tom's Kitchen
   Wolseley, The
20 Cipriani

PRIVATE CLUBS

25 Mosimann's
23 Harry's Bar
   Mark's Club
22 Morton's
   George

PRIVATE ROOMS

27 Square, The
26 Greenhouse, The
   Amaya
25 Zafferano
20 China Tang

ROOM WITH A VIEW

- 28 Waterside Inn
- 25 Foliage
- 24 Rhodes 24
- 22 Narrow, The
- 20 Galvin at Windows

SMALL PLATES

- 27 L'Atelier Joël Robuchon
- Hunan
- 26 Club Gascon
- Amaya
- 25 maze

SUNDAY LUNCH/ COUNTRY

- 28 Gravetye Manor
- 27 Le Manoir/Quat'
- Fat Duck
- Waterside Inn
- 22 Cliveden House

SUNDAY LUNCH/ TOWN

- 29 Chez Bruce
- 28 River Café
- 23 Wild Honey
- 20 Le Café Anglais
- 19 Roast

TASTING MENU

- 29 Gordon Ramsay/68 Royal
- 28 Pétrus
- 27 Rasoi Vineet Bhatia
- 26 Roussillon
- Umu

TEA SERVICE
(other than hotels)

- 26 Yauatcha
- 25 La Fromagerie
- 23 Ladurée
- 22 Wolseley, The
- 20 Sotheby's Cafe

THEATRELAND

- 27 L'Atelier Joël Robuchon
- 26 J. Sheekey
- Richard Corrigan
- 25 Barrafina
- 22 Ivy, The

WINNING WINE LISTS

- 29 Gordon Ramsay/68 Royal
- 28 Pétrus
- 27 Square, The
- 26 Greenhouse, The
- 25 Tom Aikens

BY LOCATION

BELGRAVIA

- 28 Pétrus
- 26 Amaya
- 25 Zafferano
- Ottolenghi
- Mosimann's (club)

BLOOMSBURY/ FITZROVIA

- 27 Pied à Terre
- 25 Roka
- Hakkasan
- Fino
- 24 Rasa

CANARY WHARF

- 26 Ubon
- 23 Royal China
- 22 Gaucho Grill
- 21 Gun, The
- 20 Sri Nam

CHELSEA

- 29 Gordon Ramsay/68 Royal
- 27 Rasoi Vineet Bhatia
- 25 Tom Aikens
- Aubergine
- Vama

CHISWICK

- 28 La Trompette
- 26 Le Vacherin
- 22 Devonshire, The
- 21 Annie's
- 19 Sam's Brasserie

CITY

- 26 Sweetings
- 24 Rhodes 24
- 23 Café Spice Namasté
- 1 Lombard St.
- 22 Don, The

CLERKENWELL

- 25 Moro
- 23 Eagle, The
- 18 La Porchetta
- Strada
- 17 Zetter

COVENT GARDEN

- 27 L'Atelier Joël Robuchon
- 26 J. Sheekey
- 25 Clos Maggiore
- 24 Great Queen St.
- Food for Thought

HAMPSTEAD

- 27 Jin Kichi
- 22 Gaucho Grill
- 21 XO
- 20 Artigiano
- Wells, The*

ISLINGTON

- 26 Morgan M
- 25 Ottolenghi
- 24 Rasa
- 22 Duke of Cambridge
- 21 Frederick's

KENSINGTON

- 26 Clarke's
- 24 Il Portico
- Zaika
- Ark, The
- Locanda Ottoemezzo

KNIGHTSBRIDGE

- 27 Zuma
- 26 Capital Rest.
- 25 Foliage
- 24 Park, The
- Patara

MARYLEBONE

- 26 Defune
- Michael Moore
- 25 La Fromagerie
- Locanda Locatelli
- 24 Dinings

MAYFAIR

- 27 Square, The
- Le Gavroche
- Nobu London
- 26 Alain Ducasse
- Greenhouse, The

NOTTING HILL

- 28 Ledbury, The
- 26 Assaggi
- 25 Ottolenghi
- Notting Hill Brasserie
- 24 Hereford Road

PICCADILLY

- 24 Bentley's
- 23 Yoshino
- 22 St. Alban
- Gaucho Grill
- Wolseley, The

SHOREDITCH/ SPITALFIELDS/ HOXTON

- 25 Song Que Café
- Fifteen
- 24 Hawksmoor
- 23 St. John Bread/Wine
- 22 Eyre Brothers

SMITHFIELD

- 27 St. John
- 26 Club Gascon
- 23 Comptoir Gascon
- Le Café du Marché
- 21 Smiths/Top Floor

SOHO

- 26 Richard Corrigan
- Yauatcha
- 25 Barrafina
- 24 Arbutus
- Alastair Little

SOUTH KENSINGTON

- 25 Star of India
- Cambio de Tercio
- 24 Patara
- 23 Bibendum
- Khan's of Kensington

ST. JAMES'S

- 25 L'Oranger
- Wilton's
- 24 Le Caprice
- 23 Ritz, The
- Matsuri

IN THE COUNTRY

- 28 Gravetye Manor
- 27 Le Manoir/Quat'
- Fat Duck
- Waterside Inn
- 22 Cliveden House

Top Decor Ratings

<u>29</u>	Ritz, The
<u>28</u>	Les Trois Garçons
<u>27</u>	Le Manoir/Quat'
	Gravetye Manor
<u>26</u>	Sketch/Lecture Room
	Wolseley, The
	Hakkasan
<u>25</u>	Mosimann's (club)
	Oxo Tower
	Pétrus
	Gilgamesh
	Pasha*
	Gordon Ramsay/68 Royal
	Clos Maggiore
	Rules
	Crazy Bear
	Umu*
	Waterside Inn
	Taman Gang
	Gordon Ramsay/Claridge's

Alain Ducasse
Sketch/Gallery

<u>24</u> Mark's Club (club)
Momo
Rhodes 24*
Zuma
Cliveden House
Scott's*
Le Gavroche
L'Atelier Joël Robuchon
Galvin at Windows
Wallace, The
Levant
Greenhouse, The
Blue Elephant
Cinnamon Club
Bibendum
Cheyne Walk
Annabel's (club)
China Tang

OUTDOORS

Coq d'Argent
La Famiglia
La Poule au Pot
L'Aventure
Ledbury, The

Le Pont de la Tour
L'Oranger
Manicomio
River Café
Suka

ROMANCE

Alain Ducasse
Cheyne Walk
Club Gascon
Galvin at Windows
La Poule au Pot

Le Gavroche
Les Trois Garçons
Momo
Pétrus
Rhodes W1 Rest.

ROOMS

Gilgamesh
Hakkasan
L'Atelier Joël Robuchon
Le Café Anglais
Les Trois Garçons

Ritz, The
Sake no hana
Sketch/Lecture Rm.
Wolseley, The
Zuma

VIEWS

Foliage
Galvin at Windows
Inn The Park
Le Pont de la Tour
Narrow, The

Oxo Tower
Rhodes 24
Skylon
Ubon
Waterside Inn

Top Service Ratings

28	Gordon Ramsay/68 Royal
	Oslo Court

27	Le Manoir/Quat'
	Fat Duck
	Pétrus

26	Le Gavroche
	La Genova
	Mark's Club* (club)
	Ritz, The
	Goring Dining Rm.
	Waterside Inn
	Chez Bruce
	Capital Rest.

25	Pied à Terre
	Square, The
	Clarke's
	Alain Ducasse
	Ledbury, The
	Foliage
	Mosimann's (club)

Gordon Ramsay/Claridge's
Gravetye Manor
La Trompette*
Roussillon*
Umu*
Wilton's
Il Portico
L'Oranger
River Café
Greenhouse, The
Park, The

24	Le Colombier
	J. Sheekey
	Clos Maggiore
	Dorchester/The Grill*
	Quirinale
	Tom Aikens
	Nahm
	Rasoi Vineet Bhatia
	Le Caprice

Best Buys

1. Food for Thought
2. Churchill Arms
3. Books for Cooks
4. Leon
5. New Tayyabs
6. Pepper Tree
7. Golden Hind
8. Ed's Easy Diner
9. Little Bay
10. Hache
11. Original Lahore
12. Mandalay
13. Gourmet Burger
14. La Porchetta
15. Lucky 7
16. Song Que Café
17. Diner, The
18. Busaba Eathai
19. Le Pain Quotidien
20. Pat. Valerie
21. Wagamama
22. Jenny Lo's Tea
23. Whole Foods
24. New Culture Rev.
25. Court
26. Tas
27. Gallipoli
28. Fire & Stone
29. Masala Zone
30. Wahaca
31. Chinese Experience
32. North Sea
33. Imli
34. La Fromagerie
35. Tokyo Diner
36. Mildreds
37. Jade Garden
38. Basilico
39. Pizza Express
40. Firezza

OTHER GOOD VALUES

Alounak
Baker & Spice
Bodeans
Cay tre
Cha Cha Moon
Chuen Cheng Ku
Coach & Horses
Crazy Homies
El Rincon Latino
Feng Sushi
Fish Club
Giraffe
Isarn
Itsu
Kandoo
Kastoori
Khan's
Kiasu
Kulu Kulu Sushi
Maxwell's
Napket
Nautilus Fish
New World
Nyonya
Original Tagine
Ping Pong
Porters
Raoul's
Satsuma
Seashell
Sticky Fingers
Taqueria
Ten Ten Tei
Troubador, The
Two Brothers Fish
222 Veggie Vegan
Viet Grill
Viet Hoa
Wong Kei
Yoshino

DINNER (£35 & UNDER)

Adam St.	16.50	Latium	24.50
Al Duca	25.50	La Trompette	35.00
Alloro	29.50	La Trouvaille	29.50
Artigiano	16.50	L'Aventure	28.50
Bellamy's	24.00	Le Café/Marché	31.50
Bincho Yakitori	25.00	Le Relais/Venise	19.00
Blue Elephant	33.00	Les Trois Garçons	29.00
Boisdale	18.70	Matsuri	35.00
Brackenbury	15.00	Memories of China	31.50
Brasserie Roux	24.50	Miyama	35.00
Café Japan	17.00	Mr. Kong	9.80
Café Spice Namasté	30.00	New Tayyabs	15.00
Champor	27.90	Noura	30.00
Chapter Two	24.50	Odette's	35.00
Clerkenwell Dining	14.50	Odin's	29.00
Clos Maggiore	19.50	Painted Heron	27.50
Coq d'Argent	24.50	Pasha	30.00
El Pirata	13.95	Princess Garden	35.00
Fairuz	26.95	Rasa	25.00
Fifth Floor	19.50	Royal China	30.00
Four Seasons	13.50	Salt Yard	25.00
Fung Shing	18.00	Sartoria	19.50
Glasshouse, The	35.00	Shepherd's	29.50
Good Earth	28.80	Singapura	15.00
Gopal's of Soho	22.00	Sonny's	18.50
Gravetye Manor	35.00	Spread Eagle	27.00
Il Convivio	33.50	Sri Nam	25.00
Imperial China	16.50	St. Germain	14.00
Imperial City	25.95	Tas	17.95
Inside	16.95	Vasco & Piero's	29.50
Ishbilia	30.00	Yming	22.00
Lamberts	15.00	Yoshino	19.80
La Porte des Indes	34.00	Zafferano	34.50

LUNCH (£25 & UNDER)

Arbutus	15.50	Morgan M	19.50
Café Japan	8.50	Moti Mahal	10.00
Defune	21.50	New Tayyabs	15.00
Dorchester/The Grill	25.00	Nobu Berkeley St	25.00
Enoteca Turi	14.50	Nobu London	25.00
Fifteen	25.00	Notting Hill Brass.	17.50
Glasshouse, The	23.50	Orrery	25.00
Gravetye Manor	23.00	Pied à Terre	24.50
Greenhouse, The	25.00	Quilon	15.50
Inside	11.95	Roka	25.00
J. Sheekey	24.75	Spread Eagle	16.00
La Trompette	23.50	Sumosan	22.50
La Trouvaille	16.50	Tamarind	18.95
Le Vacherin	23.50	Timo	13.90
Michael Moore	15.95	Tsunami	10.50

RESTAURANT
DIRECTORY

| | FOOD | DECOR | SERVICE | COST |

NEW **Aaya** *Japanese* — | — | — | E

Soho | 66-70 Brewer St., W1 (Piccadilly Circus) | 020-7319 3888
Gary Yau, brother of lauded restaurateur Alan Yau (Hakkasan), makes his culinary debut with this monochromatically slick, spacious Soho venue; bamboo screens twinkle with elegant beaded lights, whilst staff clad in baggy kendo pants proffer sophisticated Japanese victuals from a pricey, varied menu; N.B. the more subdued basement space houses an equally polished sushi bar.

Abbeville, The *British/European* — | — | — | M

Clapham | 67-69 Abbeville Rd., SW4 (Clapham South) | 020-8675 2201 | fax 8675 2212 | www.theabbeville.com
"Always cramped" with Clapham locals, this place is "perfect for gastropubbing", given the "incredibly cosy" digs; if the Modern European–Traditional British "food never really impresses", at least it's "above average."

Abeno *Japanese* 18 | 14 | 16 | £25

Bloomsbury | 47 Museum St., WC1 (Holborn) | 020-7405 3211 | fax 7405 3212

Abeno Too *Japanese*

Covent Garden | 17-18 Great Newport St., WC2 (Leicester Sq.) | 020-7379 1160
www.abeno.co.uk
"Who would have thought something as simple as an omelet could taste so good" enthuse fans of these "unique" Japanese in Bloomsbury ("limited seating") and Covent Garden (more casual) that emphasise okonomiyaki (sautéed eggy pancakes); since the "food is cooked at your table", the scene gets a little "hot" and smelly, but the fare's "very filling" – and "wallet-friendly" to boot.

Abingdon, The *European* 18 | 18 | 16 | £40

Kensington | 54 Abingdon Rd., W8 (Earl's Ct./High St. Kensington) | 020-7937 3339 | fax 7795 6388 | www.theabingdonrestaurant.com
"Comfy, charming" and "relaxed", this Kensington haunt is "what a gastropub should be", offering a "reliable" Modern European menu that, whilst not cheap, is a "decent price for the quality"; "but sometimes the service is spotty – don't hesitate to ask twice" if in need.

About Thyme Bar & Bistro *European* — | — | — | M

Pimlico | 82 Wilton Rd., SW1 (Victoria) | 020-7821 7504 | www.aboutthyme.co.uk
Thyme after Thyme, surveyors return to this "airy" midpriced Pimlico bistro-bar for the "wonderful welcome" and "dependable" Modern Euro–Med food, making it "a reliable local for lunch, dinner and weekend brunch; P.S. "great space upstairs for parties."

Academy *British* — | — | — | M

Piccadilly | Royal Academy of Arts | Piccadilly, W1 (Green Park/Piccadilly Circus) | 020-7300 5608 | www.royalacademy.org.uk
After "you've been to the art exhibitions", the Royal Academy's cafe can be a picture-perfect break, with its budget-minded buffet of

	FOOD	DECOR	SERVICE	COST

"fresh, appetising" Modern British fare; N.B. dinner served Fridays only, with table service (reservations required).

Acorn House ☒ *British* ▽ 19 | 16 | 16 | £35

King's Cross | 69 Swinton St., WC1 (King's Cross) | 020-7812 1842 | www.acornhouserestaurant.com

"More of this type, please" plead green-minded gourmands who support the "serious" "environmental and ethical stance" of this King's Cross eatery, applied to everything from biodegradable packaging to fresh ingredients in the "eclectic", "surprisingly good" Modern British fare; however, a few foes feel the "inspiring concept is not yet fully realised", especially given the "slow" service (the lunchtime deli-counter is a speedier option).

Adam Street ☒ *British* ▽ 20 | 22 | 20 | £39

Covent Garden | 9 Adam St., WC2 (Charing Cross) | 020-7379 8000 | fax 7379 1444 | www.adamstreet.co.uk

Blessed with the cool "cavern atmosphere" of an 18th-century vault, this low-key private club is "available to non-members for lunch" with a surcharge – which modern-day Adams deem "well worth it", as it's "quieter and more upmarket than most places in Covent Garden"; other plus points include a "good cocktail bar" (signature drink: the Oliver Twist, with an olive and a twist– get it?), "Modern British classics" and staff that "will oblige if you tell them you're in a hurry."

Addendum ☒ *European* – | – | – | E

Tower Bridge | Apex City of London Hotel | 1 Seething Ln., EC3 (Tower Hill) | 020-7977 9500 | fax 7977 9529 | www.addendumrestaurant.co.uk

"Good for a business lunch in an area without many great restaurants", this "chic" hotel near the Tower of London offers two options: a formal, low-ceilinged restaurant serving "inventive, capably executed" Modern European dishes, and a more "reasonably priced" brasserie with handsomely large windows; it "can be quiet, but nothing wrong with that."

Admiral Codrington, The *British/European* 18 | 17 | 16 | £32

Chelsea | 17 Mossop St., SW3 (South Kensington) | 020-7581 0005 | fax 7589 2452 | www.theadmiralcodrington.co.uk

"Walk past a smoky pub scene in front and find yourself in a contemporary dining room" with a "retractable summer roof" that "adds light and charm" to this "fish specialist gastropub" with a "straightforward" Modern British–European menu and clientele ranging from Sloane Rangers to "braying estate agents with red socks"; P.S. "Mossop Street can be tough to find, even for cabbies."

Admiralty, The *French* 18 | 20 | 18 | £45

Covent Garden | Somerset House | The Strand, WC2 (Temple) | 020-7845 4646 | fax 7845 4658

"It's the atmosphere you come here for" advise mateys of this "hidden", historic venue (the former admiralty offices) in Somerset House, since the New French menu – whilst "done well enough" – is "just not terribly exciting", and the "lacklustre service" and "terrible acoustics where every clink of glass is amplified" deserve a dousing as well; however, all hands are on deck for the "stunning" setting overlooking the Thames.

Aglio e Olio ● *Italian*   21 | 13 | 19 | £29

Chelsea | 194 Fulham Rd., SW10 (South Kensington) | 020-7351 0070

"It has a dive look", but this "crowded" Chelsea Italian packs them in with a well-oiled recipe of "generous portions", "authentic", "strong flavours" and "reasonable prices" for "pleasing results" – provided "you're in the mood" for a "frenetic", "buzzy atmosphere."

Z NEW Alain Ducasse   26 | 25 | 25 | £107
at The Dorchester ⓈⓂ *French*

Mayfair | The Dorchester | 53 Park Ln., W1 (Hyde Park Corner/Marble Arch) | 020-7629 8866 | www.alainducasse-dorchester.com

French super-toque Alain Ducasse "has not forgotten the smallest detail" ("love the stools for resting handbags on") at his "divine" new Dorchester venture where protégé chef Jocelyn Herland produces "passionate" New French fare, "delivered by an overwhelming number of staff" within a beige room that "spells elegance"; still, a few "quibble about a lack of wow factor" – except in the "insane prices" (it's "best enjoyed when someone else is paying"); N.B. privacy-seekers should check out the central table cocooned by a circular canopy of fibre-optic strands.

Alastair Little ●Ⓢ *British*   24 | 16 | 21 | £52

Soho | 49 Frith St., W1 (Leicester Sq./Tottenham Court Rd.) | 020-7734 5183 | fax 7734 5206

"Don't be put off by its tiny size and austere ambience" – this Soho stalwart is "still a winner after all these years" and an especially "popular media haunt" for a business lunch; chef Juliet Peston (who succeeded the eponymous Little a whilst ago) brings "the feel of home cooking" to the "honest" Modern British menu that "represents great value" and is served by "professional staff without an attitude."

Albannach Ⓢ *Scottish*   16 | 17 | 14 | £40

Soho | 66 Trafalgar Sq., WC2 (Charing Cross/Leicester Sq.) | 020-7930 0066 | fax 7389 9800 | www.albannach.co.uk

"In quite an interesting setting" – a converted bank with a Scottish theme, complete with stag-antler chandelier – this tri-level Trafalgar Square restaurant/bar/club offers a Modern European menu with traditional Sassanachs dishes (like haggis) bolstered by a "great selection of whiskies" and brought by "gorgeous waiters"; but moor to the point, snap naysayers, is the "incredibly loud" environs, "appallingly slow service" and "pricey" bill for merely "decent" fare.

Albemarle, The *British*   22 | 22 | 24 | £57
(fka Brown's Hotel - The Grill)

Mayfair | Brown's Hotel | Albemarle St., W1 (Green Park) | 020-7518 4060 | fax 7493 9381 | www.brownshotel.com

It's "a bit more modern" now, but an "old-school" air still hangs over this recently rechristened, "wonderfully Londonesque" hotel restaurant where regulars rely on Traditional British "food prepared with a delicate touch" – and served by staff that are "professional", but "without any stodginess or snobbery"; it's "very dear, but so is everything in Mayfair", and economisers can always opt for afternoon tea in the lounge instead – "the best gift you can give yourself."

Albion, The *British*

	FOOD	DECOR	SERVICE	COST
	17	17	11	£27

Islington | 10 Thornhill Rd., N1 (Angel) | 020-7607 7450 | www.the-albion.co.uk

Fans of this "Islington luvvies haunt" tout the "understated" Georgian pub's "lovely patio for summer drinking" and "reliable" Traditional British fare; what 'ales' the refurbished watering hole, some opine, is "trading on its garden" with "service that ranges from confused to nonexistent" – to call it "spotty would be overrating it."

Al Duca 🗷 *Italian*

	FOOD	DECOR	SERVICE	COST
	20	16	18	£42

St. James's | 4-5 Duke of York St., SW1 (Green Park/Piccadilly Circus) | 020-7839 3090 | fax 7839 4050 | www.alduca-restaurant.co.uk

"Busy on working days, but a paradise on weekends", this "somewhat cramped" "standby" near St. James's Square is appreciated for Italian fare that "never disappoints", mainly because of the "remarkably good value set menus" (including "one of the best theatre deals in town").

Al Hamra ● *Lebanese*

	FOOD	DECOR	SERVICE	COST
	21	14	18	£37

Mayfair | 31-33 Shepherd Mkt., W1 (Green Park) | 020-7493 1954 | fax 7493 1044

Brasserie Al Hamra 🗷 *Lebanese*

Mayfair | 52 Shepherd Mkt., W1 (Green Park) | 020-7493 1068 | fax 7355 3511
www.alhamrarestaurant.co.uk

"Popular with Middle Eastern plutocrats, cosmocrats" and "well-heeled" locals, these Shepherd Market Lebanese offer "delectable" fare, including a "tempting assortment of mezze"; even if staff are "somewhat abrupt" and the "setting ordinary", it's often "bustling" at the "particularly nice" pavement tables; P.S. whilst it's "akin to eating in a cafeteria", the Brasserie has lower prices and French charcuterie.

Alloro 🗷 *Italian*

	FOOD	DECOR	SERVICE	COST
	21	18	19	£50

Mayfair | 19-20 Dover St., W1 (Green Park) | 020-7495 4768 | fax 7629 5348

"Always a pleaser" for "better-than-average", "seasonal" Italian *cucina* that's "not abusively expensive by Mayfair standards", this "grown-up", "buzzy" "standby" draws praise for a "great wine cellar" and "wonderful bar"; those less smitten cite "enthusiastic" but "uneven service"; P.S. it "can be a bit 'suity' at lunch."

All Star Lanes *American*

	FOOD	DECOR	SERVICE	COST
	12	21	16	£29

Bloomsbury | Victoria House | Bloomsbury Pl., WC1 (Holborn) | 020-7025 2676 | fax 7025 2677 ●
Bayswater | Whiteleys Shopping Ctr. | Porchester Gdns., W2 (Paddington) | 020-7313 8360
www.allstarlanes.co.uk

"Even if you have never bowled before", this duo of "kitschy '50s-themed alleys" with a "fab retro feel" in Bloomsbury and Bayswater strike it right for "group nights out" – just expect "drinks at the cool bars" that are "expensive for bowling" and "so-so" American diner food at the booth seats; P.S. try "booking both lanes in the private room."

Almeida *French* | 19 | 17 | 18 | £47 |

Islington | 30 Almeida St., N1 (Angel/Highbury & Islington) | 020-7354 4777 | fax 7354 2777 | www.almeida-restaurant.co.uk

"An oasis of informal elegance off achingly trendy Upper Street", this "mainstay" for Almeida Theatre-goers gets a "good buzz", particularly post-curtain; however, the Classic French "*carte* is generally unchanging – a matter of reassurance to some, but disappointment to others" – and that, plus "overblown" prices and "slow service", makes it missable to many; P.S. "decor has been updated."

Alounak ● *Persian* | 22 | 13 | 15 | £22 |

Westbourne Grove | 44 Westbourne Grove, W2 (Bayswater/Royal Oak) | 020-7229 4158 | fax 7792 1219

Olympia | 10 Russell Gdns., W14 (Olympia) | 020-7603 1130

The "tight quarters" and "no-frills" decor notwithstanding, patrons proclaim this a "pleasant Persian" pair, primarily on account of the "awesome", "melt-in-your-mouth" cooking at "reasonable prices"; "bring your own wine" and "expect to wait an eternity for a table", whether in Westbourne Grove or Olympia.

☑ Al Sultan ● *Lebanese* | 23 | 16 | 20 | £36 |

Mayfair | 51-52 Hertford St., W1 (Green Park) | 020-7408 1155 | fax 7408 1113 | www.alsultan.co.uk

Despite its 23 years, this "pleasant surprise" is "less well known than many other Lebanese, but is preferable" for its "attentive service" and "authentic", "consistently delicious" cooking; some connoisseurs claim it's "not cheap for Middle Eastern fare – guess you pay for the location" in Shepherd Market.

☑ Al Waha ● *Lebanese* | 23 | 16 | 22 | £31 |

Bayswater | 75 Westbourne Grove, W2 (Bayswater/Queensway) | 020-7229 0806

"Small and packed", this "sufficiently out-of-the-way" Westbourne Grove Lebanese lures "local and faithful" fans with its "fantastic", sometimes "unusual" Middle Eastern fare and a "good wine list" to match; despite "crowded-together" tables and "dishes that arrive at random order", the prevailing plan is to "definitely return."

☑ Amaya ● *Indian* | 26 | 23 | 20 | £55 |

Belgravia | 15-19 Halkin Arcade, Motcomb St., SW1 (Knightsbridge) | 020-7823 1166 | fax 7259 6464 | www.realindianfood.com

"Deft touches with spices" and "exciting twists on classic flavours" offer a "feast for the senses" at this "suave" subcontinental small-plates specialist "tucked away in high-end Belgravia"; true, it's "incredibly expensive" and "staff can be a bit clueless", but most delight in this "dark" spot's "definitely different take" on Indian cuisine.

| | FOOD | DECOR | SERVICE | COST |

Ambassador, The *European*
| | − | − | − | M |

Clerkenwell | 55 Exmouth Mkt., EC1 (Farringdon) | 020-7837 0009 |
www.theambassadorcafe.co.uk

A "brilliantly simple" doctrine of "solid, uncomplicated" Modern European fare, a "great wine list", "knowledgeable service" and moderate prices has the "local crowd" feeling the goodwill of this laid-back Exmouth Market bistro, an "enjoyable experience" from breakfast on through to supper.

Amici Bar & Italian Kitchen *Italian*
| | ▽ 16 | 17 | 15 | £37 |

Wandsworth | 35 Bellevue Rd., SW17 (Wandsworth Common) |
020-8672 5888 | www.amiciitaly.co.uk

Offering a range of "reliable, hearty" Italian dishes, this "cute", "friendly" venue beside Wandsworth Common makes for a "pleasant" local; however, it has recently "changed hands", becoming part of the Brinkley's stable, and a few feel it's "not such good value any longer."

Anchor & Hope *British*
| | 25 | 14 | 20 | £32 |

Waterloo | 36 The Cut, SE1 (Southwark/Waterloo) |
020-7928 9898

"Rapidly becoming a culinary institution" due to its "home from home", "fresh Modern British food" – "quite simply the best pub grub" in town – this "hugely popular" Waterloo haunt with "typical pub decor" packs in the punters, who revel in service that's "informal in the best way – no fuss, but knowledgeable", and capable of getting you out "before the Old Vic" curtain nearby; true, the "no-reservations policy can result in a long wait", so the savvy anchor their hopes on Sunday lunch, which is bookable and resembles "a great family meal, without the annoying family."

Andrew Edmunds *European*
| | 22 | 20 | 20 | £39 |

Soho | 46 Lexington St., W1 (Oxford Circus/Piccadilly Circus) |
020-7437 5708

"Most would walk past and ignore" this "hidden" "Soho diehard" – pity, because they'd miss a "rustic ambience" with "lots of romantic candles" ("perfect for a second date"), a "daily changing", "great-value" Modern European menu of "simple dishes that's complemented by an extensive wine list" and "staff who know how to please"; in short, a "fantastic cubbyhole", even if it can "feel a little claustrophobic."

Z NEW Angelus M *French*
| | 23 | 17 | 19 | £55 |

Bayswater | 4 Bathurst St., W2 (Lancaster Gate) | 020-7402 0083 |
www.angelusrestaurant.co.uk

"In what used to be a pub", a front-of-house alumnus of Le Gavroche offers "an oasis of French charm", from the brasserie fare "with flair" ("the Anjou pigeon is fantastic") to the "enthusiastic staff" to the "simple outdoor seating"; all in all, a "welcome addition" to Bayswater, even if "parking is an issue" and the site overlooks a working stables, complete "with fresh horse muck."

	FOOD	DECOR	SERVICE	COST

Anglesea Arms *British*

19 | 16 | 17 | £28

Shepherd's Bush | 35 Wingate Rd., W6 (Goldhawk Rd./Ravenscourt Park) | 020-8749 1291 | fax 8749 1254

With its "relaxed, pubby atmosphere", leather couches (the one "by the fire is mint") and a "mouth-watering" Modern British menu, it's no surprise this "jolly gastropub" in Shepherd's Bush "can be crowded" ("shame it's not possible to book"); it's "dog-friendly – in fact, entirely friendly", although "service is slow."

Annabel's ●⊠ *British/French*

20 | 24 | 23 | £83

Private club; inquiries: 020-7629 1096

This "most elegant nightclub in the world" has "gone through a change of ownership" (from the late Mark Birley to Richard Caring of Le Caprice Holdings), but it remains an "iconic" "magical establishment" for Mayfair's "well-heeled and well-bred to mingle", served by "considerate staff"; yes, the "civilised" "decor beats the food" ("extremely expensive" Classic Anglo-French fare) and a handful huff it's "not kept up with the times", "but the members don't seem to care" – they just "party like it's 1999!"

Annex 3 ●⊠ *Eclectic*

- | - | - | E

Fitzrovia | 6 Little Portland St., W1 (Oxford Circus) | 020-7631 0700 | www.annex3.co.uk

Its "just-dropped-some-acid decor lends charm" to this "perfect escape from the crazy speed of Oxford Street"; however, critics call it "more of a bar than a food place", with the "fantastic drinks" in the "loud lounge" overshadowing the dining room's Eclectic fare.

Annie's *British*

21 | 21 | 22 | £32

Barnes | 36-38 White Hart Ln., SW13 (Barnes Bridge Rail) | 020-8878 2020 | fax 8876 8478

Chiswick | 162 Thames Rd., W4 (Kew Bridge Rail) | 020-8994 6848 www.anniesrestaurant.co.uk

With their "cute", "homey atmosphere" (mismatched "uncovered oak tables", etc.), this "inviting" duo in Barnes and Chiswick are "a favourite with locals" for "dependable" Modern British bistro-style fare "at reasonable prices", served from 10 AM on; "friendly, unhurried" service completes the picture, though grinches grimace they're "family-friendly – aka lots of ill-behaved children."

Aperitivo ⊠ *Italian*

- | - | - | M

Soho | 41 Beak St., W1 (Oxford Circus/Piccadilly Circus) | 020-7287 2057 | www.aperitivo-restaurants.com

"Hidden on Beak Street – thousands walk past without realising it" – this "nice bar" offers "Italian tapas, a great idea, not bad in execution" and "not too expensive" either; there's "also a good wine list."

NEW Apsleys *Italian*

- | - | - | VE

Belgravia | The Lanesborough | Hyde Park Corner, SW1 (Hyde Park Corner) | 020-7259 5599 | www.lanesborough.com

The palm trees are gone, but the impressive glass roof remains atop The Lanesborough's airy conservatory, a grand room transformed by Tihany Design into a comfortably, contemporarily elegant setting for indulging in the upscale modern Italian menu of chef Nick Bell (ex Cecconi's and Zafferano) and a 500-bin wine list; N.B. the main space is flanked by two handsome rooms for private parties.

Aquasia *Asian/Mediterranean*

| - | - | - | E |

Chelsea | Wyndham Hotel | Chelsea Harbour, SW10 (Earl's Ct.) | 020-7823 3000 | fax 7352 8174 | www.wyndham.com

A "very nice view of the marina" is the main claim to fame of this modern Asian-Med bistro at Chelsea Harbour; it's frequented primarily by hotel guests, though all can enjoy its "great deck for dining on nice evenings."

☑ Arbutus *European*

| 24 | 17 | 19 | £45 |

Soho | 63-64 Frith St., W1 (Leicester Sq./Tottenham Court Rd.) | 020-7734 4545 | www.arbutusrestaurant.co.uk

"Don't let the casual atmosphere fool you" – this "understated" Soho eatery serves "superb" Modern European fare, "creative and alluring, whilst retaining a reassuring familiarity" and backed by "a huge choice of wine by the carafe" ("brilliant idea"); "service can be spotty", but staff mostly manage "that fine balance between friendly and professional"; now "if only it were less noisy" and "cramped" – the glass-fronted surrounds are "like eating in a goldfish bowl."

Archipelago ☑ *Eclectic*

| ▽ 22 | 25 | 18 | £42 |

Fitzrovia | 110 Whitfield St., W1 (Goodge St./Warren St.) | 020-7383 3346 | fax 7383 7181

Take a "weird, wonderful" "walk to another world" when you enter this "enjoyable Fitzrovia restaurant that specialises in less-common foods" (to put it mildly) – including seared zebra, crocodile filet and a baby bee brûlée; the Eclectic edibles are dished up in an "exotic/spiritual" interior that blends golden Buddhas, peacock feathers and dwarf palm trees to great "romantic" effect.

Ark, The ☑ *Italian*

| 24 | 20 | 20 | £39 |

Kensington | 122 Palace Gardens Terrace, W8 (Notting Hill Gate) | 020-7229 4024 | fax 7792 8787 | www.ark-restaurant.com

"All those living near Notting Hill" Gate can count themselves lucky to have this "nice neighbourhood spot", a "small, cosy" room (which "can be quite romantic") with Italian fare that's "a little on the pricey side, but pleasant" – especially the "fabulous truffle menu in autumn"; it's "reliable", whether you're going two by two or "with a gaggle of friends."

Armani Caffé ☑ *Italian*

| 19 | 22 | 18 | £37 |

Knightsbridge | Emporio Armani | 191 Brompton Rd., SW3 (Knightsbridge) | 020-7584 4549 | fax 7823 8854 | www.emporioarmani.com

"You get to wander through the Emporio Armani to get" to this "hip", mirrored cafe, a "tried-and-true" choice of "model-y types" looking for "light", "healthy" Italian dishes "after a day of shopping"; but sceptics snap "the service wins no awards", and the fare – like the clothing – is "not cheap."

		FOOD	DECOR	SERVICE	COST

Artigiano *Italian* — 20 | 15 | 17 | £42

Hampstead | 12A Belsize Terrace, NW3 (Belsize Park/ Swiss Cottage) | 020-7794 4288 | fax 7435 2048 | www.etruscarestaurants.com

"A reliable oasis in a culinary desert" around Belsize Village, this "cosy neighbourhood haunt" serves Italian "comfort food" from a "menu that changes just enough from visit to visit"; unfortunately, the "ultramodern" environs get "loud during dinner hours", and whilst the servers are "friendly", a score slip suggests there are "not enough" of them.

NEW Artisan *European* — ▽ 18 | 20 | 23 | £75

Mayfair | Westbury Hotel | Bond St., W1 (Oxford Circus/Green Park) | 020-7629 7755 | fax 7499 1270 | www.westburymayfair.com

Part of the Westbury Hotel's luxurious, £20 million revamp, this bright "new dining room" boasts a "stylish" art deco look complete with parquet flooring and elegant, beaded crystal chandeliers; if the sophisticated Modern European menu "prices are very Mayfair", they're balanced by a wine list with a good spread under the £40 mark.

Asadal *Korean* — - | - | - | M

Holborn | 229-231 High Holborn, WC1 (Holborn) | 020-7430 9006 | www.asadal.co.uk

"Ignore the fact you're almost as deep as Holborn [tube] platform" – this "presentable Korean" (a spin-off from a New Malden eatery) makes up for having "no daylight in the basement" premises with "bright ideas in the kitchen department"; in particular, the "at-table BBQ is a good choice."

Asakusa 🖾 *Japanese* — ▽ 25 | 13 | 18 | £25

Camden Town | 265 Eversholt St., NW1 (Morningtown Crescent St.) | 020-7388 8533

"There's nothing polished or chic about this no-frills, cramped den lifted from a Tokyo side street" and dropped in Camden, but the "food more than makes up for it": "screamingly fresh sushi" and "simple, homestyle" dishes from "sweet, but occasionally impatient service"; it's "not for a romantic night out", but the atmosphere's "authentic", down to the "off-menu items that adorn the walls, so bring your Japanese dictionary."

Z Asia de Cuba ● *Asian/Cuban* — 21 | 23 | 18 | £57

Covent Garden | St. Martins Lane Hotel | 45 St. Martin's Ln., WC2 (Leicester Sq.) | 020-7300 5588 | fax 7300 5540 | www.chinagrillmanagement.com

"East meets West perfectly in the exquisite fusion of flavours" and "the cleverness of the drinks" at this "sleek" white-on-white Theatreland Asian-Cuban "with a turn-of-the-millennium feel" that "still brings in the crowds" a decade after its birth; true, it's "too loud", with "no shortage of attitude" amongst staff, "but there's still something that makes you come back" to this "fabulously pricey" "bling zone."

	FOOD	DECOR	SERVICE	COST

Ask Pizza *Pizza* — 15 | 13 | 15 | £19

Bloomsbury | 48 Grafton Way, W1 (Warren St.) | 020-7388 8108 | fax 7388 8112 ◗
Marylebone | 197 Baker St., NW1 (Baker St.) | 020-7486 6027
Marylebone | 56-60 Wigmore St., W1 (Bond St.) | 020-7224 3484
Mayfair | 121-125 Park St., W1 (Marble Arch) | 020-7495 7760 | fax 7495 7760
Victoria | 160-162 Victoria St., SW1 (St. James's Park/Victoria) | 020-7630 8228 | fax 7630 5218
Hampstead | 216 Haverstock Hill, NW3 (Belsize Park/Chalk Farm) | 020-7433 3896 | fax 7435 6490
Chelsea | 300 King's Rd., SW3 (Sloane Sq.) | 020-7349 9123
Putney | 345 Fulham Palace Rd., SW6 (Putney Bridge) | 020-7371 0392
South Kensington | Unit 23-24, Gloucester Arcade, SW7 (Gloucester Rd.) | 020-7835 0840
Notting Hill | 145 Notting Hill Gate, W11 (Notting Hill Gate) | 020-7792 9942
www.askcentral.co.uk
Additional locations throughout London

"Lazy and formulaic" they may be, but for a "functional quick lunch" or "dinner of convenience", this "nice and casual" Italian chain furnishes "low-priced" pizzas and pastas "you can't be bothered to make at home"; P.S. "don't forget the salads, they are excellent."

☒ Assaggi ☒ *Italian* — 26 | 15 | 22 | £54

Notting Hill | 39 Chepstow Pl., 1st fl., W2 (Notting Hill Gate) | 020-7792 5501 | fax 0870-0051 2923

Expect "celebrity sightings" of "film-producer types" and a "theatrical (in a good way) presentation of the menu" from co-owner Pietro Fraccari at this "loud-coloured", "quirky dining room" in Notting Hill; some grumble "you pay a lot for bare boards above a pub with flaking paintwork", and "getting a table is a nightmare", "but keep calling", 'cos the "fresh", "rustic" *cucina* is among "the best Italian in London."

Atami Restaurant & Bar ☒ *Japanese* — 19 | 22 | 22 | £44

Westminster | 37 Monck St., SW1 (St. James's Park) | 020-7222 2218 | www.atami-restaurant.com

"Tucked away from the London throng in the streets behind Westminster Abbey", this "chic", "modern" Japanese offers "not only the classics, but also an aspiring gastronomic menu"; given the "rather small portions", prices seem "above average", but the "bargain lunch" bento boxes are easy to swallow and the "service is charming."

Atma Ⓜ *Indian* — - | - | - | M

Hampstead | 106C Finchley Rd., NW3 (Finchley Rd.) | 020-7431 9487

"You'll want to keep to yourself" "this Indian with a difference", but "it deserves recognition" for its "well-prepared" dishes, "none too highly spiced" and all "excellent value"; just be prepared for a "noisy location right on the Finchley Road."

| | FOOD | DECOR | SERVICE | COST |

Aubaine *French* — 19 | 18 | 15 | £30

Piccadilly | 4 Heddon St., W1 (Piccadilly Circus) | 020-7440 2510 🚇

South Kensington | 260-262 Brompton Rd., SW3 (South Kensington) | 020-7052 0100 | fax 7052 0622

www.aubaine.co.uk

"More sophisticated than the usual bistro" (and perhaps more pricey), these Piccadilly and South Ken venues offer "rustic", "well-conceived French classics" all day; "service could be more professional", but the Provençal-style premises are "always crowded" with "Sloane Square princesses and their banker boyfriends", especially at the "tremendously popular weekend brunch."

Auberge du Lac Ⓜ *European/French* — ∇ 26 | 26 | 23 | £72

Welwyn | Brocket Hall | Hertfordshire | 01707 368888 | fax 01707 368898 | www.brocket-hall.co.uk

In a "beautiful location overlooking the lake and Brockett Hall" in Hertfordshire, "calm, sophisticated surroundings" create a canvas for "young chef Phil Thompson" to prepare "high-end Classic French"–Modern European fare, supported by "surprisingly decent service"; if some still claim it's "never [been] as good since Jean-Christophe Novelli left" a few years back, others insist it's "worth the drive just for the scenery."

Aubergine Ⓩ *French* — 25 | 21 | 23 | £73

Chelsea | 11 Park Walk, SW10 (Gloucester Rd./South Kensington) | 020-7352 3449 | fax 7351 1770 | www.auberginerestaurant.co.uk

"Posh, and at the same time warm and welcoming", this "clean"-lined Chelsea eatery is the home to chef William Drabble's "innovative creations" from a "world-class" New French menu; most find it "excellent in every way" – if a "bit rarefied for ordinary mortals, particularly those without expense accounts."

Automat ⬤ *American* — 18 | 19 | 17 | £35

Mayfair | 33 Dover St., W1 (Green Park) | 020-7499 3033 | www.automat-london.com

"Feels like New York has come to London" with this "train-carriage-styled" "clubby diner" whose seating options include "cosy booths or a light, airy greenhouse at the rear"; "sadly, the decor is better than the food" – "jazzed-up American-style" basics – and don't "expect too much of the service", but at least it's "reasonably priced for Mayfair."

Avenue, The ⬤Ⓩ *European* — 19 | 20 | 19 | £49

St. James's | 7-9 St. James's St., SW1 (Green Park) | 020-7321 2111 | fax 7321 2500 | www.danddlondon.com

"Chic", if somewhat "cold", this "modern, glass-fronted restaurant in the heart of St. James's" has "stood the test of time" (well, 14 years, anyway) as an "expense-account haunt" serving "simple, hearty" Modern European meals; what keeps it "heaving", however, is the "vibrant" bar – "young professionals stop in after work or the theatre."

	FOOD	DECOR	SERVICE	COST

Awana *Malaysian* — 22 | 18 | 18 | £40

Chelsea | 85 Sloane Ave., SW3 (South Kensington) | 020-7584 8880 | fax 7584 6188 | www.awana.co.uk

With its "favourable location" in Chelsea and "authentic", "lovingly presented" Malaysian food from an open kitchen ("the satay is particularly good"), this Mango Tree sibling is "worth multiple visits", even if it's "a bit pricey", "considering the small portions"; "service can be a bit slow-paced, but attentive."

Axis 🅱 *British/Eclectic* — 19 | 20 | 19 | £49

Covent Garden | One Aldwych Hotel | 1 Aldwych, WC2 (Charing Cross/Covent Garden) | 020-7300 0300 | fax 7300 0301 | www.onealdwych.com

"Usefully located under the hip One Aldwych Hotel" in Covent Garden, this "stylish" (some say "stark"), "high-ceilinged basement restaurant" makes a "sophisticated" choice "when you need to impress"; the Eclectic–Modern British menu is "a steady performer", if "not exactly value for money" warn the economical – except for the "top pre-theatre prix fixe"; P.S. beware, the "noise can be traumatic on jazz evenings."

Aziz *Moroccan* — ▽ 19 | 15 | 17 | £27

Fulham | 30-32 Vanston Pl., SW6 (Fulham Broadway) | 020-7386 0086 | fax 7610 1661 | www.delaziz.co.uk

Run by a husband-and-wife team, this "atmospheric" Fulham venue is a veritable "Moroccan wonderland", with hookah pipes in the lounge bar and "reasonably priced", "hearty North African flavours" in the dining room; it gets "buzzy" Thursdays–Saturdays when many "go for the belly-dancing" – though, if you can get up the next day, "Sunday brunch is exceptional" too.

Babylon *European* — ▽ 17 | 25 | 18 | £52

Kensington | The Roof Gdns. | 99 Kensington High St., W8 (High St. Kensington) | 020-7368 3993 | fax 7938 2774 | www.roofgardens.com

"The view and the gardens are what makes this place great" profess high-fliers about Sir Richard Branson's "castle in the air" high above Kensington, with its "better-than-average" Modern European cuisine, "romantic atmosphere" and "buzzy bar"; but dissenters dismiss it as *"Footballers' Wives* territory", not least on Friday and Saturday nights when, for a fee, diners gain access to the private nightclub one floor below.

Bacchus 🅱 *Eclectic* — 21 | 16 | 20 | £59

Hoxton | 177 Hoxton St., N1 (Old St.) | 020-7613 0477 | fax 7100 1704 | www.bacchus-restaurant.co.uk

"Fine dining in a casual gastropub setting" summarises this Eclectic, whose "bold, dashing" dishes "are more hit than miss" and staff are "friendly without being overbearing"; the vaguely "'70s-influenced decor can look pretty basic", and the Hoxton location downright "frightening", but most will bacchus up when we say this novice is "worth the effort to get to."

	FOOD	DECOR	SERVICE	COST

Baker & Spice *Bakery/Mediterranean* — 23 | 15 | 13 | £23

Belgravia | 54-56 Elizabeth St., SW1 (Sloane Sq./Victoria) | 020-7730 3033 | fax 7730 3188
Kilburn | 75 Salusbury Rd., NW6 (Queens Park) | 020-7604 3636 | fax 7604 3646
St. John's Wood | 20 Clifton Rd., W9 (Warwick Ave.) | 020-7266 1122 | fax 7266 3535
Chelsea | 47 Denyer St., SW3 (Knightsbridge/South Kensington) | 020-7589 4734 | fax 7823 9148
www.bakerandspice.com

Yes, the "prices are mind-boggling", but they really have some of "the best pastries, baked goods" and Med savouries at these "brilliant" "bespoke delis" around town; if the "service seems variable" and the communal tables "cramped", remember these are "mainly takeaway places" – and besides, "sometimes you [just] need a pricey cookie."

Balans ◑ *British* — 16 | 14 | 17 | £25

Soho | 60 Old Compton St., W1 (Leicester Sq./Piccadilly Circus) | 020-7439 2183 | fax 7734 2665
Earl's Court | 239 Old Brompton Rd., SW5 (Earl's Ct./West Brompton) | 020-7244 8838 | fax 7244 6226
Chiswick | 214 Chiswick High Rd., W4 (Turnham Green) | 020-8742 1435
Kensington | 187 Kensington High St., W8 (High St. Kensington) | 020-7376 0115 | fax 7938 4653

Balans Cafe ◑ *British*

Soho | 34 Old Compton St., W1 (Leicester Sq./Piccadilly Circus) | 020-7439 3309
www.balans.co.uk

Established in 1986, these "gay-friendly", "busy", "buzzy" bistros remain "reliable fallbacks" for brunch – they open at 8 AM (60 Old Compton Street is also "classic for a Soho night out", as it serves until dawn); if the Modern British fare is "blessedly cheap but decidedly mediocre", well, watching the "always-attractive young men" is "the main event here, as is the campy, flirtatious service."

Baltic ◑ *Polish* — 22 | 22 | 19 | £40

Southwark | 74 Blackfriars Rd., SE1 (Southwark) | 020-7928 1111 | fax 7928 8487 | www.balticrestaurant.co.uk

"For the adventurously minded, one visit won't be enough" to this Southwark citizen serving "intriguing Eastern European" (mainly Polish) dishes in a "trendy" "warehouse environment"; it's "intoxicating" "if you have a hankering for herring", but "service is a bit slow", so some "wade through" the "stylish London crowd swirling all around" for "a few flavoured vodkas and blinis at the bar."

Bam-Bou 🗷 *Pan-Asian* — 22 | 22 | 16 | £37

Fitzrovia | 1 Percy St., W1 (Tottenham Court Rd.) | 020-7323 9130 | fax 7323 9140 | www.bam-bou.co.uk

Occupying a "converted Fitzrovia townhouse" – "an exciting building with many floors" – this "chic" "Vietnamese-French colonial-themed" venue collects compliments for its "solid" spicy Pan-Asian fare, that's a "bit pricey but worth it"; some wonder "why are the staff so grumpy", but on balance, the place "makes you feel at ease."

subscribe to ZAGAT.com

	FOOD	DECOR	SERVICE	COST

Bangkok 🗷 *Thai*
▽ 25 | 15 | 19 | £26

South Kensington | 9 Bute St., SW7 (South Kensington) | 020-7584 8529
"A favourite for over 40 years that never, ever disappoints", this unpretentious South Kensington Thai is a place to "take a crowd of friends and have fun" over such "standbys" as satays, garlic-fried chicken and homemade ice creams.

Bank Westminster & Zander Bar 🗷 *European*
16 | 17 | 15 | £41

Victoria | 45 Buckingham Gate, SW1 (St. James's Park) | 020-7379 9797 | fax 7240 7001 | www.bankrestaurants.com
"Views of the courtyard fountain add to the pleasant, yet trendy atmosphere" of this "well-designed" Victoria conservatory, an "interesting place" for "pretty consistent Modern European fare"; the main quibbles: the "noisy Zander bar" (reportedly the U.K.'s longest) at the front, and "service that ranges from attentive to indifferent"; N.B. a summer 2008 refurb is mooted, outdating the Decor score.

Barnes Grill *British*
- | - | - | E

Barnes | 2-3 Rocks Ln., SW13 (Barnes Bridge Rail) | 020-8878 4488 | fax 8878 5922 | www.awtrestaurants.com
Bare-brick walls and a purple-toned hunting lodge look create a comfy feel to this Barnes member of chef-owner Antony Worrall Thompson's stable; as the name implies, it specialises in British grills, including "pretty good steaks", but malcontents mutter "the menu is a bit hit-and-miss – [sibling] Kew Grill seems so much better."

Barnsbury, The *British*
▽ 21 | 18 | 18 | £27

Islington | 209-211 Liverpool Rd., N1 (Angel) | 020-7607 5519 | fax 7607 3256 | www.thebarnsbury.co.uk
Whether it's a "cosy wintery evening by the fire or a Pimms-filled summer afternoon in the garden", this "pleasing pub off the Islington beaten track" is "always busy", thanks to a "warm welcome" and Modern British fare that's "different enough to draw people"; oh, and it's "dog-friendly" too.

🗷 Barrafina *Spanish*
25 | 19 | 20 | £38

Soho | 54 Frith St., W1 (Leicester Sq./Piccadilly Circus) | 020-7813 8016 | www.barrafina.co.uk
"The closest you'll get to Madrid in London" laud lovers of this "little" L-shaped Soho site, ever-"buzzing" with "glitzy" types eating its "expertly cooked, top-quality" tapas and other Spanish specialities; true, you'll probably endure "ridiculous" waits before getting a "coveted place at the marble bar" (tip: "check out the queue size on their webcam before you go"), and some snarl the authenticity doesn't extend to the "British Airways-type staff"; all in all, though, it's "a joy."

Bar Shu ☾ *Chinese*
23 | 18 | 17 | £37

Soho | 28 Frith St., W1 (Leicester Sq./Tottenham Court Rd.) | 020-7287 8822 | fax 7287 8858 | www.bar-shu.co.uk
"Hot, hot, hot in more ways than one", this "smart" Soho site is a rare Sichuan specialist in town, preparing "authentic", "unusual

dishes covered in vibrant red chilli" that makes them "fiery like a dragon, and refreshingly so"; although "surprisingly brusque service lets it down", most agree this "tongue-tingling" spot is "a cut above."

Basilico *Pizza*

| 20 | 9 | 15 | £19 |

Finchley | 515 Finchley Rd., NW3 (Finchley Rd.) | 080-0316 2656 | fax 7794 4737
Islington | 26 Penton St., N1 (Islington) | 080-0093 4224 ●
Clapham | 175 Lavender Hill, SW11 (Clapham Junction Rail) | 080-0389 9770 | fax 7978 4254 ●
Fulham | 690 Fulham Rd., SW6 (Fulham Broadway) | 080-0028 3531
Richmond | 178 Upper Richmond Rd., SW14 (Mortlake) | 080-0096 8202
www.basilico.co.uk

"Deserves its reputation as the best delivery outfit in London" declare enthusiasts of this "efficient" quintet and its "thin, crunchy" "real Italian pizzas" featuring the "most amazing toppings"; however, it's "strictly a takeaway option unless you like sitting on stools."

Bedford & Strand ⊠ *British/French*

| ∇ 18 | 15 | 16 | £26 |

Covent Garden | 1A Bedford St., WC2 (Covent Garden) | 020-7836 3033 | www.bedford-strand.com

"The real draw is the wine list" at this casual Covent Gardener – an old-fashioned, bistro-like wine bar whose "good" menu is a mélange of British and French staples; but "service seems to suffer" when it "gets busy and noisy after work."

Beiteddine ● *Lebanese*

| ∇ 21 | 11 | 21 | £31 |

Knightsbridge | 8 Harriet St., SW1 (Knightsbridge/Sloane Sq.) | 020-7235 3969 | fax 7245 6335 | www.beiteddinerestaurant.com

"In an unpretentious environment" (some say "boring"), this glass-fronted Knightsbridge eatery is "among the better places" for "traditional", "high-end Lebanese" victuals; if a few feel it's "expensive compared to similar restaurants" , it's still "value for money."

Belgo *Belgian*

| 18 | 16 | 16 | £25 |

Covent Garden | 50 Earlham St., WC2 (Covent Garden) | 020-7813 2233 | fax 7209 3212
Chalk Farm | 72 Chalk Farm Rd., NW1 (Chalk Farm) | 020-7267 0718 | fax 7284 4842
www.belgo-restaurants.com

"The original Belgian mussels joints", this Covent Garden and Chalk Farm duo offer an "industrial" "beer-hall atmosphere" with "cafeteria-style dining" (unless you opt to eat "on the rich side" with private, reserved tables) and "servers in monks' robes" who "sometimes rush you out, other times are too slow"; if critics call the "concept tired", those in a moules-and-frites mood maintain the menu's "basic, but brilliant" – especially the "mind-blowing beer selection."

⊠ Bellamy's ⊠ *French*

| 22 | 19 | 22 | £56 |

Mayfair | 18-18A Bruton Pl., W1 (Bond St./Green Park) | 020-7491 2727 | fax 7491 9990 | www.bellamysrestaurant.co.uk

There's "a true French feel" to this "buzzy" brasserie, blessed with a "central Mayfair location", "straightforward, but well-prepared food" and "attentive service"; yes, the "decor's a bit of a bore", but the "well-spaced tables" are welcome, so supporters say it "should be a destination - not [just] a when-all-else-fails"; P.S. try sampling the "superb" bivalves at the oyster bar.

Belvedere, The *British/French*   20 | 23 | 21 | £52

Holland Park | Holland Park, off Abbotsbury Rd., W8 (Holland Park) | 020-7602 1238 | fax 7610 4382 | www.belvedererestaurant.co.uk

"In the most beautiful setting of Holland Park" (the entrance "can be a little hard to find"), this "elegant" venue showcases "creative" Modern British–New French cuisine from "attentive", but "not too overbearing staff"; it's "a bit costly", but "picture-perfect" "for that romantic date."

Benares *Indian*   23 | 23 | 21 | £58

Mayfair | 12A Berkeley Square House, W1 (Green Park) | 020-7629 8886 | fax 7499 2430 | www.benaresrestaurant.com

"Don't plan on seeing the usual Indian menu choices" at this "posh" Mayfair venue - an "ethereal dining atmosphere with flowing water and a lily pond" - where chef-patron Atul Kochhar's "technical brilliance" ensures the "precise" "flavours dance off the plate"; staff are highly "attentive", but "get you to over-order", leading some to grouse "good grief - this place is expensive!"

Bengal Clipper ❶ *Indian*   19 | 14 | 13 | £33

Tower Bridge | Cardamom Bldg. | 31 Shad Thames, SE1 (London Bridge/ Tower Hill) | 020-7357 9001 | fax 7357 9002 | www.bengalclipper.co.uk

It might look "like a cafeteria for pensioners", but the Indian food - "a quality spin on your favourites" - "more than makes up" for it at this Shad Thames subcontinental that's been "under family ownership for donkey's years"; if service is "comically inept", at least "the pianist soothes the waiting" most days.

Benihana *Japanese*   19 | 16 | 20 | £38

Piccadilly | 37 Sackville St., W1 (Green Park/Piccadilly Circus) | 020-7494 2525 | fax 7494 1456

Swiss Cottage | 100 Avenue Rd., NW3 (Swiss Cottage) | 020-7586 9508 | fax 7586 6740

Chelsea | 77 Kings Rd., SW3 (Sloane Sq.) | 020-7376 7799 | fax 7376 7377 www.benihana.com

"You always know what to expect at this Japanese steakhouse" trio: "unfailingly energetic" "entertainers-cum-chefs catching all manner of things in their hats whilst cooking" tableside; cynics say the routine is, well, "pretty routine" by now, and you should "never mistake this for *real* Japanese food"; but it makes for "good family fun if you can afford it" ("not for a romantic date, unless you think it might not go well").

Benja ⓩ *Thai*   – | – | – | E

Soho | 17 Beak St., W1 (Oxford Circus/Piccadilly Circus) | 020-7287 0555 | fax 7287 0056

Whilst each floor has a different theme and colour scheme, a "chic, sexy atmosphere" prevails throughout this three-storey Soho site that offers an "innovative" Thai menu of "well-seasoned, perfectly cooked" dishes, served by "attentive, but not hovering staff"; it's a "good date place", with "special-treat cocktails" to lubricate the evening along.

Ben's Thai *Thai*

- | - | - | I

St. John's Wood | 15 Clifton Rd., W9 (Maida Vale/Warwick Ave.) | 020-7266 3134 | fax 7221 8799

"Cheap and tasty eats above a pub" sums up this "reliable" Thai in St. John's Wood; some "just go there for takeaways", whilst others enjoy the "authentic" food at table ("just wish they wouldn't hurry you so much" to finish it).

Bentley's *British/Seafood*

24 | 21 | 21 | £56

Piccadilly | 11-15 Swallow St., W1 (Piccadilly Circus) | 020-7734 4756 | fax 7758 4140 | www.bentleys.org

"So British and so fabulous" fawn fish fans of this long-time "Piccadilly power spot" revived by chef-owner Richard Corrigan; the "traditionally chic surroundings" comprise two parts: a "stress-free" oyster bar, with "shellfish so fresh it jumps into your mouth", and "a more intimate upstairs" with "perfectly prepared" classics; it's "certainly no bargain", and the staff swings from "friendly" to "cheeky", "but it's made up for" by "the Dover sole with soul."

Bertorelli *Italian*

16 | 15 | 15 | £32

Covent Garden | 37 St. Martin's Ln., WC2 (Covent Garden) | 020-7836 5837 | fax 7240 8462

Covent Garden | 44A Floral St., WC2 (Covent Garden) | 020-7836 3969 | fax 7836 1868 ◑

Soho | 11-13 Frith St., W1 (Leicester Sq./Tottenham Court Rd.) | 020-7494 3491 | fax 7439 9431 ◑

Fitzrovia | 19 Charlotte St., W1 (Goodge St./Tottenham Court Rd.) | 020-7636 4174 | fax 7467 8902 ⌷

Blackfriars | 1 Plough Pl., EC4 (Chancery Ln.) | 020-7842 0510 | fax 7842 0511 ⌷

City | Plantation Pl. | 15 Mincing Ln., EC3 (Bank/Monument) | 020-7283 3028 | fax 7929 5987 ⌷

www.santeonline.co.uk

"Casual", "cheap and cheerful" characterises this chain that's "like Chez Gérard, only Italian" (the same group owns both); sure, they're "a bit basic on the decor" and "the waiters could do with a week in charm school", but "the formula" is "a favourite" for a quick meal, and the Covent Garden branches are "handy" "pre- and post-theatre."

Bevis Marks ⌷ *British/Jewish*

▽ 22 | 20 | 22 | £44

City | 4 Heneage Ln., EC3 (Aldgate/Liverpool St.) | 020-7283 2220 | fax 7283 2221 | www.bevismarkstherestaurant.com

Nestled "in a courtyard next to [a historic] synagogue", this City "kosher oasis" "fills a need" with its "enjoyable" Modern British fare, along with "Jewish penicillin" (aka chicken soup) and other classics; the service and setting are equally "stylish."

subscribe to ZAGAT.com

	FOOD	DECOR	SERVICE	COST

Bibendum *French*

	23	24	21	£59

South Kensington | Michelin House | 81 Fulham Rd., SW3
(South Kensington) | 020-7581 5817 | fax 7823 7925 |
www.bibendum.co.uk

"Mr. Bib looks great on the stained-glass windows" of this "dazzling
art nouveau" dining room "in an old Michelin tyre facility" at
Brompton Cross, where chef Matthew Harris prepares "divine", "inventive" New French cuisine, supported by an "extensive wine list"
and "eager-to-please staff"; if a few "feel deflated at the flat atmosphere" and "expense-account" prices, this "grown-up" spot remains a "great staple for a posh night out."

Bibendum Oyster Bar *French/Seafood*

	21	18	17	£37

South Kensington | Michelin House | 81 Fulham Rd., SW3
(South Kensington) | 020-7589 1480 | fax 7823 7925 |
www.bibendum.co.uk

"Still shucking after all these years" (22 to be precise), this "faintly
austere" "tiled landmark" (Michelin's "old garage" at Brompton
Cross) offers a "civilised" "rest from shopping" with its "sweet, succulent oysters" and "tasty", "fresh" French fare; it's a "nice alternative to the proper restaurant" above – even if staff can make "you
feel a bit like the poor relative."

Bierodrome *Belgian*

	16	13	15	£22

Covent Garden | 67 Kingsway, WC2 (Charing Cross/Holborn) |
020-7242 7469 | fax 7242 7493 🖂
Islington | 173-174 Upper St., N1 (Highbury & Islington) |
020-7226 5835 | fax 7704 0632
Clapham | 44-48 Clapham High St., SW4 (Clapham North) |
020-7720 1118 | fax 7720 0288 ☾
www.belgo-restaurants.co.uk

"With 1,000 heavenly beers", this "brash" Belgian brigade is "probably a better bar than restaurant" – especially given the "dingy" digs
and seemingly "intentionally rude staff"; still, given the "economic"
prices, it's a place for the "young crowd" to "come for a mussels fix."

Big Easy ☾ *American*

	16	16	17	£27

Chelsea | 332-334 King's Rd., SW3 (Sloane Sq.) | 020-7352 4071 |
fax 7352 0844 | www.bigeasy.uk.com

"Bring an appetite – you forget how big those American portions
are" – to this King's Road "heaven for surf 'n' turf lovers", where the
fare is "well priced" if "executed without a whole lot of flair"; the
crab-shack setting is "great for kids" and groups, but "if you like
blending with the younger generation, remember your earplugs –
the [nightly] live music is very loud."

NEW Bincho Yakitori *Japanese*

▽	21	19	19	£30

Soho | 16 Old Compton St., W1 (Tottenham Court Rd.) | 020-7287 9111
South Bank | Oxo Tower Wharf | Barge House St., SE1 (Blackfriars/
Waterloo) | 020-7803 0858 ☾
www.bincho.co.uk

Those who go for grills salute this "superb yakitori place" on the second floor of the Oxo Tower, a "smart" if slightly "spartan" newcomer with "authentic Japanese-style nibbles", "plus more sake than you can shake a chopstick at"; its "lively", "informal atmosphere" makes it "great for groups, but not romantic couples" (despite "fantastic views" "overlooking St.Paul's"); N.B. diners can also watch the grill-masters at work at its even younger Soho spin-off.

Bistro 190 ❶ *British/Mediterranean*   − − − E

South Kensington | Gore Hotel | 190 Queen's Gate, SW7 (Gloucester Rd./South Kensington) | 020-7584 6601 | fax 7589 8127 | www.gorehotel.com

Amidst the "charming surroundings of a Victorian hotel", this "oldie but goodie" offers the "warm, welcoming atmosphere of a club", along with an "imaginative" Traditional British–Med menu and a "buzzy bar scene next door"; it's "handy for the Royal Albert Hall" nearby.

Bistrotheque *French*   20 20 20 £35

Bethnal Green | 23-27 Wadeson St., E2 (Bethnal Green) | 020-8983 7900 | fax 8880 6433 | www.bistrotheque.com

"The decor is sparse, but it's more than made up for by the lively diners" – an "interesting array of performers, body-builders and boho riffraff" – at this "converted factory" "in the middle of East End London"; "cute waiters" serve "finely tuned" French bistro fare from "the sort of menu where you want to order everything", and if some sneer at the "too-cool-for-school" scene, the weekend "transvestite cabaret adds a certain something (as well as many extra drinks to the bill)."

Black & Blue *Chophouse*   18 16 18 £30

Marylebone | 90-92 Wigmore St., W1 (Bond St.) | 020-7486 1912 | fax 7486 1913

Borough | Borough Mkt. | 1-2 Rochester Walk, SE1 (London Bridge) | 020-7357 9922

Hampstead | 205-207 Haverstock Hill, NW3 (Belsize Park) | 020-7443 7744 | fax 7443 7744

South Kensington | 105 Gloucester Rd., SW7 (Gloucester Rd.) | 020-7244 7666 | fax 7244 9993

Kensington | 215-217 Kensington Church St., W8 (Notting Hill Gate) | 020-7727 0004 | fax 7229 9359

www.blackandbluerestaurant.co.uk

"Functional", if "a bit formulaic", this "casual" chophouse chain is a "good place to placate carnivorous instincts"; the "high ceilings and comfy booths" have a "retro feel", but "getting a table can be pot-luck", as, "irritatingly, they don't take bookings."

Blah! Blah! Blah! ⓩ⌿ *Vegetarian*   − − − M

Shepherd's Bush | 78 Goldhawk Rd., W12 (Goldhawk Rd.) | 020-8746 1337 | fax 7328 3138

The "good, wholesome fare more than amply fills a hole" at this slightly "tatty" Shepherd's Bush "vegetarian oasis"; if it's "sometimes perplexing how root vegetable dishes can cost the same as a steak elsewhere", at least it "being a BYO keeps things reasonable."

| | FOOD | DECOR | SERVICE | COST |

Blakes *Eclectic* | 19 | 23 | 21 | £69 |

South Kensington | Blakes Hotel | 33 Roland Gdns., SW7 (Gloucester Rd./South Kensington) | 020-7370 6701 | fax 7373 0442 | www.blakeshotels.com

"Stylish and secluded" (so, a "good place if you don't want to be seen with a date"), this "beautiful" "dark" dining room in the basement of a South Ken hotel offers "huge", "delicious" Eclectic dishes "with an Asian twist"; it's rather "expensive", though – hence a request to "halve the portions and halve the price."

Bleeding Heart 🖾 *French* | 22 | 20 | 20 | £46 |

Farringdon | 4 Bleeding Heart Yard, off Greville St., EC1 (Farringdon) | 020-7242 8238 | fax 7831 1402

Bleeding Heart Tavern 🖾 *British*

Farringdon | 19 Greville St., EC1 (Farringdon) | 020-7242 2056 | fax 7831 1402
www.bleedingheart.co.uk

"A bit off the beaten track" in a "historic" Holborn courtyard, this venue is actually "a collection of great spots": a "cosy" bistro with "cute Swiss log cabin decor" and a more "fancy" "atmospheric" downstairs" restaurant, both serving "wholesome, satisfying" New French fare and "well-priced wines"; then there's the informal Tavern on Greville Street, "good for Traditional British soul food and a pint"; main complaint for all: "why don't they open at the weekend?"

Bloom's *Deli/Jewish* | 17 | 11 | 13 | £24 |

Golders Green | 130 Golders Green Rd., NW11 (Golders Green) | 020-8455 1338 | fax 8455 3033

This "old-fashioned, family-run" Golders Green deli remains "the only place in town for a kosher salt beef on rye", plus other "hearty" Jewish classics; whilst most take the "grumpy servers" in stride – at least "they hustle the food out" – the belicose believe the bloom's off: "well below par for what's now in the area."

Bluebird *European* | 18 | 19 | 17 | £43 |

Chelsea | 350 King's Rd., SW3 (Sloane Sq.) | 020-7559-1000 | fax 7559 1111 | www.bluebird-restaurant.co.uk

Whilst considered "more grown-up after refurbishment" in spring 2007, this "sleek" (think "Austin Powers meets the 1970s James Bond"), "roomy" eatery in a Chelsea landmark "could still do more to improve the Modern European menu" and "indifferent service"; however, the ground-floor all-day cafe, a "Sloaney staple", "continues to wow", especially with its "great outdoor space for those rare sunny days."

Blue Elephant ◗ *Thai* | 20 | 24 | 19 | £41 |

Fulham | 4-6 Fulham Broadway, SW6 (Fulham Broadway) | 020-7385 6595 | fax 7386 7665 | www.blueelephant.com

"Amaze friends, family and new flames" at this "lush tropical retreat", "complete with wooden bridges over koi-filled rivers", that looks "unlike anywhere else", especially in Fulham Broadway; given the "uneven" eats – "all the traditional Thai classics prepared every which way" – and the "dodgy service", it's a "poor value" – "but a guilty pleasure" nonetheless; P.S. it's near the Chelsea football club, so "avoid if there's a home match."

Blueprint Café *European* | 18 | 20 | 19 | £38 |

Tower Bridge | Design Museum | 28 Shad Thames, SE1 (London Bridge/ Tower Hill) | 020-7378 7031 | fax 7357 8810 | www.blueprintcafe.co.uk

"Not a cafe, but a full and fancy restaurant", this "modern", "mini-malist" museum dining room offers a Modern European menu that's "enjoyable" (especially the "good value lunch"); but some argue the "real reason to go is the exquisite view of the river and Tower Bridge" – "if you're lucky enough to get a seat on the porch."

Bodeans *BBQ* | 18 | 12 | 16 | £22 |

Soho | 10 Poland St., W1 (Oxford Circus) | 020-7287 7575 | fax 7287 4342
Clapham | 169 Clapham High St., SW4 (Clapham Common) | 020-7622 4248 | fax 7622 3087
Fulham | 4 Broadway Chambers, SW6 (Fulham Broadway) | 020-7610 0440 | fax 7610 1115
NEW **Notting Hill** | 57 Westbourne Grove, W2 (Bayswater) | 020-7727-9503
www.bodeansbbq.com

"Great big servings" of "cheap" vittles make this quartet "a true home for Americans dying for the finer art of ribs" and other barbe-cued treats; the "physical space is nothing to write home about", but "lonely expats" insist this is "the closest London gets to Dixie" – "and if you're lucky, they'll be showing U.S. football too."

Boisdale Ⓢ *British/Scottish* | 20 | 16 | 17 | £44 |

Victoria | 15 Eccleston St., SW1 (Victoria) | 020-7730 6922 | fax 7730 0548 ●
City | Swedeland Ct. | 202 Bishopsgate, EC2 (Liverpool St.) | 020-7283 1763 | fax 7283 1664
www.boisdale.co.uk

"Clubby", "self-consciously lairdlike" surrounds, decorated in red-and-green tartan ("or is that tarty?") offer a "different" setting for the "quintessential English fare" with strong Scottish supplements – "lovely meats" and "fab haggis" – at this "lively" duo in Victoria and the City; true, "service is spotty" and it's "not cheap", but a "well-stocked whisky bar" and "some very jolly jazz" most nights mollify most.

Bombay Bicycle Club *Indian* | 18 | 15 | 16 | £29 |

Hampstead | 3A Downshire Hill, NW3 (Hampstead) | 020-7435 3544 | fax 7794 3367
Clapham | 95 Nightingale Ln., SW12 (Clapham South) | 020-8673 6217 | fax 8673 9100
Holland Park | 128 Holland Park Ave., W11 (Holland Park) | 020-7727 7335 | fax 7727 7305
www.thebombaybicycleclub.co.uk

They're "more expensive than your average curry house, but they don't serve your average curry" at this Indian trio; despite the Indo-European decor, they "lack atmosphere" some say – hence the "unbeatable takeaway" proves "popular."

| | FOOD | DECOR | SERVICE | COST |

Bombay Brasserie ❂ *Indian*   22 | 22 | 21 | £43

South Kensington | Courtfield Rd., SW7 (Gloucester Rd.) | 020-7370 4040 | fax 7835 1669 | www.bombaybrasserielondon.com

Although it's been "around the block a few times", this 27-year-old in South Ken "still sets the standard" for subcontinental classics – such as "awesome curries" – proffered by "attentive, appropriate service" within rooms that evoke "a real feeling of the days of the Raj"; regulars recommend it "to introduce first-time visitors to Indian cuisine."

Bonds *French*   22 | 19 | 18 | £50

City | Threadneedles Hotel | 5 Threadneedle St., EC2 (Bank) | 020-7657 8088 | fax 7657 8100 | www.theetoncollection.com

"In a relative wilderness of good food", this New French's "flavoursome" fare is "more interesting than most City restaurants'"; the "swanky" "converted bank" venue and staff who "just let you be" make it a "location where deals get done (or at least discussed)" – mainly during the week (it serves breakfast only Saturday–Sunday).

Books for Cooks Ⓢ Ⓜ *Eclectic*   23 | 19 | 20 | £18

Notting Hill | 4 Blenheim Crescent, W11 (Ladbroke Grove/ Notting Hill Gate) | 020-7221 1992 | fax 7221 1517 | www.booksforcooks.com

"An iconic destination for serious cooks", this "teeny-tiny" cafe "located at the back of a unique bookshop" off Ladbroke Grove features "wildly exciting", "experimental" Eclectic meals (one choice per day), using recipes "taken from featured cookbooks"; it's "the biggest bargain in town – but don't tell anyone, it's busy enough."

NEW BORD'EAUX *French*   - | - | - | VE

Mayfair | Grosvenor House | Park Ln., W1 (Marble Arch) | 020-7399 8460 | www.bord-eaux.com

The Grosvenor House's new high-ceilinged, huge-windowed restaurant overlooking Park Lane is kitted out like a classic Gallic brasserie, circa 1930s; jolly chef Ollie Couillaud (ex Tom's Kitchen and The Dorchester's Grill) brings the gutsy tastes of his native Aquitaine to a "solid" Southwestern French menu that's "highly expensive, but at least has the surroundings and services to back up the top prices."

NEW Botanist, The *British*   - | - | - | E

Chelsea | 7 Sloane Sq., SW1 (Sloane Sq.) | 020-7730 0077 | www.thebotanistonsloanesquare.com

Gastropub-ateurs Ed and Tom Martin add to their portfolio (The Gun, Empress of India) this all-day brasserie in a "prime location" on Sloane Square; already there's "lots of action at the bar", whilst the beige-toned dining room, adorned with painted replicas of Sir Hans Sloane's botanical discoveries, offers an upmarket Modern British menu, delivered by "attentive", but "a bit slow service."

Bouga ❂ *Moroccan*   - | - | - | M

Muswell Hill | 1 Park Rd., N8 (Archway) | 020-8348 5609

There's a "family feel" to this neighbourhood haunt in "buzzy Crouch End", offering all the Moroccan mainstays at moderate prices, plus "great cocktails" and weekend belly dancing, amidst the candlelit contours of an Old Marrakech–themed setting.

Bountiful Cow ⧄ *Chophouse*

▽ 21 | 18 | 21 | £28

Holborn | 51 Eagle St., WC1 (Holborn) | 020-7404 0200 | fax 7404 0200
A bit "difficult to find" in a Holborn side street, this chophouse from TV chef Roxy Beaujolais offers all manner of meats, but it's the "expertly cooked and flavourful" "giant hamburgers" that get the most mention; decorated with "funky" bovine-themed film posters, the "relaxed pub"-like place also wins points for value.

⧉ Boxwood Café ◗ *British*

23 | 21 | 22 | £62

Belgravia | The Berkeley | Wilton Pl., SW1 (Hyde Park Corner/Knightsbridge) | 020-7235 1010 | fax 7235 1011 | www.gordonramsay.com
"The less-stuffy face of Gordon Ramsay" is on show at the celebrity chef's "chic, yet chilled" Berkeley hotel dining room where an "imaginative" Modern British menu with "mischievous food pairings" "meets the desires of modern customers for less-fussy fine dining"; "staff are welcoming", and if it's "not the best" in GR's stable, at least it comes "at a (marginally) lower price."

Brackenbury, The *European*

▽ 21 | 18 | 19 | £25

Hammersmith | 129-131 Brackenbury Rd., W6 (Goldhawk Rd./Hammersmith) | 020-8748 0107 | fax 8748 6159
"Perhaps not worth a special trip, but if you're out west", this "neighbourhood haunt" in Hammersmith offers "inventive", "good-value" Modern European meals with "agreeable service"; the brown-and-green interior does get "stuffed with 'meedja' types", so there's gratitude for the "outside seating in good weather."

Bradley's *British/French*

▽ 16 | 15 | 20 | £46

Swiss Cottage | 25 Winchester Rd., NW3 (Swiss Cottage) | 020-7722 3457 | fax 7435 1392 | www.bradleysnw3.co.uk
Those Swiss Cottagers who claim to be "lucky to have this as a local" cite a "reliable" Classic French–Modern British menu with "great deals" for the "pre-theatre crowd"; but others find it "hard to understand why this rather ordinary place inspires such loyalty."

Brasserie Roux *French*

21 | 19 | 19 | £47

St. James's | Sofitel St. James London | 8 Pall Mall, SW1 (Piccadilly Circus) | 020-7968 2900 | fax 7389 7647 | www.sofitelstjames.com
Benefiting from the "rather grand atmosphere" of the high-ceilinged premises, this St. James's brasserie has its supporters for "good-quality" French fare on an Albert Roux–inspired menu ("very worthwhile pre-theatre"), with "tempting wine bargains"; but cynics roux the day they visited this "expensive" place, protesting it's "not as good as it aims for – and somehow as it should be."

NEW Brasserie St. Jacques *French*

- | - | - | E

St. James's | 33 St. James's St., SW1 (Green Park) | 020-7839 1007 | fax 7839 3204 | www.brasseriestjacques.co.uk
The combo of prolific restaurateur Claudio Pulze (51 openings to his name) and consulting chef Pierre Koffmann (of the legendary La

Tante Claire) bodes well for this polished St. James's newcomer in the former Fiori space – a narrow, golden-hued room with chandeliers, well-spaced tables and plush red chairs and banquettes; the upscale French brasserie menu offers a wide spread, served in various guises from 8 AM until the kitchen pulls down the shutters at 11:30 PM.

Brasserie St. Quentin *French*

20 | 18 | 19 | £40

Knightsbridge | 243 Brompton Rd., SW3 (Knightsbridge/
South Kensington) | 020-7589 8005 | fax 7584 6064

"Beloved by regulars and shoppers alike", this "lively" "old-style brasserie" "directly across from the V&A Museum" is a "perennially good" option for "well-executed" French fare from "British-sourced foodstuffs"; if there are "no culinary exploits" here, at least "you can imagine you're in the middle of Paris."

NEW Brickhouse, The *European*

- | - | - | E

Shoreditch | Old Truman Brewery | 152C Brick Ln., E1 (Aldgate East) |
020-7247 0005 | www.thebrickhouse.co.uk

"Book a table on the mezzanine to get a bird's-eye view of the action" – "cutting-edge" club acts – at this multilevel Modern European in Brick Lane; reviewers rave about the "refreshing, non-formulaic" experience, from the airy, art-adorned "urban setting" carved out of an 18th-century brewery to the "imaginative" eats to the four beds for reclining and relaxing on the top floor.

Brinkley's *Eclectic*

14 | 15 | 16 | £33

Chelsea | 47 Hollywood Rd., SW10 (Earl's Ct./South Kensington) |
020-7351 1683 | fax 7376 5083 | www.brinkleys.com

A "favourite hangout for Chelsea girls and their companions", this Eclectic "Hollywood Road venue serves good grub" at reasonable prices – plus there's "a great wine selection if you get your bottle from the shop" next door; "charming, if sometimes haphazard staff" and a garden that's "amazing in summer and nice in winter" (it's heated) complete the picture.

Brompton Quarter Café *Eclectic*

15 | 18 | 12 | £30

Knightsbridge | 223-225 Brompton Rd., SW3 (Knightsbridge/
South Kensington) | 020-7225 2107 | www.bromptonquartercafe.com

Whilst knocking about Knightsbridge, this white-hued "hip cafe" is "handy for a shopping stop", since the Eclectic menu offers "a choice, from small things to large main meals" (there's a juice bar and patisserie as well as a restaurant); but doubters declare the "place looks much better than the food tastes" – and the way "indifferent" staff behave.

Brown Dog, The *European*

- | - | - | M

Barnes | 28 Cross St., SW13 (Hammersmith) | 020-8392 2200 |
www.thebrowndog.co.uk

Unsurprisingly, given its name, "dogs are welcome and roam the dining room" at this cosy gastropub stretching back over 150 years; the "perfectly recommendable" Modern European menu heavy "with French influences" is such "good value", the place tends to be "full of braying Barnes residents (you might want earmuffs)."

	FOOD	DECOR	SERVICE	COST

Browns *British* 16 | 17 | 16 | £34

Covent Garden | 82-84 St. Martin's Ln., WC2 (Leicester Sq.) | 020-7497 5050 | fax 7497 5005

Mayfair | 47 Maddox St., W1 (Bond St./Oxford Circus) | 020-7491 4565 | fax 7497 4564

Canary Wharf | Hertsmere Rd., E14 (Canary Wharf/ West India Quay DLR) | 020-7987 9777 | fax 7537 1341

City | 8 Old Jewry, EC2 (Bank) | 020-7606 6677 | fax 7600 5359 🛇

Tower Bridge | Shad Thames, SE1 (London Bridge) | 020-7378 1700 | fax 7378 7468

Islington | 9 Islington Green, N1 (Angel) | 020-7226 2555 | fax 7359 7306 www.browns-restaurants.com

If "nothing's too fancy, nothing's too bad either" at this "reasonable, reliable" and "relaxing" chain that offers "home-cooked" British fare in "publike settings"; if some branches look "a bit jaded now" and are "unfortunately overcome by tourists", they're still "fine for a leisurely – they don't do it any other way – lunch or dinner."

NEW **Brumus** – | – | – | E

Restaurant & Bar ◑ *European*

Piccadilly | Haymarket Hotel | 1 Suffolk Pl., SW1 (Piccadilly Circus) | 020-7470 4000 | fax 7470 4004 | www.firmdalehotels.com

A "welcome new option" for Piccadilly, this hotel eatery "tries so hard" with decor that's "quirky, but stylish" (think hot pink hues and umbrella-shaped lights) and a Modern European menu; but the "youthfulness of the staff does not play well", leaving some to conclude it's more a "place for a drink."

Brunello *Italian* ▽ 23 | 18 | 18 | £70

Kensington | Baglioni | 60 Hyde Park Gate, SW7 (Gloucester Rd./ High St. Kensington) | 020-7368 5900 | fax 7368 5701 | www.baglionihotellondon.com

"Bold decor and even bolder prices" characterise this "contemporary" hotel dining room opposite Kensington Gardens, where "you never know who might be sitting at the table next to you . . . Rod Stewart?"; the "quality" Italian cuisine veers towards comforting classics, supported by an extensively "good wine list."

Buen Ayre *Argentinean* – | – | – | M

Hackney | 50 Broadway Mkt., E8 (Bethnal Green) | 020-7275 9900 | fax 7900 3941 | www.buenayre.co.uk

"Hidden, but worth the visit" is the consensus on this "convivial", dinner-only Hackney grill where the "decor is basic, but feels right for the people (young, informal)" attracted by its "authentic", "affordable Argentinean steaks", served in portions "not for the fainthearted."

Builders Arms *British* 17 | 17 | 18 | £25

Chelsea | 13 Britten St., SW3 (Sloane Sq./South Kensington) | 020-7349 9040 | fax 7351 3181 | www.geronimo-inns.co.uk

An "eclectic local crowd" ensure this laid-back Chelsea haunt (whose "decor features sofas and easy chairs") "gets busy and boisterous", so expect the otherwise "nice" "service to get hassled at times"; foodwise, it's "perfectly fine" – British gastropub fare with a "new spin on old favourites", supported by "great Continental beers and wines, along with traditional ales."

Bull, The *European*

	FOOD	DECOR	SERVICE	COST
	-	-	-	E

Highgate | 13 North Hill, N6 (Highgate) | 0845-456 5033 | fax 0845-456 5034 | www.inthebull.biz

"Buzzing most evenings" (so "bring earplugs"), this Highgate boozer offers a "delightful" Modern European menu that "raises the usual gastropub standard so you don't mind paying that bit more"; however, dissenters would dock the wages of the "indifferent staff."

Bumpkin ● *British*

	FOOD	DECOR	SERVICE	COST
	19	17	19	£34

Notting Hill | 209 Westbourne Park Rd., W11 (Westbourne Park) | 020-7243 9818 | www.bumpkinuk.com

There's "always a scene" at this "all-rounder pleaser", "with people coming in jeans and T-shirts for a country night out in the city" (technically, Notting Hill); within the "funky", bucolic-themed "many rooms" on "several floors", "friendly, flirtatious staff serve up locally grown produce" and other "hearty British comfort foods"; whilst savouring the "warm, inviting" atmo, though, critics cry "the bill adds up far too quickly for what's essentially a great gastropub"; N.B. a second branch is planned in South Ken in September.

Buona Sera ● *Italian*

	FOOD	DECOR	SERVICE	COST
	18	15	17	£29

Battersea | 22-26 Northcote Rd., SW11 (Clapham Junction Rail) | 020-7228 9925 | fax 7228 1114
Chelsea | 289A King's Rd., SW3 (Sloane Sq.) | 020-7352 8827 | fax 7352 8827

"As long as you are able to climb into high spaces", the "double-decker tables are a fun twist" at these "buzzing" Battersea and Chelsea Italians that are "good for group outings" or even "a first date"; foodwise, there's "decent pasta and pizza, but nothing else."

☑ Busaba Eathai *Thai*

	FOOD	DECOR	SERVICE	COST
	22	19	16	£22

Bloomsbury | 22 Store St., WC1 (Goodge St.) | 020-7299 7900 | fax 7299 7909
Marylebone | 8-13 Bird St., W1 (Bond St.) | 020-7518 8080 | fax 7518 8088
Soho | 106-110 Wardour St., W1 (Piccadilly Circus/Tottenham Court Rd.) | 020-7255 8686

"An amazing accomplishment: a chain with truly great food" fawn fans of this "busy, brash" bevy of "dark, woodsy" West Enders; "although there are always queues, you never have to wait too long" before sitting down – you "share a big square table with other people" – and tucking into the "Thai fare with a twist"; and despite the "haphazard service", most leave "with the feeling of having gotten a good deal."

Bush Bar & Grill *European*

	FOOD	DECOR	SERVICE	COST
	▽ 18	17	16	£28

Shepherd's Bush | 45A Goldhawk Rd., W12 (Goldhawk Rd./Shepherd's Bush) | 020-8746 2111 | fax 8746 7114 | www.bushbar.co.uk

It "looks like a converted scout hut or tiny aircraft hangar" from the outside, and "feels a bit '90s" when inside, but this "Shepherd's

Bush staple" has a "relaxed atmosphere that belies the sophistication" of the "reasonably priced" Modern European cooking – plus there's a "snazzy bar" with "excellent cocktails."

Butcher & Grill, The British | 18 | 17 | 15 | £37

Battersea | 39-41 Parkgate Rd., SW11 (Clapham Junction Rail) | 020-7924 3999 | fax 7223 7979

NEW Wimbledon | 33 High St., SW19 (Wimbledon) | 020-8944 8269
www.thebutcherandgrill.com

A "vibrant atmosphere and juicy cuts" make it "just the job as a local drop-in spot" say supporters of this Traditional Brit/butcher's shop backing onto a Battersea dock; but sceptics snap this place "needs to deliver" more than "so-so" service and "passable food"; N.B. an offshoot is now serving 'em up in Wimbledon.

Butlers Wharf Chop House British | 22 | 20 | 19 | £40

Tower Bridge | Butlers Wharf Bldg. | 36E Shad Thames, SE1 (London Bridge/Tower Hill) | 020-7403 3403 | fax 7940 1855 | www.chophouse.co.uk

"Sit outside" and enjoy "spectacular views" of Tower Bridge and beyond on the banks of the Thames at this "buzzy" British chophouse; the "old-fashioned food" is "above average", both in quality and price – leading some to believe it tastes "better if you have an expense account" or can make use of the "excellent-value lunch."

Café Boheme ● French | 18 | 17 | 17 | £32

Soho | 13-17 Old Compton St., W1 (Leicester Sq./Tottenham Court Rd.) | 020-7734 0623 | fax 7434 3775 | www.cafeboheme.co.uk

"Busy from dawn until dusk", this "hard to get into" French cafe "hits the spot" as somewhere "cool just to hang", with "great people-watching of the Soho streets"; "atmosphere is its most redeeming trait, however" – don't expect more than "ok" eats from "rather random service", or else "stick to late-night drinks."

Café des Amis ●図 French | 19 | 19 | 19 | £35

Covent Garden | 11-14 Hanover Pl., WC2 (Covent Garden) | 020-7379 3444 | fax 7379 9124 | www.cafedesamis.co.uk

"Popular" with the "pre/post-opera hounds", this "pleasant modern French" in a "tiny alleyway" has been a "Covent Garden standby" for more than 20 years – "a reasonable choice, if not a destination"; *amis* enjoy its "ever-reliable" bistro fare "with a wine list to complement", but others find it's "more fun" to "sneak downstairs to the bar for fine cheeses and cheeky reds."

Café Japan Ⓜ Japanese | 25 | 10 | 19 | £29

Golders Green | 626 Finchley Rd., NW11 (Golders Green) | 020-8455 6854 | fax 8455 6854

"Sizable portions" of "staggeringly fresh, staggeringly good" sushi at "conveyor-belt prices" mean "it's always a struggle to get a place" at this "tiny" "jam-packed" Japanese; nevertheless, it's "worth a trip all the way to Golders Green" despite the "unpredictable hours" ("booking is more than advisable") and interior that "could do with a lick of paint"; N.B. dinner only, except at the weekend (cash-only lunch).

	FOOD	DECOR	SERVICE	COST

Cafe Med ❶ *Mediterranean* — 17 | 12 | 15 | £31

St. John's Wood | 21 Loudoun Rd., NW8 (St. John's Wood) |
020-7625 1222

"Solid Mediterranean food in a bistro setting" sums up this
St. John's Wood "standby"; area denizens deem it a "decent local if
you don't want to travel too far", given that it's "good value", the
staff are "used to dealing with kids" and there's "nice dining
alfresco", come summer.

Cafe Pacifico ❶ *Mexican* — 16 | 14 | 14 | £30

Covent Garden | 5 Langley St., WC2 (Covent Garden) | 020-7379 7728 |
fax 7379 5933 | www.cafepacifico-laperla.com

"Don't be frightened off by the scruffy decor", "too-close tables"
and the "no-reservations chaos on weekends" – this "very lively
(sometimes too lively)" Covent Garden cantina is, converts claim,
the "only plausible Tex-Mex in town"; if some quip "that's not saying
much" – well, this *is* "London and not Laredo" after all.

Café Rouge *French* — 14 | 14 | 14 | £25

Covent Garden | 34 Wellington St., WC2 (Covent Garden) |
020-7836 0998 | fax 7497 0738
Knightsbridge | 27-31 Basil St., SW3 (Knightsbridge) | 020-7584 2345 |
fax 7584 4253
Canary Wharf | 10 Cabot Sq., E14 (Canary Wharf) | 020-7537 9696 |
fax 7987 1232
Highgate | 6-7 South Grove, N6 (Highgate) | 020-8342 9797
St. John's Wood | 120 St. John's Wood High St., NW8 (St. John's Wood) |
020-7722 8366 | fax 7483 1015
Clapham | 40 Abbeville Rd., SW4 (Clapham South) | 020-8673 3399 |
fax 8673 2299
Dulwich | 84 Park Hall Rd., SE21 (West Dulwich) | 020-8766 0070
Putney | 200 Putney Bridge Rd., SW15 (Putney Bridge) | 020-8788 4257
Chiswick | 227-229 Chiswick High Rd., W4 (Chiswick Park) |
020-8742 7447 | fax 8742 7557
Shepherd's Bush | 98-100 Shepherd's Bush Rd., W6 (Shepherd's Bush) |
020-7602 7732 | fax 7603 7710
www.caferouge.co.uk
Additional locations throughout London

"Nothing spectacular, but never disappoints" sums up this ever-
"bustling" chain around town; the French fare is just "so-so bistro",
the "interiors look too choreographed" and staff seemingly "don't
care if you come back or not", but given the "good locations", it
works well "for a quick bite."

Café Spice Namasté ☒ *Indian* — 23 | 15 | 18 | £34

City | 16 Prescot St., E1 (Aldgate/Tower Hill) | 020-7488 9242 |
fax 7488 9339 | www.cafespice.co.uk

Chef-patron "Cyrus Todiwala is a genius", and it shows in the "inventive Indian food" cooked at his colourful place "near Tower Hill" (admittedly "out-of-the-way unless you're in the City"); more
controversial is the setting, a strongly hued "warehouse" that re-
minds one reviewer of "an '80s Mexican chain restaurant, best
suited to large groups."

	FOOD	DECOR	SERVICE	COST

Caldesi 🗷 *Italian* | 22 | 16 | 18 | £46 |
Marylebone | 15-17 Marylebone Ln., W1 (Bond St.) | 020-7935 9226 | fax 7935 9228

🆕 Caldesi in Campagna 🅼 *Italian*
Bray | Old Mill Ln., Berkshire | 01628 788500
www.caldesi.com

Dining at this "intimate" trattoria is "pretty close to being back in Tuscany", thanks to cuisine that offers "a true taste of traditional" fare, an "assured welcome" ("if you're a regular") and ambience that's as "good for a celebration as for a quiet dinner for two"; if some quibble it's the "kind of place you can't find fault with until you see the price", most maintain it's "one of Marylebone's best-kept secrets"; N.B. when in Bray, check out its new country cousin.

🇿 Cambio de Tercio ❶ *Spanish* | 25 | 17 | 20 | £42 |
South Kensington | 163 Old Brompton Rd., SW5 (Gloucester Rd./ South Kensington) | 020-7244 8970 | fax 7373 8817 | www.cambiodetercio.co.uk

"The darkly atmospheric room is the perfect showcase" for the "fabulous" fare at this "authentic" "awesome Spaniard" in South Ken; it's "cramped" and "annoyingly overpriced for casual tapas", but staff make you feel "like you're being served by friends", thus making it "a place to go back to again and again."

Camden Brasserie *European* | 20 | 16 | 20 | £33 |
Camden Town | 9-11 Jamestown Rd., NW1 (Camden Town) | 020-7482 2114 | fax 7482 2777 | www.camdenbrasserie.co.uk

"Still hanging in there" after 26 years, this "comfortably busy" Camden haunt is "no more or less than a good brasserie should be", with a "well-executed Modern European menu" ("rib of beef is the speciality"), a variety of varietals and "pleasant staff" – all "at fair prices."

Camerino 🗷 *Italian* | - | - | - | E |
Fitzrovia | 16 Percy St., W1 (Tottenham Court Rd.) | 020-7637 9900 | fax 7637 9696 | www.camerinorestaurant.com

There's a "good three-martini working lunch atmosphere (it's across the road from a media agency, so no wonder)" at this "family-run" Fitzrovian serving "wholesome Italian fare"; true, "service can be slow – but this food should not be hurried."

Canteen *British* | 18 | 17 | 15 | £27 |
Spitalfields | 2 Crispin Pl., E1 (Liverpool St.) | 0845-686 1122 | fax 686 1144
South Bank | Royal Festival Hall | Belvedere Rd., SE1 (Waterloo) | 0845-686 1122
www.canteen.co.uk

"Gives British food a good name" agree enthusiasts about this "casual", "convivial" spot in Spitalfields Market, with a "nice second location" at the Royal Festival Hall, where clients sit at long tables to consume savoury pies and other "homely" fare; sliding scores confirm comments about "a slipping kitchen", "scatty staff" and "no-frills" decor ("like a posh Ikea shop"), but you "don't expect the exceptional – it's a canteen, after all."

Cantina del Ponte *Italian*   18 | 17 | 18 | £36

Tower Bridge | Butlers Wharf Bldg. | 36C Shad Thames, SE1 (London Bridge/Tower Hill) | 020-7403 5403 | fax 7940 1845 | www.cantina.co.uk

"Very competent" fare "from a wood-burning oven" and "a wine list packed with Italian gems" ensures this Butlers Wharf representative of The Boot "remains a favourite" of fans; but cynics claim it's "nice, like when describing a 'nice' boyfriend": the fare's getting "pricey" (though the large "choice of pizzas can make for cheaper eats") and as for service – "it's a good job we had a table with a view, since we were given plenty of time to admire it."

Cantina Vinopolis *Eclectic/Mediterranean*   ▽ 18 | 18 | 14 | £36

South Bank | Vinopolis Museum | 1 Bank End, SE1 (London Bridge) | 020-7940 8333 | fax 7940 9339 | www.cantinavinopolis.com

"As would be expected" from an eatery in the Vinopolis Museum, there's an "extraordinary wine list" with some "excellent pairings" at this "charming" venue under the arches of a Victorian railway viaduct; the Eclectic-Med "food is quite good", plus there's usually "no need for reservations if you go late, after the bustle of tourists is over."

NEW Cape Town   ▽ 18 | 15 | 18 | £46
Fish Market *Eclectic/Seafood*

Soho | Sutherland House | 5-6 Argyll St., W1 (Oxford Circus) | 020-7437 1143 | www.capetownfishmarket.co.uk

Offshoot of a South African chain, this grey-and-blue–hued Soho newcomer "does a good job of mimicking the food we find on the western Cape" – chiefly "fresh, savoury" fish and other Eclectic edibles – expats enthuse; but lachrymose locals lament the fare's "not as tasty as it sounds on the menu."

Ⓩ Capital Restaurant, The *French*   26 | 22 | 26 | £76

Knightsbridge | Capital Hotel | 22-24 Basil St., SW3 (Knightsbridge) | 020-7591 1202 | fax 7225 0011 | www.capitalhotel.co.uk

"In a setting reminiscent of an intimate dining room in someone's home", the Capital Hotel's "hidden gem" is "always a fulfilling experience", thanks to "star" chef Eric Chavot's "seasonally attuned" New French "cuisine that never fails to excite the palate" and "devoted host"-like staff who ensure "you're well looked after"; *oui*, it's "*très* expensive", "but if getting away from pounding music is your thing, this is your venue."

Caraffini ◐Ⓩ *Italian*   22 | 17 | 22 | £41

Chelsea | 61-63 Lower Sloane St., SW1 (Sloane Sq.) | 020-7259 0235 | fax 7259 0236 | www.caraffini.co.uk

"You can't go wrong" with this "bright, breezy Italian" near Sloane Square; it's "justifiably popular" for its "jolly, central-casting waiters", "warm ambience" and "timeless" *cucina*, which, if "somewhat unoriginal" is "also quite affordable by London standards."

	FOOD	DECOR	SERVICE	COST

Caravaggio ⓩ *Italian* ▽ 15 | 15 | 14 | £43

City | 107-112 Leadenhall St., EC3 (Bank/Monument) | 020-7626 6206 | fax 7626 8108 | www.etruscagroup.co.uk

When seeking "a reliable spot" for a bout of "City power-lunching", diners "can do worse" than this weekday-only Italian – even if the art deco-ish decor is looking "dated" and the "overworked" servers are just "ok"; "but remember, no expense account, no Caravaggio."

Carluccio's Caffè *Italian* 17 | 14 | 14 | £23

Bloomsbury | 8 Market Pl., W1 (Oxford Circus) | 020-7636 2228 | fax 7636 9650

NEW **Covent Garden** | Garrick St., WC2 (Covent Garden) | 020-7836 0990 | fax 7836 0001

Marylebone | St. Christopher's Pl., W1 (Bond St.) | 020-7935 5927

Mayfair | Fenwick | 63 New Bond St., downstairs, W1 (Bond St.) | 020-7629 0699 | fax 7493 0069

Canary Wharf | Reuters Plaza | 2 Nash Ct., E14 (Canary Wharf) | 020-7719 1749 | fax 7513 1197

Smithfield | 12 W. Smithfield, EC1 (Farringdon) | 020-7329 5904 | fax 7248 5981

Islington | 305-307 Upper St., N1 (Angel) | 020-7359 8167 | fax 7354 9196

Fulham | 236 Fulham Rd., SW10 (Fulham Broadway) | 020-7376 5960 | fax 7376 3698

Putney | Putney Wharf, SW15 (Putney Bridge) | 020-8789 0591 | fax 8789 8360

Hammersmith | 5-6 The Green, W5 (Ealing Broadway) | 020-8566 4458 | fax 8840 8566

www.carluccios.com

Additional locations throughout London

There's "lots of variation by location, but generally the food's ok" at this "basic Italian" chain founded by celebrity chef Antonio Carluccio; true, the "cheerful" "staff often don't know what they're doing" and the "decor feels like high-end Ikea", with "no soft furnishings to deaden the din" of many "screaming kids"; nonetheless, all's "worth enduring" because the group "fills a critical price gap."

Carpaccio ●ⓑⓩ *Italian* 18 | 18 | 18 | £46

Chelsea | 4 Sydney St., SW3 (South Kensington) | 020-7352 3433 | www.carpacciorestaurant.co.uk

"Feeling like a neighbourhood restaurant where no one knows their neighbours" – because they're all "beautiful people" or "pretty Eurotrash" – this "crammed" Chelsea haunt is "a real scene"; whilst the dishes are "decent", it's "definitely not the place to go for great Italian food or efficient service" – or deep conversation ("you cannot talk, it's so noisy").

Casale Franco Ⓜ *Italian* - | - | - | M

Islington | 134-137 Upper St., N1 (Angel/Highbury & Islington) | 020-7226 8994 | fax 7359 1114

Entering its 20th year, this "quirky" theatrically themed "Islington Italian just keeps going", offering "amazing pizzas and friendly service" to locals and Almeida Theatre-goers alike.

	FOOD	DECOR	SERVICE	COST

Cay tre *Vietnamese* ∇ 23 | 7 | 13 | £19

Hoxton | 301 Old St., EC1 (Old St.) | 020-7729 8662 | www.vietnamesekitchen.co.uk

"Like a trip to Saigon without the jet-lag" describes the experience at this "outstanding" Vietnamese "smack bang in the middle of Old Street"; however, its "cheap food" keeps it "packed at dinner" – another reason that the "unappealing, cramped room" is "not for lingering."

Cecconi's ● *Italian* 21 | 20 | 21 | £52

Mayfair | 5A Burlington Gdns., W1 (Green Park/Piccadilly Circus) | 020-7434 1500 | fax 7434 2020 | www.cecconis.co.uk

"It's all about the scene – but the food's not bad either" at this Mayfair "classy waterhole for the beautiful people" from Nick Jones (Soho House); a "cosmopolitan crowd" congregate in the "chic green-and-black" environs for "unstuffy" Italian eats "available all day and till late" and to be "treated like a star (even though I'm not)"; it's a touch "overpriced", perhaps, but a "go-to location when many others are closed – or even when they're open."

Cellar Gascon ● 🅱 *French* - | - | - | E

Smithfield | 59 W. Smithfield, EC1 (Barbican/Farringdon) | 020-7796 0600 | fax 7796 0601 | www.comptoirgascon.com

"The small brother of Club Gascon" a couple of doors away, this "laid-back" Smithfield site also specialises in "fantastic" "Southwest French tapas-style dishes" ("foie gras aficionados are swooning"); the nibbles are "backed up by an even better wine list", with "knowledgeable sommeliers" to guide diners through some "most attractive and unusual" varietals, "with many selections available by the glass."

NEW Cha Cha Moon 🅱 *Chinese* - | - | - | I

Soho | 15-21 Ganton St., W1 (Piccadilly Circus/Oxford Circus) | 020-7297 9800

Legendary restaurateur Alan Yau continues his knack of capturing the London culinary mood with his latest: a spacious, speedy-serving Soho noodle house; the queues already lapping its shores are testimony to the appeal of its sultry, slinky look and sensibly priced, cleverly structured menu that ranges from China to Malaysia for its influences.

NEW Champagne Bar, The *British* ∇ 14 | 21 | 15 | £30

King's Cross | St. Pancras Int'l | Pancras Rd., NW1 (King's Cross/ St. Pancras) | 020-3006 1550 | www.searcystpancras.co.uk

It's a "champagne bar first, restaurant second – but you can't fault the setting" of this long, open-air newcomer stretching along a train platform in the "amazing" renovated St. Pancras International station; aside from breakfast, the menu mostly consists of Modern British nibbles from Searcy caterers to accompany the 72 brands of bubbly; and though they "could do with a couple more cheaper glasses", it's "a lovely experience" – down to "the heated seats."

	FOOD	DECOR	SERVICE	COST

Champor-Champor 🈯 *Malaysian* — ▽ 20 | 24 | 21 | £36

Tower Bridge | 62-64 Weston St., SE1 (London Bridge) | 020-7403 4600 | www.champor-champor.com

"Located in a backstreet" near London Bridge, this "quirky" eatery is "not easy to find", but those who do are rewarded by an "eclectic" "unusual interior" – "like eating in an Asian antiques shop" – and a "wildly creative" menu that melds Malaysian and other Asian fare (the name doesn't mean 'mix and match' for nothing); both cuisine and service have "some ups and downs", but it's "well worth a visit" overall.

Chancery, The 🈯 *European* — 17 | 16 | 18 | £44

Holborn | 9 Cursitor St., EC4 (Chancery Ln.) | 020-7831 4000 | fax 7831 4002 | www.thechancery.co.uk

From the Clerkenwell Dining Room team comes this discreet "oasis in the culinary desert" of Holborn, where "attendant servers" offer a "solid, but not spectacular" Modern European menu in a modern, white-walled, wooden-floored setting that can be booked for private dinners on Saturday.

Chapter Two *European* — 23 | 17 | 21 | £47

Blackheath | 43-45 Montpelier Vale, SE3 (Blackheath Rail) | 020-8333 2666 | fax 8355 8399 | www.chaptersrestaurants.co.uk

"Has never failed to delight me" gush lovers of this "reliable and reasonably priced" Blackheath haute cuisine haven whose "excellent" Modern European meals are served by staff that are "attentive, yet relaxed enough to leave you to it"; "the room lacks a bit of soul though."

Charlotte's Place *European* — – | – | – | M

Ealing | 16 St. Matthew's Rd., W5 (Ealing Broadway/Ealing Common) | 020-8567 7541 | www.charlottes.co.uk

A "cosy" renovated Victorian home houses "inventive Modern European cooking" at this "reasonable", two-storey Ealing Common local; "friendly service" adds to the "pleasant" ambience.

Chelsea Brasserie *European* — 17 | 15 | 15 | £47

Chelsea | Sloane Square Hotel | 7-12 Sloane Sq., SW1 (Sloane Sq.) | 020-7881 5999 | www.sloanesquarehotel.co.uk

With "tables looking out at Sloane Square, you almost feel like you're in Paris" at this hotel eatery with "obscure green lighting"; alas, the illusion ends with the Modern European cooking ("just not that great") and service ("unbelievably slow"); still, it's a comparatively "reasonable place in an expensive part of town", "and handy for the Royal Court Theatre" opposite.

Chelsea Bun *British* — ▽ 14 | 7 | 15 | £13

Chelsea | 9A Limerston St., SW10 (Earl's Ct./Sloane Sq.) | 020-7352 3635 | fax 7376 5158 | www.chelseabun.co.uk

Considered one of the "best places to treat a hangover", this "casual" (at best) cafe "just off King's Road" is a "place to hang over a quick, cheap meal" of "classic British fry-ups" and "sassy U.S.-style" diner fare.

	FOOD	DECOR	SERVICE	COST

Ⓩ Cheyne Walk Brasserie *French* | 23 | 24 | 21 | £49 |

Chelsea | 50 Cheyne Walk, SW3 (Sloane Sq./
South Kensington) | 020-7376 8787 | fax 7376 5878 |
www.cheynewalkbrasserie.com

"Order something done over the wood-burning fire" that dominates the "wonderfully warm", "luminous setting" of this "cosy"
Chelsea "French rustic" that also boasts a "sexy", "inviting" bar
"with river views upstairs"; be warned, though: "you can hardly
ever get a table", and the "attitude is not too welcoming, if you
are not a regular."

Ⓩ Chez Bruce *British* | 29 | 21 | 26 | £58 |

Wandsworth | 2 Bellevue Rd., SW17 (Balham/
Wandsworth Common Rail) | 020-8672 0114 | fax 8767 6648 |
www.chezbruce.co.uk

Despite relinquishing London's No. 1 Food ranking to Mr. Ramsay
this year, this "gastronomic outpost" remains "first-class" cry the
many boosters of its "brilliantly conceived" Modern British cuisine
that "never falters" – and is "phenomenal value" to boot; augmented
by "fantastic advice from the sommelier", the "high-calibre" service
is "outstandingly orchestrated", navigating the "reassuringly informal" setting; all told, it's "really worth it in Wandsworth"; P.S. those
who find it "cramped", rejoice: it's "expanding to accommodate
more tables" in summer 2008.

Chez Gérard *French* | 17 | 16 | 15 | £35 |

Covent Garden | Opera Terrace, The Market | 45 E. Terrace, WC2
(Covent Garden) | 020-7379 0666 | fax 7497 9060 ◗

Holborn | 119 Chancery Ln., WC2 (Chancery Ln.) | 020-7405 0290 |
fax 7242 2649 🗷

Mayfair | 31 Dover St., W1 (Green Park) | 020-7499 8171 |
fax 7491 3818 🗷

NEW Piccadilly | 36-40 Rupert St., W1 (Piccadilly Circus) |
020-7287 8989

Victoria | Thistle Hotel | 101 Buckingham Palace Rd., SW1 (Victoria) |
020-7868 6249 | fax 7976 6073

Fitzrovia | 8 Charlotte St., W1 (Goodge St./Tottenham Court Rd.) |
020-7636 4975 | fax 7637 4564 ◗

City | 1 Watling St., EC4 (Mansion House/St. Paul's) | 020-7213 0540 |
fax 7213 0541 🗷

City | 14 Trinity Sq., EC3 (Tower Hill) | 020-7480 5500 |
fax 7480 5588 🗷

City | 64 Bishopsgate, EC2 (Bank/Liverpool St.) | 020-7588 1200 |
fax 7588 1122 🗷

Waterloo | 9 Belvedere Rd., SE1 (Waterloo) | 020-7202 8470 |
fax 7202 8474
www.santeonline.co.uk

They "churn out cuisine with some aplomb" at this bevy of "French-
ish brasseries" around town that "don't break the bank" ("but could
be better for the price"); "service is slapdash" and "decor's a bit
tired" – though one branch offers "great views over Covent
Garden" – but "keep expectations low" and they're "unlikely to surprise, either positively or negatively."

	FOOD	DECOR	SERVICE	COST

Chez Kristof ● *French*
20 | 18 | 17 | £42

Hammersmith | 111 Hammersmith Grove, W6 (Hammersmith) | 020-8741 1177 | fax 8846 3750 | www.chezkristof.co.uk

"Holding up in an odd area" in Hammersmith, this tightly packed "neighbourhood-style brasserie" is cited for Classic French fare that's "full of flavour" (pity that "staff can appear bored" serving it); all also agree the "outside tables are a treat in summer", plus there's "plenty to keep you interested" in the next-door deli, especially the "wonderful breakfast" (served until 3 PM).

Chiang Mai *Thai*
▽ 20 | 11 | 15 | £27

Soho | 48 Frith St., W1 (Leicester Sq./Tottenham Court Rd.) | 020-7437 7444 | fax 7287 2255

"Family-run (and what a lovely family)", this "relaxed" Soho eatery is praised for its "plentiful, delicately flavoured" Thai cuisine at "cheap prices", even if "decor and atmosphere are spectacularly absent."

NEW Chicago Rib Shack ● *BBQ*
‒ | ‒ | ‒ | M

Knightsbridge | 145 Knightsbridge, SW1 (Knightsbridge) | 020-7591 4664 | www.thechicagoribshack.co.uk

A line-up of porcelain pigs painted to resemble personalities ranging from Batman to David Beckham dominates the entrance of this bi-level jolly joint, which closed down nine years ago, but has been resurrected by a group of investors in Knightsbridge; the big-hearted BBQ menu runs the gamut from burgers and smoked ribs (with kosher options) to salads and fish, supported by kid-friendly floats, shakes and smoothies; N.B. parents will appreciate the valet parking.

China Tang ● *Chinese*
20 | 23 | 20 | £64

Mayfair | The Dorchester | 53 Park Ln., W1 (Hyde Park Corner/Marble Arch) | 020-7629 9988 | www.dorchesterhotel.com

"Just walking in provides a rush of sensations" at this "glitzy, 1930s Shanghai-style" site in The Dorchester, "packed with celebs", "high-spending Russians and hotel guests"; comments on the Cantonese cuisine career from "creative" to "mediocre", but either way you "better be on an expense account" – or stick to dim sum in the "enjoyable bar"; P.S. service is "attentive, but not particularly polite", although "the sommelier's advice can avoid wine-list land mines."

Chinese Experience *Chinese*
20 | 14 | 19 | £21

Chinatown | 118-120 Shaftesbury Ave., W1 (Leicester Sq.) | 020-7437 0377 | fax 7437 0378 | www.chineseexperience.com

With not much decor to distract you, "just close your eyes and imagine you're in Hong Kong" at this busy Chinatowner, whose "wonderful", "super-fresh dim sum" is "well worth the price"; its hours and location make it a "convenient" experience for theatre-goers too.

Chisou ☒ *Japanese*
▽ 23 | 14 | 20 | £42

Mayfair | 4 Princes St., W1 (Oxford Circus) | 020-7629 3931 | www.chisou.co.uk

"Where London's Japanese denizens go" declare devotees of this medium-size monochromatic venue near Oxford Circus; it "keeps things simple" in every respect, from the functional setting to the "great sushi, sake" and cooked fare that, whilst not cheap, represents "excellent value" given it's "the real thing."

Chor Bizarre ❶ *Indian*   19 | 18 | 19 | £37

Mayfair | 16 Albemarle St., W1 (Green Park) | 020-7629 9802 | fax 7493 7756 | www.chorbizarre.com

"Authentic, family-style Indian cuisine", each dish paired with items from an "interesting wine list", makes this Mayfair subterranean subcontinental "a standout" to supporters; but reactions are less rosy to the "cluttered" antiques market–like digs: "bizarre decor indeed."

Chowki Bar & Restaurant ❶ *Indian*   17 | 12 | 13 | £25

Piccadilly | 2-3 Denman St., W1 (Piccadilly Circus) | 020-7439 1330 | fax 7287 5919

A monthly changing, "unusually varied Indian menu", offering "a sampling of various localities' cuisines" in "minimalist presentations (rather than heaped platters)", is the main draw at this Piccadilly Circus subcontinental; the environs never were much - "diners crowded together" "sharing a long table with strangers" - but sliding scores suggest the food's "not as good" of late, and it's further "let down by indifferent service."

Christopher's
Covent Garden *American/Chophouse*   19 | 18 | 19 | £40

Covent Garden | 18 Wellington St., WC2 (Covent Garden) | 020-7240 4222 | fax 7240 3357 | www.christophersgrill.com

The "classy", "clublike surroundings" of a Covent Garden Victorian building offer an "interesting take on U.S. dining", with "reliable grills, impressive seafood" and "attentive, if not particularly knowledgeable, service"; the "pricey" bill makes some grumble it's "geared around expense-accounters", excepting the "really good" pre-theatre menus and "weekend brunch, which cures all hangover blues."

Chuen Cheng Ku ❶ *Chinese*   21 | 11 | 14 | £24

Chinatown | 17 Wardour St., W1 (Leicester Sq./Piccadilly Circus) | 020-7437 1398 | fax 7434 0533 | www.chuenchengku.co.uk

"Don't be misled by the exterior" (or the interior "showing its age") - this "big" Chinatown venue boasts "blooming tasty dim sum" "served from trolleys" by staff who, despite the Service score, seem "smilier than of old"; not surprisingly, it's "incredibly popular" as "a place to go before or after the theatre", especially if "there's a large group."

Churchill Arms *Thai*   20 | 14 | 14 | £14

Notting Hill | 119 Kensington Church St., W8 (High St. Kensington/Notting Hill Gate) | 020-7727 4242 | www.fullers.co.uk

"Don't be fooled by the price" ("cheap" would be an understatement) - this "kitschy" Notting Hill pub with a "Thai in the back" and "lots of interesting memorabilia [and plants] hanging everywhere" offers "generous servings" of "good, freshly prepared" fare; "service is rushed and they look to turn over the tables very quickly" - in fact, "seating is limited to one hour."

| | FOOD | DECOR | SERVICE | COST |

Chutney Mary ◐ Indian
23 | 21 | 21 | £45

Chelsea | 535 King's Rd., SW10 (Fulham Broadway) | 020-7351 3113 | fax 7351 7694 | www.realindianfood.com

Whilst "some say it's no longer the best Indian in London, a recent revamping keeps this restaurant in the running" for reviewers who rave about the "luxurious", "innovative" cuisine at this Chelsea "standby"; when reserving, regulars "recommend seating in the conservatory", although the shimmery main room, all crystal-studded murals and candles, is "pleasant" enough; a few cynics swat the service – "although good, they can get a little lost" at times.

Chutney's Indian
▽ 23 | 13 | 18 | £34

Marylebone | 124 Drummond St., NW1 (Euston Sq.) | 020-7388 0604 | fax 7209 0627

For a "terrific deal", try the "fabulous lunch buffet" at this scruffy Euston haunt where the "wonderful Indian vegetarian" cooking is "still delicious after all these years" (25 and counting); "to avoid the crush, go early or on Saturday."

Cicada Ⓢ Pan-Asian
▽ 21 | 21 | 19 | £34

Clerkenwell | 132-136 St. John St., EC1 (Farringdon) | 020-7608 1550 | fax 7608 1551 | www.cicada.nu

This "pleasant, though unspectacular, Clerkenwell staple" "tends to please" a "chic clientele" with its "solid" Pan-Asian victuals, even if "service suffers" on the occasions when "crowds of braying media types make lunchtimes an ordeal"; P.S. the recent refurb should appease those who felt it was "looking slightly tired."

Cigala Spanish
21 | 17 | 18 | £37

Bloomsbury | 54 Lamb's Conduit St., WC1 (Holborn/Russell Sq.) | 020-7405 1717 | fax 7242 9949 | www.cigala.co.uk

"A real find in the neighbourhood" near the British Museum, this often "overlooked" "Iberian eatery" offers up "delicious peasant food", along with an "amazing selection of sherries" and "ports to accompany" the meal; "friendly staff" provide a "relaxing atmosphere."

Ⓩ Cinnamon Club Ⓢ Indian
24 | 24 | 21 | £49

Westminster | The Old Westminster Library | 30-32 Great Smith St., SW1 (Westminster) | 020-7222 2555 | fax 7222 1333 | www.cinnamonclub.com

"The curry house of politicians, Lords" and media "hacks", this "serene", "sophisticated" venue in the "former Westminster Library" (hence the "bookish decor" theme) "appeals to discerning palates" with its "inventive, exotic" Indian menu that offers "something different every time" – but is always brought by "playful, attentive service"; those who find it "too expensive" "head downstairs to the swanky lounge bar with mellow music and Bollywood movies."

Cipriani ◐ Italian
20 | 20 | 19 | £67

Mayfair | 25 Davies St., W1 (Bond St.) | 020-7399 0500 | fax 7399 0501 | www.cipriani.com

"Love it or hate it", there's "never a dull moment" at Mayfair's "home of bling", "brimming with Eurotrash" and British "beautiful people", all "posing and air-kissing"; "you don't come here for the food" – "old-time Italian with Venetian flair" at "rather expensive" prices – "but it doesn't let you down if you do"; alas, the same can't be said about the "uneven service" ("unless you are famous").

	FOOD	DECOR	SERVICE	COST

Ciro's Pizza Pomodoro ● *Pizza* | 16 | 13 | 15 | £22 |

Knightsbridge | 51 Beauchamp Pl., SW3 (Knightsbridge) | 020-7589 1278 | fax 7589 8719
City | 7-8 Bishopsgate Churchyard, EC2 (Liverpool St.) | 020-7920 9207 | fax 7920 9206 🖂
www.pomodoro.co.uk

"If you like live music and pizza", with "lots of dancing" thrown in, this "cheap and cheerful" Italian duo in Knightsbridge and the City are "frolicking spots" indeed – that is, "if you can put up with the small space and slow service."

Citrus *Mediterranean* | 19 | 17 | 19 | £45 |

Piccadilly | Park Lane Hotel | 112 Piccadilly, W1 (Green Park) | 020-7290 7364 | fax 7499 1965 | www.citrusrestaurant.co.uk

"Like the name, it's fresh and refreshing" ("unexpected for a Sheraton") at this "simple, small restaurant in a cheery setting within the Park Lane Hotel"; whilst it's "not a destination in itself", the Mediterranean menu is "creative", and coupled with "a view of Green Park" to boot.

City Café Westminster ● *European* | 17 | 18 | 16 | £31 |

Westminster | City Inn | 30 John Islip St., SW1 (Pimlico) | 020-7932 4600 | fax 7932 7575 | www.cityinn.co.uk

"The food's better than you might expect – in fact, it's exceedingly good" at this "peaceful", dark-wooded Modern European "near the Tate Britain"; its £10 prix fixe is "a wonderful value for lunch", and the Sunday brunch buffet isn't bad either.

City Miyama 🖂 *Japanese* | - | - | - | E |

City | 17 Godliman St., EC4 (St. Paul's) | 020-7489 1937 | fax 7236 0325

Whilst the "chrome-meets-fake-wood decor might not be the freshest, the sashimi thankfully is" at this "hidden gem" of a Japanese on the "edge of the City"; the recently "revamped teppanyaki menu" is worth a trip too, but regulars recommend you "go at the weekend to avoid expense-account types and enjoy excellent deals."

Clarke's 🖂 *British* | 26 | 18 | 25 | £57 |

Kensington | 124 Kensington Church St., W8 (Notting Hill Gate) | 020-7221 9225 | fax 7229 4564 | www.sallyclarke.com

As it turns 25, chef-owner Sally Clarke's Kensington "classic" is "still a delight", as "calm and orderly" as ever, with its "original" Modern British cuisine that "practically jumps from its source onto your plate", served "with attention to each individual diner"; a few grumble "the plank floors and plain decor don't justify the luxury-zone prices", but that just lets you "focus on the sublime food with no distractions" disciples declare.

Clerkenwell
Dining Room & Bar 🛃 *European* ▽ 22 | 19 | 19 | £48

Clerkenwell | 69-73 St. John St., EC1 (Farringdon) | 020-7253 9000 |
fax 7253 3322 | www.theclerkenwell.com

"They care whether you are pleased and whether you return" to this
"understated Clerkenwell" Modern European, an "all-round solid"
choice for a "pleasant, intimate" meal; perhaps the decor "lacks distinctive character", but the place "will not disappoint."

Cliveden House *British/French* 22 | 24 | 23 | £77

Taplow | Cliveden House Hotel | Berkshire | 01628 668561 |
fax 01628 661837 | www.clivedenhouse.co.uk

"Elegant and quintessentially English", this stately home-turned-
hotel set on the "beautiful" banks of the Thames at Taplow has
"much history of interest" (the Astors owned it); it also offers a
"true dining experience", either in the "romantic" subterranean
Waldo's, serving "excellent" New French fare, or the red-hued
Terrace, with its "impressive" views and more Classic Anglo-Franco
menu; "some may lament its old-school flavour, but that's precisely
why it's a classic."

🛡 Clos Maggiore *French* 25 | 25 | 24 | £50

Covent Garden | 33 King St., WC2 (Covent Garden/Leicester Sq.) |
020-7379 9696 | fax 7379 6767 | www.maggiores.uk.com

"An exceptionally romantic atmosphere", with an "unusual combination of oak panels, privet hedge", fireplaces, "hanging flowers and
a glass roof", makes this "gem in the heart of Covent Garden" "suitable for marriage proposals and other special occasions"; equally
"magical" is the "modern fine French cuisine", supported by a
"mind-boggling wine list" and "superb service"; just be sure to avoid
being "sent to the barren front area"; P.S. "now open on Sunday."

Club Bar & Dining, The 🛃 *Eclectic* - | - | - | E

Soho | 21-22 Warwick St., W1 (Oxford Circus/Piccadilly Circus) |
020-7734 1002 | www.theclubbaranddining.co.uk

"Stylish, yet approachable", with exposed brickwork and Gothic
design touches, this Soho eatery offers an Eclectic menu that
ranges from a swordfish sandwich to an entire roast pig;
however, imbibers believe it's "better for a drink" in the purple-
hued bar below.

🛡 Club Gascon 🛃 *French* 26 | 20 | 23 | £64

Smithfield | 57 W. Smithfield, EC1 (Barbican/Farringdon) | 020-7796 0600 |
fax 7796 0601 | www.clubgascon.com

Prepare for a "festival of foie gras" prepared several ways, plus other
"completely mad and unexpected" "variations on Gascon cuisine",
at this "fantastic modern French" in a marble-walled, former
Smithfield teahouse; "attentive" staff serve the small "dishes designed for sharing", which can be "imaginatively paired" with labels
from the "deep, offbeat wine list"; whilst "not as unique as when it
opened" a decade ago, still it "would be my desert island
restaurant – if cholesterol and money were no object."

	FOOD	DECOR	SERVICE	COST

Coach & Horses *British* — | — | — | M

Clerkenwell | 26-28 Ray St., EC1 (Farringdon) | 020-7278 8990 |
fax 7278 1478 | www.thecoachandhorses.com

"If you can get past the less-than-grand atmosphere, you will be rewarded with a short, simple menu" of "solid English food" – say, "a
decent meat pie washed down with warm beer" – at this "authentic
pub" "next door to the *Guardian*" in Clerkenwell; however, you hungry
types should hold your horses – "the food's a little slow to arrive."

Cocoon ●⊠ *Pan-Asian* 21 | 23 | 16 | £52

Piccadilly | 65 Regent St., W1 (Piccadilly Circus) | 020-7494 7600 |
www.cocoon-restaurants.com

This "high-energy" Piccadilly Pan-Asian "looks at first glance too hip
to be true", with its "modern, slick plastic decor", "oh-so-cool"
"retro furnishings" and "lots of models walking around" – but the fusion food (e.g. foie gras gyoza) "stands up for itself just fine"; that
said, it's "definitely more bar than restaurant" in some eyes, not
helped by the "staff who, although good-looking, are pretty daft."

Collection, The ●⊠ *Eclectic* ∇ 13 | 20 | 13 | £44

South Kensington | 264 Brompton Rd., SW3 (South Kensington) |
020-7225 1212 | fax 7225 1050 | www.the-collection.co.uk

A dramatic entrance hallway and "bar so long it looks as if it's trying
to prove something" score higher than the "overpriced" Eclectic fare
at this "buzzy" Brompton Cross warehouse haunted by "celebs and
social climbers alike"; the savvy stick to the "sensual drinks."

Como Lario ●⊠ *Italian* ∇ 21 | 17 | 17 | £47

Pimlico | 18-22 Holbein Pl., SW1 (Sloane Sq.) | 020-7730 2954 |
fax 7730 9046 | www.comolario.uk.com

"Well-presented", "honest Italian food" is the main attraction at this
low-key Sloane Square trattoria; although the "cramped tables" mean
there are "no private conversations", the "flirty waiters" make amends.

⊠ Comptoir Gascon ⊠Ⓜ *French* 23 | 20 | 19 | £33

Smithfield | 61-63 Charterhouse St., EC1 (Barbican/Farringdon) |
020-7608 0851 | fax 7608 0871 | www.clubgascon.com

"Homey, unpretentious" and "provincial French in all the right ways"
sums up this "nice little deli"/bistro (a Club Gascon sib) in
Smithfield Market, where it's "worth enduring the cramped layout"
for "authentic", "strong-flavoured" specialties of the *Sud-Ouest*, including "the very, very best goose fat chips" and "unusual wines."

Coq d'Argent *French* 22 | 23 | 18 | £54

City | 1 Poultry, EC2 (Bank) | 020-7395 5000 | fax 7395 5050 |
www.coqdargent.co.uk

"Checking in on a busy lunchtime is like lining up at the Club World
desk at Heathrow" – i.e. it's "filled with City types" – at this "airy
dining room" with an "amazing roof terrace" and "well-spaced tables for confidential meets"; the "accomplished" Classic French
menu "has really improved" of late, but remains rather "tough on the
wallet, so make sure your recruitment consultant is paying."

	FOOD	DECOR	SERVICE	COST

Costas Grill ⓩ Greek
▽ 14 | 11 | 19 | £22

Notting Hill | 12-14 Hillgate St., W8 (Notting Hill Gate) | 020-7229 3794 | www.costasgrill.co.uk

"Greek staples straight out of the '70s" and a "shabby Formica and fluorescent lighting interior" sum up this Cypriot, an "unchanging" Notting Hill fixture for decades; it's "like an old-school friend of whom one is fond – but for reasons that are not entirely clear."

NEW Côte French
- | - | - | M

Soho | 124-126 Wardour St., W1 (Oxford Circus/Tottenham Court Rd.) | 020-7287 9280

Wimbledon | 8 High St., SW19 (Wimbledon) | 020-8947 7100 www.cote-restaurants.co.uk

"Genuine, not pastiche French" fare – "well-executed and sensibly priced" – is on offer at this "simple" pair in Wimbledon and Soho; especially "recommended: the soups and fish", like the tuna niçoise.

Cottons Caribbean
▽ 19 | 17 | 20 | £30

Camden Town | 55 Chalk Farm Rd., NW1 (Chalk Farm) | 020-7485 8388

Islington | 70 Exmouth Mkt., EC1 (Angel) | 020-7833 3332 www.cottons-restaurant.co.uk

"If you like West Indian food, this is the place to go" declare converts of these sunny Caribbean siblings in Camden and Islington; others opine it's "worth visiting just for the drink", which includes an "extensive choice of rums", and the "authentic decor" (enlivened by live music at Exmouth Market branch's Rum Jungle bar).

Court Restaurant Eclectic
18 | 21 | 17 | £22

Bloomsbury | The British Museum | Great Russell St., WC1 (Russell Sq.) | 020-7323 8990 | www.britishmuseum.org

You can't beat the "spectacular surroundings" – "mummies to the right of you, books to the left" – at the British Museum's "chic", "pleasant cafe" offering "unexpectedly upscale offerings" of an Eclectic nature; service has improved to the point of being "social" now; P.S. there's also a "low-scale snack bar" that requires "fewer pounds."

Cow Dining Room, The British
21 | 16 | 17 | £34

Notting Hill | 89 Westbourne Park Rd., W2 (Westbourne Park/Royal Oak) | 020-7221 0021 | fax 7727 8687 | www.thecowlondon.co.uk

"Holy cow" cry converts to this Notting Hill eatery, which despite its name "serves such fresh seafood" "you'll eat yourself silly" ("portions aren't stingy", either); the bar specialises in "lovely oysters" and "old authentic pubby atmosphere" but is "crowded all the time", whilst "dining upstairs" in the Modern Brit restaurant "is more civilised, albeit a bit boring"; expect "iffy service" at each.

ⓩ Crazy Bear, The ⓩ Thai
20 | 25 | 16 | £44

Fitzrovia | 26-28 Whitfield St., W1 (Goodge St.) | 020-7631 0088 | fax 7631 1188 | www.crazybeargroup.co.uk

"Good to impress a date", this "sexy" Fitzrovian is a "great space", especially the "trendy downstairs bar" (complete with "cute staff" and "delicious cocktails"); "although the restaurant seems to be an afterthought", its Thai cuisine is "quite good", if "expensive"; some complain "staff are so up themselves", however; P.S. the "cool loos" with wacky mirrors are "worth a trip alone."

Crazy Homies *Mexican*

19 | 16 | 13 | £23

Notting Hill | 125-127 Westbourne Park Rd., W2 (Royal Oak/Westbourne Park) | 020-7727 6771 | fax 7727 6798 | www.crazyhomieslondon.co.uk

"Mexican is hard to find in London, but they do a decent job" at Tom Conran's "chill little" cantina in Westbourne Park Road, where the eats "for the burrito-starved" are among "the best in town"; admittedly, the "service can be stroppy" and you "might have to wait a while to sit", but at least there are "awesome" margaritas to pass the time.

Cross Keys, The ● *French*

- | - | - | M

Chelsea | 1 Lawrence St., SW3 (Sloane Sq.) | 020-7349 9111 | fax 7349 9333 | www.thexkeys.co.uk

"Always busy with locals", this Chelsea gastropub is "great for a group dinner" in the airy rear conservatory with a tree growing in the middle; but it makes critics cross, because the French fare, whilst "above-average", is "not innovative" and staff can be "pretentious."

Cru 🅜 *Mediterranean*

- | - | - | E

Hoxton | 2-4 Rufus St., N1 (Old St.) | 020-7729 5252 | fax 7729 1070 | www.cru.uk.com

"As the name implies", there are some "great wines" on offer at this converted Hoxton warehouse, adorned with walnut woods and an open kitchen; whilst the Med menu is only "average for the price", the "sharing platters and nibbles are ideal for a group of friends."

🆕 Cruse 9 🅜 *European*

- | - | - | E

Islington | 62-63 Halliford St., N1 (Highbury & Islington) | 020-7354 8099 | www.cruse9.com

A little off the beaten Islington track, this newly created building is spread over three floors – two of which are flooded with natural light from floor-to-ceiling windows – and offers a casually chic setting for Modern European cuisine with Med twists and a varied veggie selection, all from a well-travelled chef; downstairs is a comfy, cosy bar.

Cuckoo Club 🅢🅜 *European*

- | - | - | E

Piccadilly | Swallow St., W1 (Piccadilly Circus) | 020-7287 4300 | www.thecuckooclub.com

"In between the sophisticated ambience" and "impressive drinks", "we go cuckoo for the club" coo clients of this "hot, happening", purple-hued Piccadilly premises with a dance lounge below and a dining room above; however, some say "you should go for the party, not the food", as the Modern European fare is "far too complicated" and the service somewhat attitudinal.

| | FOOD | DECOR | SERVICE | COST |

Da Mario ❶ *Italian*
▽ 16 | 12 | 16 | £25

Kensington | 15 Gloucester Rd., SW7 (Gloucester Rd.) | 020-7584 9078 | fax 7823 9026 | www.damario.co.uk

"If the signs are to be believed, Princess Diana (at least once) ordered" at this "no-frills" Kensington trattoria, "always a safe bet" for "satisfying", "hearty" Italian staples "in a critically rare price range"; it's also "an ideal location for kid's parties."

Dans Le Noir 🅱 *Eclectic*
▽ 8 | 13 | 19 | £41

Clerkenwell | 30-31 Clerkenwell Green, EC1 (Chancery Ln./Farringdon) | 020-7253 1100 | www.danslenoir.com

"Eating in the pitch dark" – literally – is an "interesting idea" that's "worth a try for the experience" (or even for "a second or third date when you want to kick it up a notch") at this Clerkenwell citizen supported by the Foundation for the Blind; but opponents opine "once is enough", given that 'surprise menu' of Eclectic fare is "disappointing" and the entire "experience disorganised."

Daphne's ❶ *Italian*
22 | 21 | 22 | £50

Chelsea | 112 Draycott Ave., SW3 (South Kensington) | 020-7589 4257 | fax 7581 2232 | www.daphnes-restaurant.co.uk

"Busy, yet private at the same time", this "comfortable", "chic" "Chelsea institution" offers "a delightful wealth of choice on its Italian menu, backed up by a solid wine list" and "accommodating service"; if trendsetters titter it's more a "place to bring your parents", to devotees it's "always divine" – plus "you never know which celeb you'll see."

Daquise *Polish*
▽ 15 | 9 | 13 | £21

South Kensington | 20 Thurloe St., SW7 (South Kensington) | 020-7589 6117

The "shabby" "South Ken institution probably looks like it did 30 years ago", but "the food is why one is here": "huge portions of home-cooked Polish" cuisine (like "awesome pork knuckle") at "cheap" cost; service is "brusque, but efficient."

🆕 Daylesford Organic Café *Eclectic*
18 | 19 | 16 | £29

Knightsbridge | Harvey Nichols | 109-125 Knightsbridge, SW1 (Knightsbridge) | 020-7201 8749

St. John's Wood | Clifton Nurseries | 5A Clifton Villas, W9 (Warwick Ave.) | 020-7266 1932 🅼

Chelsea | Daylesford Organic Store | 31 Sloane Sq., SW1 (Sloane Sq.) | 020-7881 8020

Pimlico | Daylesford Organic Store | 44B Pimlico Rd., SW1 (Sloane Sq.) | 020-7881 8060

www.daylesfordorganic.com

"Very much a ladies-who-lunch venue", this burgeoning chain of "neutral-chic" ("never seen so much marble in one place!"), "fresh-faced cafes" in the town's smartest stores "gets jammed" with folks feasting on "elegant", "ecologically conscious", and – some hiss –

"overly expensive" Eclectic fare; they also feature a "feast of take-home goodies to enthrall you."

⚡ Defune *Japanese* | 26 | 15 | 22 | £57 |

Marylebone | 34 George St., W1 (Baker St./Bond St.) | 020-7935 8311 | fax 7487 3762

Sushi savants swear this "well-kept secret in Marylebone ticks all the boxes" for "amazing", "authentic" Japanese victuals in a "quiet", "clean-lined setting" that some liken to a "railway shelter"; sure, it's "killingly expensive" – especially "for what you get" the woeful whisper – but most find the "sublime" fish "worth it."

NEW Dehesa *Italian/Spanish* | - | - | - | M |

Soho | 25 Ganton St., W1 (Oxford Circus/Piccadilly Circus) | 020-7494 4170

"Spain comes to Carnaby Street" (or actually, nearby Ganton) at this new tapas bar "from the same respected stable as Salt Yard"; already a "wonderful place", it's named after woodlands where black-footed pigs roam, some of whom end up as ham on the Iberian-Italian menu; "service is slick and caring", even if the communal tables "try to squeeze too many people in."

Delfina ☒ *Eclectic* | - | - | - | E |

Borough | 50 Bermondsey St., SE1 (London Bridge) | 020-7357 0244 | www.delfina.org.uk

A "trendy, art-gallery atmosphere" (e.g. "plain, unfussy decor") pervades this "gem of a find" in an airy, 19th-century Borough chocolate factory; the Eclectic dishes are "excellent and original", and whilst it "unfortunately tends to be open only weekdays", the "luxuriously spaced tables" make it a "perfect lunchtime bolt hole if you don't want to be overheard"; N.B. they do serve dinner on Friday.

Delfino ☒ *Italian* | 20 | 12 | 17 | £29 |

Mayfair | 121A Mount St., W1 (Bond St.) | 020-7499 1256 | fax 7493 4460 | www.finos.co.uk

"Always a favourite" for wood oven-baked pizzas and other "standard pasta dishes", this "welcoming" Italian with "super-fast service" "makes a pleasant change from the chains", even if the casual, cramped space "lacks atmosphere"; wallet-watchers woefully wail "prices have crept up over recent times", but it remains "reasonable for Mayfair."

NEW Devonshire, The *British* | 22 | 18 | 22 | £37 |

Chiswick | 126 Devonshire Rd., W4 (Turnham Green) | 020-7592 7962 | www.gordonramsay.com

"A great alternative for those wanting the Gordon Ramsay experience", the second of the maestro's "pub restaurants" is in an "odd location" – residential Chiswick; but the high-ceilinged, wood-panelled space offers up "very capable cooking" of the Traditional British sort, including "wonderfully fresh prawns and pickled cockles", plus "real ales", served by "friendly staff"; just beware the slightly "berserk prices" for a pub.

	FOOD	DECOR	SERVICE	COST

dim t *Chinese*

15 | 15 | 15 | £21

NEW Victoria | 56-62 Wilton Rd., SW1 (Victoria) | 020-7834 0507
Fitzrovia | 32 Charlotte St., W1 (Goodge St.) | 020-7637 1122 |
fax 7580 1574
NEW Borough | 2 More London Pl., Tooley St., SE1 (London Bridge) |
020-7403 7000
Hampstead | 3 Heath St., NW3 (Hampstead) | 020-7435 0024 |
fax 7435 8060
Highgate | 1A Hampstead Ln., N6 (Highgate) | 020-8340 8800 |
fax 8348 1671
South Kensington | 154-156 Gloucester Rd., SW7 (Gloucester Rd.) |
020-7370 0070
www.dimt.co.uk

Whilst dominated by "solid dim sum", "they've got a wide variety of
Asian [fare] to choose from" at this "casual" Chinese chain; cynics
say they "need to smarten up their act", particularly the "patchy service", but they perform for the proverbial "quick bite"; P.S. the
"Tower Bridge branch has stunning river views."

Diner, The ● *American*

18 | 15 | 11 | £17

Soho | 18 Ganton St., W1 (Oxford Circus) | 020-7287 8962
Shoreditch | 128-130 Curtain Rd., EC2 (Old St.) | 020-7729 4452
www.goodlifediner.com

"A pretty good facsimile of a U.S. diner" is the consensus on this
couple in Soho ("buzzing with kitschy decor") and Shoreditch
("worth the trip"), where the "juicy", "cheap burgers" and late
breakfasts are "not done exceptionally well, but not terribly either";
most muttering is over the "muddled service."

Dinings ⓢ *Japanese*

24 | 14 | 24 | £40

Marylebone | 22 Harcourt St., W1 (Edgware Rd.) | 020-7723 0666 |
fax 7723 3222

"Very un-London in its simple, utilitarian decor", this "tiny, minimalist"
Marylebone Japanese is "well worth the effort to find" for its "brilliant sushi" – "superbly cut, extremely fresh" – and "meticulously
prepared tapas [size] dishes"; whilst "not cheap, it's cheaper than
other places" of this quality (the chef-owner used to be at Nobu).

Dish Dash *Lebanese/Persian*

∇ 21 | 15 | 17 | £29

Chelsea | 9 Park Walk, SW10 (South Kensington) | 020-7352 1330
Balham | 11-13 Bedford Hill, SW12 (Balham) | 020-8673 5555 |
fax 8673 7711
www.dish-dash.com

An "unusual", "wonderful variety" of Lebanese-Persian "tapas-style
small plates" and "lush cocktails" "means every visit turns up something new" at this "pretty" pair in Balham and Chelsea; both boast a
"Middle Eastern atmosphere, with belly dancers" once a month, and
a "value-for-money" experience all the time.

Diverso *Italian*

17 | 18 | 20 | £51

Piccadilly | 85 Piccadilly, W1 (Green Park) | 020-7491 2222 | fax 7495 1977

There's quite a diverso of opinion about this Italian, decorated
Tuscan-style: fans who "really like the relaxed setting" say it's "great

for the Green Park view and Piccadilly people-watching"; however, since a recent chef change, foes "find the food to be ok, but not up to the prices."

Don, The 🖾 European   22 | 20 | 21 | £47

City | The Courtyard | 20 St. Swithins Ln., EC4 (Bank/Cannon St.) | 020-7626 2606 | fax 7626 2616 | www.thedonrestaurant.co.uk

"Consistently packed with the great and the good from the City" – it's "one of the better venues open for dinner" *and* lunch – this Modern European is "hard to find, but easy to like", with "consistently high" but "not overpriced" cuisine, "unstuffy, atmospheric" premises and "staff that are a credit to the place"; there's a "good bistro downstairs" in the vaulted cellar too; P.S. the wine list includes an "interesting selection of sherries" and ports – in homage to the 1798 building's past as the Sandeman's warehouse.

Dorchester (Hotel) - The Grill *British*   24 | 21 | 24 | £69

Mayfair | The Dorchester | 53 Park Ln., W1 (Hyde Park Corner/Marble Arch) | 020-7629 8888 | fax 7317 6464 | www.dorchesterhotel.com

True, the tartan-bedecked decor can be "overpowering" ("silly pseudo-Scottish surroundings" cynics sniff), but if you "avert your eyes from the kilts on the walls", you're in for some "great Modern British fare", with "royal service to match" at "The Dorchester's polished spot"; hence, it remains "a favourite" with business-lunchers and an "older, well-heeled crowd" who don't mind the high, "standard upscale hotel" prices.

Dover Street   15 | 15 | 17 | £45
Restaurant & Jazz Bar ●🖾 *European*

Mayfair | 8-10 Dover St., W1 (Green Park) | 020-7491 7509 | www.doverst.co.uk

If "you like eating in nightclubs", "splash out and take your partner" to this "crowded" Mayfair veteran with a "Continental atmosphere" and "terrific" live jazz nightly; whilst the Modern European cooking is "not exactly high cuisine, it's not terrible either" – though, as befits a "dancing and socialising venue", the "noise inhibits conversation."

Dragon Castle *Chinese*   - | - | - | M

Kennington | 114 Walworth Rd., SE17 (Elephant & Castle) | 020-7277 3388

"In a less-than-salubrious location" – it's "the only reason to go to Walworth Road" – this "sleeping dragon" turns out "excellent dim sum" and "reliably good Cantonese" mains; all's "fairly priced", with "friendly, fast service" to boot.

Draper's Arms, The *European*   19 | 19 | 17 | £29

Islington | 44 Barnsbury St., N1 (Highbury & Islington) | 020-7619 0348 | fax 7619 0413 | www.thedrapersarms.co.uk

"Jam-packed full of yummy mummies and posh dads at weekends", this Islington Modern European is "a bit pricey for elevated pub food"; but "booking is essential", which confirms that many "enjoy a thoroughly happy experience" here – plus, it's got a "garden in the back: what more could one ask for?"

	FOOD	DECOR	SERVICE	COST

Duke of Cambridge *British*

| 22 | 21 | 15 | £28 |

Islington | 30 St. Peter's St., N1 (Angel) | 020-7359 3066 | fax 7359 1877 | www.sloeberry.co.uk

"For the same price as normal pub food, you can have sustainable food" – "hearty" Modern British edibles – at this "organic gastro-pub" in Islington; the secondhand furnishings make for a "homely", "relaxed" setting, only slightly marred by the "hit-and-miss service" ("don't go if you're in a rush").

Eagle, The *Mediterranean*

| 23 | 14 | 15 | £26 |

Clerkenwell | 159 Farringdon Rd., EC1 (Farringdon) | 020-7837 1353 | fax 7689 5882

"A small selection of daily dishes from a chalkboard – always fresh", "ingenious" and "cheap" Med fare – is what causes this Clerkenwell "classic" "to fill up fast" with "young, sometimes funky people"; it's "not a safe bet for the fussy", given the "limited menu", "cramped seating" and "rough 'n' ready" service, "but it's as good as it gets when it comes to gastropub food."

Eagle Bar Diner *American*

| 17 | 16 | 11 | £22 |

Fitzrovia | 3-5 Rathbone Pl., W1 (Tottenham Court Rd.) | 020-7637 1418 | www.eaglebardiner.com

"Very reasonable, considering the location" just off Oxford Street, this brown-hued venue offers a full-bore American diner menu, from carb-laden breakfasts to bourbon-laced drinks and "milk-shakes worth getting fat for"; but "this really is the place for burg-ers", both beef and "alternative" versions like kangaroo, ostrich and "the best veggie"; pity about the "inhospitable" staff.

e&o *Pan-Asian*

| 22 | 19 | 17 | £47 |

Notting Hill | 14 Blenheim Crescent, W11 (Ladbroke Grove) | 020-7229 5454 | fax 7229 5522 | www.rickerrestaurants.com

"Always hopping with that Notting Hill vibe", this "social hot spot" still gathers the local glitterati for its "imaginative" "Far Eastern food mix" and "fabulous dim sum" served all day at the "buzzing bar"; after eight years, foes feel it's "a little factorylike now", noting the "ego-driven service" and "overpriced" menu; even so, it's "so much fun."

Eat & Two Veg *Vegetarian*

| 16 | 16 | 15 | £20 |

Marylebone | 50 Marylebone High St., W1 (Baker St.) | 020-7258 8595 | fax 7258 8596 | www.eatandtwoveg.com

For "guilt-free eating", this Marylebone "vegetarian's paradise" pro-vides an all-day array of "meatless meals", including the "perfect re-covery brunch"; but the "diner"-style "decor doesn't blend with the menu", and some still "can't get excited" about the "bland, boring" edibles (though "when it's bad, they take it back with a smile").

Ebury Dining Room & Brasserie *European*

| ∇ 16 | 22 | 19 | £33 |

Pimlico | 11 Pimlico Rd., SW1 (Sloane Sq./Victoria) | 020-7730 6784 | fax 7730 6149 | www.theebury.co.uk

"Reasonable grub in a hip pub" sums up this "posh" place in Pimlico with an upstairs dining room – where you can "enjoy the jazz band" at the weekend – and a "brash" bar below ("great for after-work shenanigans"); a few find the Modern European eats "expensive", however.

Ebury Wine Bar & Restaurant *Eclectic*

	18	17	18	£35

Belgravia | 139 Ebury St., SW1 (Sloane Sq./Victoria) | 020-7730 5447 | fax 7823 6053 | www.eburywinebar.co.uk

"An old reliable that wears well", this Belgravia wine bar/French bistro (just reaching its 50th anniversary) is "loaded with neighbourhood regulars" who appreciate the "personable" service and "good Eclectic menu at reasonable prices"; on the downside, the "whimsical decor is a bit stale" and it can get "boisterous in the evenings."

Ed's Easy Diner *Burgers*

	17	17	18	£17

Piccadilly | London Trocadero Ctr. | 19 Rupert St., W1 (Piccadilly Circus) | 020-7287 1951 | fax 7287 6998
Soho | 12 Moor St., W1 (Leicester Sq./Tottenham Court Rd.) | 020-7439 1955 | fax 7494 0173
www.edseasydiner.co.uk

"If you want the feeling of a great ol' American diner" with "juicy", "old-fashioned burgers" and "legendary milkshakes" that are "easy on the wallet, if not the waist", try this duo in Soho and Piccadilly; but the uneasy tremble it's "getting tired", comparing the hamburgers to "thin hockey pucks on a bun."

Efes Kebab House ❶ *Turkish*

	-	-	-	I

Bloomsbury | 175-177 Great Portland St., W1 (Great Portland St.) | 020-7436 0600 | fax 7636 6293

Efes Restaurant ❶ ⬚ *Turkish*

Bloomsbury | 80-82 Great Titchfield St., W1 (Oxford Circus) | 020-7636 1953 | fax 7323 5082 | www.efesrestaurant.co.uk

"Really decent kebabs, not the usual greasy rubbish" keep regulars returning to these two "quirky" Turks (under separate ownership) in Bloomsbury; whilst "decor and ambience are nothing to write home about", the "moderate prices" and "service with a smile" compensate.

1802 *British*

	▽ 16	17	11	£24

Canary Wharf | Museum of Docklands | No. 1 Warehouse, West India Quay, Hertsmere Rd., E14 (Canary Wharf/ West India Quay DLR) | 0870-444 3886 | fax 7537 1149 | www.searcys.co.uk

"One of the pleasures of the Docklands Museum is this neighbourhood treasure next door", an old Canary Wharf tea-sorting house resembling "a well-polished aircraft hangar", serving "wholesome", if "average" Modern British "nibbles" from Searcy caterers, along with "a good selection of wine"; but beware, it turns into a "drinking frenzy after work", when it limits the menu and forbids kids.

Eight Over Eight *Pan-Asian*

	22	19	18	£47

Chelsea | 392 King's Rd., SW3 (Sloane Sq.) | 020-7349 9934 | fax 7351 5157 | www.rickerrestaurants.com

This "sister of e&o" is "one of the best picks on King's Road" – a "fabulous hot spot" with "great people-watching" and "creative" Pan-Asian cuisine in which "flavours, colours and delightful surprises abound"; a few feel the minimalist Asian "decor doesn't score", but "young professionals" hail it as a "hip" option "for a date, drink or dinner with friends."

El Blason ⌷ *Spanish* ▽ | 18 | 13 | 19 | £38 |

Chelsea | 8-9 Blacklands Terrace, SW3 (Sloane Sq.) | 020-7823 7383 | fax 7589 6313

"You are greeted like a long-lost friend even if you have never been" to this "informal" Iberian just off King's Road; it's "much loved by local residents and those at the Spanish consulate around the corner" for "decent" renditions of suckling pig and flan.

Electric Brasserie, The ● *Eclectic* 17 | 17 | 15 | £33 |

Notting Hill | 191 Portobello Rd., W11 (Ladbroke Grove/Notting Hill Gate) | 020-7908 9696 | fax 7908 9595 | www.the-electric.co.uk

"Jammed with hipsters and moviegoers" "catching a flick next door", this Notting Hill hot spot "buzzes with energy" – from the "perpetually busy" bar in front to the more "intimate" brasserie behind; though the eats "take a backseat" to the scene, the Eclectic "comfort/nursery food [offers] something for everyone" – unlike the staff, which "need to go to hospitality school."

Elena's l'Etoile ⌷ *French/Italian* 18 | 18 | 22 | £46 |

Fitzrovia | 30 Charlotte St., W1 (Goodge St.) | 020-7636 1496 | fax 7637 0122 | www.elenasletoile.co.uk

"Famous for feeding Cameron Mackintosh" and other theatrical folk, "the legendary Elena [Salvoni] continues to cast her spell over this unique London institution" in Fitzrovia; diners sit at "tables cheek by jowl" – "close your eyes and you're in Paris" – to feast on Classic French–Italian fare that fans feel is "first-rate", even if "regular restaurant-goers" growl it's "nothing special."

11 Abingdon Road *European* 19 | 17 | 19 | £38 |

Kensington | 11 Abingdon Rd., W8 (High St. Kensington) | 020-7937 0120 | fax 7937 3049

"Simple yet sharp" decor gets a "quirky" lift from the "owner's art collection" at this Sonny's sibling a few "yards from Kensington High Street"; "well-spaced" tables, "intelligent" Modern European fare and "snappy service" ("much improved in the last year") make this spot a "handy" go-to for locals "if the fridge is empty."

El Faro *Spanish* ▽ | 23 | 22 | 19 | £39 |

Canary Wharf | 3 Turnberry Quay, Pepper St., E14 (Canary Wharf) | 020-7987 5511 | www.el-faro.co.uk

"Amongst the Docklands' rather poor selection of restaurants", this entry is an "unexpected" "gem" for its "genuine Spanish" cuisine, skilfully served in a pillared room decorated with lighthouse photos and "looking out across the river" from the multiple arched windows – a "lovely" scene "on warm summer evenings."

El Gaucho *Argentinean/Chophouse* 17 | 12 | 15 | £29 |

Chelsea | Chelsea Farmers Mkt. | 125 Sydney St., SW3 (Sloane Sq./ South Kensington) | 020-7376 8514 | fax 7589 7324

(continued)

El Gaucho

South Kensington | 30 Old Brompton Rd., SW7 (South Kensington) | 020-7584 8999 | fax 7589 7324 ❶
www.elgaucho.co.uk

Sliding scores support the sense that "some of the shine has come off" this Argentinean pair, whose ranch-house look "has attitude"; still a trip to Chelsea or South Ken "beats a 16-hour flight to the pampas" "if you have a craving for steak" ("the other food's pretty ordinary").

Elistano *Italian*

| 22 | 12 | 19 | £39 |

Chelsea | 25-27 Elystan St., SW3 (South Kensington) | 020-7584 5248 | fax 7584 8965 | www.elistano.com

Expect "excellent rustic Italian food" at this well-established trattoria in a Chelsea side street – hence "a bit Sloaney", clientelewise; *amici* also admire the usually "genuine service", but the premises "need a makeover" ("outside's nicer").

Elk in the Woods *Eclectic*

| - | - | - | E |

Islington | 39 Camden Passage, N1 (Angel) | 020-7226 3535 | www.the-elk-in-the-woods.co.uk

"Hidden in Camden Passage" and surrounded by antique shops, this quirky, "cheery" all-day gastropub "mixes 1960s wallpaper with the atmosphere of a Swiss chalet" and serves "bright tasting" Eclectic fare that ranges from Danish frikadeller (meatballs) to South African kudu (antelope) with a "friendly, casual" attitude; throw in a "hip bar", and you've got "a good address in Islington."

El Pirata ❶🅩 *Spanish*

| 20 | 16 | 17 | £33 |

Mayfair | 5-6 Down St., W1 (Green Park/Hyde Park Corner) | 020-7491 3810 | fax 7491 0853 | www.elpirata.co.uk

This "small Spanish hangout" just off Piccadilly "has gone unnoticed for too long" declare disciples of its "tapas to suit all tastes", with "sangria to make the meal complete"; just "make sure you have time, though, as the service couldn't be much slower"; P.S. regulars recommend "sit upstairs – the decor and staff are much better" there.

El Rincon Latino ❶🅜 *S American/Spanish*

| - | - | - | M |

Clapham | 148 Clapham Manor St., SW4 (Clapham North) | 020-7622 0599

You're "guaranteed a good night out" at "Clapham's best-kept secret", a cramped place serving "good-value" Spanish–South American fare, especially the "very edible" tapas; "the mood is festive", "but a bit noisy for a date", perhaps.

Empress of India ❶ *British*

| ∇ 21 | 21 | 19 | £33 |

Hackney | 130 Lauriston Rd., E9 (Bethnal Green) | 020-8533 5123 | www.theempressofindia.com

Though technically a tavern (The Gun team own it), this "bright, elegantly decorated dining space" "in the oasis of Victoria Park Village" seems "more a restaurant than a gastropub"; it's always "buzzing with the local chattering classes" chowing down on "hearty" Modern British fare, served by "friendly", if "a bit vacant" staff.

	FOOD	DECOR	SERVICE	COST

Engineer, The *British* 20 | 17 | 18 | £30

Primrose Hill | 65 Gloucester Ave., NW1 (Chalk Farm) | 020-7722 0950 | fax 7483 0592 | www.the-engineer.com

"Even though it's in la-di-da-di Primrose Hill, there's surprisingly nice atmosphere" (with "the walled garden a bonus") to this "see-and-be-seen" gastropub – "one of the originals" – serving "consistently good, not great food" and "wines perfectly chosen for quaff-ability"; some pout it's "overpriced", but then the Modern Brit meals come with "cachet attached."

Enoteca Turi ⓩ *Italian* 24 | 18 | 22 | £44

Putney | 28 Putney High St., SW15 (Putney Bridge) | 020-8785 4449 | fax 8780 5409 | www.enotecaturi.com

It's "worth a trip over the river to this restaurant", which, with its "homey" vibe and "hearty, rustic fare", "feels like you're having a meal made by your Italian grandma – only she has a phenomenal wine cellar" to boot; a few suggest that success has made "the place lose the plot", citing "long waits between courses" (especially "if you're not a regular"), but positives proclaim it "a real plus for Putney."

Enterprise, The *Eclectic* ▽ 17 | 19 | 19 | £37

Chelsea | 35 Walton St., SW3 (Knightsbridge/South Kensington) | 020-7584 3148 | fax 7584 2516 | www.theenterprise.co.uk

"The haunt of ageing estate agents", "20-year-old groups and couples on dates", this gastropub has "no pretence or attitude" – just an "ok" Eclectic menu with "all the comfort classics" within an interior that "feels a bit like *The Golden Girls* were hired to decorate"; sure, it's "expensive, but then again, it *is* on Walton Street"; P.S. "watch out for long waits as they don't take reservations."

Esarn Kheaw *Thai* ▽ 25 | 9 | 16 | £25

Shepherd's Bush | 314 Uxbridge Rd., W12 (Shepherd's Bush) | 020-8743 8930 | fax 7243 1250 | www.esarnkheaw.co.uk

True, "the decor is hilariously bad, but you come for the food" – "mouth-wateringly intense" Thai cuisine "as it tastes in Thailand" – served by this "brilliant family business" near Shepherd's Bush; staff can be "quirky, but they warm up once they recognise you."

Essenza ● *Italian* ▽ 18 | 15 | 20 | £36

Notting Hill | 210 Kensington Park Rd., W11 (Ladbroke Grove) | 020-7792 1066 | fax 7792 2088 | www.essenza.co.uk

This "nice local" in Notting Hill delivers "decent", "classic Italian" *cucina* within "homely" digs; "although not as good" as Osteria Basilco and Mediterraneo, it's "often easier to get a table [here] than at its nearby sisters" – and "they don't ask you to leave" to make room for the next booking.

Eyre Brothers ⓩ *Portuguese/Spanish* 22 | 21 | 21 | £50

Shoreditch | 70 Leonard St., EC2 (Old St.) | 020-7613 5346 | fax 7739 8199 | www.eyrebrothers.co.uk

There's "always a warm welcome and a kitchen that can produce some fine Spanish-Portuguese food" at this "sleek yet comfortable"

Shoreditch eatery from the eponymous Eyres; it's a "good choice if you want something slightly different", though it "can get pricey."

☑ Fairuz *Lebanese*   22 | 14 | 16 | £33

Marylebone | 3 Blandford St., W1 (Baker St./Bond St.) | 020-7486 8108 | fax 7935 8581 | www.fairuz.uk.com

"Make sure you bring your appetite" to this "loud" Lebanese in Marylebone, proffering "huge portions" of "home eats at a reasonable price"; if staff seem "less-than-helpful", there's "takeaway instead."

Fakhreldine *Lebanese*   19 | 18 | 19 | £45

Piccadilly | 85 Piccadilly, 1st fl., W1 (Green Park) | 020-7493 3424 | fax 7495 1977 | www.fakhreldine.co.uk

It has "been around for ages" (actually, three decades) but there's a "contemporary" feel to this "classy" Lebanese "with fabulous views of Green Park", "accommodating service" and a menu showing a "modern twist" from a "chef with a light hand"; "high prices" deter some, who suggest "stick to the appetisers" and "interesting cocktails" ("the bar has inviting low seating").

Farm, The *French*   ▽ 19 | 20 | 16 | £35

Fulham | 18 Farm Ln., SW6 (Fulham Broadway) | 020-7381 3331 | fax 7386 3761 | www.thefarmfulham.co.uk

"The bright, contemporary interior complements the fresh, up-to-date" Classic French cuisine at this "great little gastropub" in Fulham; although it's "a little pricey", and "let down by variable service" at times, there's a "buzzy atmosphere", plus "you can sit outside."

Fat Badger, The *British*   ▽ 15 | 14 | 10 | £27

Notting Hill | 310 Portobello Rd., W10 (Ladbroke Grove/Westbourne Park) | 020-8969 4500 | www.thefatbadger.com

Perhaps "there are better in the area" around Notting Hill, but this "good gastropub" offers "a relaxed atmosphere, with comfy couches and big windows to see the world passing by" as you munch the Modern British meals (and the "edgy neighbourhood crowd makes the food cooler"); alas, "achingly hip staff would do better to check on the guests, rather than checking each other out."

☑ Fat Duck, The Ⓜ *European*   27 | 23 | 27 | £128

Bray | High St., Berkshire | 01628 580333 | www.fatduck.co.uk

Be "blown away by the artful combinations and intense flavours" from chef-owner Heston Blumenthal, whose "experimental" Modern European edibles "elevate the simple process of eating to a vivid, humourous experience", aided by "staff's terrific enthusiasm"; given items like foie gras 'benzaldehyde' and nitro-green tea mousse, some wonder at "paying good money for the aftermath of a science lesson" – indeed, "when the bill comes, you'll quack a lot" – but most say this "simple" Bray cottage is "to food what the Tate Modern is to art."

Feng Sushi *Japanese*   18 | 12 | 15 | £23

Borough | 13 Stoney St., SE1 (London Bridge) | 020-7407 8744 | fax 7407 8777 🗷

(continued)

(continued)

Feng Sushi

Chalk Farm | 1 Adelaide Rd., NW3 (Chalk Farm) | 020-7483 2929 |
fax 7449 9893
Fulham | 218 Fulham Rd., SW10 (Fulham Broadway) | 020-7795 1900 |
fax 7352 8262
Kensington | 24 Kensington Church St., W8 (Notting Hill Gate) |
020-7937 7927 | fax 7376 9191
Notting Hill | 101 Notting Hill Gate, W11 (Notting Hill Gate) |
020-7727 1123 | fax 7727 1125
www.fengsushi.co.uk

"After tramping around town", it's good "to grab a casual bite" at
this "surprisingly good" string of sushi-slingers, even if their rolls
"really can add up"; however, most of the "interiors are quite small",
so many prefer the "prime takeaway" ("they deliver" too).

ffiona's Ⓜ *British*   23 | 16 | 21 | £40

Kensington | 51 Kensington Church St., W8 (High St. Kensington/
Notting Hill Gate) | 020-7937 4152 | www.ffionas.com

"Fierce, funny" Ffiona Reid-Owen "seems to do it all – take your order, cook it, and provide company and stories" – at her "offbeat but
charming" Kensington corner; her Traditional British comfort food is
"fabulous", and it's all "fresh"-ly bought – so many advise "reserve
as early [a time] as possible, or items will be sold out."

Fifteen *Mediterranean*   25 | 20 | 23 | £55

Hoxton | 15 Westland Pl., N1 (Old St.) | 0871-330 1515 | www.fifteen.net

The "young chefs [in training] work hard to impress" at this "casual", "cute concept from the peripatetic Jamie Oliver", where "creative" dishes from an "enticing" Med menu are "served
enthusiastically"; whether you prefer the "smart dining room downstairs" or the "cheaper", more "buzzy" "bistro space upstairs", it's
"well worth the adventure" of heading to Hoxton.

Fifth Floor *European*   21 | 18 | 19 | £44

Knightsbridge | Harvey Nichols | 109-125 Knightsbridge, SW1
(Knightsbridge) | 020-7235 5250 | fax 0191 6019 |
www.harveynichols.com

"You wouldn't expect much from a department store" restaurant,
but the colour-changing, "chic yet comfortable atmosphere attracts
urban sophisticates" aplenty to this Modern European "atop Harvey
Nichols"; the food is "surprisingly well-executed" – even
"imaginative" – and the "amazing [prix fixes] with unlimited wine"
(at lunch and early evening) "are well worth a punt"; and if the
"decor's looking a little tired", the bar remains a "happening place to
see and be seen."

Fifth Floor Cafe *British/Mediterranean*   18 | 15 | 14 | £32

Knightsbridge | Harvey Nichols | 109-125 Knightsbridge, SW1
(Knightsbridge) | 020-7823 1839 | fax 7823 2207 |
www.harveynichols.com

Using the "same kitchen as the [adjacent] restaurant, but with a
lighter menu" of Modern British–Med fare, Harvey Nic's "hectic",

"casual" cafe is "packed with yummy mummies and shoppers" seeking "to recharge"; whilst "service varies from professional to abject indifference", it remains "relatively fast."

Fig *European*
22 | 16 | 20 | £34

Islington | 169 Hemingford Rd., N1 (Barnesbury/Caledonian Rd.) | 020-7609 3009 | www.fig-restaurant.co.uk

"When you can't be bothered to cook for yourself", this "very sweet local" in Islington (a converted grocer's) "deserves high marks" for its well-"above-average Modern European cooking" and "delightful service"; "it doesn't hurt your wallet too much either."

ℤ Fino ⚅ *Spanish*
25 | 20 | 18 | £48

Fitzrovia | 33 Charlotte St., W1 (Goodge St./Tottenham Court Rd.) | 020-7813 8010 | fax 7813 8011 | www.finorestaurant.com

"Some of the best Spanish food in London" is on offer at this dark, "hip restaurant off Tottenham Court Road"; true, "they charge superlative prices", but happy paisanos pay the pesos for the "tapas supremo" and "superb wine"; "if you don't want the formality of the tables, you can dine at the bar" – though "service can be distracted" there "as it gets busy, which it always does."

Fire & Stone ◑ *Pizza*
18 | 16 | 15 | £20

Covent Garden | 31-32 Maiden Ln., WC2 (Covent Garden/Leicester Sq.) | 0845-330 0139 | fax 020-7395 1969 | www.fireandstone.com

"If you want your pizzas unusual" – would you believe, a version "with black pudding"? – then this "big", "buzzing" Covent Garden haunt is worth a try; most clients can cope with the "canteen-style tables and chairs", though "tardy service" lets the side down.

Firezza *Pizza*
19 | 10 | 15 | £19

Islington | 276 St. Paul's Rd., N1 (Highbury & Islington) | 020-7359 7400

Battersea | 40 Lavender Hill, SW11 (Clapham Junction Rail) | 020-7223 5535

Chelsea | 116 Finborough Rd., SW10 (Earl's Ct.) | 020-7370 2255

Wandsworth | 205 Garratt Ln., SW18 (East Putney) | 020-8870 7070

Chiswick | 48 Chiswick High Rd., W4 (Turnham Green) | 020-8994 9494

Notting Hill | 12 All Saints Rd., W11 (Notting Hill Gate) | 020-7221 0020

www.firezza.com

Surveyors "love ordering by the metre" at this "gourmet pizza" chain, which also offers "interesting salads"; whilst they boast "the best delivery around, eating-in is less special"; hence, they're "generally done as takeout."

fish! *Seafood*
19 | 16 | 17 | £35

South Bank | Borough Mkt. | Cathedral St., SE1 (London Bridge) | 020-7407 3803 | fax 7357 8636 | www.fishdiner.co.uk

"If you love fish, you'll love fish!" quip followers of this glass-roofed seafooder that offers "a not-creative, but good formula" – your pick of "fresh fish, cooked as you like it with your choice of sauce"; however, the "hectic", "antiseptic" setting makes it like "eating in a fishmonger's" "in the middle of Borough Market."

	FOOD	DECOR	SERVICE	COST

Fish Club ☑ *Seafood*
— | — | — | I

Battersea | 189 St. John's Hill, SW11 (Clapham Junction Rail) |
020-7978 7115

The "best fish 'n' chips in London" swear supporters of this small,
"simple, straight-up" Battersea seafooder; these and other delights
of "fishy perfection" are "cooked as you want", and since the wet
counter receives two deliveries daily, all the fin fare's hyper-fresh.

Fish Hook *Seafood*
▽ 20 | 11 | 18 | £37

Chiswick | 6-8 Elliott Rd., W4 (Turnham Green) | 020-8742 0766 |
fax 8742 3374 | www.fishhook.co.uk

Given the cries of "consistently wonderful", surveyors seem hooked on
the fish at this "small" seafooder in Chiswick; considering the quality,
"it's probably one of the best deals in London", sweetened by the way
chef-patron Michael Nadra "comes out of the kitchen" to greet diners.

Fish Shop on St. John St. ☑ *Seafood*
▽ 18 | 14 | 17 | £36

Clerkenwell | 360-362 St. John St., EC1 (Angel) | 020-7837 1199 |
fax 7837 3399 | www.thefishshop.net

"They know how to keep it simple" at this "oasis in a culinary dry
spot" in Clerkenwell, an "airy" seafooder offering a deep-fried
"range of fish (surprise!)" with "clean, crisp flavours"; there's an
"imaginative pre-theatre prix fixe for those heading to nearby
Sadler's Wells"; service is "ok, friendly at least."

FishWorks *Seafood*
19 | 13 | 17 | £36

Marylebone | 89 Marylebone High St., W1 (Baker St.) | 020-7935 9796 |
fax 7935 8796
NEW Piccadilly | 7-9 Swallow St., W1 (Piccadilly Circus) | 020-7734 5813
Primrose Hill | 57 Regents Park Rd., NW1 (Chalk Farm) | 020-7586 9760
Islington | 134 Upper St., N1 (Angel/Highbury & Islington) |
020-7354 1279 | fax 7226 8269
Battersea | 54 Northcote Rd., SW1 (Clapham Junction Rail) |
020-7228 7893
Chelsea | 212 Fulham Rd., SW10 (South Kensington) | 020-7823 3033
Fulham | 177 New King's Rd., SW6 (Parsons Green) | 020-7384 1009
Richmond | 13-19 The Square, TW9 (Richmond) | 020-8948 5965
Chiswick | 6 Turnham Green Terrace, W4 (Turnham Green) |
020-8994 0086 | fax 8994 0778
www.fishworks.co.uk

Your dinner "can be ordered off the fishmonger's counter and be
cooked to specification" at these fast-spawning fish houses; but
even friends feel the food's "freshness is really the only reason for
dining here, as the uncomfortable surroundings and disinterested
staff create an 'off' whiff"; P.S. tip: "order the specials, as they
outshine some of the standards on the menu."

Flaneur ☒ *European*
24 | 20 | 17 | £34

Farringdon | 41 Farringdon Rd., EC1 (Farringdon) | 020-7404 4422 |
fax 7831 4532 | www.flaneur.com

A "bistro in a gastronomic shop – brilliant!" say boosters of this
Farringdon Road "foodie heaven" offering "fantastic" Modern
European fare in an "airy", low-lit space "relatively free of back-

ground noise"; it's only "marred by inept service" – "staff seem to have misunderstood the slow food movement" – but at least "you can do your shopping at the same time" you're waiting.

Floridita ●⊠ *Cuban* | 17 | 19 | 16 | £43 |

Soho | 100 Wardour St., W1 (Tottenham Court Rd.) | 020-7314 4000 | fax 7314 4040 | www.floridita.co.uk

Although it's "more *Footballers' Wives* than Havana", this large, "loud"-with-live-music Latino in Soho "remains reliable" for a "fun, funky" chance to dance; the "overpriced" food gives "just a nod to real Cuban cooking", and "takes an age to arrive", but it's "a sidelight to the rum drinks and encounters" anyway.

Foliage *European/French* | 25 | 23 | 25 | £75 |

Knightsbridge | Mandarin Oriental Hyde Park | 66 Knightsbridge, SW1 (Knightsbridge) | 020-7201 3723 | fax 7235 2001 | www.mandarinoriental.com/london

"Offering leafy views of Hyde Park", the Mandarin Oriental's "sleek", airy dining room makes a "glorious" setting for chef Chris Staines' "delicate", "spectacularly delicious Modern European–Classic French cuisine", along with "want-for-nothing", "swish service"; sure, the "bill can set you back", and "walking through the crowded bar" at the front is a bugbear, but otherwise, this site is "superlative in every category."

Food for Thought ⊄ *Vegetarian* | 24 | 11 | 17 | £12 |

Covent Garden | 31 Neal St., WC2 (Covent Garden) | 020-7836 9072

"Serving for over 30 years", it "looks like an old-school vegetarian restaurant, but the flavours are modern and interesting" at this meat-free mecca that's "a must for the health-conscious"; yes, the Covent Garden "cafterialike basement" is "pretty grotty and cramped", and service "canteen-style", but fans "forgive all, for it's the most wholesome best-value food in London" – and the Best Buy in the Survey.

Forge, The ● *European* | 18 | 20 | 18 | £42 |

Covent Garden | 14 Garrick St., WC2 (Covent Garden/Leicester Sq.) | 020-7379 1432 | fax 7379 1530 | www.theforgerestaurant.co.uk

A cousin to Le Café du Jardin and Le Deuxième nearby, this Modern European has forged some friendships with those who call it a "welcome addition" to Covent Garden, with "relaxing" ambience and an "interesting wine list" – though steely hearted surveyors say the food's "not up to scratch"; still, few deny its "wonderful pre-theatre: staff are skilled at getting you fed and in your seat for the curtain."

Fortnum's Fountain *British* | 17 | 16 | 16 | £32 |

St. James's | Fortnum & Mason | 181 Piccadilly, W1 (Green Park/ Piccadilly Circus) | 020-7973 4140 | fax 7437 3278 | www.fortnumandmason.co.uk

After a much-heralded revamp, Fortnum & Mason's all-day dining room (with its own entrance "at the Jermyn Street corner") "looks updated and polished" – yet surveyors (and lower scores) suggest "it seemed to work better" before: "service is rushed, and portions can be small"; but if you need a "return to Traditional British comfort food", "surrounded by well-dressed ladies", it remains "handy."

Four Seasons Chinese Chinese
22 | 9 | 13 | £24

Bayswater | 84 Queensway, W2 (Bayswater) | 020-7229 4320 | fax 7229 4320

"Everyone orders the justly famous roast duck" at this "hugely popular" Queensway Chinese, which "offers some of the most authentic food in London" – and at "low prices" to boot; just "be prepared for substandard service" and to "get there early to avoid lines."

Foxtrot Oscar British
∇ 15 | - | 13 | £36

Chelsea | 79 Royal Hospital Rd., SW3 (Sloane Sq.) | 020-7352 4448 | fax 7351 1667 | www.gordonramsay.com

This "favourite Chelsea eatery", established 1980, was "renovated and reopened by Gordon Ramsay" in early 2008; alas, "all the charm seemed to have evaporated" cry critics – "it's more tempting to look at your fellow diners than to actually eat" the Traditional British meals (though they're "good" enough); at least the decor, which "reminded some of a nicely decorated cab office", has gotten a softer, warmer look post-Survey.

Franco's ⊠ Italian/Mediterranean
19 | 16 | 21 | £50

St. James's | 61 Jermyn St., SW1 (Green Park) | 020-7499 2211 | fax 7495 1375 | www.francoslondon.com

A "solid standby for business" types, thanks to its "clublike atmosphere" and "staff who make you feel important", this confidential Jermyn Street stalwart (a sib of next door Wilton's) prepares "surprisingly good" Italian-Med cuisine "with a modern twist", even if it is "wildly overpriced."

Frankie's Italian Bar & Grill Italian
14 | 18 | 16 | £37

Knightsbridge | 3 Yeoman's Row, SW3 (Knightsbridge) | 020-7590 9999 | fax 7590 9900

Marylebone | Selfridges | 400 Oxford St., lower ground fl., W1 (Bond St.) | 0800-123 400

Putney | 263 Putney Bridge Rd., SW15 (Putney Bridge) | 020-8780 3366 Ⓜ

Chiswick | 68 Chiswick High Rd., W4 (Stamford Brook) | 020-8987 9988 | fax 8987 9911

www.frankiesitalianbarandgrill.com

Developed in partnership with top jockey Frankie Dettori, this quartet in the Marco Pierre White stable is "popular with families" for "quick" Italian-American eats served amidst a "vast array of shiny material (including super-sized glitter balls" and mosaics); alas, naysayers are "not inspired", suggesting "Frankie should stick to riding."

Franklins British
- | - | - | M

Kennington | 205-209 Kennington Ln., SE11 (Kennington) | 020-7793 8313

Dulwich | 157 Lordship Ln., SE22 (East Dulwich Rail) | 020-8299 9598

www.franklinsrestaurant.com

Frank foes feel it's "nothing to write home about", but devotees dub this "buzzing" "little local" "East Dulwich's best" for "really good

Modern British food" served at the back of "a cosy pub"; the younger, more spacious branch boasts a pretty courtyard in "the heart of Kennington."

Frederick's ☒ *British/European* | 21 | 23 | 19 | £56 |

Islington | 106 Camden Passage, N1 (Angel) | 020-7359 2888 | fax 7359 5173 | www.fredericks.co.uk

Maintaining a "high reputation after all these years", this "Islington institution" is "always a pleasure", especially for its "conservatory-style room" ("a jewel-box of a glass house"); the "varied" Modern British–Euro "meals are fit for a king – ok, maybe a prince" – and if the "service can be a bit hit-and-miss", it's a "great place to take the parents" or for special occasions (they have a civil marriage license, so you can even have the wedding there).

French Horn *British/French* | ▽ 21 | 24 | 23 | £66 |

Sonning | French Horn Hotel | Berkshire | 01189 692204 | fax 01189 442210 | www.thefrenchhorn.co.uk

In a "dreamy location by the river" Thames, this Berkshires family-run 19th-century inn an hour outside London is "worth the trip" for "lovely" Classic French–British cuisine ("stick to the duck", "roasted right in front of you over an open fire"), an "excellent wine cellar" and "comforting" service; even if it "just falls short" of its "fancy prices", it's "great for impressing."

French House, The ☒ *French* | ▽ 17 | 17 | 16 | £43 |

Soho | 49 Dean St., W1 (Piccadilly Circus/Tottenham Court Rd.) | 020-7437 2477 | fax 7287 9109 | www.frenchhousesoho.com

Walking up to this "Soho classic" (as De Gaulle did during World War II) situated above a "cosy" pub is like climbing "a culinary stairway to heaven" – if your idea of bliss is an "old-fashioned, authentic French bistro"; it "serves nothing but standards, like confit de canard, but does it so well."

Frontline *British* | - | - | - | E |

Paddington | 13 Norfolk Pl., W2 (Paddington) | 020-7479 8960 | fax 7479 8961 | www.thefrontlineclub.com

"Much-needed in still-developing Paddington", this establishment sits below a private journalists' club – and the cameraman-owner's "wonderful photos adorn the walls, to keep you entertained" whilst you wait for the staff ("often missing in action at the frontline") to bring the "spectacularly hit-or-miss", almost "too English food" to table; the minimal markup policy on the wine is definitely "outstanding", though.

Fung Shing ● *Chinese* | 23 | 11 | 18 | £31 |

Chinatown | 15 Lisle St., WC2 (Leicester Sq.) | 020-7437 1539 | fax 7743 0284 | www.fungshing.co.uk

"Divine seasonal specials", "unusual foods like eel done well" and "authentic" Cantonese standards served by "smiling waiters" have made this Chinatown veteran a "family favourite" for decades; it's also "great for pre- or post-theatre dining", even if the "tired" setting "looks like the set from a bad Peter Sellers movie."

Gaby's ⊟ *Jewish/Mideastern*

FOOD	DECOR	SERVICE	COST
-	-	-	I

Covent Garden | 30 Charing Cross Rd., WC2 (Leicester Sq.) | 020-7836 4233

"When there isn't time for a more swept-up place", theatre-goers trek to this small late-night veteran in a "handy location" in Leicester Square; it's "reliable" for Middle Eastern and Jewish "down-home" delicatessen, "but there's no atmosphere except for the staff's mood."

Galicia ●Ⓜ *Spanish*

FOOD	DECOR	SERVICE	COST
19	13	17	£26

Notting Hill | 323 Portobello Rd., W10 (Ladbroke Grove) | 020-8969 3539

"As soon as you walk in the door, you're in Spain" sigh supporters of this "straightforward, no-frills" place in Notting Hill; there's "terrific tapas" and other "down-to-earth Galician food", offered up at "unbeatable value", with a "lively" vibe thrown in.

Gallipoli *Turkish*

FOOD	DECOR	SERVICE	COST
18	18	16	£21

Islington | 102 Upper St., N1 (Angel) | 020-7359 0630 | fax 7704 0496
Islington | 107 Upper St., N1 (Angel) | 020-7226 5333 Ⓜ
Islington | 120 Upper St., N1 (Angel) | 020-7359 1578 | fax 7704 0496
www.gallipolibazaar.com

It's "like walking into Istanbul" at this "atmospheric" Turkish with "three locations in Upper Street" - each "a favourite with locals, and understandably so", thanks to "plentiful portions" of "easy-going food" at a "bargain" price; if "service can be hit-and-miss", it's not surprising given they're often "overcrowded" with "lively" groups.

Galvin at Windows Restaurant & Bar *French*

FOOD	DECOR	SERVICE	COST
20	24	21	£70

Mayfair | London Hilton on Park Ln. | 22 Park Ln., W1 (Hyde Park Corner) | 020-7208 4021 | www.galvinuk.com

Nesting atop the Hilton Park Lane with "breathtaking" vistas "across Hyde Park and Buckingham Palace", this "serene" dining room "breaks the rule that good food and great views don't go together", with a New French menu that offers "something for everyone", and "polished service"; foes find it "a tad fussy - to justify the high prices", perhaps; but there's solace in the "sophisticated" bar.

Ⓩ Galvin Bistrot de Luxe *French*

FOOD	DECOR	SERVICE	COST
23	20	19	£47

Marylebone | 66 Baker St., W1 (Baker St.) | 020-7935 4007 | fax 7486 1735 | www.galvinuk.com

"Big and buzzing", Baker Street's French "favourite" "does not call itself de Luxe for nothing": it "elevates basic bistro fare to a new level", and serves it in an "upscale setting" of "banquettes and starched wine linen", "with upmarket prices" to match; "don't go if you have a deadline - service is slow", but otherwise, this "convivial" citizen "deserves all the credit it receives."

Garbo's *Swedish*

FOOD	DECOR	SERVICE	COST
▽ 17	15	20	£35

Marylebone | 42 Crawford St., W1 (Baker St./Marylebone) | 020-7262 6582 | fax 7262 6582

"Swedish expats love this place, so they must be doing something right" at this "friendly" Marylebone veteran serving "steady"

| | FOOD | DECOR | SERVICE | COST |

Scandinavian savouries (the savvy say "stick to the simple dishes"); the "old-fashioned" setting is "comfortable, if a little claustrophobic", with that elk's head staring down at you from the wall.

☑ Gate, The ⊠ *Vegetarian*   25 | 15 | 21 | £32

Hammersmith | 51 Queen Caroline St., W6 (Hammersmith) | 020-8748 6932 | www.thegate.tv

Even carnivores crave the cooking at this veteran that's "difficult to find" (hint: it's behind the Apollo Theatre) "but worth it" for "wonderful vegetarian" vittles that are amongst "the most innovative in London", "full of life and pleasing to the eye"; what's less pleasing is the "environment, too well-scrubbed to be warm" – though "at lunch, the bulding's light compensates for this."

☑ Gaucho Grill *Argentinean/Chophouse*   22 | 20 | 19 | £44

Holborn | 125-126 Chancery Ln., WC2 (Chancery Ln.) | 020-7242 7727 | fax 7242 7723 ⊠

Piccadilly | 25 Swallow St., W1 (Piccadilly Circus) | 020-7734 4040 | fax 7734 1076 ☽

Canary Wharf | 29 Westferry Circus, E14 (Canary Wharf) | 020-7987 9494 | fax 7987 9292

City | 1 Bell Inn Yard, EC3 (Bank/Monument) | 020-7626 5180 | fax 7626 5181 ⊠

City | 5 Finsbury Ave., EC2 (Liverpool St.) | 020-7256 6877 | fax 7256 5410 ⊠

NEW Tower Bridge | 2 More London Riverside, SE1 (London Bridge) | 020-7407 5222 | fax 7407 5166

Hampstead | 64 Heath St., NW3 (Hampstead) | 020-7431 8222 | fax 7431 3714

Chelsea | 89 Sloane Ave., SW3 (South Kensington) | 020-7584 9901 | fax 7584 0045

Richmond | The Towpath | The Towpath Richmond Riverside, TW10 (Richmond) | 020-8948 4030 | fax 8948 2945 ☽ www.gaucho-grill.com

Their decor of "cowhide upholstery and wall coverings" may "border on the Disneyesque", but there's no naysaying the "menu dominated – rightly – by the wonderful steaks" ("don't try anything else") plus a "daunting collection of Argentine wines" at this "lively" Latin American chain; "some may moo at the prices", and staff "can get busier than they can handle", but overall, gauchos grin it's "great to see them expanding, but not diminishing in quality."

Gay Hussar ⊠ *Hungarian*   19 | 18 | 19 | £36

Soho | 2 Greek St., W1 (Tottenham Court Rd.) | 020-7437 0973 | fax 7437 4631 | www.gayhussar.co.uk

It's an "institution for Hungarian food, but there's far from institutional cooking" – in fact, the fare's "improved over our last visit" – at this Soho "dowager" that remains "reliable, especially to those who've been coming for 40 years"; a "noisy" crowd of "excited intelligentsia and socialites" are "served promptly", and if it's "more a cultural than culinary experience" now, the "old-school" decor festooned with politicians' cartoons – "like a caricature museum" – "really does contribute to an enjoyable experience."

	FOOD	DECOR	SERVICE	COST

Geales Fish Restaurant *Seafood*

20 | 13 | 17 | £26

Notting Hill | 2 Farmer St., W8 (Notting Hill Gate) | 020-7727 7528 |
fax 7229 8632 | www.geales.com

"Whilst the new look is a bit too 'uptown' for its history" as a "quint-essential fish 'n' chips" shop, foodwise this Notting Hill seafooder "has been rescued" by its "new owners" (including chef Garry Hollihead); it now offers quite a "decent" selection of "fresh" fin fare, along with classic "sides of mushy peas", etc. at "easy-on-the-wallet" prices.

George Ⓢ *European*

22 | 22 | 23 | £63

Private club; inquiries: 020-7491 4433

"Find a member and go" to "this private, yet very public club" (thanks to its high-profile clientele) in a "terrific location in the centre of [Mayfair's] hedge-fund community"; the Modern European kitchen turns out "simple food cooked perfectly", staff show "attention to detail without overdoing it" and don't forget the "bar area - classy, contemporary and great fun."

Getti *Italian*

14 | 13 | 15 | £43

Marylebone | 42 Marylebone High St., W1 (Baker St./Bond St.) |
020-7486 3753 | fax 7486 7084

St. James's | 16-17 Jermyn St., SW1 (Piccadilly Circus) | 020-7734 7334 |
fax 7734 7924 Ⓢ

www.getti.com

"Not a destination for foodies, but not bad neighbourhood eateries either" sums up this "simple" "non-fussy" pair of Italians in St. James's and an "upmarket area of Marylebone"; "so-so service" lets the side down, but Jermyn Street's prix fixes are "great deals pre-theatre."

Giardinetto Ⓢ *Italian*

- | - | - | E

Mayfair | 39-40 Albemarle St., W1 (Green Park) | 020-7493 7091 |
fax 7493 7096 | www.giardinetto.co.uk

Some "impressive" Italian dishes and a "huge selection of wines" are the main appeal of this "expensive" Mayfair eatery; but foes find the glass-and-metal "minimalist" surrounds are "too trendy by far (and not even that attractive)", and overall, "something seems missing."

Ⓩ Gilgamesh *Pan-Asian*

19 | 25 | 15 | £41

Camden Town | The Stables, Camden Mkt. | Chalk Farm Rd., NW1
(Camden Town/Chalk Farm) | 020-7482 5757 | www.gilgameshbar.com

"Enormously high ceiling", pillars, carved woods and tapestries: the "fantasy-world" decor is "definitely over the top – but that's the point" of this "huge" Camden Pan-Asian, "the trendy place" du jour; "neither the food nor the service match the splendid" surrounds – the former offers "more style than substance", the latter "needs a course in hospitality" – but "admit it, who wouldn't want to eat in a restaurant named after a Sumerian hero?"

Giovanni's ●Ⓢ *Italian*

20 | 16 | 19 | £37

Covent Garden | 10 Goodwin's Ct., WC2 (Covent Garden) |
020-7240 2877

"What a find (when you can find it)" fawn fans of this "old-fashioned Italian" "in an alley off St. Martin's Lane" that's "always a cosy pleasure" for "simple, home-cooked" fare ("at reasonable prices for the location") and "personalised service" from "gregarious host-owner", Pino Ragona; "a real luvvies place", it's a "favourite after a play" as well.

Giraffe *Eclectic*

| 16 | 14 | 16 | £21 |

Marylebone | 6-8 Blandford St., W1 (Baker St./Bond St.) | 020-7935 2333 | fax 7935 2334

Spitalfields | Spitalfields Mkt. | Unit 1, Crispin Pl., E1 (Liverpool St.) | 020-3116 2000 | fax 3116 2001

Waterloo | Royal Festival Hall | Unit 1 & 2, Riverside Level 1, SE1 (Waterloo) | 020-7928 2004 | fax 7620 1952

Hampstead | 46 Rosslyn Hill, NW3 (Hampstead) | 020-7435 0343 | fax 7431 1317

Muswell Hill | 348 Muswell Hill Broadway, N10 (Highgate) | 020-8883 4463 | fax 8883 1224

Islington | 29-31 Essex Rd., N1 (Angel) | 020-7359 5999 | fax 7359 6158

Battersea | 27 Battersea Rise, SW11 (Clapham Common/ Clapham Junction Rail) | 020-7223 0933 | fax 7223 1037

Richmond | 30 Hill St., TW9 (Richmond) | 020-8332 2646 | fax 8332 9171

Chiswick | 270 Chiswick High Rd., W4 (Turnham Green) | 020-8995 2100 | fax 8995 5697

Kensington | 7 Kensington High St., W8 (High St. Kensington) | 020-7938 1221 | fax 7938 3330

www.giraffe.net

Additional locations throughout London

"Healthy food, child-friendly, rapid service, lots of convenient venues" – small wonder this herd of bright-hued, music-filled Eclectics "stands tall in its field" of chain eateries; but cynics suggest whilst it's "good for families, if you're not in one, don't go", and even supporters say it could use "a shake-up – screaming kids need new colouring mats."

NEW Giusto *Italian*

| - | - | - | M |

Marylebone | 43 Blandford St., W1 (Baker St.) | 020-7486 7340 | www.giustorestaurant.com

Taking over Spighetta's old space, this first venture from former staffers at The Oak is already "a great addition to the restaurant flora in Marylebone, with a small but attractive menu" of pizzas from a prominent wood-fired oven and other "well-priced", "modern Italian" dishes; the rustic, terra-cotta–floored basement also contains a casual bar with a *cicchetti* menu of tapas-style dishes.

Glasshouse, The *European*

| 25 | 22 | 22 | £55 |

Richmond | 14 Station Parade, TW9 (Kew Gdns.) | 020-8940 6777 | fax 8940 3833 | www.glasshouserestaurant.co.uk

In an area with "a lack of decent restaurants", this "serene spot in Kew" ("close to the Gardens") "shines" with a "carefully crafted", "sophisticated" Modern European menu served by "professional staff" within a multiwindowed, "lovely, sunny room"; "it's pricey, but you get your money's worth – not only because of the fine food, but because of the pleasant ambience" radiated by this "sparkling" "gem."

	FOOD	DECOR	SERVICE	COST

Golden Dragon ● *Chinese* — 20 | 13 | 15 | £26

Chinatown | 28-29 Gerrard St., W1 (Leicester Sq./Piccadilly Circus) | 020-7734 2763 | fax 7734 1073

"Hong Kong through and through", this Chinatown behemoth "gets extremely crowded" on account of "some seriously good food" and "lots of dim sum"; if "the service goes erratically from rush to snail's pace", you "can't get more authentic than this" cuisinewise – and it's "great value" too.

◪ Golden Hind ⊠ *Seafood* — 23 | 10 | 17 | £15

Marylebone | 73 Marylebone Ln., W1 (Bond St.) | 020-7486 3644

If this Marylebone seafooder "feels like an institution" – it is: "since it opened in 1914", it's served "some of the freshest and best fish 'n' chips" around; the "drab" decor's enlivened by the "family atmosphere" and the "presence of an art deco fryer" (no longer used), so "the only negative is, no beer" (but you can bring your own").

Goldmine ● *Chinese* — - | - | - | M

Bayswater | 102 Queensway, W2 (Bayswater) | 020-7792 8331

Although it's a relative newcomer to the ranks of "Chinese on Queensway", this "casual" eatery with an "ex-Four Seasons Chinese chef at its helm" assumes "the mantle as the place for Cantonese roasted duck par excellence" (even if "other dishes are ordinary"); it's also credited as an "amazing value."

Good Earth, The *Chinese* — 21 | 15 | 19 | £37

Knightsbridge | 233 Brompton Rd., SW3 (Knightsbridge/South Kensington) | 020-7584 3658 | fax 7823 8769

Finchley | 143-145 The Broadway, NW7 (Mill Hill Rail) | 020-8959 7011 | fax 8959 1464

www.goodearthgroup.co.uk

"Gorge yourself as if you haven't eaten in a week" at this Mandarin pair in Knightsbridge and Finchley, which have "been reliable for eons" (well, decades) for "big portions" of "quality food" in "better-than-average" Asian digs; but a few grouse this "good earth needs some nurturing", especially the "hit-or-miss service."

Gopal's of Soho ●⊠ *Indian* — ▽ 20 | 9 | 16 | £26

Soho | 12 Bateman St., W1 (Leicester Sq./Tottenham Court Rd.) | 020-7434 1621 | fax 7434 0840

"Memories of the British Raj are alive" at this "old standby" in Soho, where the "Indian fare" includes "good veggies"; "there are more distinctive places now", but it still comes "recommended."

◪ Gordon Ramsay at Claridge's *European* — 26 | 25 | 25 | £90

Mayfair | Claridge's Hotel | 45 Brook St., W1 (Bond St.) | 020-7499 0099 | fax 7499 3099 | www.gordonramsay.com

"Perfect for that push-the-boat-out evening", Gordon Ramsay's "high-ceilinged", art deco-"opulent" dining room at Claridge's represents "celebrity chefdom at its finest", offering "sublime" Modern European "taste explosions", served by staff who seem to "enjoy the experience as much as you do"; perhaps it's "not as good as

[GR's] Royal Hospital Road location", which may be why it seems "insanely expensive", but "you get looked after so well the price becomes less relevant."

☑ Gordon Ramsay at 68 Royal Hospital Rd. ⌧ *French*

29 | 25 | 28 | £111

Chelsea | 68 Royal Hospital Rd., SW3 (Sloane Sq.) | 020-7352 4441 | fax 7352 3334 | www.gordonramsay.com

"He may not be there every day" (other restaurants to open, TV shows to star in, etc.), but Gordon Ramsay's "original emporium" in Chelsea "remains true to his cooking credo and intensity" – and has regained London's No. 1 for Food title to prove it; the "amazing", "ambrosial" New French fare is served within a white-on-white "jewel box" setting by staff that rank as the No. 1 for Service, neither "shunning the first-time visitor nor fawning over the regular" (thanks to "charming" manager Jean-Claude Breton); just remember to "bring a large sack of gold bullion" to settle up.

☑ Goring Dining Room *British*

25 | 23 | 26 | £58

Victoria | Goring Hotel | 15 Beeston Pl., SW1 (Victoria) | 020-7396 9000 | fax 7834 4393 | www.goringhotel.co.uk

Expect a "range of diners from families to tycoons" to "members of the Lords" at this "gracious" hotel dining room near Victoria Station; "superbly done", "professionally and unobtrusively served" Traditional British fare and a "well-balanced wine selection" make it an "excellent all-rounder"; P.S. they do a "wonderful breakfast."

Gourmet Burger Kitchen *Burgers* (aka GBK)

19 | 11 | 13 | £16

Covent Garden | 13-14 Maiden Ln., WC2 (Covent Garden) | 020-7240 9617 | fax 7240 3908

Hampstead | 200 Haverstock Hill, NW3 (Belsize Park) | 020-7443 5335 | fax 7443 5339

Hampstead | 331 West End Ln., NW6 (West Hampstead) | 020-7794 5455 | fax 7794 4401

Battersea | 44 Northcote Rd., SW11 (Clapham Junction Rail) | 020-7228 3309 | fax 7978 6122

Fulham | 49 Fulham Broadway, SW6 (Fulham Broadway) | 020-7381 4242 | fax 7381 3222

Putney | 333 Putney Bridge Rd., SW15 (Putney Bridge) | 020-8789 1199 | fax 8780 1953

Richmond | 15-17 Hill Rise, TW10 (Richmond) | 020-8940 5440 | fax 8940 5772

Wimbledon | 88 The Broadway, SW19 (Wimbledon) | 020-8540 3300 | fax 8543 1947

Bayswater | 50 Westbourne Grove, W2 (Bayswater/Royal Oak) | 020-7243 4344 | fax 7243 4234

Chiswick | 131 Chiswick High Rd., W4 (Turnham Green) | 020-8995 4548 | fax 8995 4572

www.gbkinfo.com

Additional locations throughout London

Although it's "a gourmet experience in relative terms", for the London "burger lover, this is as good as it gets" – "tender" and

"lush", with "inventive" sauces; as the "semi-service" "chain prolif-
erates", punters pout the patties "have gone down in quality", and
why, oh "why can't the chips be better?", but "dream prices"
pacify most protesters.

Goya ● Spanish
16 | 13 | 17 | £32

Belgravia | 2 Eccleston Pl., SW1 (Victoria) | 020-7730 4299
Pimlico | 34 Lupus St., SW1 (Pimlico) | 020-7976 5309
www.goyarestaurant.co.uk

"Easy on the wallet and tasty on the belly", these two tapas bars in
Pimlico and Belgravia are "fun for a quick snack and hello to chums";
even if the Spanish menu and decor are not much better than "basic", "all the waiters are friendly."

☑ Gravetye Manor British
28 | 27 | 25 | £70

East Grinstead | Gravetye Manor | Vowels Ln., West Sussex |
01342 810567 | fax 01342 810080 | www.gravetyemanor.co.uk

"As traditional as it comes", this "gorgeous Elizabethan manor set in
the beautiful Sussex countryside" is a "stunning backdrop" for the
hotel's "intimate, oak-panelled" dining room, with its "mind-
blowing" Modern British dishes using organic, "fresh-from-their-
own-garden veggies and herbs" ("the taste difference really is
there"); those not to the manor born also appreciate the "friendly,
knowledgeable" staff and "talented sommelieuse"; P.S. it makes a
"wonderful stopover on the way to Gatwick."

Great Eastern Dining Room ☒ Asian
16 | 18 | 17 | £44

Shoreditch | 54-56 Great Eastern St., EC2 (Liverpool St./Old St.) |
020-7613 4545 | fax 7613 4137 | www.greateasterndining.co.uk

A "lively atmosphere in the heart of coolness" (aka Shoreditch) ensures this e&o sibling is "still going strong" after 11 years; friends
find the Asian fusion food "interesting" (e.g. chocolate pudding with
green tea ice cream), but critics carp the place "thinks it's much
more than it is" – especially the "snooty", "spasmodic service."

Great Queen Street ☒ British
24 | 16 | 20 | £34

Covent Garden | 32 Great Queen St., WC2 (Covent Garden/Holborn) |
020-7242 0622 | fax 7404 9582

"Great gastropubbing on Great Queen Street" summarises the sentiment about this woody, blood-red relative of a certain famed pub;
in fact, it's "just like the Anchor & Hope, but you can reserve" a
chance to feast on the "flavoursome" fare; is "this the new British
cuisine or 'olde' cuisine reinvented? who cares – it's first-rate"; only,
do something about the "hideous noise level", please.

Green & Red Bar & Cantina Mexican
∇ 19 | 11 | 14 | £32

Bethnal Green | 51 Bethnal Green Rd., E1 (Liverpool St./Shoreditch) |
020-7749 9670 | fax 7749 9671 | www.greenred.co.uk

"Young and noisy (in a nice way)", this Bethnal Green cantina is
about "as good as Mexican gets in London" with its "inventive",
if "maybe a bit pricey", menu and "killer tequila bar"; in sum, "a
good place to start a night out" before hitting the "heart
of Shoreditch cool."

	FOOD	DECOR	SERVICE	COST

Green Cottage *Chinese* ▽ 18 | 9 | 12 | £26

Finchley | 9 New College Parade, Finchley Rd., NW3 (Finchley Rd./
Swiss Cottage) | 020-7722 5305

"It's harder than you can imagine to find a good Chinese, but Green
Cottage is just that" profess Finchley fans of this "reliable" veteran;
it's "always busy" with "lots of locals" enjoying the "good-
value" BBQ meats.

☒ Greenhouse, The ☒ *French* 26 | 24 | 25 | £77

Mayfair | 27A Hay's Mews, W1 (Green Park) | 020-7499 3331 |
fax 7499 5368 | www.greenhouserestaurant.co.uk

"Off a little mews" in Mayfair, a "most peaceful garden sets the scene
for what's to follow": "imaginative", "complex New French cuisine,
[cooked] with a deft touch" and served "like a classy, well-
choreographed ballet"; the "wine list is outrageously big" – and outrageously priced, some snap – but otherwise, this "tranquil spot" "only
gets better each year"; P.S. a perpetual "power-lunch" place, its
"new understated, contemporary decor" "makes it great for
romantic evenings" now too.

Green Olive, The *Italian* ▽ 23 | 16 | 20 | £45

St. John's Wood | 5 Warwick Pl., W9 (Warwick Ave.) | 020-7289 2469 |
fax 7289 2463

It's "like dining at a friend's house" to visit St. John's Wood's "little-
known" "sister to Red Pepper" that works "great for a quiet night
with the wife"; the menu offers "lovely Italian dishes, with fantastic
wines", and the staff's "caring attitude is appreciated."

Green's ☒ *British/Seafood* 23 | 20 | 23 | £52

St. James's | 36 Duke St., SW1 (Green Park/Piccadilly Circus) |
020-7930 4566 | fax 7930 2958 | www.greens.org.uk

"Some might think it a bit stuffy and 'old-boyish'", but the
"St. James's aristocracy" are "never disappointed" in the "excellent
English fare" – "the "solid seafood's a specialty" – "attentive service" and "sedate setting" of this "landmark" ("owned by Camilla's
ex-brother-in-law"); the "clubby" "green-leather" decor, whilst
"perfect for business", is "not very exciting though."

Greig's ◕ *British/Chophouse* ▽ 17 | 13 | 15 | £48

Mayfair | 26 Bruton Pl., W1 (Bond St.) | 020-7629 5613 | fax 7495 0411 |
www.greigs-restaurant.com

"If meat is for you", so may be this Mayfair chophouse, which for
nearly 60 years has set "a good standard for British food and service" within clubby digs (oak panelling and stained-glass window
provide "early evening atmosphere"); still, some shrug it off as "expensive, but nothing special."

Grenadier, The *British* 17 | 21 | 18 | £30

Belgravia | 18 Wilton Row, SW1 (Hyde Park Corner) | 020-7235 3074

This "venerable" watering hole is "almost impossible to find" – and
"if you don't know how, I'm not going to tell you" say selfish surveyors, because it's already "packed" with travellers ("used to be a

Belgravia pub, now more of a tourist attraction" foes fume); the "British pub fare's standard", but "hauntingly wonderful" "atmosphere abounds" (watch out for the "headless grenadier's ghost"), plus the "Bloody Marys are not to be missed."

Greyhound, The Ⓜ *British/European* ▽ 23 | 18 | 18 | £39

Battersea | 136 Battersea High St., SW11 (Clapham Junction Rail) | 020-7978 7021 | fax 7978 0599 | www.thegreyhoundatbattersea.co.uk

"Whether it's a gastropub or a restaurant with a bar is questionable", but why debate when this "buzzy" Battersea haunt offers "imaginative" Modern British–European fare (including "rather macho" dishes like smoked salmon and eels or mutton neck) and "interesting wines"; but the belligerent bark about the "fluctuating service."

Groucho Club, The Ⓩ *British* 18 | 19 | 20 | £45

Private club; inquiries: 020-7439 4685

An "'in' place for the media elite" and "great for star-spotting", this colourful (literally and figuratively) Soho private club is open all day, serving Modern British fare that gets "an A for effort" from friends, a D for "disappointing" from foes; "but you don't go for the food" here – "the action takes place at the two funky bars."

Grumbles *British/French* - | - | - | M

Pimlico | 35 Churton St., SW1 (Pimlico/Victoria) | 020-7834 0149 | fax 7834 0298 | www.grumblesrestaurant.co.uk

This "sweetly cosy local" in Pimlico makes a "great winter-warmer eatery", with a "varied menu" of French bistro and Traditional British "comfort dishes"; P.S. tip: "upstairs is less cramped" than down.

Guinea Grill Ⓩ *British/Chophouse* 21 | 17 | 20 | £50

Mayfair | 30 Bruton Pl., W1 (Bond St.) | 020-7499 1210 | fax 7491 1442 | www.theguinea.co.uk

"Just the place for a clubby, macho" meal, this "intimate" "quintessential British establishment" in Mayfair "provides safe harbour" for "well-prepared" chophouse fare – "heavy on steaks" and "amazing steak and kidney pie"; but it's getting "tattered around the edges", and many bemoan the menu prices ("a guinea will buy you nothing here").

Gun, The ● *British* 21 | 18 | 16 | £35

Canary Wharf | 27 Coldharbour, E14 (Canary Wharf) | 020-7515 5222 | www.thegundocklands.com

"It may bill itself as a pub, but the kitchen" produces "solid (in a good way)" Modern British cuisine at this "fine example of a gastropub" at Canary Wharf; even if "service can be achingly slow", the "cool, laid-back local crowd" seem undeterred as they occupy the "lovely old-school dining room" – though "in summer the riverside patio is the real winner", with its "great views of the Dome" and Portuguese barbecue.

Gung-Ho ● *Chinese* ▽ 19 | 16 | 19 | £32

Hampstead | 328-332 West End Ln., NW6 (West Hampstead) | 020-7794 1444 | fax 7794 5522

In Hampstead, this "lively Chinese full of local families" is a moderate option for "high-quality" fare (which "can be spicy, so watch out");

even if it "could do with a face-lift", regulars revel in its reliability: "you know exactly what you'll get, and they never disappoint."

Hache *Burgers*
20 | 14 | 14 | £16

Camden Town | 24 Inverness St., NW1 (Camden Town) | 020-7485 9100
NEW **Chelsea** | 329-331 Fulham Rd., SW10 (South Kensington) | 020-7823 3515
www.hacheburgers.com

"The best of the burger chains" bellow boosters of this duo in Camden Town (lots of chandeliers) and Chelsea ("loud, too loud") whose "U.S.-style" menu offers "lots of variety", with "vegetarian, chicken and fish versions available"; they're a bit "expensive for a burg and chips", "but a nice indulgence" nonetheless.

Haiku ⊠ *Pan-Asian*
19 | 19 | 14 | £45

Mayfair | 15 New Burlington Pl., W1 (Oxford Circus) | 020-7494 4777 | www.haikurestaurant.com

"They could do with a few more light bulbs" at this oh-"so-dark" multilevel venue in an "odd location just off Regent Street"; diners also need light shed on the Pan-Asian menu that, whilst "solid", "casts far too wide a net" – "sushi followed by curry, anyone?" – and is compounded by "slow, inefficient service"; with prices "geared towards the corporate credit card", many stick to the "buzzy bar downstairs."

⊠ Hakkasan ● *Chinese*
25 | 26 | 20 | £59

Bloomsbury | 8 Hanway Pl., W1 (Tottenham Court Rd.) | 020-7927 7000 | fax 7907 1889

"Don't let the alley location put you off" – this "dreamy, dark" "Shanghai brothel"-ish Bloomsbury basement ("like something out of *Blade Runner*") "lives up to its reputation" as an "über-cool", "sexy spot" whose "superb" Chinese fusion cuisine "justifies the cost"; yes, the music is "waaaay too loud" – "waiting for a table is a test of your patience and ears" – and "staff irritatingly remind you of the two-hour policy from the second you sit down"; nevertheless, converts "can't wait to go back."

Halepi ● *Greek*
19 | 11 | 17 | £32

Bayswater | 18 Leinster Terrace, W2 (Lancaster Gate/Queensway) | 020-7262 1070 | fax 7262 2630

"For traditional Greek [fare], it fits the bill" say advocates of the "crowded, chaotic and casual" Bayswater taverna, whose decor is reminiscent of a "basement converted to a rec room"; whilst it remains "affordable", however, a slipping score supports those who grimace "the food's going a bit down-hill" – perhaps it's become "a victim of its own success"?

Hand & Flowers, The *British/French*
∇ 23 | 19 | 22 | £44

Marlow | 126 West St., Buckinghamshire | 01628 482277

Whilst the feel is "more pubby than restaurant", this "beautiful place in Marlow" is "wonderfully welcoming and atmospheric" (exposed beams, etc.), providing a "relaxed environment" in which to savour a "delicious menu" of New French–Modern British fare "with imaginative twists."

	FOOD	DECOR	SERVICE	COST

NEW Haozhan *Chinese*
23 | 17 | 19 | £34

Chinatown | 8 Gerard St., W1 (Leicester Sq.) | 020-7434 3838 | www.haozhan.co.uk

"Chic-ish decor" and "smiley service in a sea of sourpusses" make this "modern" yearling something "a bit different for Chinatown"; add in "good value", "delicately flavoured versions of traditional dishes" ("the homemade tofu is silky perfection") from an ex-Hakkasan chef, and you have a "great addition" to the neighbourhood.

Harbour City ❂ *Chinese*
18 | 13 | 17 | £27

Chinatown | 46 Gerrard St., W1 (Leicester Sq./Piccadilly Circus) | 020-7439 7859 | fax 7734 7745

There are "lots of Chinese eating here, so you know it's authentic" claim converts to this Chinatown Cantonese; they've got "some of the best dim sum around" at "a fairly reasonable price", but staff "tend to serve very quickly (so don't order everything at once)."

Hard Rock Cafe ❂ *American*
14 | 20 | 15 | £26

Piccadilly | 150 Old Park Ln., W1 (Green Park/Hyde Park Corner) | 020-7629 0382 | fax 7629 8702 | www.hardrock.com

"If you have to go to a Hard Rock, this is the one" opine reviewers of this "high-octane" Piccadilly premises, the "first of an institution" and a "must for any rock 'n' roller", thanks to the memorabilia museum across the street; there are "no other redeemable qualities" – just "basic American fare" that's the "same the world over", plus "servers who act like they're rock stars and you're an annoying stalker."

Harlem ❂ *American*
∇ 12 | 17 | 13 | £24

Notting Hill | 78 Westbourne Grove, W2 (Bayswater/Queensway) | 020-7985 0900 | fax 7985 0901 | www.harlemsoulfood.com

"Funky and cosy, with a great bar and entertainment downstairs", this Notting Hill eatery is "more about the atmosphere than the food" – "hearty" Harlem-inspired American eats that are "disappointing to anyone who has tasted the real stuff"; "the people-watching is better."

NEW Harrison's *Eclectic*
∇ 15 | 17 | 13 | £41

Balham | 15-19 Bedford Hill, SW12 (Balham) | 020-8675 6900 | www.harrisonsbalham.co.uk

Sam Harrison, owner of Sam's Brasserie & Bar, did not look far for the name of his second venture, a casually chic, brown-hued refurb of Balham Kitchen & Bar; ranging from crab linguini to plum crumble, the all-day menu is viewed as "decent", but "not particularly interesting", and the service "has some teething problems."

Harry Morgan's *Deli/Jewish*
15 | 13 | 14 | £29

Knightsbridge | Harrods | 87-135 Brompton Rd., SW1 (Knightsbridge) | 020-7730 1234
Fitzrovia | 6 Market Pl., W1 (Oxford Circus) | 020-7580 4849 🅢
St. John's Wood | 29-31 St. John's Wood High St., NW8 (St. John's Wood) | 020-7722 1869
www.harryms.co.uk

They got "chicken soup that's better than your nana's" and the "best salt beef" at his traditional Jewish deli in St. John's Wood and its younger, "crowded" branches; so "what's not to like?" – how about "prices that are on the high side", and service that runs the gamut from "friendly" to "rude."

Harry's Bar ●⑤ *Italian* | 23 | 22 | 23 | £77 |

Private club; inquiries: 020-7408 0844

New owner Richard Caring and "new chef Michele Lombardi had big shoes to fill" taking over this "posh" private club in Mayfair, one of the late Mark Birley's stable; but so far the "old-time flair" seems intact, from the "fine" Northern Italian food and "out-of-the-box wine list" to the "intimate service"; if younglings yelp it "needs jazzing up", loyalists name it "a never-ending classic" – albeit one that's "really lost the plot with the prices."

Hartwell House *British* | - | - | - | VE |

Aylesbury | Hartwell House | Oxford Rd., Buckinghamshire | 01296 747444 | fax 01296 747450 | www.hartwell-house.com

"So romantic", this "country house hotel" makes a "spectacular place for afternoon tea" or "formal dining" in a lemon-coloured salon; staff are "well trained", and the Modern British fare is "good for the area" – a "blissful" bit of Buckinghamshire.

Hat & Feathers ⑤ *European* | - | - | - | E |

Clerkenwell | 2 Clerkenwell Rd., EC1 (Barbican) | 020-7490 2244

"Love the lively bar, love the quiet and elegant upstairs, love the food" fawn fans of this Clerkenwell Modern European, a characterful 1870 boozer revamped with Victorian faux gas lights, large mirrors and gold-leaf cornicing; it's "expensive for what you get", however.

☑ Hawksmoor ⑤ *Chophouse* | 24 | 17 | 20 | £47 |

Shoreditch | 157 Commercial St., E1 (Liverpool St./Shoreditch) | 020-7247 7392 | www.thehawksmoor.com

"Once you get over the dreadful location and dreary interior", sit back and savour "the best steak in London" served by this Shoreditch grill; it's usually "buzzing" with a "local crowd", well-lubricated by the cocktails, including "a great range of mint juleps."

Haz ● *Turkish* | 22 | 17 | 19 | £31 |

City | 9 Cutler St., E1 (Liverpool St.) | 020-7929 7923 | fax 7623 5132

"Those unfamiliar with Turkish cuisine will thrill at the delightful aromas and presentation" at this "busy" City haunt, also praised for "incredibly speedy service" and "reasonable prices"; all in all, it's "great for a business lunch", plus they "do takeaway too"; just beware: it "can get a bit smoky – from the grill."

🆕 Hereford Road *British* | 24 | 16 | 20 | £39 |

Notting Hill | 3 Hereford Rd., W2 (Bayswater/Queensway) | 020-7727 1144 | www.herefordroad.org

A "St. John-trained chef-owner produces in a similar vein to his alma matter" at this newcomer off Westbourne Grove, where you "need to be hungry" to handle the "rustic", "superbly cooked Modern British fare" (i.e. big on braised meats and sticky puddings); however, staff are "curiously mixed", alternating between "approachable" and "self-importance personified", whilst the "drab" "room lacks any atmosphere."

	FOOD	DECOR	SERVICE	COST

NEW Hibiscus ☒ *French* 24 | 20 | 22 | £69

Mayfair | 29 Maddox St., W1 (Oxford Circus) | 020-7629 2999 | www.hibiscusrestaurant.co.uk

"The transition from Shropshire has been immaculate" for chef-patron Claude Bosi's celebrated New French, now an "oasis of calm" in Mayfair; with signatures like foie gras ice cream and fir-stuffed quail, his "food sounds like a joke, but tastes like a dream" and, led by wife Claire, his "staff have brought Ludlow friendliness with them"; true, "some dishes don't work", and the "prices – *sacrebleu!*" but the majority cry "welcome to London, Claude! can I have some more sausage roll?"

High Road Brasserie *European* 19 | 22 | 16 | £36

Chiswick | High Road House | 162-166 Chiswick High Rd., W4 (Turnham Green) | 020-8742 7474 | www.highroadhouse.co.uk

"Always attended" by "animated, happy customers", this "noisy" all-day Chiswick brasserie ("not the place for intimate dialogue") makes a "decent place for a hearty bite" of Modern European fare; however, "the attitude-laden service can spoil it" for some; P.S. note the "nice pavement seating for warmer days."

Hinds Head *British* 22 | 17 | 20 | £41

Bray | The High St., Berkshire | 01628 626151 | fax 01628 623394 | www.hindsheadhotel.co.uk

Now "under the co-direction of Heston Blumenthal of The Fat Duck" nearby, this "oldie worldly" Traditional Brit in Bray is worth a heads-up – and in fact "the place to be Sunday lunchtime"; "don't be tricked into thinking it's pub grub – it's Heston's twist on home-cooked treats" (e.g. "to-die-for triple-cooked chips"); some quip it "may be the most expensive gastropub in England" – but it "really works."

NEW Hix Oyster & Chop House *British* - | - | - | E

Farringdon | 36-37 Greenhill Rents, Cowcross St., EC1 (Farringdon/Barbican) | 020-7017 1930 | fax 7017 1931 | www.restaurantsetcltd.co.uk

Around the corner from Smithfield Market, Mark Hix (respected ex-chef-director of Caprice Holdings) has opened this earthy eatery evoking old London oyster and chophouses via a Traditional British menu featuring the likes of mutton chop curry, bubble and squeak and beef-and-oyster pie – all of which are already "flying out the door"; the wine list offers value, with some options served by the carafe.

Home House ● *British/European* - | - | - | VE

Private club; inquiries: 020-7670 2100

"Not your usual gentlemen's club (there are youngish people around)", this "stunning setting" in Portman Square offers a "blissful respite" from the world with its Oriental rugs, crystal chandeliers and other elements of 18th-century splendour; malcontents mutter the Modern British–European menu is "overpriced", but there's "really reasonable bar food" downstairs and "great staff" throughout.

	FOOD	DECOR	SERVICE	COST

Hot Stuff ☒ *Indian*
— | — | — | M

Kennington | 19 Wilcox Rd., SW8 (Vauxhall) | 020-7720 1480 |
www.eathotstuff.com

It's "nothing to look at – indeed you may wonder if you are in the
right place" – but this "teeny", "no-frills" Vauxhalll Indian, with its
"cafe, Formica-style tables", is "worth seeking out" for a "genuine
gourmet curry experience" at "fish 'n' chip shop prices"; what's
more, it's BYO, with a store next door to bring in your choice of tipple.

Hoxton Apprentice *Eclectic*
— | — | — | M

Hoxton | 16 Hoxton Sq., N1 (Old St.) | 020-7749 2828 | fax 7749 2829 |
www.hoxtonapprentice.com

This "worthwhile concept" – whereby "young people are given a
chance to blossom under close tutelage in the [restaurant]
business" – earns applause for its "endearing service" and "decent",
"flexible Eclectic menu"; the "cool" Hoxton premises (a former
Victorian school) are enlivened by live music four days a week.

Hoxton Grille, The *British/French*
▽ 15 | 19 | 13 | £32

Shoreditch | Hoxton Hotel | 81 Great Eastern St., EC2 (Old St.) |
020-7739 9111 | www.grillerestaurants.com

A "laid-back place in a cool hotel" in Hoxton, decorated with "odd
combinations of furniture" and exposed brick, this venue's French-
inflected British menu offers "something for everyone" – even if it's
all "a bit hit-and-miss"; service tends to be "forgetful" and "slow",
but "the people-watching is good, so it's ideal if you're having dinner
with a dullard."

☒ Hunan ☒ *Chinese*
27 | 13 | 20 | £48

Pimlico | 51 Pimlico Rd., SW1 (Sloane Sq.) | 020-7730 5712 |
fax 7730 8265 | www.hunanlondon.com

"The only way to dine" at this "quiet, intimate" Pimlico Chinese is to
"put yourself in the hands" of chef-owner Michael Peng who brings
"a roller coaster of flavours" from a "sophisticated", "authentic"
menu "until you can eat no more"; that, and an "incredibly fairly
priced wine list", makes up for "long waits between dishes" and "decor that could use some updating."

Hush ❶ *British/French*
14 | 18 | 16 | £43

Mayfair | 8 Lancashire Ct., W1 (Bond St.) | 020-7659 1500 |
fax 7659 1501 | www.hush.co.uk

This "vibrant place" in Mayfair "draws a young, good-looking
crowd", primarily to its "great outdoor space" in a discreet cobble-
stone courtyard and "buzzy" lounge bar; there's also a Modern
British brasserie and Classic French–Italian "upstairs restaurant", but
both offer "average food and service" – so most "go here to drink."

Ikeda ☒ *Japanese*
▽ 26 | 9 | 20 | £47

Mayfair | 30 Brook St., W1 (Bond St.) | 020-7629 2730 | fax 7490 5992

"Such a basic setting doesn't fit with the super-posh Brook Street
scene" outside, but what does fit like a glove is the "expensive, but
exquisite traditional Japanese food", including "possibly the highest-

quality sushi in London"; "chefs yelling at each other behind the bar in broken English gives it character."

☑ Il Bordello *Italian* 23 | 13 | 21 | £29

Wapping | 81 Wapping High St., E1 (Wapping) | 020-7481 9950
"Consistency, consistency, consistency" characterises this corner of "little Italia in Wapping", aka "carb central" for its "huge" – almost "terrifying" – portions of pizza and pasta; "friendly staff are part of the cheery" if "chaotic" atmosphere, and whilst "the decor isn't anything special, when the place is full, who notices?"

Il Convivio ☒ *Italian* 22 | 19 | 22 | £46

Belgravia | 143 Ebury St., SW1 (Sloane Sq./Victoria) | 020-7730 4099 | fax 7730 4103 | www.etruscarestaurants.com
Whilst it's a decade old, this Italian still feels like "a find in Belgravia" for its "innovative", "chic" *cucina* (e.g. black spaghetti with lobster, white espresso ice cream), served by "cordial" staff "in an open, inviting atmosphere"; the main criticism amongst the *convivio* comments: it's "not cheap."

Il Falconiere ●☒ *Italian* ▽ 15 | 12 | 17 | £34

South Kensington | 84 Old Brompton Rd., SW7 (Gloucester Rd./ South Kensington) | 020-7589 2401 | fax 7589 9158 | www.ilfalconiere.co.uk
"Perfect for a decent dinner with little fuss" attest *amici* of this Italian "across the street from Christie's", with its "tables pinched together" and "service that's efficient, if somewhat disinterested"; just "don't order anything where fresh ingredients are important."

Il Portico ●☒ *Italian* 24 | 17 | 25 | £37

Kensington | 277 Kensington High St., W8 (High St. Kensington) | 020-7602 6262 | www.ilportico.co.uk
"A neighbourhood favourite", "this family-run restaurant makes you feel right at home" cry Kensingtonians who crave its "classic" "savoury, satisfying" Italian dishes and "heartfelt service"; best of all, "the bill still leaves some change for the homemade desserts."

Imli *Indian* 19 | 16 | 18 | £22

Soho | 167-169 Wardour St., W1 (Tottenham Court Rd.) | 020-7287 4243 | fax 7287 4245 | www.imli.co.uk
It's an "excellent concept": "Indian-style tapas" with "interesting twists" at "outstanding prices" proclaim proponents of this "trendy, cool" Tamarind offshoot; staff are "relaxed and helpful", and whilst some find the "extremely orange decor" "odd", most salute this "spicy, not stodgy" Soho subcontinental.

Imperial China ● *Chinese* 21 | 18 | 17 | £27

Chinatown | 25A Lisle St., WC2 (Leicester Sq./Piccadilly Circus) | 020-7734 3388 | fax 7734 3833 | www.imperial-china.co.uk
"An attempt to upgrade the Chinatown experience that works" declare devotees of this venue with "modern" earth-toned decor, "out-of-this-world dim sum" and "better-than-average Cantonese" cuisine; "it's huge, so you can always get a seat", though that means

	FOOD	DECOR	SERVICE	COST

"superstore-style service" as well; but "if you hire one of the private rooms, you can also indulge in a little karaoke."

Imperial City ❑ Chinese
▽ 23 | 20 | 15 | £34

City | Royal Exchange, Cornhill, EC3 (Bank) | 020-7626 3437 | fax 7338 0125 | www.orientalrestaurantgroup.co.uk

"The wonderful red brick vaulted ceilings" below the Royal Exchange provide an interesting backdrop to this "good business lunch place in the City" serving an "extremely tasty Western type of Chinese food"; only the "offhand service" lets the side down.

Inaho ❑ Japanese
▽ 25 | 9 | 12 | £38

Bayswater | 4 Hereford Rd., W2 (Bayswater/Queensway) | 020-7221 8495

It's "like being in a Japanese family's home" to visit this Bayswater Asian, which "dishes up the most delectable morsels"; the "disinterested service" doesn't help the "tiny cubbyhole" digs, but disciples declare "to expand would be to detract" from the experience.

Incognico ❑ French
21 | 18 | 18 | £47

Soho | 117 Shaftesbury Ave., WC2 (Leicester Sq./Tottenham Court Rd.) | 020-7836 8866 | fax 7240 9525 | www.incognico.com

Just by Cambridge Circus, this "clubby feel"-ing, often-"overlooked" venue is "wonderfully convenient for the theatre", offering "terrific Classic and New French" brasserie fare; still, some find it "shockingly expensive" now that there are "no more prix fixe" options.

Indian Zing Indian
- | - | - | M

Hammersmith | 236 King St., W6 (Ravenscourt Park) | 020-8748 5959 | www.indianzing.co.uk

Aiming to be "a dining rather than just a feeding experience", this "upmarket Indian" in Hammersmith is "recommended" for its "imaginative" cuisine (e.g. monkfish tikka) "from a talented chef"-owner, and the "amazing ambience" of its contemporary, bright decor.

Indigo ● European
21 | 21 | 21 | £45

Covent Garden | One Aldwych Hotel | 1 Aldwych, WC2 (Charing Cross/Covent Garden) | 020-7300 0400 | fax 7300 1001 | www.onealdwych.com

"Get a table next to the railing and enjoy an unimpaired view of the lobby bar below" at the One Aldwych Hotel's "cool" mezzanine Modern European, serving "substantial" meals "with international flavour to business travellers"; "the decor and setting help justify the price tag", as does "smart, friendly" staff.

Inn The Park British
18 | 20 | 16 | £36

St. James's | St. James's Park, SW1 (St. James's Park) | 020-7451 9999 | fax 7451 9998 | www.innthepark.com

"Overlooking the lake and trees" "in the heart of St. James's Park", this biparte Oliver Peyton–owned pavilion sees "tourists mingling with government officials"; but it's a "strange concept" – those "in the restaurant section are a table away from [cafeteria] tray-wielding patrons", the Traditional British "food's nothing memorable" and the service "spotty"; "an idyllic setting", "but that's about it."

	FOOD	DECOR	SERVICE	COST

Inside ☒ *European* ▽ 25 | 17 | 17 | £33

Greenwich | 19 Greenwich South St., SE10 (Greenwich) | 020-8265 5060 |
www.insiderestaurant.co.uk

"Close to Greenwich station, this small, unobtrusive restaurant"
delights locals with its "fresh", "unfussy" Modern European fare and
"reasonable service" in "simple" premises; whilst the bare floors make
it "a bit noisy", boosters believe it "the best in this part of London."

Isarn *Thai* - | - | - | E

Islington | 119 Upper St., N1 (Angel) | 020-7424 5153 | www.isarn.co.uk
In an "unassuming" stretch of Upper Street, this "upmarket Thai"
(owned by restaurateur Alan Yau's sister) is a "cool", "serene" site
that's "head and shoulders above [others] in terms of the authenticity"
of its "interesting" food; "perfect to grab a bite before a movie" nearby.

Ishbilia *Lebanese* 22 | 13 | 16 | £35

Belgravia | 9 William St., SW1 (Knightsbridge) | 020-7235 7788 |
fax 7235 7771 ◐

Knightsbridge | Harrods | 87-135 Brompton Rd., 2nd fl., SW1
(Knightsbridge) | 020-7893 8598
A "standard Lebanese menu done to a high standard" – and at "reasonable prices for the area" – is the formula at this "little bit of Beirut"
in Belgravia and its Harrods offshoot; the service can seem "surly",
but "if you are a regular, they always remember you"; N.B. the Decor
score doesn't reflect a post-Survey rehab at William Street.

Ishtar ◑ *Turkish* ▽ 19 | 19 | 21 | £30

Marylebone | 10-12 Crawford St., W1 (Baker St.) | 020-7224 2446 |
www.ishtarrestaurant.com
This Turk "ticks a lot of boxes": "pleasant atmosphere", "light, luscious
food" and "courteous service"; if some lament it "lacks zing", at
least there's "value for money" at this "modern" Marylebone venue.

Island Restaurant & Bar *British* - | - | - | M

Bayswater | Royal Lancaster Hotel | Lancaster Terrace, W2
(Lancaster Gate) | 020-7551 6070 | fax 7551 6071 |
www.islandrestaurant.co.uk
Offering "generous portions" of "well-prepared" classic and
Modern British fare, this "solid performer" is considered "the most
reliable and reasonable restaurant in the area" around Bayswater; if
"service is a little inconsistent", it doesn't distract from the light-
filled, "smart, but relaxed" digs with Hyde Park views.

itsu *Japanese* 17 | 14 | 15 | £22

Soho | 103 Wardour St., W1 (Oxford Circus/Piccadilly Circus) |
020-7479 4794 | fax 7479 4795

Canary Wharf | Cabot Pl. E., 2nd fl., E14 (Canary Wharf) | 020-7512 5790 |
fax 7512 5791 Ⓢ

Chelsea | 118 Draycott Ave., SW3 (South Kensington) | 020-7590 2400 |
fax 7590 2403
www.itsu.co.uk

"One of the better conveyor-belt sushi chains", this swinging '60s-
style string remains "a staple" for "sparklingly fresh" victuals and

Japanese cooked fare; the edibles are "not premium, but the self-serve [system] makes for easy eating", whilst the "wonderful bento" boxes for takeaway create "the trendiest picnic."

☑ Ivy, The ◗ *British/European*

| | 22 | 21 | 23 | £58 |

Covent Garden | 1-5 West St., WC2 (Leicester Sq.) | 020-7836 4751 | fax 7240 9333 | www.the-ivy.co.uk

"Once you successfully navigate the Byzantine reservation system" and snag a seat in the "dark-wood-panelled inside", this "timeless" Theatreland "thespian stalwart" will "pamper you in an understated way"; whilst "surprisingly good", the "homely" Modern British–Euro cuisine is perhaps "not worthy of what they charge"; "but then you don't come here to just eat – you come to experience the dependably star-studded energy."

Jade Garden ◗ *Chinese*

| | 21 | 15 | 18 | £23 |

Chinatown | 15 Wardour St., W1 (Leicester Sq./Piccadilly Circus) | 020-7437 5065 | fax 7429 7851 | www.londonjadegarden.co.uk

"It hums, it sings, it's noisy – it's like Hong Kong" at this "crowded" Chinatown stalwart, with "pretty decent" dim sum and "inexpensive" Mandarin mains; disregard staff that are "even rude to native speakers (that's telling you something)"; oh, and "don't forget to pretend you know what you're ordering."

Jenny Lo's Tea House ☒⇥ *Chinese*

| | 21 | 12 | 17 | £20 |

Belgravia | 14 Eccleston St., SW1 (Victoria) | 020-7259 0399

Some say "it's more like a takeaway place", but "for people who are comfortable with basic decor and communal tables", this "real jewel" in Belgravia from Ken Lo's daughter, Jenny, offers a "solid experience" of "fresh, quick, healthy" Chinese fare at "great value."

NEW Jimmy's *British*

| | - | - | - | M |

Chelsea | 386 King's Rd., SW3 (Sloane Sq.) | 020-7351 9997 | www.jimmyschelsea.com

A young husband-and-wife team are behind this *petit* newcomer in Chelsea, which lays on a "stunning" prix fixe Modern British menu with some unusual combos – e.g. "roast chicken, amazing with a lovage and potato salad"; the "cool" split-level setting boasts modern design – eccentric wall art, resin chairs – juxtaposed with a Louis XV chandelier; in pleasant weather, the front windows open for pavement dining.

Jim Thompson's *Thai*

| | ▽ 16 | 18 | 15 | £29 |

Putney | 408 Upper Richmond Rd., SW15 (East Putney) | 020-8788 3737 | fax 8788 3738 | www.jim-thompsons-putney.co.uk

Jim Thompson's Green Dragon *Thai*

Finchley | 889 Green Lns., N21 (Southgate) | 020-8360 0005 | fax 8364 3006 | www.greendragon-winchmore.co.uk

Jim Thompson's Hand & Flower *Thai*

Fulham | 617 King's Rd., SW6 (Fulham Broadway) | 020-7731 0999 | fax 7731 2835 | www.thehandandflower.co.uk

"Fun in a tacky, touristy way", this Thai trio comes laden with Asian artefacts for sale; the "quirky" "decor is the best thing going" for it protest purists – "go for a pint by all means, but get your curry elsewhere."

	FOOD	DECOR	SERVICE	COST

☒ Jin Kichi Ⓜ *Japanese* — 27 | 12 | 18 | £32

Hampstead | 73 Heath St., NW3 (Hampstead) | 020-7794 6158 |
fax 7794 6158 | www.jinkichi.com
This "little hole-in-the-wall" in Hampstead "transports you directly to
Downtown Tokyo", partly because it's "packed and noisy", but more
importantly because of its "out-of-this-world", "proper Japanese"
victuals (the "sashimi's always fresh" but "the yakitori excels"); just
"make sure to order everything at once, or you may find that extra
piece of sushi takes a one-hour wait."

Joe Allen Ⓞ *American* — 16 | 18 | 18 | £37

Covent Garden | 13 Exeter St., WC2 (Covent Garden) | 020-7836 0651 |
fax 7497 2148 | www.joeallenrestaurant.com
A is for Joe Allen, adored by "A-listers treading the boards", although
the old Theatrelander is all "about the atmosphere", rather than the
"average" if "always reliable" American eats, or poster-adorned decor
"in need of a spruce-up"; P.S. ask for the "off-the-menu burger."

Joe's *Mediterranean* — - | - | - | E

South Kensington | 126 Draycott Ave., SW3 (South Kensington) |
020-7225 2217 | fax 7584 1133 | www.joseph.co.uk
"Ladies who lunch" are a regular fixture at this casual Brompton
Cross bistro, set opposite its owner, the Joseph store; whilst the
Mediterranean meals are merely "reliable", "no one expects any
wow in their food" – though some oomph might be appreciated in
staff that are "good-looking, but not trained."

Joe's Restaurant Bar *British* — 19 | 18 | 18 | £35

Knightsbridge | Joseph | 16 Sloane St., SW1 (Knightsbridge) |
020-7235 9869 | fax 7235 3218 | www.joseph.co.uk
A "multicultural melting pot of rich Londonites, topped off with
fresh food and polite service" summarises the "upscale" scene at
this "healthy" Modern Brit basement cafe; as its locale in the Joseph
store suggests, it's also "quite an expensive place" where the "portions are sized for models, not men."

Joy King Lau Ⓞ *Chinese* — 18 | 10 | 12 | £22

Chinatown | 3 Leicester St., WC2 (Leicester Sq./Piccadilly Circus) |
020-7437 1133 | fax 7437 2629
This "crowded" Chinatown veteran "may not look like much" – it's
"rather glum" in truth – but it "just sticks to doing good, old-fashioned
dim sum well", along with "inexpensive" Cantonese mains; "service
is efficient, if a little offhand" (even so, "expect to queue").

☒ J. Sheekey Ⓞ *Seafood* — 26 | 21 | 24 | £56

Covent Garden | 28-32 St. Martin's Ct., WC2 (Leicester Sq.) |
020-7240 2565 | fax 7497 0891 | www.j-sheekey.co.uk
Located down a "Dickensian" alleyway, the "ultimate clubby"
Covent Gardener "looks uninspiring from the outside, but inside it
creates a cosy atmosphere, with wood panelling, signed photos"
and "tables that are bit close together (but they're all [occupied by]
celebrities, so who cares?)"; the fare's "nothing fancy, nothing

adventurous – just superb seafood", admittedly "expensive" but "artfully prepared" and served by "suave, witty staff" who'll "get you to the theatre on time – if you can bear to leave."

Julie's ◗ British
17 | 22 | 18 | £43

Holland Park | 135 Portland Rd., W11 (Holland Park) | 020-7229 8331 | fax 7229 4050 | www.juliesrestaurant.com

"The real draw is the atmosphere" at this "deeply romantic" "institution", "one of the prettiest spots in Holland Park" with its rabbit warren of "cosy", "small rooms" and "great outdoor eating space"; but as some feel the "pricey" cuisine "does not live up to expectations", perhaps it's no surprise this Modern Brit is "better for drinks than dinner."

Just St. James's ⓩ British
20 | 22 | 19 | £47

St. James's | 12 St. James's St., SW1 (Green Park) | 020-7976 2222 | fax 7976 2020 | www.juststjames.com

A St. James's "converted bank lobby's" "impressive, opulent space" adds a "big wow factor" to this Modern Brit with "good food and a good-looking crowd"; given the "noisy atmosphere" and "spotty service", however, many feel it's "really more of a drinking space than a restaurant"; N.B. downstairs is Just Oriental, an Asian eatery/lounge with a DJ.

Kai Mayfair Chinese
23 | 20 | 22 | £55

Mayfair | 65 S. Audley St., W1 (Bond St./Marble Arch) | 020-7493 8988 | fax 7493 1456 | www.kaimayfair.co.uk

Mayfair's "high-class Chinese never fails to impress", not least because its "inventive", albeit "extraordinarily priced", cuisine is "spectacularly served" with "dry ice and special effects"; the "gracious service makes one feel like a regular within a visit or two", and the "setting's lovely", if a bit "dated" (though the twice-weekly "harpist is a nice touch").

Kandoo ◗ Persian
- | - | - | M

Marylebone | 458 Edgware Rd., W2 (Edgware Rd.) | 020-7724 2428 | fax 7724 6769

Family-run, traditionally decorated and offering "great hospitality", this "solid neighbourhood restaurant" on Edgware Road serves "authentic", "reliable Persian" fare with some "tasty specialities"; "the fact it's BYO helps keeps the cost down."

Kastoori African/Indian
- | - | - | M

Balham | 188 Upper Tooting Rd., SW17 (Tooting Bec/Tooting Broadway) | 020-8767 7027

Fans "never tire of" this "wonderful African-Indian run by a lovely family" for 20 years in Tooting; the secret is the "well-spiced", "unusual" menu – "all vegetarian, but meat eaters don't seem to mind."

Kensington Place British
19 | 13 | 17 | £39

Kensington | 201-209 Kensington Church St., W8 (Notting Hill Gate) | 020-7727 3184 | fax 7229 2025 | www.kensingtonplace-restaurant.co.uk

"Horribly noisy – and proud of that fact", this "light, bright establishment" soldiers on as a "neighbourly" Notting Hill Gate Modern Brit;

some sob since "the departure of its long-time chef [and owner], it's just not the same" – "cooking has suffered" and "service is on autopilot" – but steady scores support those who insist "though changed, all's still good."

NEW Kensington Square Kitchen ☒ *British*

— | — | — | M

Kensington | 9 Kensington Sq., W8 (High St. Kensington) | 020-7938 2598 | www.kensingtonsquarekitchen.co.uk

Offering "calm and comfort", this new all-day cafe on two "small", pastel-hued floors in leafy Kensington Square is the creation of Sara Adams, whose health-conscious Modern British menu offers a "well-executed", wallet-friendly selection of brunch fare, small plates and more substantial daily specials; N.B. last orders at 6 PM.

NEW Kenza ●☒ *Lebanese/Moroccan*

— | — | — | E

City | 10 Devonshire Sq., EC2 (Liverpool St.) | 020-7929 5533 | www.kenza-restaurant.com

Its name means 'treasure' in Arabic, and this latest venture from Tony Kitous (Levant, Pasha) is a "truly sumptuous venue hidden away in the City", all rich colours, wood carvings, heady incense and intimate alcoves; indeed, to early reviewers, the main "reason to visit is the opulent decor", which overshadows the "simple" "mix of Moroccan and Lebanese" dishes; P.S. "make sure you catch the belly dancing show" nightly in the "totally fab bar."

Kettners ● *Eclectic*

15 | 20 | 18 | £30

Soho | 29 Romilly St., W1 (Leicester Sq.) | 020-7734 6112 | fax 7287 6499 | www.kettners.com

"Opulent dining rooms and tinkling piano" "kind of mask the average food" at this historic townhouse, a "true Soho icon" now owned by Pizza Express; still, it's "always buzzing" with punters chomping on "posh pizza" and other Eclectic eats; plus the "cosy champagne bar" makes "a great place to meet."

Kew Grill *British*

— | — | — | E

Richmond | 10B Kew Green, TW9 (Kew Gdns.) | 020-8948 4433 | fax 8605 3532 | www.awtrestaurants.com

In "comfortable surroundings that match the area perfectly", this rustic Kew venue – run by celebrity chef Antony Worrall Thompson and wife Jay – is "great for meat eaters", but "dull if you don't want beef"; some also believe this Modern Brit could offer "more welcoming service."

Khan's ● *Indian*

21 | 9 | 13 | £19

Bayswater | 13-15 Westbourne Grove, W2 (Bayswater/ Queensway) | 020-7727 5420 | fax 7229 1835 | www.khansrestaurant.com

Since 1977, this "Indian food factory" has been a halal haven for "tried-and-true", "inexpensive" eats; whilst critics khan no longer stand certain aspects – "tired" decor, "curt staff" (maybe "rudeness is part of the allure"?) and "worst of all – no alcohol served", "locals and tourists alike flock" to this "cavernous" Bayswater "stalwart."

	FOOD	DECOR	SERVICE	COST

Khan's of Kensington ● *Indian* | 23 | 14 | 16 | £27 |

South Kensington | 3 Harrington Rd., SW7 (South Kensington) |
020-7584 4114 | fax 7581 2900

"Inspired food" at a "reasonable price" keeps this South Ken Indian
going; but several say it's a "great place to pick up takeaway – then
you don't have to deal with the lazy service" and "boring" decor.

Kiasu *Pan-Asian* ▽ 21 | 13 | 17 | £18 |

Bayswater | 48 Queensway, W2 (Bayswater) | 020-7727 8810 |
www.kiasu.co.uk

A mixture of "Malaysian/Singaporean/Indonesian" eats will "take
you to the Far East" at this "bustling" Bayswater venue; "fascinating
and well-prepared", the food is of "a much higher standard than
comparably priced Asian restos", even if the "on-a-budget decor"
and "efficient, but not exceptional service" are more "typical."

Kiku *Japanese* | 23 | 12 | 20 | £46 |

Mayfair | 17 Half Moon St., W1 (Green Park) | 020-7499 4208 |
fax 7409 3359 | www.kikurestaurant.co.uk

Some of "the most authentic" Japanese food in town, served "with a
smile", makes this Mayfair Japanese a "favourite" of "visiting busi-
nessmen" and locals alike; "particularly strong in sushi and hot
pots", the cuisine's not cheap, though the set "lunch menu is excellent value"; if the digs seem "bright, almost sexless", well, that only
adds to its "traditional" appeal.

Kobe London ● *Japanese* ▽ 19 | 18 | 19 | £37 |
(fka Kobe Jones)

Bloomsbury | St. Giles Hotel | 111A Great Russell St., WC1
(Tottenham Court Rd.) | 020-7300 3250 | fax 7300 3254

"Whether you go for the sushi or one of the hot dishes", this "really
nice looking" haunt "hidden off Tottenham Court Road" offers
Japanese fare in "surprising combinations" (think green tea salmon
or sake-infused trifle); just beware –"although it doesn't seem expensive", the bill ends up being "a bit pricey."

Koi *Japanese* | 21 | 19 | 19 | £50 |

Kensington | 1E Palace Gate, W8 (Gloucester Rd./High St. Kensington) |
020-7581 8778 | fax 7589 2788

For "fantastic teppanyaki" and "decent sushi in Kensington", locals
rely on this "pleasant" Japanese adorned with traditional low tables
and floor mats; if the "speedy service" is maybe "*too* speedy", at
least that makes it ideal "for a quick bite on the way home."

Konstam at the Prince Albert ☒ *British* ▽ 23 | 17 | 14 | £37 |

King's Cross | 2 Acton St., WC1 (King's Cross) | 020-7833 5040 |
www.konstam.co.uk

The way chef-owner Ollie Rowe "insists on local ingredients is not
posturing, it really works" at this King's Cross Modern Brit whose
"interesting" cuisine is sourced within the M25, supported by a
"good selection" of English wine; dominated by dangly chain fixtures, the "bizarre decor is endearing" . . . eventually.

	FOOD	DECOR	SERVICE	COST

Kulu Kulu Sushi 🖹 *Japanese* — 19 | 11 | 12 | £23

Covent Garden | 51-53 Shelton St., WC2 (Covent Garden) | 020-7240 5687 | fax 7240 5687

Soho | 76 Brewer St., W1 (Piccadilly Circus) | 020-7734 7316 | fax 7734 6507

South Kensington | 39 Thurloe Pl., SW7 (South Kensington) | 020-7589 2225 | fax 7589 2225

"Fresh, refreshing [victuals] that excite the taste buds" are on offer at this trio – "one of the best of the robo-sushi" chains; if the "cramped surroundings" lack charm, the "price is very reasonable" – plus there's "lovely service when you ask for your own favourites."

NEW Kyashii at Kingly Club 🖹 *Japanese* — – | – | – | VE

Covent Garden | 4 Upper St. Martin's Ln., WC2 (Covent Garden/ Leicester Sq.) | 020-7836 5211 | www.kinglyclub.com

The success of entrepreneur Dezzi McCausland's private Soho spot (also named Kingly Club) has spawned an offshoot for the public near Leicester Square; the glitzy, glass-fronted premises include a basement eatery, flanked by dramatic aquariums and serving pricey Japanese fare from chef Andrew Lassetter (ex Cocoon); upstairs lies a lounge endowed with natural light from floor-to-ceiling windows.

La Bouchée *French* — 21 | 14 | 17 | £35

South Kensington | 56 Old Brompton Rd., SW7 (South Kensington) | 020-7589 1929 | fax 7584 8625

"It's always a pleasure to revisit this reliable" South Ken site serving "authentic, delicious" French bistro fare at "fair value"; there are downsides: it's "dark and crowded" ("great for hearing other peoples' conversations") and "difficult to find the staff's friendly side" sometimes, "but you will come out of here with a smile on your face."

La Brasserie *French* — 18 | 16 | 14 | £34

South Kensington | 272 Brompton Rd., SW3 (South Kensington) | 020-7581 3089 | fax 7581 1435 | www.labrasserielondon.com

This "crowded" Brompton Cross veteran comes bearing all "the charm and defects of many a Parisian brasserie": the former includes "traditional, no-nonsense" fare ("predictable, but sometimes that is just what one wants"); the latter, "worn ambience" and waiters who veer from "indifferent to rude."

L'Accento Italiano 🖹 *Italian* — – | – | – | E

Bayswater | 16 Garway Rd., W2 (Bayswater/Queensway) | 020-7243 2201 | fax 7243 2201

"A neighbourhood staple for those in-the-know" confide the cognoscenti about this "quaint" "little" Italian that's "great in the summer when the doors open" onto its quiet Bayswater street; the "daily prix fixe menu is the way to go" to avoid otherwise upscale prices.

La Collina *Italian* — ∇ 24 | 18 | 26 | £31

Primrose Hill | 17 Princess Rd., NW1 (Chalk Farm) | 020-7483 0192

"Just what Primrose Hill needed – quality Italian fare for decent prices" purr patrons pleased with this young Piedmontese; service, too, is "very amiable indeed", but given the slightly "cramped surroundings", some prefer to "eat in the garden" when the "better days of spring and summer arrive."

Ladbroke Arms *European*

19 | 18 | 17 | £29

Notting Hill | 54 Ladbroke Rd., W11 (Holland Park/Notting Hill Gate) | 020-7727 6648 | fax 7727 2127 | www.ladbrokearms.com

With "well-cooked" Modern European fare, a "cosy environment" and a hip local "Euro crowd", this Notting Hill gastropub is "always a pleasure", with the added perk of a front patio for "eating outside on a nice day"; "service can be hit-and-miss, depending on time of day."

Ladurée *French*

23 | 22 | 16 | £30

Knightsbridge | Harrods | 87-135 Brompton Rd., ground fl., SW1 (Knightsbridge) | 020-7893 8293 | fax 3155 0112 | www.laduree.com

"As if anyone needed an excuse to go", this "delectably decorated" "Harrods-based outpost" of the Paris patisserie is "rightly famous for its macaroons" – "heavenly items" "made by angels" – as well as applauded for its "well-thought-out" Classic French menu of "light, hot dishes"; whilst pastry "perfection doesn't come cheap", and "service can be slow", most just "love the whole experience."

La Famiglia ❶ *Italian*

21 | 15 | 20 | £42

Chelsea | 7 Langton St., SW1 (Fulham Broadway/Sloane Sq.) | 020-7351 0761 | fax 7351 2409 | www.lafamiglia.co.uk

"It feels like you've been whisked away to a big, bustling Tuscan family" at this "cosy", "cosseting" Chelsea "cantina" complete with tent-covered courtyard; an "extensive, not too expensive" menu spans all the "favourite" staples, and if dissenters declare it "desperately needs a shake-up", the majority are glad it "never changes."

La Figa *Italian*

∇ 22 | 14 | 21 | £26

Canary Wharf | The Mosaic | 45 Narrow St., E14 (Limehouse DLR) | 020-7790 0077

"Take a big appetite" to this "Italian fixture" "five minutes walk from Limehouse DLR station", where "generous helpings" of "tasty, well-presented food" and a "friendly atmosphere" add up to a "brilliant" local option, even if there's "nothing special" about the setting itself.

La Fromagerie Café *European*

25 | 17 | 17 | £25

Marylebone | 2-6 Moxon St., W1 (Baker St.) | 020-7935 0341 | fax 7935 0341 | www.lafromagerie.co.uk

"Some of the most knowledgeable cheese purveyors in the city" can be found at this Marylebone "fabulous store" where a "tiny cafe space at the rear" has diners "eating elbow to elbow" (everyone's "glad they are expanding" as we write); the "irresistible", "imaginative" Modern European dishes are made with "produce available to purchase", and if the "prices will kill you, the food is to die for."

La Genova ⧈ *Italian*

25 | 20 | 26 | £47

Mayfair | 32 N. Audley St., W1 (Bond St.) | 020-7629 5916 | fax 7629 5916 | www.lagenovarestaurant.com

With a "personable owner" who "makes you feel right at home", "fresh, mouth-watering" Italian fare and a "noteworthy wine list full of bright" ideas, this "comfortable", "old-style" trattoria makes a "real find off Oxford Street", "even though it's a bit pricey"; "decor is pleasant, if not gorgeous."

Lamberts British

▽ 21 | 17 | 22 | £51

Balham | 2 Station Parade, Balham High Rd., SW12 (Balham) | 020-8675 2233 | www.lambertsrestaurant.com

Despite residing "on the wrong side of the tracks in Balham", this "child-friendly, whilst still sophisticated" Modern Brit is an "excellent find" for "reliable", "reasonably priced" fare, "using top-drawer seasonal produce"; it's also "surprisingly difficult to book . . . must be a good sign."

NEW Landau, The European

▽ 25 | 25 | 25 | £66

Marylebone | The Langham | Portland Pl., W1 (Oxford Circus) | 020-7965 0165 | www.thelandau.com

Entering via an evocatively lit corridor lined with wine racks, diners discover a "beautiful", oval-shaped room of grandly attired tables and a view onto Portland Place at "this delightful newcomer to The Langham hotel"; chef Andrew Turner's "innovative" Modern European menus offer "great grazing" choices, matched by "divine service", making this a "wonderful place for a relaxing celebration dinner."

Langan's Bistro ⧄ British/French

19 | 18 | 21 | £42

Marylebone | 26 Devonshire St., W1 (Baker St.) | 020-7935 4531 | fax 7493 8309 | www.langansrestaurants.co.uk

"A classical bistro that never fails to bring enjoyment", this Marylebone veteran prepares "plentiful", "reliable" Traditional British–French fare; despite the "original art and photography of [founder] Langan's friends, such as David Hockney", the place is "getting a little shabby around the edges", but it still appeals as "a safe haven from the overly hip."

Langan's Brasserie ⧄ British/French

19 | 20 | 18 | £50

Mayfair | Stratton House | Stratton St., W1 (Green Park) | 020-7491 8822 | fax 7493 8309 | www.langansrestaurants.co.uk

"No longer trendy, but still buzzing", this "brash" Mayfair "institution" remains "dependable for business or an evening out", complete with an "interesting crowd mix"; the "classic" Anglo-French "comfort" menu is "reliable, if nothing great", whilst "service can be brusque, but professional enough"; whatever its faults ("lots of tourists", "coasting on prior triumphs"), most say, "please don't change a thing."

Langan's Coq d'Or Bar & Grill British/French

▽ 18 | 15 | 20 | £42

Earl's Court | 254-260 Old Brompton Rd., SW5 (Earl's Ct.) | 020-7259 2599 | fax 7370 7735 | www.langansrestaurants.co.uk

Comprising a formal restaurant and enclosed terrace grill/bar, this little-known Earl's Court outpost of the Langan's group makes "a good 'regular' place" to "sit and watch the world pass" by; the kitchen is "comfort-food central", churning out "consistent" British-French bistro classics.

	FOOD	DECOR	SERVICE	COST

NEW L'Anima ⊠ Italian — — — E

City | 1 Snowden St., EC2 (Old St./Liverpool St.) | 020-7422 7000 |
www.lanima.co.uk

Chef Francesco Mazzei (ex St. Alban) helms this new upscale Italian
on the City/Shoreditch border; since the name means 'soul', expect
hearty fare like Mazzei's signature pasta dish: zitoni with n'duja
(soft, spicy salami) and fried aubergine; in contrast, the space, designed by architect Claudio Silvestrin, is chic and minimal, with
limestone floors, porphyry walls and white leather chairs; N.B. it's
also open for breakfast, either healthy Med or hearty English.

Lansdowne, The European — 17 | 17 | 15 | £28

Primrose Hill | 90 Gloucester Ave., NW1 (Chalk Farm) | 020-7483 0409 |
fax 7586 1723

A "typical Primrose Hill crowd" congregate at this split-level gastropub with a split personality – "the lively pub downstairs has a totally
different feel than the mellow upstairs dining room"; but if supporters
smile it's "still as hip as ever", a fallen Food score supports sceptics
who snarl the Modern European fare is "not as good as it used to
be", and "service can be hit-or-miss."

La Perla Bar & Grill Mexican — 19 | 15 | 19 | £36

Covent Garden | 28 Maiden Ln., WC2 (Charing Cross/Covent Garden) |
020-7240 7400 | fax 7836 5088
Fitzrovia | 11 Charlotte St., W1 (Tottenham Court Rd.) | 020-7436 1744 |
fax 7436 1911
www.cafepacifico-laperla.com

Miles from Mexico they may be, but this "lively" Covent Garden and
Fitzrovia duo "draw the crowds" with a "good-quality, quickly served
attempt at Tex-Mex cuisine"; still, some feel it's all "focused more
around the bar than the food", thanks to the "vast tequila selection."

Z NEW La Petite Maison Mediterranean — 25 | 19 | 19 | £56

Mayfair | 54 Brooks Mews, W1 (Bond St.) | 020-7495 4774 |
www.lpmlondon.co.uk

A "great mix of patriarchs, matriarchs, bright young things and dates",
plus a celebrity or two, crowds into this "copy of the South of France
original", making it "very much an 'it' place" du jour (with the "strato-
spheric prices" to match); all hail the "simple, classic Med food" –
"the whole chicken with foie gras is a must-have" – even if some are
"not convinced by the concept of sharing plates", or of "bringing the
courses when they're cooked, rather than together"; all in all,
though, this "vibrant" yearling is "like a breath of fresh air to Mayfair."

La Porchetta Pizzeria Pizza — 18 | 10 | 16 | £16

Holborn | 33 Boswell St., WC1 (Holborn) | 020-7242 2434 ⊠
Clerkenwell | 84-86 Rosebery Ave., EC1 (Angel) | 020-7837 6060 |
fax 7837 6200
Muswell Hill | 265 Muswell Hill Broadway, N10 (Highgate) |
020-8883 1500 ●
Islington | 141-142 Upper St., N1 (Angel/Highbury & Islington) |
020-7288 2488

(continued)

(continued)

La Porchetta Pizzeria

Stoke Newington | 147 Stroud Green Rd., N4 (Finsbury Park) |
020-7281 2892 | fax 7837 6200

"These guys know how to make pizza" aver advocates of the
"awesome"-sized offerings at this "scruffy-looking" Italian chain; "a
favourite place for the office party", its "noise vols can get high" and
the "youthful" service "chaotic", but when food is this "cheap", no
one is complaining.

La Porte des Indes ● *Indian* 21 | 23 | 20 | £39

Marylebone | 32 Bryanston St., W1 (Marble Arch) | 020-7224 0055 |
fax 7224 1144 | www.laportedesindes.com

It's "worth the visit for the lush tropical decor" alone ("sit next to the
marble staircase, looking at the waterfall") at this "touristy"
Marylebone Indian, but the fare, with its "unique French influences",
won't disappoint either; "service could be more attentive", though,
and it's a "bit pricey" unless you go for the prix fixes or lunchtime
"bargain buffets" ("a jolly feast for families").

La Poule au Pot *French* 21 | 22 | 19 | £44

Pimlico | 231 Ebury St., SW1 (Sloane Sq.) | 020-7730 7763 |
fax 7259 9651

For "a touch of old-fashioned romance" ("my marriage has been re-
invigorated here every year"), this "dark, cosy" Pimlico Green
"neighbourhood bistro" "never disappoints", offering a "hearty",
"decent execution of French country classics" from "waiters who
smile and make jokes"; the outside patio is "sooo good in summer",
but "avoid downstairs like the plague."

L'Artiste Muscle *French* ▽ 20 | 11 | 14 | £29

Mayfair | 1 Shepherd Mkt., W1 (Green Park) | 020-7493 6150

The "decor and menu have hardly changed since the '70s, but this
"nice little place in Shepherd Market" is "full of Gallic charm, the
wonderful aroma of fresh garlic" and "great value" French bistro
fare; main gripe: it gets "too crowded to let you stay for coffee!"

La Rueda ● *Spanish* 15 | 11 | 15 | £29

Clapham | 66 Clapham High St., SW4 (Clapham Common/
Clapham North) | 020-7627 2173 | fax 7627 2173
Fulham | 642 King's Rd., SW6 (Fulham Broadway) | 020-7384 2684 |
fax 7384 2684
www.larueda.co.uk

"Don't be surprised to find only Spanish being spoken at the next table" of these Clapham and Fulham Iberians, "excellent for chilling
out over" "theme-park tapas" and "solid, if uninspiring" mains; "service ranges from appalling to acceptable depending on how busy
they are", but they come into their own at "large parties", which they
"frequently have year-round."

☑ L'Atelier de Joël Robuchon ● *French* 27 | 24 | 24 | £83

Covent Garden | 13-15 West St., WC2 (Leicester Sq.) |
020-7010 8600

(continued)

☑ La Cuisine *French*

Covent Garden | L'Atelier de Joël Robuchon | 13-15 West St., 1st fl., WC2
(Leicester Sq.) | 020-7010 8600
www.joel-robuchon.com

Enjoy "a serious workout for the eyes and the taste buds" at "true genius" chef-restaurateur Joël Robuchon's "slick, chic and expensive" New French; bringing a "cutting-edge to Covent Garden", his "mini-portions of perfection" are "served by people who obviously care", either in the "elegant" kitchen-themed, dinner-only La Cuisine or the "dark" ground-floor L'Atelier ("less formal", but "much better" some say); "high prices are the only dampener" – "not everyone wants to sit on stools to spend this kind of money" – otherwise, it's a "memorable" "delight."

Latium ☒ *Italian* | 23 | 18 | 21 | £61 |

Fitzrovia | 21 Berners St., W1 (Goodge St.) | 020-7323 9123 |
fax 7323 3205 | www.latiumrestaurant.com

"They greet you like long lost friends" at this trattoria "tucked behind Oxford Street", "one of the best" in the area for "impeccable", albeit "expensive" Italian fare, including an "amazing fish ravioli"; all's served amidst fresh flowers and pictures of food on the walls.

☑ La Trompette *European/French* | 28 | 22 | 25 | £53 |

Chiswick | 5-7 Devonshire Rd., W4 (Turnham Green) | 020-8747 1836 |
fax 8995 8097 | www.latrompette.co.uk

"Sound *la trompette*" for this "professionally run" yet "unpretentious" bit of "Paris in Chiswick", whose "sophisticated" Modern European–New French cuisine represents "*une triomphe*" of "culinary genius and class"; it's supported by an "excellent wine list" "across all price ranges and regions", "lovely" hardwood decor and "quick, well-informed staff"; and since all of this "would be twice the price in the West End", it's definitely "worth the journey" out.

La Trouvaille ☒ *French* | ▽ 25 | 17 | 18 | £37 |

Soho | 12A Newburgh St., W1 (Oxford Circus) | 020-7287 8488 |
fax 7434 4170 | www.latrouvaille.co.uk

"Reminiscent of Paris' Rive Gauche eateries", this sunny Soho spot features "wonderfully flavoured", "fine food with a French flounce", at "very fair prices for the quality" and served by "snazzy waiters with senses of humour"; they've got to "dispense with the world's most uncomfortable chairs", though.

Launceston Place *British* | - | - | - | E |

Kensington | 1A Launceston Pl., W8 (Gloucester Rd.) | 020-7937 6912 |
fax 7938 2412 | www.danddlondon.com

D&D London's reincarnation of this Kensington classic, which opened just as our Survey closed, has involved a "cool, comfortable" refurb of the rabbit warren of rooms, now transformed with bitter chocolate walls, gold-and-beige fabrics and art; the keys to the kitchen have been handed to Tristan Welch (ex Pétrus) who's augmenting the "well-executed" Modern British menu with regional classics from around the Isles (e.g. Long Horn beef and cheddar cobbler); patrons can watch him in action from a plasma screen in the 10-seater private dining room.

NEW L'Autre Pied ☒ European

▽ | 23 | 16 | 21 | £49

Marylebone | 5-7 Blandford St., W1 (Bond St.) | 020-7486 9696 | www.lautrepied.co.uk

Offering an "imaginatively prepared" Modern European menu that's "an obvious heritage from its big brother, Pied à Terre, if not quite as elaborate or intensely flavoured", this "cool, new addition to Marylebone" is already "abuzz with a young, happy clientele", enjoying the "friendly service"; however, a few feel it's "a bit over-priced", considering the digs ("you could share a fork with the person next to you!").

L'Aventure ☒ French

24 | 18 | 19 | £50

St. John's Wood | 3 Blenheim Terrace, NW8 (St. John's Wood) | 020-7624 6232 | fax 7625 5548

Despite – or because of – its "charmingly obscure location" in St. John's Wood, this "intimate, very Parisian" venue "keeps up a high standard year after year", "turning out authentic Classic French food with aplomb", abetted by "personal, if somewhat arrogant service"; it's the perfect place "for that niche between a super-special and an everyday eating-out experience."

Le Boudin Blanc French

22 | 18 | 18 | £44

Mayfair | Shepherd Mkt. | 5 Trebeck St., W1 (Green Park) | 020-7499 3292 | fax 7495 6973 | www.boudinblanc.co.uk

"Noisy and crowded, yes – but seriously great bistro food" sums up this "quirky"-looking, "dependable French"; the cuisine and the "marvellous candlelit atmosphere" "more than make up for the inconsistent service and the feeling you're sharing a table with three different parties" (to relieve the squeeze, "eat outdoors in quaint Shepherd Market").

NEW Le Café Anglais ❶ French

20 | 22 | 15 | £48

Bayswater | Whiteleys Shopping Ctr. | 8 Porchester Gdns., W2 (Queensway) | 020-7221 1415 | www.lecafeanglais.co.uk

"In a rather off-the-beaten-track location" (e.g., Whiteleys), this "interesting newcomer" offers a "classy, glassy and slick" setting for French brasserie fare that's "lovely plain" – though there are "fancier, more exciting things too"; "service is a bit shaky" and the "bill can be higher than expected", but overall, it's "another hit for Rowley Leigh", ex Kensington Place; P.S. "the rotisserie makes a great centrepiece for the open kitchen."

Le Café du Jardin ❶ European

19 | 17 | 16 | £38

Covent Garden | 28 Wellington St., WC2 (Covent Garden) | 020-7836 8769 | fax 7836 4123 | www.lecafedujardin.com

"Conveniently located in Covent Garden", this stalwart serves a "solid", "midrange" Modern European menu; even if "seating is close enough to rub elbows" and "service is variable", all concede its "bargain" prix fixe is "perfect before a show" (or after).

Le Café du Marché ⊠ *French*   23 | 21 | 18 | £45

Smithfield | 22 Charterhouse Sq., EC1 (Barbican) | 020-7608 1609 |
fax 7251 8575 | www.cafedumarche.co.uk

"Those in-the-know" about this "secluded" Smithfield site applaud
its "romantic" atmosphere – "wooden beams" and "soft live
music" – as well as its "lovely comfort food" *à la française,* which includes a "cheese trolley that virtually wheels itself to your table", so
"if you are dieting, go someplace else."

☑ Le Caprice ◗ *British/European*   24 | 21 | 24 | £57

St. James's | Arlington House | Arlington St., SW1 (Green Park) |
020-7629 2239 | fax 7493 9040 | www.le-caprice.co.uk

"The pace is slick and the people-watching unrivalled" at this "perennially chic" St. James's "post-theatre favourite", set in a "classy
black-and-white art deco room" ("perhaps a little dated"); its
Modern British–Euro "menu of urban staples" offers a "satisfying,
sometimes even really memorable experience", courtesy of service
that "makes you feel a million dollars without charging the earth";
and if it's a bit "like a busy club", it's one that everybody wants
to belong to.

Le Cercle ⊠ Ⓜ *French*   23 | 21 | 18 | £50

Chelsea | 1 Wilbraham Pl., SW1 (Sloane Sq.) | 020-7901 9999 |
fax 7901 9111 | www.clubgascon.com

"Minimalist on decor, maximalist on the taste buds", this "discreet" ("black dress, dahling") Sloane Square site stars an "unusual" New French menu of "shareable tapas" with a "strong
Southwest emphasis"; those "little plates can get expensive",
but the prix fixe "lunch is a breathtaking bargain"; P.S. "beg or
bribe for a corner booth."

Le Colombier *French*   21 | 19 | 24 | £49

Chelsea | 145 Dovehouse St., SW3 (South Kensington) | 020-7351 1155 |
fax 7351 5124 | www.lecolombier-sw3.co.uk

Constituting "a corner of France in Chelsea", this "friendly local" is
"perfect for a romantic dinner" with its "thoroughly reliable" bistro
menu offering "loads of possibilities", matched by a "clever wine
list" and "nice atmosphere"; the large front terrace in particular is
"always a pleasure."

☑ Ledbury, The *French*   28 | 23 | 25 | £70

Notting Hill | 127 Ledbury Rd., W11 (Notting Hill Gate/Westbourne Park) |
020-7792 9090 | fax 7792 9191 | www.theledbury.com

"A perfect place for a first, or a 5,001st, date" declare devotees of
this "classy, almost-world-class" venue that "adds glamour to a
less-than-glamourous end of" Notting Hill; as a rising Food rating re-
veals, chef Brett Graham's "worth-every-penny", "sophisticated"
New French menu just keeps getting better – even "better than sibling The Square's" some say – and it's "served up with no attitude,
just discreet, helpful staff"; the "swish, modern decor" may be "a bit
ordinaire", but it affords "sufficient room between tables, so that a
quiet dinner for two stays that way."

| | | FOOD | DECOR | SERVICE | COST |

Le Deuxième ❶ *European*
20 | **17** | **22** | **£36**

Covent Garden | 65A Long Acre, WC2 (Covent Garden) | 020-7379 0033 | fax 7379 0066 | www.ledeuxieme.com

"Close enough to the Royal Opera House to hear the high Cs", this "safe bet for lunch or pre-theatre" is "more sophisticated than most in Covent Garden", given its "formal service", "consistent" Modern Euro menu and "civilised" if "relatively featureless setting"; best of all, "the accounts department won't give you flack about your expenses."

Lee Ho Fook ❶ *Chinese*
18 | **13** | **15** | **£25**

Chinatown | 15-16 Gerrard St., W1 (Leicester Sq./Piccadilly Circus) | 020-7494 1200 | fax 7494 1700

"So this is what Warren Zevon was talking about" (in 'Werewolves of London') reveal rock-oriented reviewers about this "crowded" "Chinatown institution", which for 40-odd years has dished dim sum and Mandarin mains that are "decent", if "a bit pricey for the quality"; to avoid "slow service", "try dropping in on off-hours" – the 3 AM closing time makes it ideal "if you want some Chinese after a pub crawl."

❷ Le Gavroche ▣ *French*
27 | **24** | **26** | **£98**

Mayfair | 43 Upper Brook St., W1 (Marble Arch) | 020-7408 0881 | fax 7491 4387 | www.le-gavroche.co.uk

"If you like eating in the lap of luxury", this "timeless" Mayfair "institution" gives any meal "a real sense of occasion", with "crème de la crème" cooking that "sets the standard of Classic French cuisine" in the capital, capped by "legendary service" that, "without being cloying", "makes every customer feel like a king"; sophisticates sigh it's "so old hat", especially the subterranean setting, and it's certainly "not for the faint of wallet", but legions of fans profess it "faultless in every way"; P.S. "the set lunch is a steal."

❷ Le Manoir aux Quat'Saisons *French*
27 | **27** | **27** | **£97**

Great Milton | Le Manoir aux Quat'Saisons Hotel | Church Rd., Oxfordshire | 01844 278881 | fax 01844 278847 | www.manoir.com

"Deservedly an icon" declare disciples of this 15th-century "manor house converted into a luxurious boutique hotel in the heart of Oxfordshire"; there are "not enough superlatives" to describe chef-owner Raymond Blanc's "simply stunning" New French cuisine nor the "divine gardens" ("growing the same vegetables you eat") nor the "splendid service"; in short, it's "a must-visit place, even if only once in a lifetime (but do save up to go more often)."

Le Mercury ❶ *French*
16 | **14** | **15** | **£25**

Islington | 140A Upper St., N1 (Angel/Highbury & Islington) | 020-7354 4088 | fax 7359 7186 | www.lemercury.co.uk

"Always busy, and for good reason", this "cosy" Islington "standby" "hits the right note" with its New French fare at near-"bargain" prices – hence it's as "popular with starving paupers and students" as it is with "couples and large groups."

	FOOD	DECOR	SERVICE	COST

Lemonia ◗ *Greek* | 18 | 15 | 19 | £30 |

Primrose Hill | 89 Regent's Park Rd., NW1 (Chalk Farm) | 020-7586 7454 | fax 7483 2630

"Always a hustling, bustling place", this "cheerful" "Primrose Hill institution" "treats you like family", rustling up "reliable", "great-value" Greek fare that covers "all the favourites"; there's also a "lovely place to sit in the sun" (perhaps preferable to the "noisy" interior).

Leon *Mediterranean* | 19 | 15 | 15 | £15 |

Covent Garden | 73-74 The Strand, WC2 (Covent Garden) | 020-7240 3070 | fax 7240 9988

Marylebone | 275 Regent St., W1 (Oxford Circus) | 020-7495 1514

Soho | 35 Great Marlborough St., W1 (Oxford Circus) | 020-7437 5280

City | 12 Ludgate Circus, EC4 (Blackfriars) | 020-7489 1580 | **Ⓢ**

NEW City | 86 Cannon St., EC4 (Cannon St.) | 020-7623 9699 | **Ⓢ**

Spitalfields | 3 Crispin Pl., E1 (Liverpool St.) | 020-7247 4369 | fax 7377 1653

NEW South Bank | 7 Canvey St., SE1 (Blackfriars) | 020-7620 0035
www.leonrestaurants.co.uk

Take "wholesome, tasty" "guilt-free" "foods from ethical producers", "served at "McDonald's speed and at not much more than McDonald's prices", and you see why this Med chain actually provides "a joyful fast-food experience"; its "cool" bric-a-brac–laden decor "even attracts the odd minor celeb."

Le Pain Quotidien *Bakery/Belgian* | 18 | 15 | 14 | £18 |

NEW Covent Garden | 174 High Holborn, WC1 (Holborn/ Tottenham Court Rd) | 020-7486 6154

Marylebone | 72-75 Marylebone High St., W1 (Baker St./Regent's Park) | 020-7486 6154

Soho | 18 Great Marlborough St., W1 (Oxford Circus/Piccadilly Circus) | 020-7486 6154 | fax 7486 6164

South Bank | Royal Festival Hall | Belvedere Rd., SE1 (Waterloo) | 020-7486 6154

NEW King's Cross | St. Pancras Int'l | 81 Euston Rd., NW1 (King's Cross/ Russell Sq.) | 020-7486 6154 ◗

Chelsea | 201-203 King's Rd., SW3 (Sloane Sq./South Kensington) | 020-7486 6154

NEW South Kensington | 15-17 Exhibition Rd., SW7 (South Kensington) | 020-7486 6154

Kensington | 9 Young St., W8 (High St. Kensington) | 020-7486 6154
www.lepainquotidien.com

"Fast becoming a staple" around town, this cafe/deli chain – "the best Belgian thing since Hercule Poirot" – offers a taste of "informal country-style dining" with "huge" communal tables, "tasty tartines" and other "bakery-type" fare; but "it gets very crowded", so don't be surprised by the "so-so service."

Le Palais Du Jardin ◗ *French* | 21 | 21 | 19 | £43 |

Covent Garden | 136 Long Acre, WC2 (Covent Garden/Leicester Sq.) | 020-7379 5353 | fax 7379 1846 | www.lpdj.co.uk

"Opened in the early '90s", this "bustling, modern brasserie" is "ageing nicely", as rising scores suggest; occupying a "deceptively large" space – especially "in summer when the front is opened up" – it caters to a "country-cousinish clientele" with a New French menu that's "good and reliable", if "too dear" – but then it has a perfect perch: "just around the corner from Covent Garden", but "far enough from the plaza not to be manic."

Le Pont de la Tour ● *French/Seafood* | 20 | 21 | 18 | £58 |

Tower Bridge | Butlers Wharf Bldg. | 36D Shad Thames, SE1 (London Bridge/Tower Hill) | 020-7403 8403 | fax 7940 1835 | www.lepontdelatour.co.uk

Its "spectacular setting on the Thames", basking "in the reflected light of Tower Bridge", makes this Classic French a "solid choice for quality dining"; if pessimists posit the *pont* "feels a little passé", especially given the "sky-high prices", its "wide choice of seafood" and "deep, varied wine list" remain "reliable for an all-round special occasion."

☑ Le Relais de Venise l'entrecôte *French* | 22 | 16 | 15 | £32 |

Marylebone | 120 Marylebone Ln., W1 (Bond St./Marylebone) | 020-7486 0878 | fax 7486 0879 | www.relaisdevenise.com

"The whole restaurant is eating the same thing" at this Parisian "elbow-to-elbow" export to Marylebone, with its "single-minded" menu of steak frites served with an "exceptional special sauce"; even if the "slapdash service" from "cute waitresses" lets the side down, the "simple formula works", especially if "you need a quick French fix."

L'Escargot ●☒ *French* | 23 | 23 | 21 | £55 |

Soho | 48 Greek St., W1 (Leicester Sq./Tottenham Court Rd.) | 020-7437 6828 | fax 7437 0790 | www.whitestarline.org.uk

It's "class all the way" at this Soho "sweet spot" – an "informal ground-floor" brasserie and "upstairs dining room with an unusual art collection" – where "wonderful" Classic French cooking and a "wine list thicker than *Gone With the Wind*" ensure a "fine-dining experience"; true, the "service can vary", from "seamless" to "at a snail's pace", but the "great pre-theatre menus" mollify many.

☑ Les Trois Garçons ☒ *French* | 21 | 28 | 20 | £59 |

Shoreditch | 1 Club Row, E1 (Liverpool St.) | 020-7613 1924 | fax 7012 1236 | www.lestroisgarcons.com

Adorned with "handbags floating from chandeliers and a great Victorian bar", the "hallucinatory decor" – think *Alice in Wonderland* on steroids – at this "outlandish" Shoreditch eatery is "so theatrical, one expects the food to be as tacky" – but the game-heavy Classic French fare is actually "really good" (albeit "pricey"); if some "snooty staff" get the thumbs-down ("we were shushed for laughing too loudly"), the "extravagant owners make it a treat"; besides, there's "nothing like eating boar with a boar's head supervising."

Le Suquet ● *French/Seafood* | 22 | 14 | 19 | £47 |

Chelsea | 104 Draycott Ave., SW3 (South Kensington) | 020-7581 1785 | fax 7225 0838

The "fish swims in daily" to this "unpretentious, charming" Brompton Cross "stalwart" serving "super", "simply prepared"

Gallic classics (at "prices that make the eyes water"); true, the "South of France in the '60s" decor looks "a bit worn at the edges", but the fact "nothing changes here" is just "fine" for most.

L'Etranger *French*

FOOD	DECOR	SERVICE	COST
23	20	21	£52

South Kensington | 36 Gloucester Rd., SW7 (Gloucester Rd.) | 020-7584 1118 | fax 7584 8886 | www.etranger.co.uk

"Wonderfully inventive" and "stylishly presented", "the cooking is an unusual blend of French sophistication with an Asian twist" at this "best-kept secret" on Gloucester Road; those who aren't strangers to it "love the wine list and helpful staff"; however, they advise "avoid the back room, as it vibrates from the disco downstairs."

☑ Le Vacherin *French*

FOOD	DECOR	SERVICE	COST
26	21	24	£50

Chiswick | 76-77 South Parade, W4 (Chiswick Park) | 020-8742 2121 | fax 8742 0799 | www.levacherin.co.uk

"Underrated and overlooked" (except by us) in a part of Chiswick "lacking serious restaurants", this "very French" eatery is appreciated for its "terrific classic cooking" that's "not too heavy"; the fare, along with "diligently discreet service", makes it "worth the price."

Levant ➊ *Lebanese*

FOOD	DECOR	SERVICE	COST
21	24	16	£48

Marylebone | Jason Ct. | 76 Wigmore St., W1 (Bond St.) | 020-7224 1111 | fax 7486 1216 | www.levant.co.uk

With "lovely belly dancers", "sultry decor and huge platters of mezze, you really do feel a million miles away from Marylebone" at this "seductive" Lebanese; whilst the emphasis is less on the dishes than the "decadent setting" ("often becomes a harem late at night" purr pickup artists), it does offer a "lovely feast"; "on the downside", the "set menus are pricey" and the "service mediocre."

Levantine ➊ *Lebanese*

FOOD	DECOR	SERVICE	COST
-	-	-	M

Paddington | 26 London St., W2 (Paddington) | 020-7262 1111 | fax 7402 4039 | www.levant.co.uk

"More peaceful and friendly than older sister" Levant (though it also has a belly dancer nightly), this "cosy" "Paddington location makes a great date place for close conversation mixed with delicious mezzes" and other "authentic Middle Eastern food with a twist of Europe" amidst flowers, floating candles and Lebanese antiques.

Light House *Eclectic*

FOOD	DECOR	SERVICE	COST
-	-	-	E

Wimbledon | 75-77 Ridgeway, SW19 (Wimbledon) | 020-8944 6338 | fax 8946 4440 | www.lighthousewimbledon.com

This "reliable local favourite", "very popular" with "horsey Wimbledonites" (it's next door to a riding stables), trades in a "quality offering" of Eclectic edibles; but the less-enlightened claim the "overpriced" menu is for those with "more money than sense."

L'Incontro ➊ *Italian*

FOOD	DECOR	SERVICE	COST
▽ 21	19	20	£53

Pimlico | 87 Pimlico Rd., SW1 (Sloane Sq.) | 020-7730 3663 | fax 7730 5062 | www.lincontro-restaurant.com

"Genuine" Italian cuisine, along with a "first-rate wine list with good-value labels", is the focus of this "pleasant place" in Pimlico, which "now has more buzz, and better service"; nevertheless, an "inconsistent" kitchen causes naysayers to snap it's "not worth the cost."

Little Bay ● *European*   21 | 20 | 19 | £20

Farringdon | 171 Farringdon Rd., EC1 (Farringdon) | 020-7278 1234 | fax 7278 5368
Kilburn | 228 Belsize Rd., NW6 (Kilburn Park) | 020-7372 4699 | fax 7223 6131 ⊟
Battersea | 228 York Rd., SW11 (Clapham Junction Rail/ Wandsworth Town Rail) | 020-7223 4080 | fax 7223 6131
Fulham | 140 Wandsworth Bridge Rd., SW6 (Parsons Green) | 020-7751 3133 | fax 7223 6131
www.little-bay.co.uk

"Mood-enhancing", "fine bistro fare" at "budget" prices keeps them coming to this "cheerful" chain of Modern Euro eateries; whilst their decor varies, from Farringdon's "opulent" Greco-Roman style to Kilburn's candlelit atmosphere, they "consistently" offer "a cheap night out with plenty of atmosphere."

Little Italy ● *Italian*   16 | 15 | 19 | £30

Soho | 21 Frith St., W1 (Leicester Sq./Tottenham Court Rd.) | 020-7734 4737 | fax 7734 1777 | www.littleitalysoho.co.uk

This "little cafe with lots of life" – especially when it "spills out into the street in the warm months" – offers "ok", if "pricey-for-the-quality" Italian staples; "what makes it a good option is staying until the wee hours", as "the downstairs plays cheesy pop" until 4 AM – perfect for "when you fancy a mad Soho night out with your mates."

Livebait *Seafood*   19 | 15 | 16 | £33

Covent Garden | 21 Wellington St., WC2 (Covent Garden) | 020-7836 7161 | fax 7836 7141 ⓩ
Waterloo | 43 The Cut, SE1 (Waterloo) | 020-7928 7211 | fax 7928 2279
www.santeonline.co.uk

"Unquestionably fresh fish" ("could have swum up the Thames that morning") baits the hook of this "noisy" seafood duo in Waterloo and Covent Garden; whilst it "looks stark with all the tiles" and service can be "slapdash", "it does what it says on the tin", and for "fair prices" too.

Living Room, The ● *European*   17 | 19 | 18 | £28

Piccadilly | 3-9 Heddon St., W1 (Oxford Circus/Piccadilly Circus) | 020-7292 0570 | fax 7851 0897 | www.thelivingroomw1.co.uk

There is indeed a "relaxed living-room style" to this "funky" Piccadilly bar/brasserie in a converted post office; the Modern European menu offers "nothing to complain about, but nothing special" either – and is "actually a bit expensive"; so some suggest "sticking to bar snacks" and listening to the bands playing nightly.

☙ Locanda Locatelli *Italian*   25 | 22 | 23 | £62

Marylebone | Hyatt Regency London - The Churchill | 8 Seymour St., W1 (Marble Arch) | 020-7935 9088 | fax 7935 1149 | www.locandalocatelli.com

"Hats off to Signor Locatelli" cheer chef-owner Giorgio's groupies, as his Portman Square venue "remains one of the best Italians in

London", with "warm" staff serving "intense", "innovative" fare from the northern regions; the David Collins–designed digs are "classic, comfortable – like an Armani suit", offering a chance to "look at the powerful and famous of London"; so what if "you'll pay for the company you keep" – just "sell granny's pearls and head here for a divine treat."

Locanda Ottoemezzo ☒ *Italian*   24 | 17 | 23 | £46

Kensington | 2-4 Thackeray St., W8 (High St. Kensington) | 020-7937 2200 | fax 7937 9871 | www.locandaottoemezzo.co.uk

"In a funky corner" of Kensington, this "romantic neighbourhood hideaway" offers "fantastic Italian food", especially "when truffles are in season"; "service is friendly and prompt" within a homelike space "with sophisticated movie posters making good conversation starters"; in contrast, prices can be "a conversation stopper", but converts claim "the cuisine's worth every penny."

Loch Fyne *Seafood*   21 | 14 | 17 | £31

Covent Garden | 2-4 Catherine St., WC2 (Covent Garden) | 020-7240 4999 | fax 7240 4499 | www.lochfyne.com

"More a brasserie than a loch", this "solid seafooder in the heart of Theatreland" is "a bright, loud" place for a "quick meal" at "reasonable prices"; if the "hurry-up" service and "formulaic" fare give it "the feel of a chain" – well, it *is* one, with over 40 branches throughout the U.K.

L'Oranger ☒ *French*   25 | 22 | 25 | £71

St. James's | 5 St. James's St., SW1 (Green Park) | 020-7839 3774 | fax 7839 4330 | www.loranger.co.uk

"One of the best French restaurants in London" – certainly "the best in St. James's" – this "expensive" "institution" makes "you feel transported to Paris" with its "hard-to-fault" fare ("inventive starters, fairly classic mains"), "comfortable" yet "elegant surroundings" complete "with skylight and garden" and "super-attentive service", including a "friendly sommelier who likes diners to try his new acquisitions"; it's *un peu* "old-fashioned – but who ever said that was bad?"

Lou Pescadou ●☒Ⓜ *French/Seafood*   – | – | – | M

Earl's Court | 241 Old Brompton Rd., SW5 (Earl's Ct.) | 020-7370 1057 | fax 7244 7545

"Everyone goes for the fish, which is tops" – though there's some "excellent French food" too – at this quirky Earl's Court eatery where "friendly owners" cater to a clientele of "mostly regulars."

L-Restaurant & Bar *Spanish*   – | – | – | M

Kensington | 2 Abingdon Rd., W8 (High St. Kensington) | 020-7795 6969 | fax 7795 6968 | www.l-restaurant.co.uk

Those "impressed by this little"-known venue just off Kensington High Street cite "delightful Spanish-inspired" tapas made from "simple, quality ingredients"; other pluses include "friendly staff" and "elegant decor", which features an impressive, retractable glass roof and stone flooring.

	FOOD	DECOR	SERVICE	COST

Luciano ☒ *Italian* | 19 | 17 | 15 | £51 |

St. James's | 72-73 St. James's St., SW1 (Green Park) | 020-7408 1440 | fax 7493 6670 | www.lucianorestaurant.co.uk

With a mix of "beautiful people" and "business suits", Marco Pierre White's "sophisticated" St. James's venue is an "all-round winner" to fans who fawn over its "fabulous bar", "varied" Italian menu and "deep wine list"; but critics claim this "overpriced", "chaotic" *cucina* "misses the mark" ("not sure if it's a restaurant or drinks place").

Lucio *Italian* | 22 | 19 | 24 | £50 |

Chelsea | 257-259 Fulham Rd., SW3 (South Kensington) | 020-7823 3007 | fax 7823 3009

Patron Lucio Altana "is always on hand to provide a warm welcome" to his "friendly" Fulham Road site, attracting "ladies who lunch" and "B-list" celebrities with "an aura of calm" across its understated premises; the Italian *cucina* is "enjoyable" – "if never exciting", foes fume – but a score rise confirms the service is "better than before."

Lucky 7 *American/Burgers* | 21 | 15 | 14 | £19 |

Notting Hill | 127 Westbourne Park Rd., W2 (Royal Oak/Westbourne Park) | 020-7727 6771 | fax 7727 6798 | www.lucky7london.co.uk

It "feels like you're stepping into a small American diner" at Tom Conran's "vintage-y" Notting Hill spot, which gets "a bit chaotic" (notably "at weekends, given the horrific queues"), but is "great for a burger" and a "filling milkshake"; "you cannot beat it for price" either.

Made in Italy ◑ *Italian* | 20 | 13 | 13 | £26 |

Chelsea | 249 King's Rd., SW3 (Sloane Sq./South Kensington) | 020-7352 1880 | www.madeinitalygroup.co.uk

"Bring your sense of humour" to this "frenetic" Chelsea trattoria; "tables are scarce (with nowhere to wait)" and "service is poor", but the "great atmosphere" and "rustic" Italian staples (starring "*delizioso* pizza") make it a "perennial favourite", and "good value" to boot.

Magdalen ☒ *European* | 23 | 17 | 21 | £41 |

Borough | 152 Tooley St., SE1 (London Bridge) | 020-7403 1342 | fax 7403 9950 | www.magdalenrestaurant.co.uk

In an "out-of-the-way stretch" between London and Tower bridges, this "charming modern bistro" is "a great addition to the SE1 scene"; its "intelligently done" Modern European menu, backed by a "wide-ranging, well-sourced wine list" is full of "food you could eat every day, at a price that almost makes it possible."

Maggie Jones's *British* | 19 | 20 | 18 | £38 |

Kensington | 6 Old Court Pl., W8 (High St. Kensington) | 020-7937 6462 | fax 7376 0510

"The candlelight, pine tables and eclectic seating" create a "super-cosy, adorable country" look to this Kensington place, appropriately serving "giant portions" of "rustic", "rather heavy" Traditional British "comfort food" (like "old-fashioned roasts"); even if the "service is lacking" and "prices are dear", it remains "a funky favourite."

	FOOD	DECOR	SERVICE	COST

Ma Goa Ⓜ Indian
22 | 15 | 21 | £27

Putney | 242-244 Upper Richmond Rd., SW15 (East Putney) |
020-8780 1767 | www.ma-goa.com

The "innovative" Goan "food's always full of flavour" at this
"family-run, with a welcoming feel" Putney Indian; "good with
children", "courteous staff" compensate for "cramped" environs.

Malabar ◐ Indian
22 | 13 | 21 | £28

Notting Hill | 27 Uxbridge St., W8 (Notting Hill Gate) | 020-7727 8800 |
www.malabar-restaurant.co.uk

Its "unpretentious" digs are "cramped", but mem sahibs don't
mind, because the menu – "not in-your-face Indian food, but a
subtler interpretation" – is so "fresh and inventive" at this eatery
"tucked away in Notting Hill"; "helpful, friendly service"
enhances the experience.

Malabar Junction Indian
23 | 20 | 21 | £32

Bloomsbury | 107 Great Russell St., WC1 (Tottenham Court Rd.) |
020-7580 5230 | fax 7436 9942 | www.malabarjunction.com

Near the British Museum, this "enchanting space with a glass ceiling
and plants" (don't worry, it's "better than it looks from the outside")
offers an "ambitious menu" of "unconventional, light, yet truly authentic" Keralan fare ("good for vegetarians") from southern India;
"service is very friendly" as well.

Mandalay Ⓧ Burmese
23 | 10 | 20 | £18

Marylebone | 444 Edgware Rd., W2 (Edgware Rd.) | 020-7258 3696 |
fax 7258 3696

"The second time you go, you'll be a 'regular'" as far as the "wonderfully friendly owners" of this "tiny Burmese" in Marylebone are con-
cerned; decorwise, it looks more "like a cafe", but it's set apart by its
"fantastic" fare – "I've no idea if it is authentic, but it is delicious" –
at a "price that's difficult to find fault with."

Mandarin Kitchen ◐ Chinese
24 | 9 | 14 | £31

Bayswater | 14-16 Queensway, W2 (Bayswater/Queensway) |
020-7727 9012 | fax 7727 9468

"Every seafood lover must make a pilgrimage to this temple of crus-
taceans, highlighted by the most flavourful lobster" "in various
preparations" (the "lobster noodles remain its raison d'être"); the
Queensway digs might look "shockingly spartan and dilapidated",
but it remains "legendary" amongst Chinese haunts, "with
a dedicated following."

Mango Tree Thai
21 | 20 | 19 | £41

Victoria | 46 Grosvenor Pl., SW1 (Hyde Park/Victoria) | 020-7823 1888 |
fax 7838 9275 | www.mangotree.org.uk

"Snazzy Thailand comes to London" in the form of this "trendy"
Victoria Station venue (i.e. "hip"-looking, but in "need of some
soundproofing"); the "extensive menu" includes "interesting dishes
alongside staple standards", and is overseen by staff that, whilst
"always polite", get "too busy for their own good."

	FOOD	DECOR	SERVICE	COST

Manicomio *Italian*
19 | 16 | 17 | £41

Chelsea | 85 Duke of York Sq., SW3 (Sloane Sq.) | 020-7730 3366 | fax 7730 3377 | www.manicomio.co.uk

With "crisp, contemporary surroundings" and a "wonderful" terrace, this "busy" Italian in the old Duke of York Barracks near Sloane Square makes a "useful" stop "whilst shopping"; otherwise, some would avoid the "above-standard" but "uneven" fare and "generally rather frantic" service; N.B. a larger second location was due to debut in Gutter Lane in July 2008.

Mao Tai ● *Pan-Asian*
▽ 23 | 19 | 19 | £44

Fulham | 58 New King's Rd., SW6 (Parsons Green) | 020-7731 2520 | fax 7471 8992 | www.maotai.co.uk

"After a fire in 2007, this Parsons Green eatery has reinvented itself", and fans find it "even better" than before; the setting may be "minimalist", but the Pan-Asian dishes are "true delicacies", from the "sophisticated Southeast Asian" eats to the "delicious" Chinese dim sum; it's "a little pricey", but worth "saving for a special blowout."

NEW Marco ⊠Ⓜ *French*
- | - | - | E

Fulham | Chelsea Football Club Complex | Stanford Bridge, Fulham Rd., SW6 (Fulham Broadway) | 020-7915 2929 | www.marcorestaurant.co.uk

If Chelsea FC now has Marco Pierre White's name in lights, it's not to herald his football skills, but his culinary ones - as evidenced in this new venture, a disco-esque setting with tinted windows, mirrored ceiling and Swarovski crystal-clad pillar; the approachable Classic French menu features several MPW signatures - "a particular highlight is the pigeon with foie gras" - alongside some British delights (especially on match days), as an "expert sommelier recommends" from a wine list that caters as much to the connoisseur as to the quaffer.

Mark's Club ⊠ *British/French*
23 | 24 | 26 | £73

Private club; inquiries: 020-7499 2936

"Rubbing shoulders with top industrialists, the upper classes and minor royalty", "you'll feel you're one of the privileged few to enter" this "elite" private club in a "charming, cosy" Mayfair townhouse (now one of Richard Caring's "clutch of establishments"); the "quality" Classic French-British fare is "simple but delicious" and staff "cannot be copied for graciousness and comfort" - "I take my butler to show him what we want at home."

Maroush ● *Lebanese*
22 | 12 | 16 | £27

Knightsbridge | 38 Beauchamp Pl., SW3 (Knightsbridge) | 020-7581 5434 | fax 7723 3161

Marylebone | 1-3 Connaught St., W2 (Marble Arch) | 020-7262 0222

Marylebone | 21 Edgware Rd., W2 (Marble Arch) | 020-7723 0773 | fax 7723 3161

Marylebone | 4 Vere St., W1 (Bond St.) | 020-7493 5050 | fax 7723 3161

Marylebone | 62 Seymour St., W1 (Marble Arch) | 020-7724 5024 | fax 7723 3161

subscribe to ZAGAT.com

(continued)
Maroush
Marylebone | 68 Edgware Rd., W2 (Marble Arch) | 020-7224 9339 |
fax 7723 3161
www.maroush.com
This long-time Lebanese chain "can always be counted on" for a
"veritable feast" of "classic cuisine" at "relatively inexpensive"
rates; "open very late", they're a "3 AM staple for a shawarma" –
indeed, many "go for the longer hours rather than the food."

Marquess Tavern, The *British*   - | - | - | M
Islington | 32 Canonbury St., N1 (Highbury & Islington) | 020-7354 2975 |
www.themarquesstavern.co.uk
"The quality of the ingredients shines through" the Traditional
British cuisine at this "casual" Islington pub dating back to the
1850s; an airy "glass-ceiling dining room", "knowledgeable servers
and a great beer list" add to its appeal as an "awesome place to meet
up with friends for a chill evening."

Masala Zone *Indian*   19 | 14 | 17 | £20
NEW **Covent Garden** | 48 Floral St., WC2 (Covent Garden) |
020-7379 0101 | fax 020-7836 0202
Soho | 9 Marshall St., W1 (Oxford Circus/Piccadilly Circus) |
020-7287 9966 | fax 7287 8555
NEW **Camden Town** | 25 Parkway, NW1 (Camden Town) |
020-7267 4422 | fax 020-7267 8833
Islington | 80 Upper St., N1 (Angel) | 020-7359 3399 | fax 7359 6560
Earl's Court | 147 Earl's Court Rd., SW5 (Earl's Ct.) | 020-7373 0220 |
fax 7373 0990
www.masalazone.com
"Loud, happening spots for young and old to enjoy authentic, well-
priced Indian fare" sums up this string of "spicy" street-fare specialists
("the Thalis are the absolute best"); "decor varies by location" –
from "colourful" to "cheerless" – and "efficiency varies by visit", but
overall, it lands in the zone for a "quick, filling" meal.

Matsuri *Japanese*   23 | 16 | 20 | £50
Holborn | 71 High Holborn, WC1 (Holborn) | 020-7430 1970 |
fax 7430 1971 🖫
St. James's | 15 Bury St., SW1 (Green Park) | 020-7839 1101 |
fax 7930 7010
www.matsuri-restaurant.com
With tableside-prepared teppanyaki and sushi that garner "high
marks for style and even higher marks for substance", these "authentic" Japanese in St. James's ("a bit sterile") and Holborn (more
"elegant") come "highly recommended" as "places to entertain",
especially "on the company credit card."

Maxwell's 🌑 *American*   18 | 18 | 18 | £25
Covent Garden | 8 James St., WC2 (Covent Garden) | 020-7836 0303 |
fax 7379 5035 | www.maxwells.co.uk
Large and "lively", this Covent Garden veteran "is a hub of activity",
drawing in families, teens and tourists with its American diner–style

fare that's "not bad" "for a quick bite"; on weekend nights, the "fantastic bar" features "really loud music."

Z maze *French*   25 | 22 | 23 | £70

Mayfair | The Marriott Grosvenor Sq. | 10-13 Grosvenor Sq., W1
(Bond St.) | 020-7107 0000 | fax 7107 0001 | www.gordonramsay.com
Chef "Jason Atherton is the genius behind the gastronomical
fireworks" – "dazzling mouthfuls" of "Asian-accented" New French
"tapas-sized plates" – at this "chic" yet "casual" Grosvenor Square
venue "from the Gordon Ramsay stable"; sure, "it's a bit pricey",
"particularly if you are used to filling up", but "professional service",
"fantastic cocktails" and a "positive atmosphere" add up to an
"a-mazing" grazing place.

NEW maze Grill *Chophouse*   - | - | - | VE

Mayfair | The Marriott Grosvenor Sq. | 10-13 Grosvenor Sq., W1
(Bond St.) | 020-7495 2211 | fax 7592 1603 | www.gordonramsay.com
Firebrand chef-restaurateur Gordon Ramsay sets another blaze in
Mayfair with this take on an American steakhouse adjoining his
maze; "beautiful" banquettes and warm, elegant hues set the stage
for chef Jason Atherton's upscale menu of beef cooked over coal and
finished in a searing broiler plus an array of stylish starters and "delicate
small plates"; N.B. a 12-seat table of solid English oak offers a
unique peek into the kitchen.

Medcalf *British*   - | - | - | M

Clerkenwell | 40 Exmouth Mkt., EC1 (Angel/Farringdon) | 020-7833 3533 |
fax 7833 1321 | www.medcalfbar.co.uk
Set in an old butcher's shop, this "trendy" Exmouth Market haunt is
"not for the fussy", but does feature a "Modern British menu of robust,
interesting" fare; if you want to "just relax and enjoy the food",
though, better "get in early before the nighttime-scene crowds" kick in.

Mediterraneo ● *Italian*   21 | 15 | 18 | £36

Notting Hill | 37 Kensington Park Rd., W11 (Ladbroke Grove) |
020-7792 3131 | fax 7243 3630 | www.mediterraneo-restaurant.co.uk
"The neighbourhood Italian if you live in heaven" gush Notting Hill
amici of this "crowded" "classic that never changes" its "homely
dishes" ("wonderful sea bass") or "accessible service"; "cramped
conditions" aside, it's "a good alternative when [nearby sister]
Osteria Basilico is booked."

Mela ● *Indian*   21 | 15 | 20 | £25

Covent Garden | 152-156 Shaftesbury Ave., WC2 (Leicester Sq.) |
020-7836 8635 | fax 7379 0527 | www.melarestaurant.co.uk
Take "a tour of India" via the "mélange of regional dishes" offered by
this "delectable" subcontinental; "attentive but not pushy" service,
a "remarkable value" prix fixe and its location 'twixt Covent Garden
and Soho make it perfect "for the pre-theatre set."

Memories of China *Chinese*   22 | 18 | 19 | £43

Belgravia | 65-69 Ebury St., SW1 (Victoria) | 020-7730 7734 |
fax 7730 2992

| | FOOD | DECOR | SERVICE | COST |

(continued)

Memories of China

Kensington | 353 Kensington High St., W8 (High St. Kensington) |
020-7603 6951 | fax 7603 0848
www.memories-of-china.co.uk

Nearly 30 years old, this "dependable" Belgravia "favourite" (with a younger Kensington offshoot) is "still serving decent Chinese grub for Western palates" in a scene that's "more neighbourly than hip"; naysayers note that it's "not memorable", except for its "bracing prices", to which regulars respond the "set menus are the way to go."

Menier Chocolate Factory Ⓜ *British*

| | 16 | 16 | 21 | £30 |

Southwark | 51-53 Southwark St., SE1 (London Bridge) | 020-7407 4411 |
fax 7378 1713 | www.menierchocolatefactory.com

An "atmospheric location" (a historic chocolate factory) and "relaxed, attentive service" make this cafe in a Southwark arts centre a "nice retreat before or after" one of the "Menier's fine performances"; but whilst some feel the "quirky" Modern British menu "isn't just for the theatre crowd", others claim it's "not a destination in itself."

Meson Don Felipe Ⓩ *Spanish*

| 20 | 17 | 17 | £25 |

Waterloo | 53 The Cut, SE1 (Southwark/Waterloo) | 020-7928 3237 |
fax 7736 9857

"One of the few remaining real tapas places like you'd find in Barcelona", this "lively" Waterloo "warhorse" gets "packed", thanks to "affordable" Spanish fare, "good finos and manzanillas" and a "flamenco guitarist" "stuffed into the smallest loft ever"; "brusque service" ruffles a few feathers, especially during the "rush-hour crowds", but it's "convenient" "as a pre- or post-theatre stop" (the National's nearby).

Mestizo ❶ *Mexican*

| | 23 | 18 | 17 | £27 |

Camden Town | 103 Hampstead Rd., NW1 (Warren St.) | 020-7387 4064 |
fax 7383 4984 | www.mestizomx.com

"Take some friends and share the huge servings" of "superb, well-priced" fare ("including excellent tacos") at this lively, "authentic Mexican" in Camden Town; service is "friendly", if sometimes "sluggish."

Metrogusto *Italian*

| - | - | - | E |

Islington | 11-13 Theberton St., N1 (Angel/Highbury & Islington) |
020-7226 9400 | fax 7226 9400 | www.metrogusto.co.uk

"Inventive" Italian cooking ("almost flawless at the price") with "lively if eccentric service" makes this "intimate" Islingtonian "just as a neighbourhood restaurant should be" – and "the best thing is the owner, who knows everybody."

Met Su Yan *Pan-Asian*

| - | - | - | E |

Golders Green | 134 Golders Green Rd., NW11 (Golders Green) |
020-8458 8088 | www.metsuyan.co.uk

"Filling a kosher Asian food niche" for "the Golders Green crowd", this venue "keeps its Jewish customer base coming back for more", even if it's "costly for what you get"; whether Japanese or Chinese, "the taste is authentic – *sans* shrimp or pork", of course.

Mews of Mayfair *British*   19 | 20 | 19 | £49

Mayfair | 10-11 Lancashire Ct., New Bond St., W1 (Bond St./Oxford Circus) | 020-7518 9388 | fax 7518 9389 | www.mewsofmayfair.com

"Start with drinks downstairs at the excellent bar, and move up" to the "elegant", "creamy white" dining room of this "sleeper" in a Mayfair mews; the "surprisingly good", though "a bit expensive", Modern British fare is served by "young enthusiastic staff", and if the "dining room seems a little staid", no worries – the basement lounge "is completely different."

Meza ●☒ *Mediterranean*   ▽ 13 | 18 | 13 | £37

Soho | 100 Wardour St., W1 (Tottenham Court Rd.) | 020-7314 4002 | fax 7314 4040 | www.mezabar.co.uk

Ratings may not fully reflect that this large, airy Soho space (above Floridita) has been "newly refurbished"; but so far, the switch from Spanish to Mediterranean meals has met mixed reactions from surveyors – ranging from "worth it" to "nothing special"; one thing that hasn't changed are the boisterous DJ nights from Thursday to Saturday.

☑ Michael Moore ●☒ *Eclectic*   26 | 16 | 24 | £58

Marylebone | 19 Blandford St., W1 (Baker St./Bond St.) | 020-7224 1898 | fax 7224 0970 | www.michaelmoorerestaurant.com

"Larger-than-life" chef-owner "Michael Moore is always coming out with something new to tempt you" from his "creative" Eclectic menu at this slightly "cramped" Marylebone eatery; "the cost, whilst relatively high, represents value for money", especially since "all the staff make everyone feel special."

Mildreds ☒ *Vegetarian*   22 | 12 | 16 | £22

Soho | 45 Lexington St., W1 (Oxford Circus/Piccadilly Circus) | 020-7439 2392 | fax 7439 2392 | www.mildreds.co.uk

Even "absolute carnivores love" this "long-time vegan standard" near Piccadilly Circus, "a quaint place to grab a bite" of "wholesome food" and a sip of "excellent organic wine" – "and it won't blow the bank, either"; however, it can get "crammed" (the fact that it takes "no bookings" doesn't help matters), and "service depends on who is working."

Mimmo d'Ischia ●☒ *Italian*   18 | 14 | 19 | £54

Belgravia | 61 Elizabeth St., SW1 (Sloane Sq./Victoria) | 020-7730 5406 | fax 7730 9439 | www.mimmodischia.co.uk

"With all the cheesy pictures on the wall, you wouldn't think it was a very good place – but you'd be wrong" say loyalists who laud this "loveable Italian where you feel part of the family" as you tuck into "huge portions" of "old-style" eats; no, you'd be right, hiss hostiles who've downgraded the scores of this Belgravia "stalwart", citing not just the "tattered decor" but the "overpriced", "quantity-over-quality" *cucina*.

	FOOD	DECOR	SERVICE	COST

Mint Leaf *Indian*

19 | 22 | 19 | £54

St. James's | corner of Haymarket & Suffolk Pl., SW1 (Piccadilly Circus) | 020-7930 9020 | fax 7930 6205 | www.mintleafrestaurant.com

"A dark stairway leads you down to a chic bar and dimly lit dining interior, buzzing with the noise of a young crowd" at this "sexy, sultry" Haymarket haunt; if the Indian "food is not as good as I'd hoped", it still offers "a different twist to 'going for a curry'"; just be aware that the "creative" "cocktails send the bill rocketing."

Mitsukoshi *Japanese*

19 | 13 | 19 | £44

Piccadilly | Mitsukoshi Department Store | 14-20 Lower Regent St., SW1 (Piccadilly Circus) | 020-7930 0317 | fax 7839 1167 | www.mitsukoshi-restaurant.co.uk

In a basement setting that "perfectly reproduces the typical Japanese department store restaurant look (rather bleak)", this low-key Piccadilly Asian boasts "charmingly well-mannered" staff to serve "authentic, distinctive" dishes with "very reasonable" set menus.

Miyama *Japanese*

23 | 12 | 19 | £43

Mayfair | 38 Clarges St., W1 (Green Park) | 020-7499 2443 | fax 7491 1569

"A quiet haven, mostly visited by Japanese", this "subdued" bi-level Mayfair Asian offers "traditional" raw and cooked dishes alike ("nothing like great shabu-shabu on a cool night"); "such fabulous food – and yet such a clapped-out interior."

Momo ❶ *African*

19 | 24 | 16 | £43

Piccadilly | 25 Heddon St., W1 (Piccadilly Circus) | 020-7434 4040 | fax 7287 0404 | www.momoresto.com

"Dancing on chairs is to be expected" at this "full-on taste of North Africa" off Regent Street, complete with "loud music" and a "casbahlike environment to chill out" in; if it's "popular more for the ambience than the food" – "you either love their menu or hate it" – or "so-so" service, it remains "really good for a group" with a "sense of adventure"; P.S. "downstairs is a private club", an "ex-Madonna spot."

Mon Plaisir 🅩 *French*

19 | 17 | 17 | £39

Covent Garden | 21 Monmouth St., WC2 (Covent Garden/Leicester Sq.) | 020-7836 7243 | fax 7240 4774 | www.monplaisir.co.uk

For "the genuine feel of France in Covent Garden", theatre-goers trek to this old-timer, a "solid" choice for "bourgeois cuisine" with "heavy flavours" and "no surprises" ("exactly as we like it"); there's also "speedy service" for the pre-curtain crowd.

Montpeliano ❶ *Italian*

18 | 17 | 21 | £49

Knightsbridge | 13 Montpelier St., SW7 (Knightsbridge) | 020-7589 0032 | fax 7838 0268

With a "conservatory-type room" and "quirky decor" dominated by "beautiful pictures of Hollywood stars", this "1970s Italian" in Knightsbridge "never disappoints" fans of its "simple" *cucina*; but modernists moan this "old standby" "seems a bit tired in all aspects."

	FOOD	DECOR	SERVICE	COST

Monza *Italian* ▽ | 18 | 17 | 18 | £55

Knightsbridge | 6 Yeoman's Row, SW3 (Knightsbridge/South Kensington) |
020-7591 0210 | fax 7591 0210 | www.monza-restaurant.co.uk
Its location down a Knightsbridge backstreet makes this "intimate
Italian" "a favourite for *les liaisons dangereuses*" – even if the Formula
One–themed decor seems ill-suited to romance.

☑ Morgan M Ⓜ *French* | 26 | 18 | 22 | £60

Islington | 489 Liverpool Rd., N7 (Highbury & Islington) | 020-7609 3560 |
www.morganm.com
"It makes all the difference in the world that culinary genius/propri-
etor Morgan M actually rolls up his sleeves in the kitchen" of this
"fine-dining oasis" "in a remote part of Islington"; his "magical" New
French fare "gladdens the palate", removing any sting from some
"snooty" staffers (usually, though, "service is spot-on"); P.S. "the
garden menu is seriously good" for vegetarians.

☑ Moro Ⓢ *Mediterranean* | 25 | 18 | 22 | £45

Clerkenwell | 34-36 Exmouth Mkt., EC1 (Angel/Farringdon) |
020-7833 8336 | fax 7833 9338 | www.moro.co.uk
A "genius, traditional yet creative combo of Spanish and Moroccan"
dishes, all "served with care and attention", ensures this Exmouth
Market Med "is enjoyable in all respects" – except for the "elbow-to-
elbow", "canteen-style" seating, perhaps.

Morton's Ⓢ *French* | 22 | 23 | 23 | £63

Private club; inquiries: 020-7518 2982
"Find a member (if you are not one already)" to gain access to this
private club that's equally "good for power lunches" or a "romantic
experience", given its "lovely view of Berkeley Square"; the New
French dishes "deserve a special mention for freshness and selection", and they're "beautifully presented" by "friendly staff";
P.S. "not to be confused with the international steak chain."

Mosaico Ⓢ *Italian* | - | - | - | E

Mayfair | 13 Albemarle St., W1 (Green Park/Piccadilly Circus) |
020-7409 1011 | fax 7493 0081 | www.mosaico-restaurant.co.uk
"Neither too fussy or too informal", this low-profile, "classy Italian
in classy Mayfair" makes a "solid business-lunch type of place" with
"impressive" fare (including a "good-value set meal") and "happy-
to-see-you" service.

Moshi Moshi Sushi *Japanese* | 19 | 10 | 13 | £23

Canary Wharf | Canary Wharf Waitrose | Canada Pl., E14 (Canary Wharf) |
020-7512 9201 | fax 7512 9685
City | Unit 24, Liverpool St. Station, upper level, EC2 (Liverpool St.) |
020-7247 3227 | fax 7247 3227 Ⓢ
www.moshimoshi.co.uk
"Run by people who care more about fish than look-alike restaurant"
rivals, this "conveyor-belt" Japanese duo "above Liverpool Street
Station" and "inside the Canary Wharf Waitrose's food hall" are
"worth the slightly premium prices" for their "tasty sushi"; just "be
prepared to queue during lunchtime."

		FOOD	DECOR	SERVICE	COST

☑ Mosimann's ⑤ *Eclectic* — 25 | 25 | 25 | £64

Private club; inquiries: 020-7235 9625

It "feels like a special occasion when you walk into" this "exquisite private dining" club in a "re-fitted church" in Belgravia, where chef-owner "Anton Mosimann does things of considerable integrity" with his Eclectic menu (which "changes little, but why should it when it's this good?"); staff's "excellent", and the decor's "elegant" – so "can you really ask for more? maybe make it a non-member restaurant?"

Motcombs *Eclectic* — 20 | 17 | 19 | £44

Belgravia | 26 Motcomb St., SW1 (Knightsbridge/Sloane Sq.) | 020-7235 6382 | fax 7245 6351 | www.motcombs.co.uk

"This place has been around forever" (over 40 years in fact) and "doesn't try to be anything it isn't" – just a "clubby", "comfortable" "very Belgravia" drinking/dining option that "locals love" as a "great place to meet people", especially at the upstairs wine bar; food-wise, the Eclectic menu is "basic" but "always dependable."

Moti Mahal ⑤ *Indian* — ∇ 25 | 21 | 24 | £40

Covent Garden | 45 Great Queen St., WC2 (Covent Garden/Holborn) | 020-7240 9329 | fax 7836 0790 | www.motimahal-uk.com

"An inventive blend of traditional and new Indian cuisine" is the trump card of this "modern"-looking (you can "watch the chefs cook" in the glass-enclosed kitchen) Covent Gardener; near-"impeccable service" and "reasonable prices" for the area add to this "posh" place's appeal.

Mr. Chow ◐ *Chinese* — 22 | 19 | 19 | £61

Knightsbridge | 151 Knightsbridge, SW1 (Knightsbridge) | 020-7589 7347 | fax 7584 5780 | www.mrchow.com

"The decor is a bit long in the tooth" (all "the black lacquer scares me"), the "service stand-offish" and the prices just "silly", but this Knightsbridge Mandarin "lives up to its own celebrity and reputation in terms of food quality" – indeed, "one gets easily addicted" to its Peking duck and noodles; hence, it remains home to both an "über-trendy" and "business-meetings crowd" "busy looking at each other."

Mr. Kong ◐ *Chinese* — 21 | 11 | 17 | £28

Chinatown | 21 Lisle St., WC2 (Leicester Sq.) | 020-7437 7341 | www.mrkongrestaurant.com

"Newly refurbed" after a "kitchen fire shut them down" last year (the decor scores higher, though it's still "dull"), this "affordable" veteran venue offers Cantonese fare that's "still fresh, good" and "not the usual run-of-the-mill Chinatown dishes"; there's "quick service if you're in a rush", and with last orders at 2 AM, it's a "good late-night option."

Mu *European* — - | - | - | VE

(fka Mju)

Knightsbridge | Millennium Hotel Knightsbridge | 17 Sloane St., 1st fl., SW1 (Knightsbridge) | 020-7201 6330 | fax 7201 6353 | www.millenniumhotels.co.uk

Deemed "a nice surprise for a hotel restaurant", this "pricey" Knightsbridge dining room offers "experimentally good" Modern

European fare with some "funky" combinations (e.g. foie gras with raspberry sorbet), backed by a new-world wine list; but malcontents mutter it's "missing something – vibe?"

☒ Nahm *Thai*

FOOD	DECOR	SERVICE	COST
24	21	24	£65

Belgravia | Halkin Hotel | 5 Halkin St., SW1 (Hyde Park Corner) | 020-7333 1234 | fax 7333 1100 | www.nahm.como.bz

It might clock in "at a hundred times the price in Thailand", but this "royal Thai" titillates with truly "outstanding", "innovative" dishes, served by "knowledgeable staff"; if some feel the "functional" Belgravia hotel setting is a "downside", and it "should be better" given the big bill, the majority deem it "worth it (in the same sense that Dom Perignon is worth it)."

Nam Long-Le Shaker ●☒ *Vietnamese*

FOOD	DECOR	SERVICE	COST
-	-	-	M

South Kensington | 159 Old Brompton Rd., SW5 (Gloucester Rd./South Kensington) | 020-7373 1926 | fax 7373 6046

"An old friend" to many for its "lively late-night [bar] scene" ("love those Flaming Ferrari cocktails"), this "funky" South Kensingtonian also offers Vietnamese vittles that are "good (enough)."

Nancy Lam's Enak Enak *Indonesian*

FOOD	DECOR	SERVICE	COST
-	-	-	M

Battersea | 56 Lavender Hill, SW11 (Clapham Common/Clapham Junction Rail) | 020-7924 3148 | fax 8241 6710 | www.nancylam.com

"Outrageous behaviour from the owner", TV chef Nancy Lam, when she's in residence adds "an extravagance of kitsch" to the "competent cuisine" of this Indonesian eatery; most think its "worth a journey with friends and family" to Battersea.

Nando's *Portuguese*

FOOD	DECOR	SERVICE	COST
-	-	-	I

Bloomsbury | 57-59 Goodge St., W1 (Goodge St.) | 020-7637 0708
Covent Garden | 66-68 Chandos Pl., WC2 (Charing Cross/Covent Garden) | 020-7836 4719
Marylebone | 113 Baker St., W1 (Baker St.) | 020-3075 1044
Bethnal Green | 366 Bethnal Green Rd., E2 (Bethnal Green) | 020-7729 5783
Blackheath | 16 Lee High Rd., SE13 (Lewisham Rail) | 020-8463 0119
Camden Town | 57-58 Chalk Farm Rd., NW1 (Chalk Farm)
Swiss Cottage | 252-254 West End Ln., NW6 (West Hampstead Rail) | 020-7794 1331
Islington | 324 Upper St., N1 (Angel)
Brixton | 59-63 Clapham High St., SW4 (Clapham Common/Clapham North) | 020-7622 1475
Bayswater | 63 Westbourne Grove, W2 (Bayswater/Royal Oak) | 020-7313 9506
www.nandos.co.uk
Additional locations throughout London

Rapidly expanding "all over London, this chain" is "great for families", or any punter panting for poultry Portuguese-style, with its simple formula of "consistently good", "excellent-value" flame-grilled "chicken in pitta, buns or plain", marinated in "amazing peri-peri" (that's chilli-chilli) sauce; "you order at the counter", after which "pleasant, helpful" staff "bring the food when it is ready."

	FOOD	DECOR	SERVICE	COST

Napket *Sandwiches* | - | - | - | I

NEW Mayfair | 6 Brook St., W1 (Bond St./Oxford Circus) |
020-7495 8562 Ⓢ
NEW Piccadilly | 5 Vigo St., W1 (Piccadilly Circus) |
020-7734 4387
Chelsea | 342 Kings Rd., SW3 (South Kensington) | 020-7352 9832
www.napket.com

A "great concept for fast food" fawn fashionistas of this new chichi
chain: "amazingly fresh salads", sandwiches and cakes compiled
from artfully arranged food displays, then served amidst a swank
setting of gauze-wrapped chandeliers, clear chairs and "imaginative
iPod stations" on the communal tables; self-styled suppliers of 'snob
food', they're "all the rage" "to avoid the riffraff" when you lunch.

Narrow, The *British* | 22 | 20 | 19 | £31

Limehouse | 44 Narrow St., E14 (Limehouse DLR) | 020-7592 7950 |
www.gordonramsay.com

It's "difficult to get a table on the spur of the moment, which under-
mines the point of a gastropub"; that said, this Limehouse "old-style
English" boozer, which was Gordon "Ramsay-d" last year, is "a
pleasant experience", with "absolutely delicious" "fantastic value"
"comfort food" and a "surprisingly comprehensive wine list"; if "staff
are friendly, but somewhat distracted", "truly outstanding views" of
the Thames from the recently "reworked terrace" compensate.

National Dining Rooms, The *British* | 20 | 20 | 19 | £36

Soho | The National Gallery, Sainsbury Wing | Trafalgar Sq., WC2
(Charing Cross) | 020-7747 2525 | fax 7747 2496 |
www.thenationalcafe.com

"When you've overdosed on art" in the National Gallery, take a
break at its "airy" dining room with a "delightful" view of Trafalgar
Square and "well-sourced, interestingly cooked" Modern British fare
"that any museum would be proud of"; even if staff "don't move
faster than the portraits on the wall", most agree it's a "fine choice"
"for a quiet, grown-up lunch" (dinner on Wednesday only).

Nautilus Fish Ⓢ *Seafood* | ▽ 22 | 6 | 19 | £22

Hampstead | 27-29 Fortune Green Rd., NW6 (West Hampstead) |
020-7435 2532

A cross between a "sit-down restaurant" and "a chippy", this West
Hampstead seafooder "is not posh", but it is "one of those rare food
bargains in London", serving "fresh, light" fish 'n' chips, alongside a
"fine choice" of other "fried or grilled" options.

New Culture Revolution *Chinese* | 18 | 10 | 15 | £17

Islington | 42 Duncan St., N1 (Angel) | 020-7833 9083
Chelsea | 305 King's Rd., SW3 (Sloane Sq.) | 020-7352 9281
Notting Hill | 157-159 Notting Hill Gate, W11 (Holland Park/
Notting Hill Gate) | 020-7313 9688
www.newculturerevolution.co.uk

"Tried and tested (maybe it should be called Old Culture Revolution
now?)", this "cheap" Chinese trio please the masses with "noodles
and dumplings galore", all "freshly prepared" and served "quick";

they're "great after work or a low-key date with those unimpressed by capitalist baubles" (the surrounds are pretty "utilitarian").

☒ New Tayyabs ◐ *Pakistani*   28 | 14 | 16 | £18

Whitechapel | 83-89 Fieldgate St., E1 (Aldgate/Whitechapel) | 020-7247 6400 | fax 7377 1257 | www.tayyabs.co.uk

"Why bother with Brick Lane" when there's this "wonderful" Whitechapel warhorse whose "authentic Pakistani food" is "absolutely tops"; there's "always a queue", it's always "cramped" and you "always feel like you're getting rushed out", but the cuisine "quality makes you look past any shortcomings."

New World ◐ *Chinese*   19 | 12 | 13 | £22

Chinatown | 1 Gerrard Pl., W1 (Leicester Sq.) | 020-7434 2508 | fax 7287 8994

This huge Cantonese "stands out from the crowd" of Chinatowners for its "super-consistent dim sum" in daytime; it's a "great place to take visitors who'll be bemused by the airline-style trolleys", piloted by servers who may be "rude", but are "always quick."

Nicole's ⧉ *European/Mediterranean*   21 | 16 | 21 | £49

Mayfair | Nicole Farhi | 158 New Bond St., W1 (Bond St./Green Park) | 020-7499 8408 | fax 7409 0381

"For a quick bite amongst the fashionable crowd", this "lively" eatery "in the basement of Nicole Farhi" has a "simple", "reasonably priced" Modern European–Med menu that's "better than you might expect" – even if sceptics sniff the store should "stick to clothes."

☒ Nobu Berkeley St ◐ *Japanese*   26 | 22 | 20 | £70

Mayfair | 15 Berkeley St., W1 (Green Park) | 020-7290 9222 | fax 7290 9223 | www.noburestaurants.com

"The coolest of the London Nobus", this branch near Berkeley Square swings with a "terrific scene", both at the "stylish downstairs bar" jammed with "hedge fund managers, their rich clients" and "eye candy" (which includes the "cute staff") and in the upstairs dining room, with its "exciting" Japanese-Peruvian fare, "super sushi and wood-fired oven delights"; if it's "not as perfect as the Old Park Lane" original – in particular, "the service can be spotty with attitude" – both the prices and the setting are "more relaxed."

☒ Nobu London *Japanese*   27 | 20 | 22 | £75

Mayfair | Metropolitan Hotel | 19 Old Park Ln., W1 (Hyde Park Corner) | 020-7447 4747 | fax 7447 4749 | www.noburestaurants.com

"Despite it's being a big-name celebrity hangout, the cuisine remains top-notch" at Nobu Matsuhisa's "fine-dining mainstay" in Mayfair; the "simple" yet "inspired" Japanese-Peruvian creations and "inventive" sushi are presented by "polite but not obsequious" servers amidst "sophisticated", if slightly "dated" decor; given the number of Nobus nowadays, it's "getting to feel like an international chain" cynics say, but the quality's just "so damn consistent", few really care – even if they have to "pay exorbitant sums"; P.S. some "prefer to eat at the sushi bar where they've always found space without reservations."

	FOOD	DECOR	SERVICE	COST

Noor Jahan *Indian* | 22 | 13 | 20 | £31 |

South Kensington | 2A Bina Gdns., SW5 (Gloucester Rd./
South Kensington) | 020-7373 6522

Paddington | 26 Sussex Pl., W2 (Lancaster Gate) | 020-7402 2332 |
fax 7402 5885 ☻

Though lacking "the glitz of new places", this fortysomething, "frenetic" duo in South Kensington and Paddington provide "properly
cooked", "reliable and affordable" Indian fare and service that, "despite being busy, doesn't rush you when you're done."

NEW Northbank *British* | - | - | - | E |

Blackfriars | 1 Paul's Walk, EC4 (Blackfriars) | 020-7329 9299 |
www.northbankrestaurant.com

In a secluded spot by the Millennium Bridge, this newcomer "tries hard
to be sophisticated", with a "great view over the river to the Tate
Modern" and sleek decor (smoked mirrors, funky retro lighting); pio-
neering proponents call the West Country–oriented British menu a
"huge improvement since the days of Just The Bridge", its predeces-
sor, whilst the more pessimistic pout about "patchy service."

Z North Sea ⑤ *Seafood* | 24 | 13 | 19 | £23 |

Bloomsbury | 7-8 Leigh St., WC1 (King's Cross/Russell Sq.) |
020-7387 5892 | fax 7388 9770

A "long-time favourite for sit-down fish 'n' chips" ("if the fish were
any fresher, they'd swim"), this Bloomsbury seafooder "off the
beaten tourist path" is a "simple place, but good for the basics"; the
"dated decor isn't so bad given the back-dated prices."

Notting Grill *British/Chophouse* | 21 | 17 | 20 | £47 |

Notting Hill | 123A Clarendon Rd., W11 (Holland Park/Ladbroke Grove) |
020-7229 1500 | fax 7229 8889 | www.awtrestaurants.com

This "cosy Notting Hill favourite" run by TV chef Antony Worrall
Thompson features "fantastic beef" and a speciality roast pig ("runs
out early") on a "consistent" chophouse menu; the "friendly atmosphere" makes it "most enjoyable", now if only it weren't "so tough to
find a taxi to take your full tummy home" non-W11 residents whimper.

Notting Hill Brasserie *European* | 25 | 22 | 23 | £50 |

Notting Hill | 92 Kensington Park Rd., W11 (Notting Hill Gate) |
020-7229 4481 | fax 7221 1246

"Perfect for a romantic dinner à deux or a convivial one with friends",
this "nicely laid-out" place in Notting Hill offers an "upscale", but "not
outrageously expensive" experience of Modern European cuisine
"that tastes as good as it looks" brought by staff that are "almost in-
visible (in a good way)"; the jazz "pianist in the front is a nice touch."

Noura *Lebanese* | 20 | 17 | 18 | £40 |

Knightsbridge | 12 William St., SW1 | 020-7235 5900

Mayfair | 16 Curzon St., W1 (Green Park) | 020-7495 1050 |
fax 7495 1055 ☻

Piccadilly | 122 Jermyn St., SW1 (Piccadilly Circus) | 020-7839 2020 |
fax 7839 7700 ☻

(continued)

(continued)

Noura

Victoria | 16 Hobart Pl., SW1 (Victoria) | 020-7235 9444 |
fax 7235 9244 ◐
www.noura.co.uk

"Full of locals, media people and Arabian princesses", these "buzzy"
Lebanese have a "vast menu" of "delicious" dishes, proffered by
staff who are "attentive without being unctuous"; however, pessimists point out that "portions are big, but so are the prices."

Nozomi ◑ *Japanese*

| 19 | 21 | 15 | £58 |

Knightsbridge | 15 Beauchamp Pl., SW3 (Knightsbridge) | 020-7838 1500 |
fax 7838 1001 | www.nozomi.co.uk

"Footballers, wags and wannabes" wearing "more Dolce & Gabbana
than you can shake a stick at" "can all be seen here" at this "chichi"
Knightsbridge Japanese; "the food's ok" and the "service anony-
mous", but it's "the place to be today, so "enjoy whilst it's still hot",
and "don't forget to empty your piggy bank."

NEW Number Twelve ⊠ *European*

| - | - | - | M |

Bloomsbury | Ambassadors Hotel | 12 Upper Woburn Pl., WC1 (Euston) |
020-7693 5425 | fax 7388 9930 | www.numbertwelverestaurant.co.uk

The recent modernisation of the Ambassadors Hotel includes this
airy eatery/lounge with low-slung purple lighting that serves refined
Modern European cuisine with Italian leanings, boosted by "great-
value" prix fixes; early reports find it "a little bland", but it makes a
"great location for St. Pancras" and Euston stations nearby – indeed
dinner service begins at 5:30 PM with commuters in mind.

Nyonya *Malaysian*

| ∇ 22 | 14 | 17 | £22 |

Notting Hill | 2A Kensington Park Rd., W11 (Notting Hill Gate) |
020-7243 1800 | fax 7243 2006 | www.nyonya.co.uk

Ok, it's "not the most comfortable", "but the food is delicious
and cheapish" at this Notting Hill Malaysian; consisting of
"cramped" counters and stools to sit on, it works "best for a
quick bite pre–going out."

Odette's Ⓜ *European*

| 20 | 16 | 21 | £46 |

Primrose Hill | 130 Regent's Park Rd., NW1 (Chalk Farm) | 020-7586 8569 |
fax 7586 8362 | www.odettesprimrosehill.com

Fans feel the relatively "new management" (which arrived in 2007)
have made a "great success" of this Primrose Hill veteran, introduc-
ing a "creative" Modern European menu and "bright" yellow-hued
decor; but some advise "forget the upstairs silver service and head
downstairs to the wine cellar for an intimate setting" and an
additional tapas-bar menu.

Odin's ⊠ *British/French*

| 20 | 22 | 23 | £48 |

Marylebone | 27 Devonshire St., W1 (Baker St.) | 020-7935 7296 |
fax 7493 8309 | www.langansrestaurants.co.uk

"No fireworks – just soothing and pleasant" at this "intimate"
Marylebone stalwart ("owned by the Langan's people") that resembles a "classic English drawing room"; the "solid, reliable"

Traditional British–French fare is "well served", making this a "solid" site "for a special occasion."

Old Bull & Bush, The *European* | 12 | 18 | 13 | £27 |

Hampstead | Northend Rd., NW3 (Golders Green/Hampstead) | 020-8905 5456 | www.thebullandbush.co.uk

This "comfortable", "tarted-up pub" gets "packed", thanks to its 18th-century "historic setting" "not far from Hampstead Heath" (there's "great outdoor seating too"); "shame about the haphazard service" and "hit-or-miss" Modern European fare.

☑ Oliveto *Italian* | 21 | 14 | 18 | £33 |

Belgravia | 49 Elizabeth St., SW1 (Sloane Sq./Victoria) | 020-7730 0074 | fax 7823 5277 | www.olivolondon.com

"Huge thin-crust pizzas with creative toppings" and other "dependably delicious", "authentic Sardinian" dishes, "served with warmth and knowledge", pull "the posh set" to this "convivial" if "cramped" and "noisy" Belgravia Italian.

Olivo *Italian* | 19 | 13 | 16 | £39 |

Victoria | 21 Eccleston St., SW1 (Victoria) | 020-7730 2505 | www.olivolondon.com

An "Italian menu with a difference" makes this "sprightly" Sardinian near Victoria Station a "good neighbourhood standby"; "nothing to write home about", but it's "always full, which says something."

Olivomare ☒ *Italian/Seafood* | 21 | 19 | 18 | £43 |

Belgravia | 10 Lower Belgrave St., SW1 (Victoria) | 020-7730 9022 | www.olivolondon.com

"Make sure you're looking for seafood as there is hardly anything else on the menu" of "stunning simplicity" at this Sardinian "sister to Olivo and Oliveto"; the "stark interior" ("everything's in white") is "not to everybody's taste" (especially since it's "too noisy"), plus "service can be slow", but as it's relatively "reasonably priced" – especially the "luscious Sardinian wines" – most greet this as "a great addition" to Belgravia.

1 Lombard Street ☒ *French* | 23 | 21 | 20 | £53 |

City | 1 Lombard St., EC3 (Bank) | 020-7929 6611 | fax 7929 6622 | www.1lombardstreet.com

"Check out the who's who in finance" at this "civilised" City dweller that boasts "the Bank of England as a neighbour" (is that why they "feel they can charge a lot"?) and a New French menu with "plenty of choice", presented by staff who "love to serve", albeit at a "snail-like" pace; if it's "not as much fun as the Brasserie" up front, its "central location is in its favour."

1 Lombard Street Brasserie ☒ *European* | 19 | 18 | 18 | £44 |

City | 1 Lombard St., EC3 (Bank) | 020-7929 6611 | fax 7929 6622 | www.1lombardstreet.com

Whilst "noisier than the restaurant" it fronts, due to "great buzzy atmosphere" and, alas, "terrible acoustics", this "relaxed" brasserie-cum-bar under domed skylights is nonetheless "perfect for a business lunch" or "quick meeting with a head-hunter" over "reliable" Modern European fare; however, "service can be hit-or-miss", and it's all "a little overpriced" (as a "regular City haunt" tends to be).

One-O-One *French/Seafood* | 23 | 17 | 21 | £65 |

Knightsbridge | Sheraton Park Tower | 101 Knightsbridge, SW1 (Knightsbridge) | 020-7290 7101 | fax 7201 7884 | www.oneoonerestaurant.com

"With cool decor befitting the marine theme" of its menu, this "recently renovated space" in the Sheraton Park Tower is touted for its "toe-curlingly good, delicate" seafood, although a few find the French-accented *petits plats* "concept confusing – not quite small plates, but not quite regular size either"; the "bargain business lunch" belies the "overpriced hotel" image.

NEW Only Running Footman *British* | 18 | 16 | 16 | £34 |

Mayfair | 5 Charles St., W1 (Green Park) | 020-7499 2988 | www.therunningfootman.biz

"From the owners of The Bull" comes this "convivial" newcomer with a "lively bar scene downstairs" ("a good place to pick up a hedge-fund boy" or girl) and "slightly uninteresting", "square room upstairs" serving "meaty", "hearty Traditional British fare"; the "friendly staff" "are still learning the ropes", but given that it's "in the middle of Mayfair, without the Mayfair prices", several suggest you "run there"; N.B. the name refers to the 18th-century custom of torch-bearing servants dashing ahead of a carriage to light the road.

Oriel *European* | 15 | 16 | 14 | £31 |

Chelsea | 50-51 Sloane Sq., SW1 (Sloane Sq.) | 020-7730 2804 | fax 7730 7966

"Try to land a window table to watch the action on Sloane Square" at this "usually crowded" "brasserie-cum-bar"; "if you can take the decibels, cheek-by-jowl" seating and "slow service", the "plain" Modern European fare will do for a "pit stop after shopping."

Original Lahore Kebab House ● *Pakistani* | 25 | 8 | 16 | £17 |

Whitechapel | 2-10 Umberston St., E1 (Aldgate East/Whitechapel) | 020-7481 9737 | fax 7265 0718

Highgate | 148-150 Brent St., NW4 (Hendon Central) | 020-8203 6904 www.lahore-kebabhouse.com

"Still the best of the East End's Pakistani curry caffs despite expanding to 10 times its original size", this Whitechapel wonder is "worth searching out" for "unsurpassed" "grilled meats and breads hot from the tandoor" at "dirt-cheap" prices (being BYO helps too); whilst "the wait to get a table can be annoying", once in, you're served by some of the "nicest people"; N.B. the Hendon Central sibling is smaller.

Original Tagine 🗷 *Moroccan* | - | - | - | E |

Marylebone | 7A Dorset St., W1 (Baker St.) | 020-7935 1545

"If you are looking for belly dancers and cushion seating, don't bother" booking this "modern" Marylebone Moroccan – it's the "unspeakably good", "perfectly seasoned tagines" that are "the main draw" (though the "lively" setting, with "beautifully tiled" tables and "doors that open onto the street in summer", is nice enough); "what the servers lack in smoothness, they more than make up for in enthusiasm."

Orrery *French* | 24 | 21 | 23 | £67 |

Marylebone | 55 Marylebone High St., W1 (Baker St./Regent's Park) | 020-7616 8000 | fax 7616 8080 | www.orreryrestaurant.co.uk

What with "smart, updated French cuisine" ("don't miss the cheese trolley"), "chilled-out waiters" and "a jewellike setting above the Conran's" in Marylebone, this "peaceful haven" is "perfect for a romantic date"; of course, it comes at a "high cost, but it's worth it all" advocates agree; post-Survey, "however, a new chef has been installed, which could change views."

Orso ● *Italian* | 19 | 16 | 18 | £44 |

Covent Garden | 27 Wellington St., WC2 (Covent Garden) | 020-7240 5269 | fax 7497 2148

"A gathering place for the theatre crowd" (but "avoiding thundering hordes of tourists"), this '80s Theatreland eatery gets you to the show on time with "respectable", "unpretentious Italian food" and "cheerful" servers; if the place seems "a bit passé", the plus side is there's "no 'sorry we're booked' b.s."

☑ Oslo Court ☒ *French* | 26 | 17 | 28 | £52 |

St. John's Wood | Charlbert St., off Prince Albert Rd., NW8 (St. John's Wood) | 020-7722 8795 | fax 7586 7695

"Enjoy being pampered in this fluffy pink temple to a bygone age", a "wonderfully eccentric" St. John's Wood eatery that runs "like a well-oiled machine"; expect to "leave the table groaning" after "generous portions" of Classic French fare that "wouldn't have been adventurous in the '60s", but is amazing anyway (the "highlight is the dessert presentation"); yes, the "decor's like a Berni Inn" and it's "surprisingly busy at all times" with "seniors and celebrations", but "you can't beat it for old-fashioned decadence."

Osteria Antica Bologna *Italian* | ▽ 17 | 12 | 15 | £29 |

Battersea | 23 Northcote Rd., SW11 (Clapham Junction Rail) | 020-7978 4771 | fax 7978 4771 | www.osteria.co.uk

Well, it might look "old hat", but this "neighbourhood bistro" in Battersea serves up "good, rustic Italian" victuals ("specials are best"); sceptics say "standards have slipped" of late, especially servicewise; P.S. "don't get stuck in the corridor area."

☑ Osteria Basilico ● *Italian* | 22 | 17 | 18 | £36 |

Notting Hill | 29 Kensington Park Rd., W11 (Ladbroke Grove/ Notting Hill Gate) | 020-7727 9957 | fax 7229 7980 | www.osteriabasilico.co.uk

"They serve all the classics", including "earthy" pizzas, at this "noisy" Notting Hill Italian, with a "cosy" – ok, "quite claustrophobic" – atmosphere; service is "spotty", even "pretty arrogant sometimes", but "once they know you, you are treated like family"; hence, "tables are hard to come by."

	FOOD	DECOR	SERVICE	COST

Osteria dell'Arancio *Italian* ▽ 20 | 18 | 14 | £42

Chelsea | 383 King's Rd., SW1 (Sloane Sq./South Kensington) | 020-7349 8111 | fax 7349 8123 | www.osteriadellarancio.co.uk

"It looks and feels like a cafe", but this whimsical World's End Italian is welcomed for its "wholesome", "authentic" cooking and "excellent wine list", dominated by Marche region labels; staff is "friendly", but sometimes "it seems like it was their first time" at table; at least the artwork, including a portrait of Queen Elizabeth II with a salami crown, is diverting.

NEW Osteria Stecca *Italian* – | – | – | E

St. John's Wood | 1 Blenheim Terrace, NW8 (St. John's Wood) | 020-7328 5014 | www.osteriastecca.com

Well-travelled chef Stefano Stecca (most recently at Brunello) returns to the Rosmarino site, taking over the St. John's Wood space as debutant owner; he's offering tastes of his native Romagna region on a polished Italian menu featuring reasonably priced prix fixe options; the elegant, white-walled venue is on the petite side, but gets a boost from an airy conservatory and terrace, as well as a bar serving hot and cold snacks.

Ⓩ Ottolenghi *Bakery/Mediterranean* 25 | 16 | 15 | £26

NEW Belgravia | 13 Motcomb St., SW1 (Knightsbridge) | 020-7823 2707 | fax 020-7235 0152

Islington | 287 Upper St., N1 (Angel) | 020-7288 1454 | fax 7704 1456

Notting Hill | 63 Ledbury Rd., W11 (Notting Hill Gate) | 020-7727 1121 www.ottolenghi.co.uk

"One enters with the intention to be virtuous and eat those great vegetables, but gets corrupted by the desserts on display" at these cafe/bakeries that "dare you to find something that isn't perfection" among the "sweet and savoury Mediterranean-toned" delights; less ideal is the service ("if only staff would smile more"), "military cafeteria-style communal tables" and "cramped conditions" (it's the "HQ of the stroller brigade"), so "best to opt for takeaway."

Ⓩ Oxo Tower *European* 21 | 25 | 20 | £58

South Bank | Oxo Tower Wharf | Barge House St., SE1 (Blackfriars/Waterloo) | 020-7803 3888 | fax 7803 3838 | www.harveynichols.com

"Perfect for a romantic night", to "impress clients" or just to "rest after walking the South Bank walk", the "breathtaking panoramic view" across the river to St. Paul's is "the reason to go" to this "simple, stylish" setting; "solid service" supplies the Modern European food that, if "not high on the creative side" is "quite good" – and "almost worth" "the limb it'll cost."

Ⓩ Oxo Tower Brasserie *Asian/Mediterranean* 18 | 22 | 17 | £47

South Bank | Oxo Tower Wharf | Barge House St., SE1 (Blackfriars/Waterloo) | 020-7803 3888 | fax 7803 3838 | www.harveynichols.com

"If you happen to be next to the window", "the views can't be beaten" from this 8th-floor South Bank brasserie; "the rest is silence" – or would be, if it weren't for the "clattery acoustics" "due to the bar", with its nightly live jazz; Shakespearean sarcasm aside, however, most say the "service is ok" and the Asian-Med food "above average", if "expensive" for the quality.

Özer Restaurant & Bar ➊ Turkish | 17 | 16 | 18 | £27 |

Marylebone | 5 Langham Pl., W1 (Oxford Circus) | 020-7323 0505 | fax 7323 0111 | www.sofra.co.uk

"Tasty, tender Turkish fare" "with a Western twist" is the reason why mezze mavens "always come back to" this "accommodating" Sofra group-owned site just off Regent Street; but the Ottoman-style decor is "a bit over the top" for some tastes.

NEW Pacific Oriental ⊠ Asian Fusion | - | - | - | E |

City | 52 Threadneedle St., EC2 (Bank) | 0871-704 4060 | www.orientalrestaurantgroup.co.uk

From the owners of Imperial City comes this reincarnated, relocated Asian, "gone upmarket" in its glitzy new digs (think columns, palm trees and gauzy curtains); a former City bank, the multilevel premises feature a brasserie and a formal restaurant with "surprisingly good" East-meets-West fare ranging from sushi to steamed pudding; despite "teething problems, it will become a favourite" early reports predict.

Painted Heron, The Indian | 23 | 18 | 20 | £39 |

Chelsea | 112 Cheyne Walk, SW1 (Sloane Sq.) | 020-7351 5232 | fax 7351 5213 | www.thepaintedheron.com

The "strange name belies" the "imaginative dishes" "suitable for an educated palate" at this "modern" Indian on Chelsea Embankment ("hard to find"); add in "friendly service" and it's clear why it's "not to be missed" – just "better be sure you can stand those spices."

Palmerston, The British | - | - | - | M |

Dulwich | 91 Lordship Ln., SE2 (East Dulwich Rail) | 020-8693 1629 | fax 8693 9662 | www.thepalmerston.net

"A shining example of the sensitively converted gastropub", this East Dulwich haunt with "oak-panelled atmosphere" beckons with an "excellent" Modern British menu that makes use of "locally sourced, seasonal food"; a few feel "prices are steep for what you get" – especially if you go digging into the quite "decent wine list."

NEW Pantechnicon Rooms, The European | - | - | - | E |

Belgravia | 10 Motcomb St., SW1 (Knightsbridge/Hyde Park Corner) | 020-7730 6074 | www.thepantechnicon.com

The Thomas Cubitt team have taken over the Turks Head boozer on a cosy, cobbled Belgravia street, offering upscale Modern European gastropub fare in two contrasting spaces; the bright, functional downstairs bar is tightly packed with high tables and stools, whilst upstairs is a clean-lined dining room with big windows, muted colours and traditional fixtures and fittings.

Papillon ➊ French | 21 | 19 | 18 | £45 |

South Kensington | 96 Draycott Ave., SW3 (South Kensington) | 020-7225 2555 | fax 7225 2554 | www.papillonchelsea.co.uk

In between the "very French" cuisine and the "classic" setting, you "could easily be in Paris" (vs. Brompton Cross) when you visit this bistro run by "charismatic owner" Soren Jessen, also of 1 Lombard Street; despite some "delightful preparations", however, overall "uneven experiences" make some feel it's "not worth a trip if you don't live locally" (and indeed, service seems better "if you're 'known'").

	FOOD	DECOR	SERVICE	COST

Pappagallo *Italian* ▽ 23 | 18 | 20 | £43

Mayfair | 54-55 Curzon St., W1 (Green Park) | 020-7629 2742 | fax 7493 4387 | www.pappagallocurzon.co.uk

"A wonderful place to while away a winter evening", this "pretty" green/grey–toned Mayfair "local" offers a "good selection of Italian cuisine", including "some unusual, if expensive selections"; "warm" service augments the "inviting" ambience.

NEW Paradise by way of Kensal Green *British* - | - | - | M

Kilburn | 19 Kilburn Ln., W1 (Kensal Green) | 020-8969 0098

Taking its name from the final line of a G.K. Chesterton poem, this "charming" Kilburn gastropub features dressed-down decor accented with Victorian touches (chandeliers, gilded mirrors, velvet drapes); the traditional ambience is offset by a Modern British menu as well as entertainment, both live and DJ-spun, several nights a week.

Park, The *Pan-Asian* 24 | 23 | 25 | £60

Knightsbridge | Mandarin Oriental Hyde Park | 66 Knightsbridge, SW1 (Knightsbridge) | 020-7201 3722 | fax 7235 2001 | www.mandarinoriental.com/london

"Everything at the Mandarin Oriental is done well, and this is no exception" enthusiasts say of the hotel's "beautiful", bright all-day dining room with "gorgeous views of Hyde Park" and a "brilliant", "unusual menu with heavy Pan-Asian influences", supported by service that's "gracious to all"; P.S there are also "fantastic special offers here", like unlimited wine from the sommelier's selection.

Pasha *Turkish* ▽ 19 | 16 | 19 | £32

Islington | 301 Upper St., N1 (Angel/Highbury & Islington) | 020-7226 1454 | fax 7226 1617

An "easily overlooked Upper Street stalwart", this "modern"-looking haunt is all about "traditional Turkish hospitality combined with" "mezzerific" Med fare; N.B. not to be confused with the similarly named eatery in South Ken.

Z Pasha ● *Moroccan* 21 | 25 | 15 | £46

South Kensington | 1 Gloucester Rd., SW7 (Gloucester Rd.) | 020-7589 7969 | fax 7581 9996 | www.pasha-restaurant.co.uk

"You can't help but feel you are in the Middle East" at this "warm", "exotic" Gloucester Road Moroccan where nightly "belly dancers that aren't bad to look at", "outside smoking pipes" and pretty "good food" set a "party mood"; however, some joke the place is "more like 'posh-a'", given the prices; P.S. it's "great for groups", so the amorously inclined should "ask for one of the booths for a romantic night."

	FOOD	DECOR	SERVICE	COST

Passione ⊠ *Italian*
22 | 13 | 19 | £45

Fitzrovia | 10 Charlotte St., W1 (Goodge St.) | 020-7636 2833 | fax 7636 2889 | www.passione.co.uk

"Eating here is always a pleasure" proclaim patrons passionate about this "Italian with a big heart" (despite "tight quarters") "in the middle of Fitzrovia"; some are "surprised at how expensive everything is", but the "fantastic food" and "willing-to-go-the-extra-mile service" "are worth it"; P.S. tip: "upstairs is more private and rarely full."

⊠ Patara *Thai*
24 | 19 | 20 | £36

Knightsbridge | 9 Beauchamp Pl., SW3 (Knightsbridge/South Kensington) | 020-7581 8820 | fax 7581 2155

Mayfair | 3-7 Maddox St., W1 (Oxford Circus) | 020-7499 6008 | fax 7499 6007

Soho | 15 Greek St., W1 (Leicester Sq./Tottenham Court Rd.) | 020-7437 1071 | fax 7437 1089

South Kensington | 181 Fulham Rd., SW3 (South Kensington) | 020-7351 5692 | fax 7351 5692
www.patarathailand.com

"Get your Thai fix with a civilised vibe" at this "bustling (but not too much)" quartet, serving "superb" "sophisticated" dishes "unlike anywhere else", augmented by "polite service"; if the "high standards" have "prices to match", these places remain "consistently one of the best in London."

Paternoster Chop House *British/Chophouse*
17 | 13 | 15 | £44

City | Warwick Ct., Paternoster Sq., EC4 (St. Paul's) | 020-7029 9400 | fax 7029 9409 | www.paternosterchophouse.com

"A butch steakhouse attracting City bankers", this Brit "never disappoints if expectations aren't unrealistic" advocates argue (certainly the "'beast of the day' special is always tasty"); but cynics give it the chop: "with packed-in tables, rude, hurried service" and a "deafening" noise level, it's "trading off its heavenly location close to St. Paul's."

Patisserie Valerie *French*
18 | 13 | 13 | £17

Belgravia | 17 Motcomb St., SW1 (Knightsbridge) | 020-7245 6161 | fax 7245 6161

Covent Garden | 8 Russell St., WC2 (Covent Garden) | 020-7240 0064 | fax 7240 0064

Knightsbridge | 215 Brompton Rd., SW3 (Knightsbridge) | 020-7823 9971 | fax 7589 4993

Knightsbridge | 32-44 Hans Crescent, SW1 (Knightsbridge) | 020-7590 0905

Marylebone | 105 Marylebone High St., W1 (Baker St./Bond St.) | 020-7935 6240 | fax 7935 6543

Piccadilly | 162 Piccadilly, W1 (Green Park) | 020-7491 1717

Soho | 44 Old Compton St., W1 (Leicester Sq.) | 020-7437 3466 | fax 7734 6133

City | The Pavillion Bldg. | 37 Brushfield St., E1 (Liverpool St.) | 020-7247 4906

Chelsea | 81 Duke of York Sq., SW3 (Sloane Sq.) | 020-7730 7094 | fax 7730 7094

(continued)

(continued)

Patisserie Valerie

Kensington | 27 Kensington Church St., W8 (High St. Kensington) |
020-7937 9574 | fax 7937 9574
www.patisserie-valerie.co.uk
Additional locations throughout London

"What's not to love" about the "decadent and delicious pastries"
and other "calorie-laden" delights at this "legendary" chain of
"cheapish" French bistros; sceptics snap these "coffee places trying
to be restaurants" are "not great for eating in" (i.e. "rushed, brash
service" and "indecent overcrowding"), but to most they're an "old
and valued friend", especially the "historic" Old Compton Street
branch, which "still feels like the Soho I remember."

Patterson's ⊠ *European*   24 | 20 | 22 | £49

Mayfair | 4 Mill St., W1 (Oxford Circus) | 020-7499 1308 |
fax 7491 2122 | www.pattersonsrestaurant.co.uk

"Away from the hustle and bustle" of Regent Street nearby, this
"family-owned" Mayfair Modern European is a place to "keep returning to, for fantastic food and gracious service", which "makes up
for the cramped surroundings"; all told, it's "atmospheric, classy
and 'impress someone' material."

Pearl *French*   25 | 23 | 23 | £59

Holborn | Renaissance Chancery Court Hotel |
252 High Holborn , WC1 (Holborn) | 020-7829 7000 |
fax 7829 9889 | www.pearl-restaurant.com

A "class act, at a price" characterises this chandeliered, "calm"
Holborn hotel dining room, which gleams with the "imaginative, as-
tute combinations" of chef Jun Tanaka's "memorable" New French
menu; adding to its lustre is "service that makes you feel special"
and an "excellent wine-by-the-glass selection" (pick your vintage
from the panelled 'cellar' in the centre of the room).

Pearl Liang *Chinese*   ▽ 18 | 17 | 15 | £35

Paddington | 8 Sheldon Sq., W2 (Paddington) | 020-7289 7000 |
www.pearlliang.co.uk

The "secret is out because Sunday lunch lines have started" at this
stylish "neighbourhood" yearling in a "strange location" near
Paddington Station; within its colourful decor – think fuchsia pink
hues and fish pond – it offers some "interesting renditions of classic
Chinese cuisine" at a "reasonable price", although some claim
it's only "ok."

Pellicano *Italian*   ▽ 22 | 17 | 18 | £38

Chelsea | 19-21 Elystan St., SW3 (South Kensington) | 020-7589 3718 |
fax 7584 1789 | www.pellicanorestaurant.co.uk

"With a loyal following amongst the locals", this "bright" eatery
in a "quiet street" near Chelsea Green makes a "decent neighbourhood Italian", with "enough space between tables to allow
for conversation over tasty seafood"; plus, "the prices aren't
too bad" either.

Pepper Tree *Thai*
20 | 11 | 16 | £15

Clapham | 19 Clapham Common S. Side, SW4 (Clapham Common) | 020-7622 1758 | fax 7720 7531 | www.thepeppertree.co.uk

"You may need to recalibrate the idea of cheap and cheerful" after checking out this Clapham Common Thai, with its combination of "really tasty" "decent portions" and little prices; however, the "noisy" digs and communal tables make it a "great stop to get the evening going", "rather than a romantic meal for two."

Pescatori ☒ *Mediterranean*
19 | 13 | 18 | £39

Mayfair | 11 Dover St., W1 (Green Park) | 020-7493 2652 | fax 7499 3180
Fitzrovia | 57 Charlotte St., W1 (Goodge St.) | 020-7580 3289 | fax 7580 0539
www.pescatori.co.uk

This "low-key" Med pair might look "well out of date", but they make "comfy, casual spots in the middle of 'in' spots" around Mayfair and Fitzrovia for "upmarket fish" dishes that *amici* attest "are different from the run-of-the-mill 'trat' fare" – and "served with a smile" to boot; but an across-the-board score slide supports sceptics who feel rather "hooked by the prices" for "average" eats.

Petersham, The *European*
- | - | - | VE

Richmond | Petersham Hotel | Nightingale Ln., TW10 (Richmond) | 020-8940 7471 | fax 8939 1002 | www.petershamhotel.co.uk

"Stunning Thames views", "delicate but balanced" Modern European cuisine and "lovely service" combine to make this Richmond hotel dining room "a most excellent experience", even if its "old-world charm" strikes cynics as just "old-fashioned."

Petersham Nurseries Café Ⓜ *European*
▽ 24 | 18 | 21 | £44

Richmond | Petersham Nurseries | Church Ln., off Petersham Rd., TW10 (Richmond) | 020-8605 3627 | www.petershamnurseries.com

"Never eaten in a garden centre?" – well, "belying its humble origins and dirt floor", this "casual, dog-friendly" Richmond Modern European (an actual greenhouse) offers "original", "flavoursome" fare, "fresh-tasting as you've never tasted before"; downsides are, it's "quite expensive" and only does lunch, but you can "finish the meal by wandering among the plants and herbs" you just ate.

❷ Pétrus ☒ *French*
28 | 25 | 27 | £91

Belgravia | The Berkeley | Wilton Pl., SW1 (Hyde Park Corner) | 020-7235 1200 | fax 7235 1266 | www.gordonramsay.com

"Managing to be both posh and unpretentious", The Berkeley's dining room provides a vividly coloured canvas for chef Marcus Wareing's "silky smooth execution of supreme" "modern" French dishes that are "always of the highest order"; "as its name would suggest, the wine list reads like a superb novel" and "nothing is a problem" for the "outstanding" staff; even if it will put "a big dent in your wallet", "you get what you pay for at Pétrus" – so "save up and go"; N.B. in late autumn 2008, Wareing will directly assume control of the space, and refashion it; former manager Gordon Ramsay will transfer the name to another site.

	FOOD	DECOR	SERVICE	COST

Pho ☒ *Vietnamese* — | — | — | M

NEW Fitzrovia | 3 Great Titchfield St., W1 (Oxford Circus) | 020-7436 0111 | fax 7436 2288

Smithfield | 86 St. John St., EC1 (Barbican/Farringdon) | 020-7253 7624 www.phocafe.co.uk

Noodle soup savourers go with the pho at this "cute Vietnamese" pair, the simple original near Smithfield Market and a Fitzrovia sib "with a modern interior" of bamboo tables and bright lights; both offer a "quick", well-priced menu majoring on the eponymous national dish, made from scratch and seasoned to taste; N.B. check out their coffee, made with beans that have been regurgitated by weasels.

Phoenix Palace ➊ *Chinese* 21 | 13 | 13 | £25

Marylebone | 3-5 Glentworth St., NW1 (Baker St.) | 020-7486 3515

Being "full of local Chinese testifies to the authenticity" of this "casual" Marylebone haunt, "serving the usual laundry list of dishes" – "many innovative", all "cheap", especially the "excellent dim sum"; on the downside, "the wine list needs help badly" (sake's the real specialty).

☒ Pied à Terre ☒ *French* 27 | 21 | 25 | £80

Fitzrovia | 34 Charlotte St., W1 (Goodge St.) | 020-7636 1178 | fax 7916 1171 | www.pied-a-terre.co.uk

"The *pied* may be *à terre*, but the food is heavenly" at this "Fitzrovia townhouse" where chef Shane Osborne "deserves all the accolades he gets" – and "the fortune one spends" – for his "interpretation of modern French fare" "with playful touches", backed by a "serious wine list"; all's served by "unobtrusive" but "helpful" staff in a "sophisticated", if "slightly claustrophobic" setting; "intimate rather than lively", it's "perfect for a quiet celebration."

Pigalle Club, The ☒ *European/French* ▽ 15 | 14 | 14 | £45

Piccadilly | 215 Piccadilly, W1 (Piccadilly Circus) | 020-7734 8142 | fax 7494 2022 | www.thepigalleclub.com

Surveyors "can't knock the entertainment" that plays nightly at this Piccadilly Circus supper club, named after (and decorated as) a famed 1940s cabaret; but even nostalgists note the "overpriced" Classic French–Modern Euro "food doesn't live up to" the venue.

Pig's Ear *British/French* 18 | 17 | 16 | £31

Chelsea | 35 Old Church St., SW3 (Sloane Sq.) | 020-7352 2908 | fax 7352 9321 | www.thepigsear.co.uk

Foodwise, "it makes no difference if you eat downstairs or in the [brasserielike] room upstairs", as it's all "good" – and "good-value" – at this "low-key neighbourhood" New French–Traditional British gastropub in Chelsea; but atmospherewise, the higher floor may be preferable, as "downstairs is a bit too pubby for me."

NEW Pinchito Tapas ☒ *Spanish* — | — | — | M

City | 32 Featherstone St., EC1 (Old St.) | 020-7490 0121 | www.pinchito.co.uk

A few "wish it were more like its Brighton sibling", the ab fab Pintxo People, but Spanish-seeking nibblers should still enjoy this new utilitarian-chic City Iberian with its wide choice of "great tapas – be sure to try a new type" – and "fantastic sangria"; sit at tables or at the counter ringing the open kitchen.

Ping Pong *Chinese*

| 19 | 17 | 15 | £24 |

Marylebone | 10 Paddington St., W1 (Baker St.) | 020-7009 9600 ◐
Marylebone | 29A James St., W1 (Bond St.) | 020-7034 3100 ◐
Soho | 45 Great Marlborough St., W1 (Oxford Circus) | 020-7851 6969 ◐
Fitzrovia | 48 Eastcastle St., W1 (Oxford Circus) | 020-7070 0550 ◐
Fitzrovia | 48 Newman St., W1 (Goodge St.) | 020-7291 3080
South Bank | Festival Terrace | Southbank Ctr., Belvedere Rd., SE1 (Waterloo) | 020-7960 4160 ◐
NEW **Tower Bridge** | Unit 3, Quayside, Tower Bridge House, St. Katharine's Docks, E1 (Tower Hill) | 020-7680 7850 ◐
NEW **Hampstead** | 83-84 Hampstead High St., NW3 (Hampstead) | 020-7433 0930 ◐
Notting Hill | 74-76 Westbourne Grove, W2 (Notting Hill Gate) | 020-7313 9832 | fax 7313 9849 ◐
www.pingpongdimsum.com

"Take a swing at Ping Pong" declare dim sum devotees of this young "cool, casually elegant" chain, offering "a huge selection" of 'little steamed parcels of deliciousness' – or should we say "delicious" "little parcels of steamedness"? – whichever, they're "fantastic for a quick bite" at a "fabulous price"; "the only problem is the wait" ("they don't take reservations for parties of less than eight"), but "the tea that sprouts in your cup is worth a trip in itself."

ⓩ Pizza Express *Pizza*

| 16 | 12 | 15 | £19 |

Covent Garden | 9-12 Bow St., WC2 (Covent Garden) | 020-7240 3443 | fax 7497 0131 ◐
Knightsbridge | 7 Beauchamp Pl., SW3 (Knightsbridge) | 020-7589 2355 | fax 7589 5159 ◐
Soho | 29 Wardour St., W1 (Leicester Sq./Piccadilly Circus) | 020-7437 7215 | fax 7494 2582
Blackfriars | 125 Alban Gate, London Wall, EC2 (Moorgate/St. Paul's) | 020-7600 8880 | fax 7600 8128
Battersea | 46-54 Battersea Bridge Rd., SW11 (Earl's Ct./Sloane Sq.) | 020-7924 2774
Chelsea | The Pheasantry | 152-154 King's Rd., SW3 (Sloane Sq.) | 020-7351 5031 | fax 7349 9844
Fulham | 363 Fulham Rd., SW10 (Fulham Broadway/South Kensington) | 020-7352 5300 ◐
Fulham | 895-896 Fulham Rd., SW6 (Parsons Green) | 020-7731 3117 | fax 7371 7884 ◐
Kensington | 35 Earl's Court Rd., W8 (Earl's Ct.) | 020-7937 0761 ◐
Notting Hill | 137 Notting Hill Gate, W11 (Notting Hill Gate) | 020-7229 6000 ◐
www.pizzaexpress.com
Additional locations throughout London

"The name implies casual takeaway", but "the actual offering is in fact more exciting" say fans of the "creative pizza" and other "cheap" Italian staples at this "no-frills" chain; the less-enthused say "eating here is like putting on an old pair of shoes: comforting, dependable – but then you remember why you haven't worn them" lately.

	FOOD	DECOR	SERVICE	COST

Pizza Metro ⓜ *Pizza* | − | − | − | M |

Battersea | 64 Battersea Rise, SW11 (Clapham Common/
Clapham Junction Rail) | 020-7228 3812 | fax 7738 0987

This "big" Battersea Italian gets "extremely noisy" with the constant
crowds chomping "fantastic pizza", baked in a traditional wood-
burning oven and served on a 'by-the-metre' system ("ok, a bit
gimmicky, but fun").

Pizza on the Park *Pizza* | 17 | 13 | 15 | £25 |

Belgravia | 11 Knightsbridge, SW1 (Hyde Park Corner) | 020-7235 7825 |
fax 7235 6853 | www.pizzaonthepark.co.uk

"An upscale version of Pizza Express" (which bought it in 2006), this
Italian-American "close to Hyde Park Corner" is "a decent place" for
wood-fired oven pizzas; but "when the right people are performing",
the "live jazz on certain nights" "adds another dimension" (and indeed "is better than the food").

PJ's Bar & Grill ❶ *American* | 16 | 17 | 18 | £31 |

Covent Garden | 30 Wellington St., WC2 (Covent Garden) |
020-7240 7529 | fax 7836 3426 | www.pjsgrill.net
Chelsea | 52 Fulham Rd., SW3 (South Kensington) | 020-7581 0025 |
fax 7584 0820 | www.pjsbarandgrill.co.uk

"Expect the usual pub fare, American-style" at these "noisy" "neighbourhood" hangouts in Chelsea ("perfect for Sunday brunch") and
Covent Garden ("perfect before a performance"); though sepa-
rately owned, both "can be crowded" and the "skills of the staff do
not match their beauty."

Planet Hollywood ❶ *American* | 10 | 15 | 13 | £25 |

Piccadilly | 13 Coventry St., W1 (Leicester Sq./Piccadilly Circus) |
020-7437 7639 | fax 7734 0835 | www.planethollywoodlondon.com
Jammed with "movie memorabilia and junk you can buy", this famous Piccadilly "theme restaurant" "provides an interesting decor"
even though "it's getting a little dated now"; the "average" American
burger fare is fine "if you're 15, or not from the U.K." and "need a fix
of back-home food"; otherwise, "why bother?"

Plateau *French* | 19 | 22 | 19 | £53 |

Canary Wharf | Canada Pl., 4th fl., E14 (Canary Wharf) | 020-7715 7100 |
fax 7715 7110 | www.plateaurestaurant.co.uk
Offering an "oasis from the hustle of the financial" institutions that
surround it, this New French with "expansive", "stylish" decor offers
a "good-value grill and bar" and more "elegant" dining room, both
serving "decent" eats; those whose interest has plateau-d, though,
claim "the only reason it's so busy" – and "expensive" – is that it's "one
of the few alternatives for an upscale meal around Canary Wharf."

Poissonnerie | 21 | 16 | 20 | £60 |
de L'Avenue ❶ⓩ *French/Seafood*

Chelsea | 82 Sloane Ave., SW3 (South Kensington) | 020-7589 2457 |
fax 7581 3360 | www.poissonneriedelavenue.com
"If you're looking for 'trendy', this isn't the place to come", but for a
"genteel", "gentle atmosphere", this "gorgeous old-fashioned fish

subscribe to ZAGAT.com

restaurant" at Brompton Cross fits the bill, from the Classic French preparations to the "refined service"; some sigh it seems "oh-so-tired", but the kind-hearted claim it "continues to remain a classic."

Popeseye 🗷⊅ *Chophouse*
— | — | — | M

Putney | 277 Upper Richmond Rd., SW15 (East Putney) | 020-8788 7733
Olympia | 108 Blythe Rd., W14 (Olympia) | 020-7610 4578 | fax 7376 7210
www.popeseye.com

An "example of how to stick to one thing, and do it well", this "simple", low-profile pair in Putney and Olympia use a Scottish butcher to supply "great steaks, and that's about it"; "the decor's a bit passé, but that's not what you come for."

Portal 🗷 *Portuguese*
∇ 20 | 23 | 19 | £53

Clerkenwell | 88 St. John St., EC1 (Barbican/Farringdon) | 020-7253 6950 | fax 7490 5836 | www.portalrestaurant.com

Strikingly designed, with a covered courtyard, this Clerkenwell eatery is a portal indeed into "innovative, upscale Portuguese" and other Med fare ("the house special, 20-hour cooked pork, is a sensation"), along with a "good selection of wines by the glass"; however, many patrons prefer to "plonk in the bar area for tapas and a chat" with the "laid-back – almost too so – but friendly staff."

Porters ● *British*
18 | 16 | 18 | £24

Covent Garden | 17 Henrietta St., WC2 (Covent Garden) | 020-7836 6466 | fax 7379 4296 | www.porters-restaurant.com

Have "fun sampling the interesting-sounding dishes", from bubble and squeak to spotted dick, at Lord Bradford's "safe", "solid" and "exceptional value" Covent Garden Traditional British; it's "justifiably popular with tourists" – and, admittedly, a few natives craving "food just like we got in school."

Portrait *British*
∇ 21 | 23 | 19 | £34

Soho | The National Portrait Gallery | 2 St. Martin's Pl., 3rd fl., WC2 (Charing Cross/Leicester Sq.) | 020-7312 2490 | fax 7925 0244 | www.searcys.co.uk

"Whilst it's the views that attract everyone to this spot" atop the National Portrait Gallery – a "magical" vista "over the rooftops of Trafalgar Square" – their "great" Modern British "offerings fit right in with their modern art"; just bear in mind "you are paying for the view, so enjoy it – and book in advance to get a table" that fronts it.

Potemkin ●🗷 *Russian*
— | — | — | E

Clerkenwell | 144 Clerkenwell Rd., EC1 (Chancery Ln./Farringdon) | 020-7278 6661 | fax 7278 5551 | www.potemkin.co.uk

Even if "the real stars are the simply wonderful flavoured vodkas", it's also "all good" on the menu at this red-and-purple-hued Clerkenwell Russian, which brings borscht and blinis to a city with few Soviet options; however, a few are ready to revolt over what they call "pretty shabby service."

| | FOOD | DECOR | SERVICE | COST |

Princess Garden ❶ *Chinese*
| | 22 | 18 | 19 | £48 |

Mayfair | 8-10 N. Audley St., W1 (Bond St./Marble Arch) |
020-7493 3223 | fax 7629 3130 | www.princessgardenofmayfair.com
"Favoured by the business-lunch crowd", this "Chinese with style"
"near the U.S. embassy" is "a bit pricey, but worth it" for "standard
dishes, reinvented and superbly executed"; the main debating point
is the service – "efficient" and "polite" vs. "slow and ungracious."

Prism ⌷ *British*
| | ▽ 20 | 18 | 20 | £51 |

City | 147 Leadenhall St., EC3 (Bank/Monument) | 020-7256 3888 |
fax 7191 6025 | www.harveynichols.com
"If you like art and the ambience of a large banking hall, you will enjoy"
this bright City venue – a "favourite for business", not least because,
with 120 seats, "they will never be fully booked if you need a table"
("cosy it is not"); if "nothing spectacular", the Modern British cooking and service are quite "good", and "worth the price" (a high one).

Providores, The/Tapa Room *Eclectic*
| | 22 | 16 | 18 | £40 |

Marylebone | 109 Marylebone High St., W1 (Baker St./Bond St.) |
020-7935 6175 | fax 7935 6877 | www.theprovidores.co.uk
"Wacky" Eclectic edibles, matched with "extremely nice New Zealand
wines", make for a merry time at this Marylebone fusion specialist
("Austral-Asian?") that offers "two dining options": the "always
busy", "tight" Tapa Room where you "stand in line to get a table",
and Providores, the "serene upstairs" ("more lonely", but you can
book); "too bad" about the "frankly bland" decor and "slow staff."

Quadrato *Italian*
| | - | - | - | VE |

Canary Wharf | Four Seasons Canary Wharf | 46 Westferry Circus, E14
(Canary Wharf) | 020-7510 1857 | fax 7510 1998 | www.fourseasons.com
"Customers are treated like kings and queens" – typical "Four
Seasons–quality" behaviour – at this smart, airy eatery that's something of "a secret place" in Canary Wharf; an "open kitchen provides
a stage to watch" the creation of "superb" Northern Italian fare, and
if some sigh about the slightly "soul-less" "setting just off the
lobby", few deny its status as a "go-to-impress" venue.

Quaglino's ❶ *European*
| | 18 | 21 | 16 | £54 |

St. James's | 16 Bury St., SW1 (Green Park) | 020-7930 6767 |
fax 7839 2866 | www.quaglinos.co.uk
Be "transformed into a '50s movie star on the grand sweeping staircase" of this "bustling, bold" behemoth, a St. James's fixture for 16
years; whilst the Modern European menu is "pretty consistent", it's
"not the main attraction", and as for "service – well, they tolerate
you"; in short, "a place more for the eye than a meal" – though drinks
in the "fantastic bar" above are an option too.

Quality Chop House ❶ *British/Chophouse*
| | 21 | 20 | 21 | £34 |

Farringdon | 92-94 Farringdon Rd., EC1 (Farringdon) | 020-7837 5093 |
fax 7833 8748 | www.qualitychophouse.co.uk
"Step into a time warp" – "even the cutlery feels like it's from the
1870s" – when you enter the original room of this "quirky" former

Farringdon workingman's eating house, with "old-school decor" that includes rather Dickensian bench seats (there's also a "less rustic" modern room with tables for two); the Traditional British cuisine is "competent, honest" and served with "care and attention."

Quilon *Indian*
25 | 21 | 23 | £50

Victoria | Crowne Plaza St. James Hotel | 41 Buckingham Gate, SW1 (St. James's Park/Victoria) | 020-7821 1899 | fax 7828 5802 | www.quilon.co.uk

The "pleasant interior is nothing swish", but when it comes to "perfectly cooked, delicately spiced" Southwest Indian cuisine – "quite unlike the usual, heavy food we're used to" – this venue "deserves more" credit; staff serve "with charm", and if it does "tend towards the expense-account crowd", it *is* adjacent to the corporate-y Crowne Plaza St. James.

Quirinale ☒ *Italian*
23 | 19 | 24 | £48

Westminster | 1 Great Peter St., SW1 (Westminster) | 020-7222 7080 | fax 7233 3080 | www.quirinale.co.uk

"A beacon in the gastronomic desert of Westminster", this "intimate" "underground space" is "where politicians hobnob with each other" over "imaginative" Italian cuisine brought by "charming, discreet service"; "loud at lunchtime", it seems subdued at dinner – indeed "more *fortissimo* might be better" some say.

NEW Quo Vadis ☒ *British*
- | - | - | E

Soho | 26-29 Dean St., W1 (Leicester Sq./Tottenham Court Rd.) | 020-7437 9585 | fax 7736 7593 | www.quovadissoho.co.uk

After displaying a love of all things Iberian with Fino and Barrafina, restaurateurs Sam and Eddie Hart turn Traditional British with their third venture – a revamp of the 1926 Soho stalwart; majoring on grilled meats and fish, the menu is served in a newly polished dining room with dark-tan banquettes; modern art and handsome stained-glass windows shielding diners from passing pedestrians' prying eyes; upstairs houses a pool room–equipped private club.

☒ Racine *French*
23 | 18 | 21 | £45

Knightsbridge | 239 Brompton Rd., SW3 (Knightsbridge/South Kensington) | 020-7584 4477 | fax 7584 4900

This "quintessentially French bistro" on Brompton Road "has a professional feel about it the moment you walk in", from the "punchy", "rustic" cooking, "generously served" with "Gallic charm", to the "close" but "buzzy" atmosphere "redolent of 1920s Paris"; "you can happily take your wife, girlfriend or dowager aunt"; P.S. last year's "departure of chef Henry Harris doesn't seem to have made a scrap of difference."

Rainforest Cafe *American*
11 | 21 | 15 | £25

Piccadilly | 20-24 Shaftesbury Ave., W1 (Piccadilly Circus) | 020-7434 3111 | fax 7434 3222 | www.therainforestcafe.co.uk

Although "not quite what a true rainforest is like", this "hectic" Piccadilly "playground" "keeps the little ones interested" with "fantasy" decor "full of automated animals"; adults may find it "a tough place to take", though, since the American "food is nothing to hoot about", and "they have to wait long hours to get served."

Randall & Aubin *British/Seafood* | 21 | 15 | 16 | £37 |

Soho | 14-16 Brewer St., W1 (Piccadilly Circus) | 020-7287 4447 | fax 7287 4488 | www.randallandaubin.co.uk

"Fast and flamboyant", this Soho ex-butcher's shop ("white-tiled walls", etc.) is a "fun, frantic place to grab some good, staple British grills" and "steady-as-she-goes seafood"; just bear in mind it "can be clubby and loud" at night, and the "casual service" "erratic."

Ransome's Dock *British/Eclectic* | ∇ 20 | 13 | 19 | £42 |

Battersea | 35-37 Parkgate Rd., SW11 (Sloane Sq./South Kensington) | 020-7223 1611 | fax 7924 2614 | www.ransomesdock.co.uk

Chef-owner "Martin Lam excels himself" at this unassuming Battersea dockside eatery, preparing "hearty" Modern British–Eclectic "fare with flair" – though oenophiles opine the global "wine list is the star of the show"; all's served in an "efficient" manner.

Raoul's *Mediterranean* | 20 | 15 | 13 | £23 |

St. John's Wood | 13 Clifton Rd., W9 (Warwick Ave.) | 020-7289 7313 | fax 7266 4752

Notting Hill | 105-107 Talbot Rd., W11 (Westbourne Park) | 020-7229 2400 | fax 7243 8070
www.raoulsgourmet.com

"If you don't mind the harried service" ("aloof" even at the best of times), this pair of "easy neighbourhood cafes" in St. John's Wood and Notting Hill offer a "tried-and-tested formula" of "reasonably priced", "reliable" Med fare; "the ultimate brunch venue", they can be "forgotten for dinner."

Rasa *Indian* | 24 | 13 | 19 | £33 |

Mayfair | 6 Dering St., W1 (Bond St./Oxford Circus) | 020-7629 1346 | fax 7637 0224 🗷

Fitzrovia | 5 Charlotte St., W1 (Tottenham Court Rd.) | 020-7637 0222 | fax 7637 0224

Islington | Holiday Inn King's Cross | 1 King's Cross Rd., WC1 (Farringdon/King's Cross) | 020-7833 9787 🗷

Stoke Newington | 55 Stoke Newington Church St., N16 (Stoke Newington Rail) | 020-7249 0344 | fax 7637 0224 ◑
www.rasarestaurants.com

For "a true taste adventure" that's "a million miles away from your local curry house", "you can't make a mistake coming" to this "friendly" chain, which offers "inventive, exotic South Indian (and mostly vegetarian)" fare (indeed, some branches' menus are entirely meat-free); just "don't be put off by the bright-pink decor."

☑ Rasoi Vineet Bhatia 🗷 *Indian* | 27 | 22 | 24 | £71 |

Chelsea | 10 Lincoln St., SW3 (Sloane Sq.) | 020-7225 1881 | fax 7581 0220 | www.rasoirestaurant.co.uk

"One reaches nirvana without trying" at this "transporting" townhouse in Chelsea, where owner-chef Vineet Bhatia uses a "spectacular variety of spices and flavours" to produce "adventurous", "refined" subcontinental fare – especially on the tasting menu, aka "seven courses to heaven"; add in the recently redone environs, "decorated like a peaceful candlelit temple" and "wonderful service", and "if there's a better Indian restaurant around, do let me know."

Real Greek Mezedopolio, The 🅢 *Greek*

16	12	15	£26

Hoxton | 14-15 Hoxton Mkt., N1 (Old St.) | 020-7739 8212 | fax 7739 4910

Real Greek Souvlaki & Bar, The *Greek*

Covent Garden | 60-62 Long Acre, WC2 (Covent Garden) | 020-7240-2292

Marylebone | 56 Paddington St., W1 (Baker St.) | 020-7486 0466

Clerkenwell | 140-142 St. John St., EC1 (Farringdon) | 020-7253 7234 | fax 7253 7235 🅢

Borough | Riverside House | 2A Southwark Bridge Rd., SE1 (London Bridge/Southwark) | 020-7620 0162

Putney | 31-33 Putney High St., SW15 (Putney Bridge) | 020-8788 3270 www.therealgreek.com

"Rediscover Greek food" ("true Greek, not Cypriot!") at this chain that's "a planet away from the stereotypical taverna"; the "honest" Hellenic fare is "reasonably priced", "but it's not much for your money" mutter malcontents, and it's brought "by people who don't want to be waiters"; P.S. in late 2006, the Hoxton original became Mezedopolio, a mezze-serving wine bar.

Rebato's 🅢 *Spanish*

-	-	-	M

Waterloo | 169 S. Lambeth Rd., SW8 (Stockwell) | 020-7735 6388 | www.rebatos.com

For "a genuine Spanish" experience near Stockwell, surveyors commend this unpretentious 25-year-old, with a bar serving "terrific tapas" and airy, skylit restaurant at the rear for "extremely rich, rib-sticking" and reasonably priced mains, all attended to by "lovely staff."

Red Fort *Indian*

24	21	23	£43

Soho | 77 Dean St., W1 (Oxford Circus/Tottenham Court Rd.) | 020-7437 2525 | fax 7434 0721 | www.redfort.co.uk

Fans fawn over this "fortifying Indian" in Soho, with its "innovative", "out-of-the-ordinary cuisine" – "not your mother's curry!" – and highly "attentive service"; even if the prices, like the reddish decor, veer towards the "high end", it "remains a great treat", especially "before or after the theatre."

NEW Red 'n' Hot *Chinese*

-	-	-	M

Chinatown | 59 Charing Cross Rd., WC2 (Leicester Sq.) | 020-7734 8796

From the chilly north of England comes this Southwestern Chinese hottie, offering authentically "spicy" Sichuan dishes (sliced boiled beef under chilli, fried pig intestine with red and green peppers) that are "not for the fainthearted"; early regulars advise ignore the buffet and order off the menu, and ignore the sad Chinatown locale, period.

Red Pepper *Italian*

▽ 20	11	13	£27

St. John's Wood | 8 Formosa St., W9 (Warwick Ave.) | 020-7266 2708 | fax 7266 5522

"A true local" "for the Maida Vale area", this place is "always packed", thanks to "brilliant" pizzas and other "casual" Italian eats; but the "narrowly spaced tables mean it's noisy and cramped" ("particularly downstairs"), and "service is too swift" for some tastes.

Refettorio ⊠ *Italian* — 22 | 16 | 20 | £47

Blackfriars | Crowne Plaza | 19 New Bridge St., EC4 (Blackfriars) | 020-7438 8052 | fax 7438 8088 | www.refettorio.com

"In a section of town" with limited culinary options, the Crowne Plaza's "inviting" dining room by Blackfriars Bridge makes a "trustworthy" spot for "unusual Italian concoctions", plus a "range of delicious cold meats" and cheese on display; pity that the "City location means City prices."

Refuel *European* — - | - | - | E

Soho | Soho Hotel | 4 Richmond Mews, W1 (Tottenham Court Rd.) | 020-7559 3000 | fax 7559 3003 | www.sohohotel.com

Serving three meals a day, this hotel eatery is "a good place to refuel" (ha ha) on "dependable" Modern European "fare at reasonable prices" – by Soho standards at least; however, "the eclectic decor misses the mark" for many, who reveal "the real treat are the mojitos at the adjacent bar."

Reubens *Deli/Jewish* — ▽ 15 | 10 | 13 | £35

Marylebone | 79 Baker St., W1 (Baker St.) | 020-7486 0035 | fax 7486 7079 | www.reubensrestaurant.co.uk

"Tastes like home cooking in the best possible way" are the kudos that kosher diners give the "loads of food" served at this Jewish deli in Marylebone; if sceptics snarl about the "service (or lack thereof)" and "high cost", at least "it's cheaper than a trip to Israel."

Rhodes Twenty Four ⊠ *British* — 24 | 24 | 24 | £66

City | Tower 42 | 25 Old Broad St., 24th fl., EC2 (Bank/Liverpool St.) | 020-7877 7703 | fax 7877 7725 | www.rhodes24.co.uk

"The views of London are stunning" from celebrity chef-owner Gary Rhodes' 24th-floor aerie in the City's tallest building, but the "limited" menu – "variations on classic English dishes" – "ain't half good" either (the signature bread and butter pudding "should not be missed"); the meal's "brilliantly conducted" by "relaxed waiters", and if it all "comes at a cost", at least the wine list offers "plenty for those not on expense accounts."

Rhodes W1 Brasserie *British* — ▽ 16 | 16 | 16 | £41

Marylebone | Cumberland Hotel | Great Cumberland Pl., W1 (Marble Arch) | 020-7479 3838 | fax 7479 3888 | www.garyrhodes.com

Vibrant and "rather loud", TV-chef Gary Rhodes' casual, cavernous Cumberland Hotel counterpart to his Restaurant adjacent serves "dependable Modern British grub" that, whilst "fine enough", seems "expensive for what it is"; hence, some prefer it as a drinking haunt.

Rhodes W1 Restaurant ⊠Ⓜ *British* — 23 | 21 | 23 | £74

Marylebone | Cumberland Hotel | Great Cumberland Pl., W1 (Marble Arch) | 020-7616 5930 | fax 7479 3888 | www.rhodesw1.com

A "stylish, decadent atmosphere" pervades celebrity chef Gary Rhodes' swanky, Swarovski-chandeliered venue (designed by Kelly

Hoppen) in Marble Arch; the "excellent Modern British menu makes choosing very difficult" – just "watch out for the effect on your wallet"; if the place "could do with a bit more buzz", the "unintrusive service" makes amends.

Rib Room, The *British/Chophouse* | 22 | 19 | 22 | £68 |

Belgravia | Jumeirah Carlton Tower Hotel | 2 Cadogan Pl., SW1 (Knightsbridge/Sloane Sq.) | 020-7858 7250 | fax 7823 1708 | www.jumeirahcarltontower.com

"When the carts come out and the waiters carve, it's a splendid feast" of "pricey, but utterly dependable" chophouse fare – or to put it another way, "luxuriously plain food for gourmands and fusspots" – at this "class act" in a plush Belgravia hotel; and if the "moderately constipated atmosphere" is not to everyone's taste, others say it's "just the place to calm down and feel well-fed, away from celebrity" frills.

Riccardo's *Italian* | 20 | 13 | 19 | £33 |

Chelsea | 126 Fulham Rd., SW3 (Gloucester Rd./South Kensington) | 020-7370 6656 | fax 7373 0604

Expect a "cosmopolitan crowd of mixed ages" at this "reliable" trattoria where the Italian fare is "surprisingly good, particularly the pasta", and considered "one of the best values for money in Chelsea" – hence "you don't mind the paper napkins and bare wooden tables"; "despite the place being crowded" constantly, staff "manage with verve."

☑ Richard Corrigan at | 26 | 21 | 23 | £71 |
Lindsay House ☒ *British/Irish*

Soho | 21 Romilly St., W1 (Leicester Sq./Piccadilly Circus) | 020-7439 0450 | fax 7437 7349 | www.lindsayhouse.co.uk

Chef-owner Richard Corrigan's "delightfully quirky" Soho townhouse with "hidden corners", "tiny rooms and lots of stairs to climb" is a "surefire gourmet experience", with "highly imaginative" Irish-Modern British cuisine "complemented by great service"; some seem "slightly disappointed", given the "huge prices", but it's been "a firm favourite" for a dozen years now.

Richoux *British* | 16 | 15 | 16 | £25 |

Knightsbridge | 86 Brompton Rd., SW3 (Knightsbridge) | 020-7584 8300 | fax 7589 8547
Mayfair | 41A S. Audley St., W1 (Bond St.) | 020-7629 5228 | fax 7493 4329
Piccadilly | 172 Piccadilly, W1 (Green Park/Piccadilly Circus) | 020-7493 2204 | fax 7495 6658
St. John's Wood | 3 Circus Rd., NW8 (St. John's Wood) | 020-7483 4001 | fax 7483 3810
www.richoux.co.uk

"In a setting right out of Edwardian times" (e.g. "old-fashioned"), this "classic, cutesy" chain of tearooms is a "solid standby" for Traditional British "comfort food" all day (cream tea or "breakfast is best"); if staff move at a "slow pace", that's "perfect" "after a hectic day of shopping."

| | FOOD | DECOR | SERVICE | COST |

Ristorante Semplice ☒ *Italian*   `24` `19` `24` `£56`
Mayfair | 10 Blenheim St., W1 (Bond St.) | 020-7495 1509 |
www.ristorantesemplice.com

"Simple (as the name suggests) good-quality Northern Italian food like you would prepare for a special occasion at home" – and from "a former Locanda Locatelli chef" no less – distinguishes this "intimate" spot near Oxford Street; add in "solicitous, charming" service and a "cracking wine list" (with a "sommelier who does not push expensive" labels), and you have an "absolute gem" that "deserves lots of success."

☑ Ritz, The *British/French*   `23` `29` `26` `£76`
St. James's | Ritz Hotel | 150 Piccadilly, W1 (Green Park) | 020-7300 2370 |
fax 7300 2375 | www.theritzlondon.com

"No jeans, but a tiara is acceptable" – perhaps even de rigueur – at the Ritz's "regal" Louis XVI–style venue, crowned No. 1 for Decor; "even if the Traditional British–Classic French cuisine isn't particularly innovative" (lots of tableside preparations), it's quite "well done" and proffered by incredibly "orchestrated" service ("more waiters than patrons at times!"); in short, "a special place for special times", topped off with "music and dancing in the weekend evenings"; P.S. for "the Mary Poppins of culinary experiences", there's the adjacent Palm Court's "practically perfect" afternoon tea.

Riva *Italian*   ▽ `21` `9` `20` `£49`
Barnes | 169 Church Rd., SW13 (Hammersmith) | 020-8748 0434 |
fax 8748 0434

"A steady bet" for a "low-key" meal "like the finest house-cook in Italy would make" sums up the appeal of namesake owner Andrea Riva's "small", "eccentric" Barnes stalwart; but "shabby decor" and "difficult parking" aggravate antagonists, who argue "the only reason to go is if you live in walking distance."

☑ River Café *Italian*   `28` `22` `25` `£62`
Hammersmith | Thames Wharf | Rainville Rd., W6 (Hammersmith) |
020-7386 4200 | fax 7386 4201 | www.rivercafe.co.uk

"An Italian masterpiece beside the Thames" in Hammersmith, this "bright", "bustling" legend is "larger than life", serving "gargantuan portions" of "the finest ingredients", with "perfect service to match"; so "who cares if it's a little pricey" – the "result is pure magic", and "heaven if you can sit outside on a beautiful day"; N.B. the Decor score doesn't reflect a midsummer revamp, after a fire.

Rivington Grill Bar Deli *British*   `21` `17` `18` `£39`
Greenwich | Greenwich Picturehouse Cinema |
178 Greenwich High Rd., SE10 (Greenwich) | 020-8293 9270 Ⓜ
Shoreditch | 28-30 Rivington St., EC2 (Old St.) | 020-7729 7053 |
fax 7729 7086
www.rivingtongrill.co.uk

"Energetic atmosphere" pervades this "popular" duo in "bright, cavernous" Shoreditch premises and within the Greenwich Picturehouse; despite its pedigree – same owners as The Ivy and Le

Caprice – reviewers report "uneven" experiences with the "hearty" Traditional British cooking and "friendly" but "slapdash service."

Roast - British

FOOD 19 | DECOR 22 | SERVICE 17 | COST £46

Borough | Borough Mkt. | The Floral Hall, Stoney St., SE1 (London Bridge) | 020-7940 1300 | fax 7940 1301 | www.roast-restaurant.com

"Perched above Borough Market with views towards St. Paul's" and "huge windows overlooking the bustling" scene below, this venue attracts "lots of guys in suits" with "fresh", "flavourful" fare – "a modern take on Traditional British" dishes; but "high prices" and "uppity service" "let it down" for some who "prefer the bar" with its "creative cocktails"; P.S. it's "great for brekkie if you are up in the early hours."

Rock & Sole Plaice ◐ Seafood

- | - | - | M

Covent Garden | 47 Endell St., WC2 (Covent Garden) | 020-7836 3785

For a taste of "ye olde London", try this traditional Covent Garden seafood stalwart spread over two floors ("upstairs is better, no windows downstairs"); whilst "not much to look at", it "attracts a crowd" thanks to the "many varieties" of "fresh fish 'n' chips" in "huge portions"; sure, "it's a bit pricey for what you get, but the quality is great", plus you can "sit outside on a beautiful day."

Rocket - Mediterranean

17 | 18 | 17 | £32

Mayfair | 4 Lancashire Ct., W1 (Bond St.) | 020-7629 2889 | fax 7629 2881 🖪

City | 6 Adams Ct., Old Broad St., EC2 (Bank/Liverpool St.) | 020-7628 0808 | fax 7628 0809 🖪

Putney | Putney Wharf | Brewhouse St., SW15 (East Putney) | 020-8789 7875 | fax 8789 7876

www.rocketrestaurants.co.uk

The Med menu is "nothing too fancy" – "huge salads", "über-sized pizzas" – but it "hits the spot" at this "casual", "good-value" trio in Putney (which "takes advantage of the river views"), in a Mayfair courtyard and in a "modern" City locale; staff are "good, but there's never enough of them."

Rodizio Rico ◐ Brazilian

17 | 11 | 13 | £30

Greenwich | O2 Arena | Peninsula Sq., SE10 (North Greenwich) | 020-8858 6333

Islington | 77-78 Upper St., N1 (Angel) | 020-7354 1076 | fax 7359 8952

Bayswater | 111 Westbourne Grove, W2 (Bayswater) | 020-7792 4035 | fax 7243 1401

www.rodiziorico.com

"Passed 'round on skewers", "the meat just keeps coming" ("vegans need not apply") at these "all-you-can-eat" Brazilian churrascaria joints; whilst a "decent" option "if you're on a tight budget", it's "a gimmick" growl grouches – the grub's "merely passable."

Roka ◐ Japanese

25 | 20 | 18 | £56

Fitzrovia | 37 Charlotte St., W1 (Goodge St./Tottenham Court Rd.) | 020-7580 6464 | fax 7580 0220 | www.rokarestaurant.com

"Getting a reservation is no easy task" at this "cool, slick" Fitzrovian that "sparkles with" "flash and flair", from the "sumptuous", "well-presented" Japanese dishes (meats from the exposed robata grill "are a certainty") to the "exciting atmosphere"; "service can be hit-or-miss", a bit irritating given the "sky-high prices", but it's "always full of laughing people" anyway; P.S. "don't forget you can roka-round-the-clock in the cool bar downstairs."

☒ Roussillon ☒ French   26 | 22 | 25 | £65

Pimlico | 16 St. Barnabas St., SW1 (Sloane Sq./Victoria) | 020-7730 5550 | fax 7824 8617 | www.roussillon.co.uk

This "little gem in Pimlico" – "a place where you can hear yourself speak" – offers a "fresh take on French cuisine" through chef Alexis Gauthier's "refined", "imaginative" cooking, especially on a "magnificent vegetarian tasting menu", supported by "soothing service"; although it's a "bit expensive", the set "lunch, including wine, is exceptional", "and guess what – it's also child-friendly" (kids under 12 qualify for the mini-gastronome tasting menu of six courses).

Rowley's British   20 | 16 | 19 | £40

St. James's | 113 Jermyn St., SW1 (Piccadilly Circus) | 020-7930 2707 | fax 7839 4240 | www.rowleys.co.uk

"Don't be fooled by the establishment look" – this Traditional British in Jermyn Street offers "amazing value if you like good meat, cooked simply" and served "with an endless supply of fries"; even if "more attentive service would make a perfect meal", it remains a "great place to relax" – or to get fed fast "for an early theatre dinner."

Royal China Chinese   23 | 15 | 15 | £32

Marylebone | 24-26 Baker St., W1 (Baker St.) | 020-7487 4688 | fax 7935 7893

Canary Wharf | 30 Westferry Circus, E14 (Canary Wharf) | 020-7719 0888 | fax 7719 0889

Fulham | 805 Fulham Rd., SW6 (Parsons Green) | 020-7731 0081 | fax 7384 2998

Bayswater | 13 Queensway, W2 (Queensway) | 020-7221 2535 | fax 7792 5752

www.royalchinagroup.co.uk

A decade-old "doyenne of the dim sum scene", due to its "unbelievable" selection on a "constantly changing" Cantonese menu, this "elegantly tacky" quintet ("gold and glitter" is the prevailing motif) is "jam-packed" all day long; happily the "speedy" service "churns people in and out" quickly.

☒ Royal China Club Chinese   24 | 18 | 22 | £44

Marylebone | 40-42 Baker St., W1 (Baker St.) | 020-7486 3898 | fax 7486 6977

St. John's Wood | 68 Queen's Grove, NW8 (St. John's Wood) | 020-7586 4280 | fax 7722 4750

"The upmarket version of Royal China", and certainly more "peaceful" than its sisters, this "stylish" Baker Street and Queen's Grove Chinese duo are "a must" for "decadent dim sum" and "inventive seafood combinations" (which "swim to your table" from the on-premises fish tanks); "uniquely friendly, knowledgeable staff" add to its credentials, even if a few grumble that it "costs a lot."

	FOOD	DECOR	SERVICE	COST

Royal Exchange
Grand Café & Bar ⑤ *European*

14	22	16	£34

City | The Royal Exchange | The Courtyard, EC3 (Bank) | 020-7618 2480 | fax 7618 2490 | www.royalexchangegrandcafeandbar.com

In the "stunning setting" of the old Royal Exchange's interior central courtyard, this Modern European cafe is "good for a high-class snack" of cold (mainly crustacean) dishes – even if its large atrium makes it a "bit like eating in a fishbowl"; it's also "interesting for happy-hour drinks."

R.S.J. ⑤ *British*

18	14	18	£37

Waterloo | 33 Coin St., SE1 (Waterloo) | 020-7928 4554 | fax 7401 2455 | www.rsj.uk.com

"A solid choice when in eye-distance of the National Theatre", this "nifty spot" is most "famous for its wines" ("the Loires are the real attraction"); but "staff are warm", the Modern British fare is "reliably good" and the "pre- and post-theatre menus offer excellent value."

⑤ Rules ❶ *British/Chophouse*

23	25	22	£53

Covent Garden | 35 Maiden Ln., WC2 (Covent Garden) | 020-7836 5314 | fax 7497 1081 | www.rules.co.uk

"Steeped in history", "like a Dickensian time capsule", this "venerable establishment going back hundreds of years" (211, to be precise) remains a "mega-atmospheric, still-bustling Covent Garden favourite"; even if there are "too many tourists", causing the "solicitous service" to get "frazzled" in the "tight quarters", a "well-prepared" Traditional British "comfort" menu – "filled with game" "from their own farm" – ensures it rules for business lunches, pre-theatre dinners or whenever one wants a taste of "typically English" tradition.

Sabor ❶ *S American*

-	-	-	M

Islington | 108 Essex Rd., N1 (Angel) | 020-7226 5551 | fax 7288 0880 | www.sabor.co.uk

"In an otherwise unexceptional stretch of Essex Road, this real delight" is "truly different", with its "original, tasty South American cuisine" and quirky decor of Colombian carnival masks and gold canopy; "hardworking", "friendly staff" and "fairly priced cocktails add to the positive report."

NEW Saf Restaurant & Bar ⑤ *Eclectic*

-	-	-	M

Shoreditch | 152-154 Curtain Rd., EC2 (Old St./Liverpool St.) | 020-7613 0007 | www.safrestaurant.co.uk

Staking its claim as London's first gourmet all-vegan venue, this eco-friendly, streamlined Shoreditch newcomer (from an international chain) offers a "welcome and surprising introduction to the possibilities" of animal-, dairy- and processed-free products on its midpriced Eclectic menu; the mission extends to the rear terrace – where the kitchen's herbs and flowers are grown – and to a bar offering organic cocktails and botanical and biodynamic wines.

	FOOD	DECOR	SERVICE	COST

NEW Sake no hana ❶ *Japanese* | 19 | 22 | 19 | £78 |

St. James's | 23 St. James's St., SW1 (Green Park/Piccadilly Circus) | 020-7925 8988

Dominated by striking struts of blond timber, this light-flooded, "stunning architectural" space in St. James's represents über-restaurateur Alan Yau's first Japanese venture; the "food is interesting" but "difficult" to decipher, and "mistakes are expensive at these prices" (in particular, the "drinks menu is out of control"); service also ranges from "well-trained" to "slow"; so, whilst it does seem to "please the 'in' crowd", critics claim "there's a lot of adjusting to be done."

Saki Bar & Food Emporium ⊠ *Japanese* | - | - | - | E |

Smithfield | 4 W. Smithfield, EC1 (Barbican/Farringdon) | 020-7489 7033 | fax 7489 1658 | www.saki-food.com

"Sushi good enough to make you forget you are by a meat market", plus cooked delights, are on offer at this Smithfield site that comprises a black-and-red-hued basement dining room and small, street-level deli/noodle bar; sure, it "lacks atmosphere" on occasion, but enthusiasts agree it's an "excellent Japanese"; P.S. "try the toilets" – you'll see why.

Sakura *Japanese* | 18 | 6 | 8 | £24 |

Mayfair | 9 Hanover St., W1 (Oxford Circus/Regent St.) | 020-7629 2961

With "loads of tasty sushi and light tempura" at a "good price", this "rough"-looking, "canteenlike" space near Oxford Circus is "popular with London-dwelling Japanese, which is a good sign"; what's not so popular is the staff, apparent "graduates of the Basil Fawlty school of restaurant management."

Sale e Pepe ❶⊠ *Italian* | 22 | 16 | 21 | £44 |

Knightsbridge | 9-15 Pavilion Rd., SW1 (Knightsbridge) | 020-7235 0098 | fax 7225 1210 | www.saleepepe.co.uk

Singing, "saucy staff and a celebrity from time to time" add to the character of this "exuberant" Knightsbridge "institution" that "still gives a great performance" when it comes to "huge plates" of "all those Italian favourites as you want them to be"; just bear in mind, with "crowded" quarters and "close tables", it does get "quite loud."

Salloos ❶⊠ *Pakistani* | 23 | 14 | 19 | £44 |

Belgravia | 62-64 Kinnerton St., SW1 (Hyde Park Corner/Knightsbridge) | 020-7235 4444

For over 30 years, this "terrific, upscale Pakistani on an easy-to-miss side street" in Belgravia has been known for "spicy" "northwestern frontier cuisine at its best"; though this family-run venue's "no bargain", the "passionate service" makes it feel "like eating at your grandmother's."

Salt Yard ⊠ *European* | 21 | 15 | 18 | £37 |

Fitzrovia | 54 Goodge St., W1 (Goodge St.) | 020-7637 0657 | fax 7580 7435 | www.saltyard.co.uk

"Not for the faint-of-hearing", this Fitzrovian spread over two "very busy" floors places "an emphasis on tapas" ("oh, those

	FOOD	DECOR	SERVICE	COST

courgette flowers!") that "elevates the concept to a new level"; there are also "reasonably priced" Modern Euro mains served by "accommodating staff."

Salusbury Pub & Dining Room *Italian* — | — | — | M

Kilburn | 50-52 Salusbury Rd., NW6 (Queen's Park) | 020-7328 3286

"Well-thought-out", "homemade"-tasting Italian "gastropub grub" "compensates for the noise and folksy decor" that's looking "rather jaded" at this "popular" (some say "too popular") Queen's Park haunt; N.B. their deli next door sells mainly organic fare.

Sam's Brasserie & Bar *European* 19 | 18 | 20 | £33

Chiswick | Barley Mow Ctr. | 11 Barley Mow Passage, W4 (Chiswick Park) | 020-8987 0555 | fax 8987 7389 | www.samsbrasserie.co.uk

It's "still a bit of a secret in Chiswick", but those who know the "omnipresent" Sam Harrison's "bright" brasserie – where "anyone from grandma to trendsetters" feels at home – appreciate its "imaginative" Modern Euro menu; but foes fret about "appalling acoustics" ("none of our party could hear each other") and find it "overpriced."

San Lorenzo ●🗷⊄ *Italian* 20 | 18 | 18 | £62

Knightsbridge | 22 Beauchamp Pl., SW3 (Knightsbridge) | 020-7584 1074 | fax 7584 1142

San Lorenzo Fuoriporta *Italian*

Wimbledon | 38 Wimbledon Hill Rd., SW19 (Wimbledon) | 020-8946 8463 | fax 8947 9810
www.sanlorenzo.com

"Some people love it, some people don't get it", but Mara and Lorenzo Berni's Knightsbridge "institution" "still packs them in", offering "the occasional celebrity sighting"; "behind the hype and hoopla is some very good Italian food" and "gracious" service, although it's "annoying" they "still do not accept credit cards"; P.S. the branch run by the Berni boys remains "a staple" during Wimbledon.

Santa Lucia ● *Italian* — | — | — | M

Chelsea | 2 Hollywood Rd., SW10 (Earl's Ct./South Kensington) | 020-7352 8484 | fax 7351 2390 | www.madeinitalygroup.co.uk

"An Italian neighbourhood place", this "cosy" Chelsea venue serves up pizza that's "the Real McCoy, like they don't make no more" and "reasonably priced" to boot; but sometimes it becomes "too crowded", and decorators dis the Neapolitan farmhouse look as "tired."

Santa Maria del Sur *Argentinean* — | — | — | E

Battersea | 129 Queenstown Rd., SW8 (Clapham Common) | 020-7622 2088 | fax 7627 8544 | www.santamariadelsur.co.uk

"Battersea equals Buenos Aires" at this atmospheric, "authentic Argentinean" (formerly connected to Buen Ayre) that's "miles apart from the standardised gaucho grills"; "many have lost evenings to the great wine, red meat" and "friendly service" here.

	FOOD	DECOR	SERVICE	COST

Santini ⏺ *Italian*

| | 21 | 18 | 20 | £53 |

Belgravia | 29 Ebury St., SW1 (Victoria) | 020-7730 4094 |
fax 7730 0544 | www.santini-restaurant.com

In the "foodie desert that is Victoria", this "long-time neighbour-hood Italian" a stone's throw away delights disciples with its "good, not faddish food" and "beautiful patio" (especially "now the traffic flow has been changed"); but cynics find it an "over-priced, overhectic" venue, with "service that's efficient, but could be more amiable."

Sarastro ⏺ *Mediterranean*

| | 12 | 22 | 16 | £32 |

Covent Garden | 126 Drury Ln., WC2 (Covent Garden) | 020-7836 0101 |
fax 7379 4666 | www.sarastro-restaurant.com

"Kitschy", "theatrical surroundings draw the theatre-going crowd" to this "quirky" Drury Lane "tourist trap", which features live opera twice a week; but when it comes to the culinary show, even fans mutter the "mediocre" Mediterranean "food could be so much better."

Sardo ⓩ *Italian*

| | 21 | 15 | 20 | £46 |

Fitzrovia | 45 Grafton Way, W1 (Warren St.) | 020-7387 2521 |
fax 7387 2559 | www.sardo-restaurant.com

"Luscious Sardinian cuisine", "authentic and imaginative", sets apart this "lively" "neighbourhood Italian" in Fitzrovia; the "small" surroundings can be "claustrophobic", but all appreciate "polite staff" and a "wine list full of affordable choices" from The Boot.

Sardo Canale *Italian*

| | 21 | 20 | 20 | £41 |

Primrose Hill | 42 Gloucester Ave., NW1 (Camden Town/Chalk Farm) |
020-7722 2800 | fax 7722 0802 | www.sardocanale.com

"Always a pleasure to visit" sigh supporters of this "real Sardinian experience on the canal" near Regent's Park, thanks to food that's "savoury" – even "a little adventurous" – an "outstanding wine" list and staff who "serve with a flourish"; sitting outdoors is "super for a summer day's meal."

Sartoria ⓩ *Italian*

| | 20 | 20 | 19 | £49 |

Mayfair | 20 Savile Row, W1 (Oxford Circus/Piccadilly Circus) |
020-7534 7000 | fax 7534 7070 | www.sartoriabar.co.uk

This "large, airy dining room plus bar" has a "sophisticated", if "sub-dued" ambience as it serves "consistent" Italian fare and wines; whilst "not a destination", it's "ideal for business or treating elderly relatives", as all leave "feeling as good as any of the bespoke suits made next door on Savile Row."

Satsuma *Japanese*

| | 19 | 15 | 18 | £22 |

Soho | 56 Wardour St., W1 (Leicester Sq./Piccadilly Circus) |
020-7437 8338 | fax 7437 3389

The "communal seating invites camaraderie" at this "convivial" can-teen in Soho, where a "young, hip crowd" congregate for "easy-on-the-wallet" Japanese fare, including "killer bento boxes" and now noodles; the "no-nonsense" service is "handy in a hurry."

| | FOOD | DECOR | SERVICE | COST |

Sauterelle ⊠ French
| | - | - | - | E |

City | The Royal Exchange | The Courtyard, mezzanine level, EC3 (Bank) | 020-7618 2483 | fax 7618 2490 | www.restaurantsauterelle.com

A "great setting in the Royal Exchange", overlooking the historic courtyard, makes an "unusual" backdrop for the "fresh", fish-oriented cuisine at this Classic French; if a handful find it "slightly disappointing given the grand" surrounds, most agree it's "a good experience overall" (even if the "toilets are far away").

Scalini ● Italian
| 23 | 17 | 21 | £52 |

Chelsea | 1-3 Walton St., SW3 (Knightsbridge/South Kensington) | 020-7225 2301 | fax 7581 4224

As it turns 21, this trattoria "around the corner from Harrods" remains one of "the buzzing-est Italians" around, with "great celebrity-spotting" and "plenty of eye candy" squeezed "sardine-style" into seats; the "old-style" food's "as good as ever", though rising costs make it seem "a bit overpriced" now; what irks most, however, are the "acoustically appalling" digs that "badly need an update."

⊠ Scott's Seafood
| 24 | 24 | 22 | £68 |

Mayfair | 20 Mount St., W1 (Bond St./Green Park) | 020-7495 7309 | fax 7629 5457 | www.scotts-restaurant.com

"On ultrafashionable Mount Street", this "institution" has been "tastefully revived" by Caprice Holdings (J. Sheekey, The Ivy) into a "slick", "spot-the-celeb" and "power-broker heaven", with "quite beautiful" oak-panelled and leather decor and "artfully prepared" seafood "lavishly displayed on the large central bar"; though slightly "snobby", the "spot-on service" "compensates for the steep prices"; P.S. "eating at the bar is also pleasant, should booking a table prove too taxing."

Seashell Seafood
| 20 | 11 | 15 | £23 |

Marylebone | 49-51 Lisson Grove, NW1 (Marylebone) | 020-7224 9000 | fax 7724 9071 | www.seashellrestaurant.co.uk

It looks "nothing fancy" ("shabby" in truth) and "service is painfully slow", but this Marylebone veteran offers the "quintessential London" experience of "perfectly fried fish accompanied by the typical" trimmings, like "top-notch chips" or "delicious mushy peas."

1707 Wine Bar British
| 21 | 20 | 22 | £31 |

St. James's | Fortnum & Mason | 181 Piccadilly, W1 (Green Park/Piccadilly Circus) | 020-7734 8040 | fax 7437 3278 | www.fortnumandmason.co.uk

Named for Fortnum's birth year, this classy bar in the refurbished retailer's fresh Food Hall is "worth the stop" for a "reprieve from the hustle and bustle of Piccadilly"; its chic David Collins design, "quality" Traditional British bites and "worth-the-stop wine bar" – including hundreds of bottles from the adjacent shop at cost plus corkage – all add up to a "good place for pre-theatre" or post-hamper shopping.

	FOOD	DECOR	SERVICE	COST

Shanghai Blues ● *Chinese*

24 | 22 | 20 | £42

Holborn | 193-197 High Holborn, WC1 (Holborn) | 020-7404 1668 | fax 7404 1448 | www.shanghaiblues.co.uk

It's "not exactly on the beaten path", but surveyors don't need to be shanghai-ed to visit this Holborn haven, given its "succulent morsels of modern Oriental food" – from the daytime dim sum to the evening mains – "served with gracious precision" within chic" "Chinese-European decor"; the woeful wonder "why it costs so much", but "in a part of London that needs quality eateries", it comes "highly recommended."

Shepherd's ⊠ *British*

23 | 20 | 22 | £52

Westminster | Marsham Ct., Marsham St., SW1 (Pimlico) | 020-7834 9552 | fax 7233 6047 | www.langansrestaurants.co.uk

"Although the old boys' club atmosphere might not be to everyone's taste", this "hidden jewel" in Westminster is "the place to spot politicians after a hard time with the whips", enjoying a "really good" Traditional British menu that combines "nursery food" and more "grown-up" dishes; whilst it's "pricey", a "fine wine list" and "service beyond reproach" help the yes-votes carry the day.

Shogun Ⓜ *Japanese*

- | - | - | VE

Mayfair | Millennium Hotel Mayfair | Adam's Row, W1 (Bond St.) | 020-7493 1255 | fax 7493 1877 | www.millenniumhotels.com

The "owner greets everyone as an old friend" at this "authentic Japanese experience" in a Mayfair basement, and whilst the "decor is rather depressing", it's a "consistent performer" when it comes to "excellent food"; but beware, "the bill can mount up alarmingly."

Signor Sassi ● *Italian*

21 | 16 | 21 | £48

Knightsbridge | 14 Knightsbridge Green, SW1 (Knightsbridge) | 020-7584 2277 | fax 7225 3953

It's "fun to watch the waiters" "sing to the diners" at this "always full and noisy" Knightsbridge trattoria; if the "nothing-too-fancy" Italian *cucina* is "not cheap", it's "well executed"; P.S. "is what you want not on the menu? – no problem, they'll make it for you!"

Silks & Spice *Malaysian/Thai*

16 | 13 | 16 | £27

Camden Town | 28 Chalk Farm Rd., NW10 (Camden Town/Chalk Farm) | 020-7482 2228 | fax 7482 3382

The Southeast Asian fare's only "average", but it's spiced by "generous portions" and "wide variety" at this Camden Town venue; go with a group of friends and you won't notice the "less-than-impressive environment" and that "service is lacking at times."

Simpson's-in-the-Strand *British*

20 | 22 | 22 | £51

Covent Garden | 100 The Strand, WC2 (Charing Cross) | 020-7836 9112 | fax 7836 1381 | www.simpsonsinthestrand.co.uk

"You may not be inspired, but your tummy will be satisfied and your soul will feel good" at this slightly "faded" but still "classic" taste of "olde England" in The Strand; within its "wonderful period setting" with "the snug feel of a club", "solicitous staff" bring meaty mains from the "estimable rolling carvery" (plus "some lighter dishes now"); "for a first-time tourist willing to spend, it's an absolute must."

Singapore Garden *SE Asian*

FOOD	DECOR	SERVICE	COST
19	16	17	£33

Swiss Cottage | 83-83A Fairfax Rd., NW6 (Swiss Cottage) | 020-7328 5314 | fax 7624 0656 | www.singaporegarden.co.uk
An "updated design" "has given a new spark of life" to this quarter-century-old Asian; though set in "out-of-the-way" Swiss Cottage, it's "almost a destination" in its own right, thanks to its "offbeat" but "lovely" Singaporean-Malay menu, proffered by "charming, pretty waitresses."

Singapura ⊠ *SE Asian*

FOOD	DECOR	SERVICE	COST
∇ 20	14	17	£30

Blackfriars | 1-2 Limeburner Ln., EC4 (Blackfriars/St. Paul's) | 020-7329 1133 | fax 7236 1805
City | 78-79 Leadenhall St., downstairs, EC3 (Aldgate/Tower Hill) | 020-7929 0089 | fax 7621 0366
www.singapuras.co.uk
"If you want a real lunch", with "delightful", "modern Thai-Singaporean" dishes and "tables spaced far enough apart to have a conversation without being overheard", this unpretentious pair of East Londoners ticks all the right boxes – including the one marked "reasonably priced"; N.B. only the Blackfriars branch serves dinner.

Sitaaray ●⊠ *Indian*

FOOD	DECOR	SERVICE	COST
-	-	-	M

Covent Garden | 167 Drury Ln., WC2 (Covent Garden/Holborn) | 020-7269 6422 | www.sitaaray.com
A "fantastic cinematic theme", complete with "Bollywood films screened in the background" dominates this "buzzy" sibling of Tamarai (a floor below) in Covent Garden; foodwise, the "great-value" Indian menu majors on a "mind-boggling selection of succulent kebabs", even if critics quip there's "enough oil in every dish to power my four-wheel drive."

Six13 ⊠ *Eclectic/Kosher*

FOOD	DECOR	SERVICE	COST
-	-	-	E

Marylebone | 19 Wigmore St., W1 (Bond St./Oxford Circus) | 020-7629 6133 | fax 7629 6135
"You don't leave feeling hungry" after sampling the Eclectic menu running the gamut from sushi to steaks at this kosher venue (hence, no dairy products) in Marylebone; despite a "nice" olive-and-tan, art deco-ish setting, it is "too expensive" for some wallets.

Sketch – The Gallery ⊠ *European*

FOOD	DECOR	SERVICE	COST
17	25	18	£66

Mayfair | 9 Conduit St., W1 (Oxford Circus) | 020-7659 4500 | fax 7629 1698 | www.sketch.uk.com
"Still cool, but no longer hot" say surveyors of the supper-only section of the "splendiferous" Sketch townhouse in Mayfair, where the video wall art, "bar from outer space" and *Body Snatcher*-like toilets" "are always a talking point"; pity that the Modern European food is "not as interesting as the decor" – "when you finally get it" (perhaps aliens also have abducted the staff, "as they never seem to be around").

	FOOD	DECOR	SERVICE	COST

☑ Sketch – The Lecture
Room & Library ☒Ⓜ *European*

`21` `26` `22` `£96`

Mayfair | 9 Conduit St., W1 (Oxford Circus) | 020-7659 4500 |
fax 7629 1684 | www.sketch.uk.com

From the leather-studded walls to the crystal-encrusted loos, this
"whimsical, enchanting" Modern European in Mayfair is "like going
first-class on a surreal ocean liner"; but the "highly quirky cuisine,
[whilst] obviously masterminded by a genius" (consultant chef
Pierre Gagnaire) and served by "intelligent" staff, "does not justify
the astronomical prices" – or the *petit* portions cry critics who confess
to a "desire for a cheeseburger afterwards"; P.S. some seek solace in
the 1,000-label "wine list that separates the men from the boys."

Skylon *European*

`19` `23` `18` `£46`

South Bank | Southbank Ctr. | Belvedere Rd., SE1 (Waterloo) |
020-7654 7800 | www.skylonrestaurant.co.uk

"Divided into two areas, the restaurant and the grill" (most prefer the
former), this "great space" makes a "welcome addition to the South
Bank"; boasting "a beautiful view of the Thames", "the room's the best
part of the experience", trumping the "truncated" menu of "delicate"
Modern European dishes and "correct" service; still, it's all good
enough for theatre-goers, who trumpet "there's no more excuse to
have a bad meal before or after a performance" at the National or RFH.

Smiths of Smithfield –
Dining Room ☒ *British*

`21` `19` `17` `£37`

Smithfield | 67-77 Charterhouse St., 2nd fl., EC1 (Barbican/Farringdon) |
020-7251 7950 | fax 7236 0488 | www.smithsofsmithfield.co.uk

One of several dining options in the building opposite Smithfield
Market, this Modern British "meat-lover's paradise" is a "huge room
with great energy" and "the place to go" for "incredible cuts" and
staples like a "perfect pork belly"; unlike the pricier upstairs, however, "here your steak costs £12 rather than £28, the difference being smaller portions and less choice."

Smiths of Smithfield –
Top Floor *British/Chophouse*

`21` `19` `20` `£52`

Smithfield | 67-77 Charterhouse St., 3rd fl., EC1 (Barbican/Farringdon) |
020-7251 7950 | fax 7236 0488 | www.smithsofsmithfield.co.uk

You "have to be a serious carnivore", since "superb steaks" star at
this unashamedly meat-heavy Traditional Brit; but foes fume that
the rest of the menu is "nothing out of the ordinary, given the price
range" – in particular, "side dishes could be improved"; and whilst
the "lovely terrace" offers "breathtaking views" "over the roofs of
Smithfield", the "spartan" brick interior makes the place "vibrant or
loud depending on your point of view."

Smollensky's *Chophouse*

`16` `16` `17` `£36`

Covent Garden | 105 The Strand, WC2 (Charing Cross/Covent Garden) |
020-7497 2101 | fax 7836 3270
Canary Wharf | 1 Reuters Plaza, E14 (Canary Wharf) | 020-7719 0101 |
fax 7719 0060

(continued)

Smollensky's

Hammersmith | Bradmore House | Queen Caroline St., W6 (Hammersmith) | 020-8741 8124 | fax 8741 5695 www.smollenskys.com

This imported chain seems to have an identity crisis: it pulls in office parties and "the after-work crowd" with "great cocktails" and disco or "live music", but it's also "suitable for all ages" with clowns at the Sunday kids' brunch; still, diners have no doubts about the "standard American steaks and burgers" – "about as memorable as what your brother-in-law got you last Christmas" – and the "slapdash service."

Snazz *Chinese*

| - | - | - | E |

King's Cross | 37 Chalton St., NW1 (Euston/King's Cross) | 020-7388 0808 | fax 7388 8080 | www.newchinaclub.co.uk

"Impressively hot, authentic Sichuan cooking" with "plenty of interesting choices on the menu" (from 'fruit-fragrant sea bass' to 'strange-flavoured rabbit') gets the thumbs-up at this green-walled, bi-level Euston venue; don't expect a snazzy layout though: decor's mostly a few evocative photos of rural China on the walls and some simple street seating.

Snows on the Green ⓩ *British*

| ▽ 21 | 17 | 20 | £31 |

Shepherd's Bush | 166 Shepherd's Bush Rd., W6 (Hammersmith) | 020-7603 2142 | fax 7602 7553 | www.snowsonthegreen.co.uk

"Thank heaven for Snows" – "the oasis in our desert" sigh Brook Green locals of this "relaxed" bistro; the Modern British menu changes with the seasons but "signature dishes like foie gras and fried egg" are perennial favourites; one aspect gets an icy reception: the sometimes graphic black-and-white Bill Brandt photos ("not every diner's cup of tea").

Sofra *Turkish*

| 19 | 13 | 17 | £27 |

Covent Garden | 36 Tavistock St., WC2 (Covent Garden) | 020-7240 3773 | fax 7836 6633
Marylebone | 1 St. Christopher's Pl., W1 (Bond St.) | 020-7224 4080 | fax 7224 0022
Mayfair | 18 Shepherd St., W1 (Green Park) | 020-7493 3320 | fax 7499 8282
St. John's Wood | 11 Circus Rd., NW8 (St. John's Wood) | 020-7586 9889 | fax 7586 8778
www.sofra.co.uk

The signature "mezze is a riot of fresh tastes" at this "reliable Turkish chain" around town; purists pout the fare's "not as authentic as it should be", but it does "provide value for money that can't be beaten in central London"; alfresco options in some locations compensate for "rather cramped surroundings."

Soho House ● *British*

| 19 | 20 | 20 | £42 |

Private club; inquiries: 020-7734 5188

"It's members only", but once inside the "quirky Georgian townhouse", it's "star-spotting all the way" at this Soho scenester (indeed, the "volume level of the media folk can be irritating");

"courteous servers" offer up Modern British "food that's better than you'd expect", and whilst it's "quite expensive, you're paying for the chance to chat to a Hollywood A-lister over the toilet basins."

Solly's *Mideastern*
19 | 12 | 14 | £26

Golders Green | 148A Golders Green Rd., NW11 (Golders Green) | 020-8455 2121 | fax 8455 0061

Fire swept this Golders Green stalwart in September 2007, leaving shawarma-savouring surveyors "as gutted as the top floor"; but now it's back, and "Israelis tell us it's as good as it gets" for a "quick bite" of "kosher Middle Eastern food"; though it's obviously redecorated, some still say "the best option is takeaway."

Song Que Café *Vietnamese*
25 | 4 | 15 | £16

Shoreditch | 134 Kingsland Rd., E2 (Old St.) | 020-7613 3222

Expect to "fight for a table" at this "popular Vietnamese alongside others of the same cuisine on Kingsland Road", as its "consistently perfect food" is "as authentic as you are likely to get" on this isle and for prices that let you "relive your student days"; less memorable is the "kitsch, bordering on tacky" setting and "rushed service", but on the upside, that means "you'll often not wait long" for a table.

Sonny's *European*
22 | 20 | 22 | £46

Barnes | 94 Church Rd., SW13 (Hammersmith) | 020-8748 0393 | fax 8748 2698 | www.sonnys.co.uk

A "consistently warm welcome" and "delicious" dishes make Barnes' "homey neighbourhood" Modern European a "delightful venue for a get-together"; claiming it's too "samey with other nice restaurants", critics "wouldn't make a special effort" to head here, but "it's a prime candidate whenever you're in this part of London."

Sophie's
21 | 18 | 18 | £32

Steakhouse & Bar ● *American/Chophouse*

Chelsea | 311-313 Fulham Rd., SW10 (South Kensington) | 020-7352 0088 | fax 7349 9776 | www.sophiessteakhouse.co.uk

This "boisterous local hangout for the Fulham Road set" is "perpetually packed" with "young Sloanes" who rave about the British "cracking bits of meat" ("great steaks" to you and me) and the "excellent desserts" ("ask for the banoffee pie"); the "no-booking policy means it's a no-no for big groups", but the waits make for a "buzzing bar scene"; P.S. the "American-style weekend brunches" are "more relaxed."

Sotheby's Cafe ▣ *British*
20 | 15 | 21 | £34

Mayfair | Sotheby's Auction House | 34 New Bond St., W1 (Bond St./Oxford Circus) | 020-7293 5077 | fax 7293 6993 | www.sothebys.com

A good bid during the day (it serves breakfast, "lunch and tea only"), this "upscale", "tiny spot" off the lobby in Sotheby's is "handy for Bond Street shoppers and auction-goers" who peruse the catalogues over "rich" Modern British food; but what really ups its estimate is the "wonderful people-watching", with many "art movers-and-shakers to view."

		FOOD	DECOR	SERVICE	COST

Souk Bazaar ❶ *African*   ▽ 17 | 21 | 16 | £28

Soho | 27 Litchfield St., WC2 (Leicester Sq.) | 020-7240 1796 |
fax 7240 3382

Souk Medina ❶ *African*

Covent Garden | 1A Short's Gdns., WC2 (Covent Garden) |
020-7240 1796
www.soukrestaurant.net

"Walking through caves makes you feel you are on an Indiana Jones-
style mission to dine" at this North African duo, whose "kasbah setting" is a world away from the West End; "be prepared to sit on the
floor" and balance "decently priced", "delightful food" on "woven
mats", "with hookah and coffee afterward"; P.S. "belly dancers
abound" Thursday–Saturday.

Spago ❶ *Italian*   18 | 11 | 16 | £34

South Kensington | 6 Glendower Pl., SW7 (South Kensington) |
020-7225 2407

"This hideaway near South Kensington station" is "just what you
need" for a "casual" meal of "dependable", "good-value" Italian
fare – especially "if you love real, thin-crust pizza"; led by an "eager-
to-please owner", they make you feel "like an old friend" too.

Spencer Arms, The ❶ *British*   - | - | - | M

Putney | 237 Lower Richmond Rd., SW15 (Barnes Rail/Putney Bridge) |
020-8788 0640 | www.thespencerarms.co.uk

"A decent place for a pint and meal near Putney Bridge" sums up this
site with a "delightful Victorian environment" and Traditional British
grub that's "more than a cut above the pub-food level"; but some are
up in arms about the "hit-and-miss quality" and "slow service."

Spiga ❶🗷 *Italian*   17 | 13 | 14 | £28

Soho | 84-86 Wardour St., W1 (Leicester Sq./Piccadilly Circus) |
020-7734 3444 | fax 7734 3332 | www.vpmg.net

Supporters swear this "Soho standby" is a "reliable if unexciting
Italian" that's "good for a business-type lunch", especially given the
"gentle pricing"; but foes fume the food's "not what it used to be",
and the "tacky" decor "needs freshening up."

Spread Eagle, The *French*   ▽ 24 | 24 | 17 | £48

Greenwich | 1-2 Stockwell St., SE10 (Greenwich) | 020-8853 2333 |
fax 8293 1024 | www.spreadeaglerestaurant.com

The "new ownership and decor have made this into a special place
again" declare devotees of this historic Greenwich site (dating back
to the 1600s), which, "despite the gastropub exterior", houses a
"really good restaurant", with "excellent modern French food"; however, sometimes the service seems "too quick for a relaxed meal."

🗷 Square, The *French*   27 | 23 | 25 | £87

Mayfair | 6-10 Bruton St., W1 (Bond St./Green Park) | 020-7495 7100 |
fax 7495 7150 | www.squarerestaurant.com

Get "the feel of being in the centre of London's power elite" at
this "clean, modern space" in Mayfair, where chef-owner Philip
Howard's "impeccable" New French cooking – "creative and

classical at the same time" – is matched by "spot-on, professional" staff and an "amazing wine list" with "many half-bottles"; sure, it's "not cheap" and "others may have a slight edge on decor and service", but this "wonderfully sophisticated" venue "delivers every time."

Sri Nam ☒ *Thai* | 20 | 16 | 15 | £31 |

Canary Wharf | 10 Cabot Sq., E14 (Canary Wharf) | 020-7715 9515 | fax 7715 9528 | www.orientalrestaurantgroup.co.uk

"Nicely positioned between the dives and the unaffordable of Canary Wharf", this "solid Thai" soldiers on, with staff who are "whizzed off their feet at lunchtime"; it's "a good place to catch a bite to eat and a beer after work", but be sure to "go upstairs for less noise."

St. Alban ● *European* | 22 | 18 | 24 | £55 |

Piccadilly | 4-12 Regent St., SW1 (Piccadilly Circus) | 020-7499 8558 | www.stalban.net

"Everything works perfectly" at this "cool" "sibling of The Wolseley" in Piccadilly, from the "tempting" Modern European fare to the "friendly, without being overfamiliar" staff; some feel "let down by the room" – "like an airport lounge", albeit a "first-class" one (which means "lots of space between tables") – but the consensus is: "what's not to like" about this "hot spot"?

☒ Star of India ● *Indian* | 25 | 18 | 18 | £35 |

South Kensington | 154 Old Brompton Rd., SW5 (Gloucester Rd./ South Kensington) | 020-7373 2901 | fax 7373 5664

"Not your typical Indian by any means", this "low-key" South Kensington stalwart "has been serving superb food for many years" (57, in fact), and at a "reasonable price" too; yes, "seating's a bit crowded" "albeit comfortable", so all in all, a "sparkling" experience is assured.

St. Germain *French* | ∇ 22 | 21 | 19 | £33 |

Farringdon | 89-90 Turnmill St., EC1 (Farringdon) | 020-7336 0949 | fax 7336 0948 | www.stgermain.info

Set in a 19th-century print house, this spacious, "seriously nice" player on the Farringdon foodie scene lures a "lively crowd in the evenings" with "French brasserie–style comfort food", served in a monochrome mod "open space" of black-and-white checkerboard floors, striped walls and hanging lamps.

Sticky Fingers *American* | 17 | 22 | 19 | £25 |

Kensington | 1A Phillimore Gdns., W8 (High St. Kensington) | 020-7938 5338 | fax 7937 0145 | www.stickyfingers.co.uk

Just off Kensington High Street, this "home-away-from-home for hungry [U.S.] expats" appeals to "those who want a good, burger-type meal and to Rolling Stones aficionados" (Bill Wyman helped start the place, which is adorned with the band's artefacts); but the non-musical mutter "unless you're seriously into rock memorabilia, the main selling point is its child-friendliness."

	FOOD	DECOR	SERVICE	COST

St. James's Restaurant *British*

20 | 20 | 21 | £41

St. James's | Fortnum & Mason | 181 Piccadilly, 4th fl., W1 (Piccadilly Circus) | 020-7734 8040 | fax 7437 3278 | www.fortnumandmason.co.uk

Expect to find "beautiful, ageing ladies-who-lunch and pish-posh gentlemen who dine" at Fortnum & Mason's restored-to-"elegance" eatery, "far away from the maddening crowd" on the fourth floor; the "fine, old-fashioned" British menu of "comfort food" is "pretty good" – with afternoon tea absolutely "amazing" – and comes with "well-executed" service to boot.

☑ St. John ☒ *British*

27 | 18 | 23 | £48

Smithfield | 26 St. John St., EC1 (Farringdon) | 020-7251 0848 | fax 7251 4090 | www.stjohnrestaurant.com

"If you want the whole hog, literally", this "convivial" Smithfield Modern Brit caters to "adventurous eaters" with an "innovative, nose-to-tail" menu – "a vegetarian's nightmare, but a carnivore's dream" – "and then there's baked goods", too, all served by "no-nonsense" staff; the "canteen-style", "clinical surroundings" are "not as comfortable as I'd like", given the "steep prices" – but otherwise, "this place is offaly good"; N.B. a midsummer 2008 revamp may outdate the Decor score.

St. John Bread & Wine *British*

23 | 14 | 18 | £37

Spitalfields | 94-96 Commercial St., E1 (Liverpool St.) | 020-7251 0848 | fax 7247 8924 | www.stjohnbreadandwine.com

"For the adventurous", this "relaxed" St. John offspring in Spitalfields – "more sweaters than suits here" – echoes its parent with a "highly original" Modern British menu that "utilises everything remotely edible" in "offal-land" (albeit with "less-sophisticated dishes"); sure, the plain, "contemporary setting" gets "loud and crowded, but that's part of the charm"; P.S. "breakfasts are delicious", as well.

Strada *Italian*

18 | 15 | 16 | £24

Holborn | 6 Great Queen St., WC2 (Holborn) | 020-7405 6293 | fax 7405 6284

Marylebone | 9-10 Market Pl., W1 (Oxford Circus) | 020-7580 4644 | fax 7580 7877

Mayfair | 15-16 New Burlington St., W1 (Oxford Circus) | 020-7287 5967 | fax 7287 6047

Clerkenwell | 8-10 Exmouth Mkt., EC1 (Farringdon) | 020-7278 0800 | fax 7278 6901

Islington | 105-106 Upper St., N1 (Angel/Highbury & Islington) | 020-7226 9742 | fax 7226 9187

Clapham | 102-104 Clapham High St., SW4 (Clapham North) | 020-7627 4847 | fax 7720 2153

Clapham | 11-13 Battersea Rise, SW11 (Clapham Junction Rail) | 020-7801 0794 | fax 7801 0754

Earl's Court | 237 Earl's Court Rd., SW5 (Earl's Ct.) | 020-7835 1180 | fax 7835 2093

Fulham | 175 New King's Rd., SW6 (Parsons Green) | 020-7731 6404 | fax 7731 1431

(continued)

(continued)

Strada

Wimbledon | 91 Wimbledon High St., SW19 (Wimbledon) |
020-8946 4363
www.strada.co.uk
Additional locations throughout London

"Think the Starbucks of pizza" and you have this ever-expanding chain whose "imaginative" Italian *cucina* "exudes quality ingredients" at such a "fair price", some treat it as "our second kitchen"; yes, "service is variable", "whether it's busy or quiet", and some locations are "looking in need of a refresh", but most agree this "family-orientated" operation "makes a useful local."

Suka ◑ *Malaysian*

- | - | - | VE

Fitzrovia | Sanderson Hotel | 50 Berners St., W1 (Oxford Circus/
Goodge St.) | 020-7300 1444 | fax 7300 1488 |
www.morganshotelgroup.com

Residing in the former Spoon spot in the Sanderson Hotel, this "well-thought-out", slickly designed venue with "outside seating in the atrium" has a "great vibe" (it helps that the renowned "Long Bar is just beside" it); cuisinewise, NYC chef Zak Pelaccio's "trendy twist on Malaysian food" "leaves you wanting more" – "for your money" malcontents mutter.

Sumosan ◑ *Japanese*

24 | 18 | 18 | £55

Mayfair | 26 Albemarle St., W1 (Green Park) | 020-7495 5999 |
fax 7355 1247 | www.sumosan.com

"Trendy" it may be, but this minimalist Mayfair venue is also blessed with "amazing, truly genuine Japanese" cuisine; even if the service has "embarrassing" lapses, and the "mouth-watering food" commands "eye-watering prices", it makes a "decent alternative" to others of its ilk – plus it can be "easier to get into."

☑ Sweetings ☒ *British/Seafood*

26 | 18 | 22 | £39

City | 39 Queen Victoria St., EC4 (Bank/Mansion House) |
020-7248 3062

The "unique old London fish-house atmosphere at this lunch-only City establishment" is "still packing 'em in after all these years" (120 to be precise); "expect elbow to elbow seating", "waiters in white butcher's aprons" and a seafood menu that's "simple, but there's no denying the quality"; however, they take no reservations, so "whether you can stand the wait is up to you."

☑ Taman Gang ◑☒ *Pan-Asian*

21 | 25 | 18 | £53

Mayfair | 141 Park Ln., W1 (Marble Arch) | 020-7518 3160 |
fax 7518 3161 | www.tamangang.co.uk

With stone walls and candlelight, this Balinese-themed Pan-Asian (the name is Indonesian for 'Park Lane') is a "cool space with cool cocktails" coo converts who find it "great for a date or a catch-up"; if some sneer the "food is losing its shine", loyal gangsters advise "stick with the [small dishes] and drinks, and there'll be no disappointment."

	FOOD	DECOR	SERVICE	COST

Tamarai 🗷 Ⓜ *Pan-Asian*

	20	16	13	£41

Covent Garden | 167 Drury Ln., WC2 (Covent Garden/Holborn) | 020-7831 9399 | fax 78381 5710 | www.tamarai.co.uk

Given that this Pan-Asian basement "feels like a nightclub", it's no surprise that the "great atmosphere" attracts a "trendy crowd" to Covent Garden; however, diners are divided on the "creative" menu ("magnificent" vs. "mediocre") – and the service is roundly regarded as "amateurish."

🗷 Tamarind ● *Indian*

	25	21	24	£54

Mayfair | 20 Queen St., W1 (Green Park) | 020-7629 3561 | fax 7499 5034 | www.tamarindrestaurant.com

"After all these years", this "sublime" subterranean subcontinental with "Mayfair levels of class and buzz" still attracts discerning diners with Indian "classics done right" ("the biryani is a must-try") and "delicately spiced" "contemporary interpretations", accompanied by service "fit for a raj"; just ensure you "come with a fistful of quid – the *puris* here aren't for the poor."

Tapas Brindisa 🗷 *Spanish*

	24	14	16	£28

Borough | Borough Mkt. | 18-20 Southwark St., SE1 (London Bridge) | 020-7357 8880 | www.brindisa.com

"Wooden tables" groan with "world-class ham and cheese plates", "delicious chorizo sandwiches" and other "morsels of deliciousness", "so fresh it's like they're bringing the supplies in [straight] from Borough Market at the back door" of this "hectic but heavenly" Iberian idyll; the only thing marring this much-loved *lugar* are its "long lines" ("no reservations" taken) – but amigos assure us "it's worth the wait."

Taqueria *Mexican*

	22	11	16	£23

Notting Hill | 139-143 Westbourne Grove, W11 (Notting Hill Gate) | 020-7229 4734 | www.coolchiletaqueria.co.uk

"Don't expect Tex-Mex – that's not the point" of this Notting Hill taco tavern; rather, it's about "authentic Mexican" fare – "they use fresh, lively ingredients and [even] make their own tortillas" on premises – that many call "the best in London"; whilst "well-priced", "portions are extremely small" – so, best "think of this as a cafe with tapas."

Tartine *French*

	▽ 17	16	16	£29

Chelsea | 114 Draycott Ave., SW3 (South Kensington) | 020-7589 4981 | fax 7589 5048 | www.tartine.co.uk

This "modern", "social" sandwich bar is where Chelsea's "young, hip and rich go to show off the new bling"; although praised for its "*très chic*", "cool decor", most concur that the "simple French tartines" are "reasonable but not notable."

Tas ● *Turkish*

	20	16	18	£21

Bloomsbury | 22 Bloomsbury St., WC1 (Tottenham Court Rd.) | 020-7637 4555 | fax 7637 2226

Farringdon | 37 Farringdon Rd., EC1 (Farringdon) | 020-7430 9721

(continued)

(continued)

Tas

South Bank | 72 Borough High St., SE1 (London Bridge) | 020-7403 7200 | fax 7403 7022

Waterloo | 33 The Cut, SE1 (Southwark) | 020-7928 1444 | fax 7633 9686

Tas Pide ❷ *Turkish*

South Bank | 20-22 New Globe Walk, SE1 (London Bridge) | 020-7928 3300 | fax 7261 1166

www.tasrestaurant.com

"Good-value" set menus, "many mezze to pick from" and "lots of tasty vegetarian" options, all with "fantastically fresh" ingredients and "served at dervish speed", make this fast-expanding Turkish chain "great with a group", or perfect for "a quick pre/post-theatre meal."

Tate Britain Restaurant *British* (aka Rex Whistler Restaurant)

| 19 | 20 | 17 | £34 |

Westminster | Tate Britain | Millbank, SW1 (Pimlico) | 020-7887 8825 | fax 7887 8902 | www.tate.org.uk

"Go for the Whistler and the wine list" say fans of this Modern Brit on Millbank, where along with the "lovely mural-decorated room" (by artist Rex Whistler) and vino, Tate gallery-goers gaze upon "good English food prepared without too much fuss or sauces"; the only blot on the landscape? "pretty rough" service.

Tate Modern *European*

| 17 | 20 | 16 | £32 |

South Bank | Tate Modern | Bankside, 7th fl., SE1 (Blackfriars/London Bridge) | 020-7887 8888 | www.tate.org.uk

"The view, the view, the view" exalt art lovers who make the trip to the "usually mobbed" Tate Modern's "top-floor restaurant for lunch or tea"; you go for the vista, "but the Modern European food's not bad", and that, combined with the rotating murals (currently by James Aldridge), furnishes "a feast for your eyes and stomach."

Tendido Cero *Spanish*

| ∇ 16 | 15 | 18 | £38 |

South Kensington | 174 Old Brompton Rd., SW5 (Gloucester Rd./South Kensington) | 020-7370 3685 | www.cambiodetercio.co.uk

"Informal and friendly", this lively-coloured little sister to Cambio de Tercio, directly opposite Old Brompton Road, offers "much better value", provided you prefer a meal of "very good tapas"; even so, some sulky *señors* say it's "a bit pricey", but locals "like it as a late-night option" on weekends.

NEW Tendido Cuatro *Spanish*

| - | - | - | E |

Fulham | 108-110 New King's Rd., SW6 (Parsons Green/Putney Bridge) | 020-7371 5147

The popular South Ken Spanish duo Cambio de Tercio and Tendido Cero have been joined by a new Parsons Green sibling proffering a similarly unassuming (but not inexpensive) formula of gutsy Iberian tapas served in a homespun, wooden-floored setting with a strident mix of lilac, red and ochre colouring; there are a few pavement tables for those undeterred by noisy New King's Road.

	FOOD	DECOR	SERVICE	COST

Tentazioni ⑤ *Italian* ▽ 24 | 18 | 22 | £44

Tower Bridge | Lloyd's Wharf | 2 Mill St., SE1 (London Bridge/Tower Hill) | 020-7237 1100 | fax 7394 5248 | www.tentazioni.co.uk

"What dreams are made of" rave reviewers who revere the offerings at this "off-the-track" modern Italian in Tower Bridge that's "worth the trek", especially since a recent redo; the "great degustation menu", complete with "perfectly matched" wines, is ideal for the indecisive, and they'll even "amend it for allergies" – just a typical part of the "very friendly" service.

Ten Ten Tei ⑤ *Japanese* ▽ 23 | 6 | 14 | £19

Soho | 56 Brewer St., W1 (Piccadilly Circus) | 020-7287 1738

This "little-known" Soho "gem" reels in raw fish fans with high-scoring sushi and sashimi and "great Japanese" cooked items as well; the decor might be "shabby" but believers bear it for the "bargain prices."

NEW Terranostra Cucina Italiana ⑤ *Italian* - | - | - | E

City | 27 Old Bailey, EC4 (St. Paul's/City Thameslink Rail) | 020-3201 0077 | www.terranostrafood.co.uk

Set in a former pub, slap bang in the centre of the City, this new rustic Italian retreat specialises in Sardinian cuisine; expect simple but effective dishes such as malloreddus alla Campidanese, a traditional pasta of the region served with sausage and accompanied with warm southern European service.

Texas Embassy Cantina *Tex-Mex* 14 | 16 | 15 | £25

St. James's | 1 Cockspur St., SW1 (Charing Cross/Piccadilly Circus) | 020-7925 0077 | fax 7925 0444 | www.texasembassy.com

Those in "need of a burrito fix" mosey on over to this "funky faux Western" off Trafalgar Square; but once you get past the "nice atmosphere, the experience rapidly declines"; if the "slowest service" allows, start with the "good margaritas – after several, you might not notice" how "mediocre" the Tex-Mex fare is.

NEW Texture ⑤ Ⓜ *European* ▽ 21 | 19 | 24 | £69

Marylebone | 34 Portman St., W1 (Marble Arch) | 020-7224 0028 | www.texture-restaurant.co.uk

"Part culinary lab, part gourmet" restaurant – "it may seem they're trying too hard" at this modernistic Modern European in Marylebone, brainchild of an Icelandic chef and a French sommelier, both ex Le Manoir – and indeed, some "experimental dishes" (e.g. Anjou pigeon with bacon popcorn) provide "more texture than taste"; but the "absolutely excellent" champagne tasting menu finds favour (the bar has 90 brands of bubbly), as does the "professional, assured service", so overall, an "impressive new arrival" for "adventurous diners."

T.G.I. Friday's ◐ *American* 12 | 12 | 14 | £25

Covent Garden | 25-29 Coventry St., W1 (Piccadilly Circus) | 020-7839 6262 | fax 7839 6296

Covent Garden | 6 Bedford St., WC2 (Charing Cross/Covent Garden) | 020-7379 0585 | fax 7240 3239

(continued)

(continued)

T.G.I. Friday's

Fulham | Fulham Broadway Ctr. | 472 Fulham Rd., SW6 (Fulham Broadway) | 020-7385 0470 | fax 7385 8230
www.tgifridays.com

"You know what you're getting" at this American export that's "good for a quick meal" or, cheerleaders chime, watching the "flair bartenders toss their stuff"; but many more say skip the "bland burgers and fried everything", wondering "why go here? even on Friday?"

Thai Square *Thai*

18 | 16 | 17 | £28

Covent Garden | 148 The Strand, WC2 (Covent Garden) | 020-7497 0904 ●🅢

Mayfair | 5 Princes St., W1 (Oxford Circus) | 020-7499 3333

Soho | 27-28 St. Anne's Ct., W1 (Tottenham Court Rd.) | 020-7287 2000 ●🅢

St. James's | 21-24 Cockspur St., SW1 (Charing Cross/Piccadilly Circus) | 020-7839 4000 ●

City | 1 Great St. Thomas Apostle, EC4 (Mansion House) | 020-7329 0001 🅢

City | 136-138 Minories, EC3 (Tower Hill) | 020-7680 1111 | fax 7680 1112 🅢

Islington | 347-349 Upper St., N1 (Angel) | 020-7704 2000

Putney | 2-4 Lower Richmond Rd., SW1 (Putney Bridge) | 020-8780 1811 | fax 8780 1211

Richmond | 29 Kew Rd., TW9 (Richmond) | 020-8940 5253 | fax 8940-4258

South Kensington | 19 Exhibition Rd., SW7 (South Kensington) | 020-7584 8359
www.thaisq.com

Whilst there may be "many better Thais" in town, the success of this "fast-growing chain" lies in its "dependable, affordable food" and "good locations" (the "lovely river views" at Putney win particular praise); "tasty dishes" served in "bustling" Asia-inspired surroundings make it equally "great for girls' nights out" or an "express lunch."

Theo Randall at The InterContinental *Italian*

23 | 16 | 22 | £55

Mayfair | InterContinental Park Ln. | 1 Hamilton Pl., W1 (Hyde Park Corner) | 020-7318 8747 | www.theorandall.com

"Great food, dodgy room" summarises the sentiment about this "modern" Mayfair venue; the "simple", "well-crafted" Italian cuisine is "reminiscent of the River Café" where chef Theo Randall cut his teeth – but happily "cheaper" (indeed, at £21, a set lunch of "perfect homemade pasta" is "a steal"); sadly, the "cavernous and impersonal" hotel space is simply "the wrong environment" for it.

Thomas Cubitt, The *British*

21 | 20 | 20 | £35

Belgravia | 44 Elizabeth St., SW1 (Victoria) | 020-7730 6060 | fax 7730 6055 | www.thethomascubitt.co.uk

"You'd be blessed to have this as your local" laud lovers of this bi-level place offering the best of Brit to "chic Belgravians"; snack on traditional treats in the "busy" ground-floor pub where "gorgeous floor-to-ceiling windows open up in summer", or have a "civilised", more modern meal in the "romantic" restaurant above; wherever you perch, expect "cheerful service" and "nice ambience."

NEW Three Bridges ⊠ Italian | - | - | - | M |

Battersea | 153 Battersea Park Rd., SW8 (Vauxhall/Battersea Park Rail) | 020-7720 0204 | fax 020-7627-1169 | www.thethreebridges.com

In a desolate stretch of Battersea, this unpretentious new Italian offers simple decor – wooden floor, tables and chairs, etc. – but strikes a more ambitious tone on its polished Northern Italian menu from chef/co-owner Antonio Lombardi; the strong wine list includes labels from little-known local producers from around The Boot.

Timo ⊠ Italian | ▽ 27 | 18 | 25 | £49 |

Kensington | 343 Kensington High St., W8 (High St. Kensington) | 020-7603 3888 | fax 7603 8111 | www.timorestaurant.net

"Easily overlooked" "at the western end of Ken High Street", this Italian is "just right after a busy day"; the patron here "knows his stuff" and that's reflected in the "pleasant" staff that "work hard" within the "bright decor"; "tasty", "modern" dishes and a "solid wine selection" leave even the most demanding *molto contento.*

Tokyo Diner ⬤ Japanese | 16 | 12 | 14 | £18 |

Chinatown | 2 Newport Pl., WC2 (Leicester Sq.) | 020-7287 8777 | fax 7434 1415 | www.tokyodiner.com

"Simple to the point of barren", this canteen on a corner of Chinatown is still a "great choice for those on a budget" given its "perfectly ok, if not marvellous" "Japanese street food", "with the advantage that tipping is absolutely forbidden"; however, sliding scores suggest it's "gone downhill" of late (especially the "weak sushi").

Tom Aikens ⊠ French | 25 | 22 | 24 | £89 |

Chelsea | 43 Elystan St., SW3 (South Kensington) | 020-7584 2003 | fax 7584 2001 | www.tomaikens.co.uk

"Like a mad scientist's experiment gone terribly right" rave reviewers enraptured by the "rich" New French cuisine at "creative chef-owner" Tom Aikens' "smart black-and-white setting" in Chelsea; "don't eat anything all day" – "the amuse-bouches alone are a meal" and "the petit fours should be called petit twenty-fours"; if foes fume there's "too much froth and foam" in the "fussy" fare, most rave this is "a restaurant to be reckoned with"; oh, and if you're not one of the "expense-account crowd", go for the equally "impressive set lunch."

NEW Tom Ilic Ⓜ European | ▽ 24 | 9 | 16 | £37 |

Battersea | 123 Queenstown Rd., SW8 (Queenstown Road Rail) | 020-7622 0555 | www.tomilic.com

"Rents must be cheap in Battersea – that's the only way chef-owner Tom Ilic can cook food this good at this price" posit patrons about the "lovely and light" dishes at this new Modern European; if the "service seems a bit overwhelmed on occasion", most "chalk it up to the teething problems" of new places; "but the biggest letdown is the decor, which [doesn't] do justice to the magic done in the kitchen."

	FOOD	DECOR	SERVICE	COST

Tom's Deli *Eclectic* — 16 | 13 | 13 | £23

Notting Hill | 226 Westbourne Grove, W11 (Notting Hill Gate) | 020-7221 8818 | fax 7221 7717 | www.tomconranrestaurants.co.uk
This "cute", crowded cafe is where the "moneyed" of Notting Hill "pretend to be ordinary Joes"; "if you can get a table", it's a "great spot for a weekend brunch" featuring "fantastic poached eggs" and other Eclectic delights; but better be quick, as "you'll feel the pressure to leave."

Tom's Kitchen ● *British* — 22 | 17 | 17 | £41

Chelsea | 27 Cale St., SW3 (South Kensington) | 020-7349 0202 | www.tomskitchen.co.uk
"Delicious" British "comfort food" (albeit at "an uncomfortable price") is the star of Tom Aikens' "don't-mind-if-I-share-your table", "informal offering" off the King's Road; if only the service weren't "slightly sniffy" and "the yummy mummies would keep their screaming children out" (but "don't try to complain – it's so noisy no one will hear you").

NEW Tom's Place *British/Seafood* — 18 | 16 | 14 | £24

Chelsea | 1 Cale St., SW3 (South Kensington) | 020-7351 1806 | www.tomsplace.org.uk
Tom Aikens' "third Chelsea venture" is this "ethical" and "mildly kitschy" take on the time-honoured fish 'n' chippy; sustainably sourced "fresh fish" comes fried (or grilled for "fat phobics") with the usual sides – chips, mushy peas, etc; whilst it's "pricier than a traditional chipper", it's "worth [it for] a treat every once in a whilst."

Tootsies *American* — 13 | 12 | 12 | £21

Marylebone | 35 James St., W1 (Bond St.) | 020-7486 1611 | fax 7935 4957
Blackheath | Brent Cross Shopping Ctr. | Prince Charles Dr., NW4 (Brent Cross) | 020-8203 9942
Hampstead | 196-198 Haverstock Hill, NW3 (Belsize Park) | 020-7431 3812 | fax 7794 8478
Clapham | 36-38 Abbeville Rd., SW4 (Clapham South) | 020-8772 6646 | fax 8772 0672
Putney | Putney Wharf | The Piazza, 30 Brewhouse Ln., SW1 (Putney Bridge) | 020-8788 8488 | fax 8788 6636
Wimbledon | 48 High St., SW19 (Wimbledon) | 020-8946 4135 | fax 8947 7936
Chiswick | 148 Chiswick High Rd., W4 (Turnham Green) | 020-8747 1869 | fax 8987 0486
Notting Hill | 120 Holland Park Ave., W11 (Holland Park) | 020-7229 8567
www.tootsiesrestaurants.co.uk
Despite efforts by the owners of GBK, nose-diving scores suggest "the revamp has not been altogether successful" at this "cheap" American-style diner chain; the expanded "menu is trying to offer too much", the new pastel-hued decor is "too cute" and service "leaves a lot to be desired"; still, the "specialty milkshakes and burgers" are bound to please the "kidsville" crowd.

	FOOD	DECOR	SERVICE	COST

Toto's ● *Italian*
23 | 19 | 22 | £52

Chelsea | Walton House | Walton St. at Lennox Garden Mews, SW3 (Knightsbridge) | 020-7589 2062 | fax 7581 9668

For over 20 years, this "quiet" and "gracious" Italian "hideaway" has been "a steady performer" on the Chelsea culinary scene; "always comfortable in a good way", it really comes into its own in the summer when the "accommodating" staff serve the "deftly executed" dishes in the "prettiest garden."

Trinity *European*
▽ 26 | 18 | 24 | £41

Clapham | 4 The Polygon, SW4 (Clapham Common) | 020-7622 1199 | fax 7622 1166 | www.trinityrestaurant.co.uk

"Appreciative locals" who rued the passing of Thyme "heartily recommend" the Clapham return of this particular holy trinity – chef-owner Adam Byatt, his "original", "elegant" Modern European food and the "friendly, informed" staff that accompany it; need divine inspiration? try the "brilliant", "inventive" tasting menu – perfect for "serious foodies who don't have a serious budget."

Troubadour, The *Eclectic*
▽ 18 | 21 | 17 | £22

Earl's Court | 265 Old Brompton Rd., SW5 (Earl's Ct.) | 020-7370 1434 | fax 7341 6329 | www.troubadour.co.uk

"Utterly unique", this troubadour to Earl's Court – a coffeehouse founded in the '50s – was the site of Dylan's London debut and has barely changed since; its bona fides as an arty bohemian "oasis" live on with a packed programme of music and poetry most evenings; the Eclectic fare plays second fiddle, but there's a "fantastic brunch" at the weekend, especially when you can "sit in the garden."

Truc Vert *French*
17 | 15 | 13 | £29

Mayfair | 42 N. Audley St., W1 (Bond St.) | 020-7491 9988 | fax 7491 7717

"U.S. embassy types and Mayfair hedge fund managers" welcome the "change of pace" at this "quiet French bistro", a "rustic", "really cute place" that's "charming for a light lunch" or breakfast; if you'd prefer to picnic in nearby Hyde Park, get it to go at the on-site deli.

Tsunami *Japanese*
▽ 26 | 16 | 16 | £41

Clapham | 5-7 Voltaire Rd., SW4 (Clapham North) | 020-7978 1610 | fax 7978 1591 | www.tsunamirestaurant.co.uk

A wave of praise washes over this "minimalist" Clapham Japanese for its "fantastically fresh sushi" that's "reasonably priced" if you "go before 7 PM" (20% off); whilst the decor was streamlined last year, the "service is still not up to scratch."

Tuttons Brasserie *British/French*
19 | 16 | 17 | £31

Covent Garden | 11-12 Russell St., WC2 (Covent Garden) | 020-7836 4141 | fax 7379 9979 | www.tuttons.com

"In the thick of Covent Garden", this "bustling" British-French brasserie is "not worth a special trip"; but it offers a "reliable" pre-/post-theatre supper, or "comforting food for the weary shopper", plus an opportunity to "watch the world go by."

	FOOD	DECOR	SERVICE	COST

Two Brothers Fish 🅂🄼 *Seafood*
22 | 9 | 16 | £22

Finchley | 297-303 Regent's Park Rd., N3 (Finchley Central) |
020-8346 0469 | fax 8343 1978 | www.twobrothers.co.uk
"Simple", "flavourful" fish 'n' chips and a "friendly", "busy atmosphere" make it "worth the schlep to Finchley" and this seafood "institution"; but "good luck finding a table" as "it gets packed early on with a lively middle-aged crowd" who blot out the "tired-looking decor" with bottles of the house white ("a local secret" from the namesake "two brothers' own vineyard").

202 *European*
18 | 17 | 14 | £29

Notting Hill | Nicole Farhi | 202 Westbourne Grove, W11
(Notting Hill Gate) | 020-7727 2722 | fax 7792 9217
"Watch out for well-known faces sitting behind outsized shades" at this "relaxed" cafe in the "fashionable" Nicole Farhi store; the "health-conscious" Modern European menu is "done with competence and some flourish, but is a little beside the point" to the "beautiful people brunching, with the outside tables being the premium" place to be.

222 Veggie Vegan *Vegetarian*
- | - | - | M

Fulham | 222 North End Rd., W14 (West Kensington) | 020-7381 2322 |
www.222veggievegan.com
"Huge portions" of "scrumptious vegetarian fare" from a "simple menu" that includes a lunchtime "buffet with good variety" draws voracious vegans and others to Ghanaian-born chef-owner Ben Asamani's wallet-friendly Fulham eatery; it's a "tight space", but worth the squeeze for "amazing desserts."

2 Veneti 🅂 *Italian*
▽ 19 | 20 | 20 | £43

Marylebone | 8-10 Wigmore St., W1 (Bond St./Oxford Circus) |
020-7637 0789
Two citizens of the city of canals (get the name, now?) offer "authentic Venetian food, served with grace and humour" to Marylebone via this "pleasant" trattoria featuring an Italian menu that navigates "from fine to very good indeed"; it's also "handy for Wigmore Hall" concerts.

🆉 Ubon by Nobu 🅂 *Japanese*
26 | 23 | 20 | £56

Canary Wharf | 34 Westferry Circus, E14 (Canary Wharf) |
020-7719 7800 | fax 7719 7801 | www.noburestaurants.com
As "the only real choice for lunch on the Wharf", this younger sibling of Nobu serves "City fliers" with the "same superb Japanese-Peruvian dishes" (including "exquisite sushi" and the "phenomenal black miso cod"); the only blots on the "breathtaking views" over the Thames are the "high-pressure staff" and the high-priced offerings, so either order the "excellent-value bento box" or "don't forget the corporate card."

Uli *Pan-Asian*
▽ 26 | 14 | 21 | £32

Notting Hill | 16 All Saints Rd., W11 (Ladbroke Grove) | 020-7727 7511
"Tucked away off Portobello" Road, this "tiny", "family-owned" Pan-Asian is a "great date place"; "popular with the Boho set", "it's hard

	FOOD	DECOR	SERVICE	COST

to get a table" but, once seated, expect "superb" dishes like chile lobster tempura to be served by "attentive, friendly" staff.

☑ Umu ☒ *Japanese* — 26 | 25 | 25 | £90

Mayfair | 14-16 Bruton Pl., W1 (Bond St.) | 020-7499 8881 | www.umurestaurant.com

A "chic, cosy" "bijoux box dining room" houses this "authentic Japanese gem hidden away" in a Mayfair mews (and "what an experience" it is, "not just for kaiseki") though those renowned tasting menus are pretty "exquisite" – but for sushi that's "a work of art", all preferably paired with a "sake selection without peer" and served by "staff who know what they're talking about and seem to care" too; of course it's "off-the-chart expensive – but worth it" virtually every reviewer adds; P.S. "if dinner's out of your budget, lunch can give you a spark."

Union Cafe *British/Mediterranean* — 19 | 17 | 19 | £33

Marylebone | 96 Marylebone Ln., W1 (Bond St.) | 020-7486 4860 | fax 7935 1537 | www.brinkleys.com

It's no wonder this "welcoming" Marylebone cafe is often "crowded": it's where "well-cooked" Brit "comfort food" (roast chicken, sausage and mash) meets a "modern" Med menu (seafood linguini, mushroom risotto) amidst "buzzy atmosphere"; "even more of a pleasure is the excellently priced wine list" (e.g. "without the usual shocking markups").

NEW Upper Deck *British* — - | - | - | M

Covent Garden | London Transport Museum | Covent Garden Piazza, WC2 (Covent Garden) | 020-7598 1355 | www.ltmuseum.co.uk

In service only since November 2007, this London Transport Museum cafe/bar serves as a midday – or even last – stop for weary travellers; in fair weather, picnic on the piazza; otherwise, enjoy iconically named cocktails (a Routemaster, anyone?) and a basic Brit menu – sandwiches, salads and just snacks in the evenings – on seats upholstered in fabric copied from 1930s tube trains.

Upstairs Bar & Restaurant ☒☒ *French* — - | - | - | M

Brixton | 89B Acre Ln., SW2 (Brixton/Clapham North) | 020-7733 8855 | www.upstairslondon.com

It may be a "short menu" but the New French cooking is long on taste and "delivered with confidence and flair" *français* at this venue with sophisticated yet cosy, coffee-and-cream decor (complete with roaring fireplace); it's become a destination diner for those on the Brixton/Clapham border.

NEW Urban Turban *Indian* — ∇ 17 | 17 | 14 | £37

Notting Hill | 98 Westbourne Grove, W2 (Bayswater/Royal Oak) | 020-7243 4200

"Just what the area needs" nod Notting Hillites about this new "inventive Indian", the brainchild of star chef Vineet Bhatia; if "not as impressive, it's more accessible than Rasoi Vineet Bhatia", with "tasty" tapas-style menus at "relatively reasonable prices", and a vibrantly coloured, "buzzy atmosphere"; however, "service needs to be smoothed out."

	FOOD	DECOR	SERVICE	COST

Vama ❶ *Indian* | 25 | 17 | 20 | £38 |

Chelsea | 438 King's Rd., SW10 (Sloane Sq.) | 020-7565 8500 | fax 7565 8501 | www.vama.co.uk

"If your mum were Indian, you'd wish she cooked like this" declare devotees of this decade-old, "upscale" Punjabi on the outskirts of Chelsea ("don't try to walk from the station"); "it's worth the cab ride" for "consistently" "high-quality" curries and lamb dishes, brought by "helpful staff"; "on a nice evening, get a table near the street."

NEW Vanilla 🖲 *European* | - | - | - | E |

Fitzrovia | 131 Great Titchfield St., W1 (Great Portland St.) | 020-3008 7763 | www.vanillalondon.com

Not many have made their way to this new subterranean Modern European in Fitzrovia, but with dishes like 10 spices tuna and scallops with Chinese pear and black pudding, the cuisine's clearly anything but plain vanilla (the "inventive chef" did some time at The Square); "excellent service" operates within a dramatic monochrome setting.

Vasco & Piero's Pavilion 🖲 *Italian* | 21 | 13 | 19 | £42 |

Soho | 15 Poland St., W1 (Oxford Circus) | 020-7437 8774 | fax 7437 0467 | www.vascosfood.com

"Serious" Umbrian cuisine fans "pack into this place", politely ignoring "surroundings not meant to impress"; but the blunt deem the "decor incredibly tired" – and declare that whilst this may be "one of the better Italians around Soho", it's still "nothing to write home about."

Veeraswamy *Indian* | 23 | 21 | 20 | £44 |

Mayfair | Victory House | 99-101 Regent St., W1 (Piccadilly Circus) | 020-7734 1401 | fax 7439 8434 | www.realindianfood.com

"Bite-size appetisers like flavour bombs" make an explosive start to a "well-seasoned" meal full of "interesting twists" at this "grande dame of Indian restaurants" "overlooking Regent Street"; some of the "highly unusual" "dishes don't occasionally justify the price tag" but "super service" in conjunction with the "funky" look "evocative of a 1920s maharajah's palace" means that overall, the experience is "smart and slick."

Via Condotti *Italian* | 19 | 17 | 21 | £54 |

Mayfair | 23 Conduit St., W1 (Oxford Circus) | 020-7493 7050 | fax 7409 7985 | www.viacondotti.co.uk

Opinion is split on this Italian venue on "the Mayfair scene"; some reviewers reckon its "accomplished seasonal cooking" and "affordable set menus" make "you really think you're in Rome", whilst naysayers needle that it's "overpriced" for "nothing special."

Viet Grill ❶ *Vietnamese* | - | - | - | I |

Shoreditch | 53 Kingsland Rd., E2 (Old St.) | 020-7739 6686 | www.vietnamesekitchen.co.uk

"There are better restaurants on Kingsland Road" but this "cheap, cheerful" sibling of Cay tre pulls in punters pining for Saigon with "good, reliable" "Vietnamese staples"; some slate the service, but with small bills and big dishes (like the "amazing bun sa", a lemongrass and rice vermicelli combo), it keeps 'em coming back.

Viet Hoa ● *Vietnamese* ▽ 18 | 4 | 13 | £16

Shoreditch | 70-72 Kingsland Rd., E2 (Old St.) | 020-7729 8293

"If you've come for decor or service, go home; if you've come for some of the best Vietnamese food in London, you're in the right place" advise advocates of this "no-frills" Shoreditch site that's "always busy" 'cos it "produces the goods" "at a very reasonable price."

Villandry *French* 22 | 18 | 19 | £32

Bloomsbury | 170 Great Portland St., W1 (Great Portland St.) | 020-7631 3131 | fax 7631 3030 | www.villandry.com

"A smorgasbord of food offerings" and dining experiences awaits you at this tripartite "homey, rustic French" on Great Portland Street; whether you want a "cute shop" for "gourmet" groceries and takeaway, "a light snack" or a "fancy restaurant", this "safe haven from the chaos of shopping" "never disappoints."

Vineyard at Stockcross *British/French* ▽ 25 | 21 | 24 | £88

Newbury | Vineyard at Stockcross | Stockcross, Berkshire | 01635 528770 | fax 01635 528398 | www.the-vineyard.co.uk

With 2,000-odd labels on offer, "the wine has always been the star" at this "intoxicating" venue in Berkshire; but some imbibers insist the Classic French–Modern British "food has caught up well", "reflecting seasonal specialities on the great-value" prix fixes; all agree you should "stay at the adjacent hotel – so no problem sampling the list!"

Vingt-Quatre ● *Eclectic* 13 | 9 | 13 | £25

Chelsea | 325 Fulham Rd., SW10 (South Kensington) | 020-7376 7224 | fax 7352 2643 | www.vingtquatre.co.uk

"It's ok, unless everywhere else is closed or full – then you're delighted" to squeeze into this "crowded" Chelsea Eclectic that's open *vingt-quatre* hours a day; "service is erratic", "but where else do you go for salmon and scrambled eggs or a fry-up at 4 in the morning?"

Vinoteca *European* - | - | - | M

Farringdon | 7 St. John St., EC1 (Farringdon) | 020-7253 8786 | www.vinoteca.co.uk

Life's "always busy and buzzy" at this wine bar close by Smithfield Market, thanks to a "huge", "fantastic list with appealing choices across the cost and taste spectrum" (and available to purchase from their adjacent shop), along with "excellent", "flavoursome" Modern European nibbles, such as "platters of Spanish hams and other sharing-type dishes", emanating from a "tiny on-view kitchen"; "the only drawback is you can't book, and there isn't much room to wait."

Vivat Bacchus ☒ *European* 20 | 20 | 22 | £48

City | 47 Farringdon St., EC4 (Chancery Ln./Farringdon) | 020-7353 2648 | fax 7353 3025 | www.vivatbacchus.co.uk

"City workers", including lots of local "Lovells lawyers", love the "phenomenal wine list" ("ask for a tour of the cellar") that accompanies the "interesting", "South African–inspired" Modern European menu here; you'll also "have a ball going into the cheese room and choosing your own platter"; such participation, plus "passionate service", compensates for "prices that are looking a little bit greedy."

Ζ Wagamama *Japanese*   19 | 13 | 16 | £18

Bloomsbury | 4 Streatham St., WC1 (Tottenham Court Rd.) | 020-7323 9223 | fax 7323 9224
Covent Garden | 1 Tavistock St., WC2 (Covent Garden) | 020-7836 3330 | fax 7240 8846
Knightsbridge | Harvey Nichols | 109-125 Knightsbridge, SW1 (Knightsbridge) | 020-7201 8000 | fax 7201 8080
Marylebone | 101 Wigmore St., W1 (Bond St.) | 020-7409 0111
Soho | 10A Lexington St., W1 (Oxford Circus/Piccadilly Circus) | 020-7292 0990
Blackfriars | 109 Fleet St., EC4 (Blackfriars/St. Paul's) | 020-7583 7889 Ⓢ
City | 1 Ropemaker St., EC2 (Moorgate) | 020-7588 2688 Ⓢ
Camden Town | 11 Jamestown Rd., NW1 (Camden Town) | 020-7428 0800 | fax 7482 4887
Islington | 40 Parkfield St., N1 (Angel) | 020-7226 2664
Kensington | 26 Kensington High St., W8 (High St. Kensington) | 020-7376 1717
www.wagamama.com
Additional locations throughout London

Even folks who "don't usually buy into chains" make an exception for these "minimalist but functional" Japanese; theirs is a "noisy", "get on and eat", "mess hall ambience", but for "steaming bowls" of "noodle-ish-ous" "Asian-influenced fare" that "fills the stomach without emptying the wallet", "it's almost impossible to find better"; the much-imitated communal seating means you're "elbow-to-elbow" with an "eclectic mix of clientele", and service is still "a lottery", but with one on "almost every corner", it's no surprise they're London's Most Popular for the third year in a row.

NEW Wahaca *Mexican*   20 | 18 | 18 | £24

Covent Garden | 66 Chandos Pl., WC2 (Charing Cross/Leicester Sq.) | 020-7240 1883 | www.wahaca.co.uk

The "festive" (some feel "frenetic") atmosphere of this "cute", "cheap 'n' cheerful" *cantina* basement brings Central America to Covent Garden in the shape of *tostados* and *taquitos* that touts trumpet are "the closest London gets to real Mexican food"; "they don't take reservations, which is annoying" – and means "you'll have to wait" – but after a couple of "wonderful" margaritas from the "lively and personable" staff, it's all *bueno*.

Wallace, The *French*   18 | 24 | 14 | £30

Marylebone | Wallace Museum Collection | Hertford Hse., Manchester Sq., W1 (Baker St./Bond St.) | 020-7563 9505 | www.thewallacerestaurant.com

"Hidden within the Wallace Museum" is this "charming", "calm" eatery whose atrium setting allows visitors to "enjoy a delightful alfresco meal without being subject to the elements"; the Classic French menu may be "typical upscale-museum fare", but it works well enough "for a relaxed lunch away from the Oxford Street bustle"; N.B. dinner served Friday–Saturday only.

Wapping Food *European*
∇ 19 | 26 | 18 | £54

Docklands | Wapping Hydraulic Power Station | Wapping Wall, E1 (Wapping) | 020-7680 2080 | www.thewappingproject.com

It's not the "small but titillating" Modern European menu that draws diners to this former Wapping power station – rather, the "fabulous, mad industrial interior" "enhanced by frequently changing art installations" is the main attraction; that said, it's "one of the few places that does an NY-style brunch", so weekends are "packed with New Yorkers" apparently unfazed by the "haphazard but charming" service.

NEW Warrington, The *British*
- | - | - | M

St. John's Wood | 93 Warrington Crescent, W9 (Maida Vale/ Warwick Ave.) | 020-7592 7960 | fax 7592 1603 | www.gordonramsay.com

When this Victorian, marble-pillared boozer reopened last winter, St. John's Wood denizens were delighted to discover a Gordon Ramsay gastropub on their doorstep; but whilst some rate the Traditional Brit food as "definitely a cut above" the competition, others find it only "ordinary" (even "allowing for teething problems"), and service can be a kitchen nightmare – "poor" pipe up punters.

NEW Water House *European*
- | - | - | E

Hoxton | 10 Orsman Rd., N1 (Old St.) | 020-7033 0123 | www.waterhouserestaurant.co.uk

It's eco-a-go-go at this new solar-powered, '60s-styled sibling to Acorn House; the Modern European menu is packed with sustainably sourced fish, seasonal vegetables and other low carbon impact delicacies, whilst the wine is organic or biodynamic and the water is of the filtered tap variety; early reports deem it "a worthy addition" to the Hoxton scene, with a "canalside location that comes into its own when the sun comes out."

NEW Waterloo Brasserie ● *French*
∇ 19 | 21 | 14 | £43

Waterloo | 119 Waterloo Rd., SE1 (Waterloo) | 020-7960 0202 | www.waterloobrasserie.co.uk

Proximity to the Old Vic makes this new black-and-burnt-orange–hued, "stunningly decorated" French fancy a favourite with the "cool" theatre crowd; but given reports of "annoyingly amateurish service", don't count on finishing your côte de boeuf before curtain up – instead, opt for post-performance prandials or else, "go on a patient stomach."

⊠ Waterside Inn Ⓜ *French*
27 | 25 | 26 | £111

Bray | Waterside Inn | Ferry Rd., Berkshire | 01628 620691 | fax 01638 784710 | www.waterside-inn.co.uk

"Some places are timeless", and one such is this Bray bastion of "classically correct" French cuisine, "every mouthful of which is superb" and served by staff with "unimaginable attention to detail" and, ideally, with something from the *formidable* "wine list with a reasonable selection of half-bottles"; "the slightly jaded decor is the only letdown", so the trick is to "get a table by the window", the better to drink in the "idyllic setting on the banks of the Thames" (and to "brace yourself for the bill").

Waterway, The *European*

▽ | 15 | 18 | 14 | £27

St. John's Wood | 54 Formosa St., W9 (Warwick Ave.) | 020-7266 3557 | fax 7266 3547 | www.thewaterway.co.uk

"Beautiful, pretty things" are drawn to the "great canalside location" of this St. John's Wood "summer drinking hole" where a change of ownership has upped the food stakes with "generous portions" of Modern European favourites like "light, silky pumpkin soup"; still, sceptics sniff it's "overpriced for a place in the middle of a council estate."

Wells, The *European*

20 | 19 | 19 | £33

Hampstead | 30 Well Walk, NW3 (Hampstead) | 020-7794 3785 | www.thewellshampstead.co.uk

It may be Hampstead, but "friendly staff" and a "cosy, intimate" atmosphere that welcomes man and beast alike ("they even have dog food on the menu") create a "village" feel at this Modern European gastropub; a "more formal" restaurant upstairs serves the same "creative, flavourful" dishes, but most opt to lounge below on the "comfy sofas" or the "peaceful" patio.

Westbourne, The *Eclectic*

18 | 14 | 10 | £27

Notting Hill | 101 Westbourne Park Villas, W2 (Royal Oak/ Westbourne Park) | 020-7221 1332 | fax 7243 8081 | www.thewestbourne.com

"Definitely a destination gastropub", this Notting Hill boozer "is heaving" with "deafening hordes" who come for "great outdoor socializing almost any time of the year" on the "un-publike" heated terrace; the Eclectic grub is "decent"; despite "the most obnoxious staff in London."

NEW Whole Foods Market *Eclectic*

18 | 12 | 14 | £17

Kensington | Barkers Bldg. | 63-97 Kensington High St., W8 (High St. Kensington) | 020-7368 4500 | www.wholefoods.com

It's "finally in the U.K." enthuse expats enamoured of this Kensington branch of the American organic grocer/deli, aka "Shangri-la for the healthy generation"; "huge" and "spacious", it resembles a "busy airport lounge" with crowds consuming "a great variety" of "sophisticated" foods ranging from salads to sushi to tapas; many mutter that for "food court decor and self-service", it's "overpriced", but bear in mind, it's essentially "a shop, not a restaurant."

NEW Wild Honey *British*

23 | 19 | 20 | £47

Mayfair | 12 St. George St., W1 (Bond St./Oxford Circus) | 020-7758 9160 | fax 7493 4549 | www.wildhoneyrestaurant.co.uk

"What Modern British cooking should be all about – simple, tasty, well-cooked" hum gourmet bees buzzing around this "oak-panelled" Mayfair "sibling to Arbutus"; regulars are in raptures about the "unbelievable value" prix fixes, and the "genius" in serving the "delightful" wine list "by 250-ml. carafe"; the only sting is the slightly "soulless" atmosphere occasioned by sometimes "slip-shod service."

	FOOD	DECOR	SERVICE	COST

☑ Wilton's ☒ *British/Seafood*   25 | 22 | 25 | £68

St. James's | 55 Jermyn St., SW1 (Green Park/Piccadilly Circus) | 020-7629 9955 | fax 7495 6233 | www.wiltons.co.uk

"So old-school it's actually cool", this "unbelievably traditional" St. James's "institution" dating back to the mid-1700s is "renowned" for a "consistent standard" of "classic British" dishes "with a healthy bias towards outstanding fish"; even though "your wallet feels the strain" and the "immaculate service" can be "stuffy" ("I received instruction to put my suit coat back on"), most declare all's "how it should be" here.

Wòdka ◑ *Polish*   21 | 16 | 20 | £36

Kensington | 12 St. Albans Grove, W8 (High St. Kensington) | 020-7937 6513 | fax 7937 8621 | www.wodka.co.uk

"When in London, do as the Polish do" at this Kensington kickback where "delicious waitresses" serve "delightful" traditional dishes and even better "untraditional flavoured vodkas", like cherry and horseradish; you "could drink here for hours" trying all the "great shots"; of course, "you may need a bit of help to get up . . ."

☑ Wolseley, The ◑ *European*   22 | 26 | 21 | £48

Piccadilly | 160 Piccadilly, W1 (Green Park) | 020-7499 6996 | fax 7499 6888 | www.thewolseley.com

With its "buzzing atmosphere", "unique, grand setting" ("Viennese-style" cafe "meets former bank" in Piccadilly) "and always some celebrity-spotting", this "well-oiled machine" remains "hot, hot, hot"; whilst some growl it's "more glamour than good food" here, the Modern European "comfort" menu "covers the gamut" from "brilliant breakfasts" to "delicious dinners", so "you can eat cheap and cheerful or top-end", and the "service is surprisingly friendly"; it's "impossible to book", of course, but "their policy of keeping tables for walk-ins is a wonderful touch."

Wong Kei ◑≠ *Chinese*   17 | 6 | 7 | £14

Chinatown | 41-43 Wardour St., W1 (Leicester Sq./Piccadilly Circus) | 020-7437 8408

"Walk in, be rudely ordered to go upstairs, sit at a table with seven other strangers, order food, food arrives, eat and get the bill while you're finishing, leave" – that's the drill at this veteran Chinatown Chinese; it's "not the warmest in terms of ambience" or service ("ask for a fork and you're asking for trouble"), but the "basic food" "remains remarkable value", so "that's why we keep going."

Wright Brothers' Oyster & Porter House ☒ *Seafood*   - | - | - | E

Borough | 11 Stoney St., SE1 (London Bridge) | 020-7403 9554 | www.wrightbros.eu.com

"They know seafood, bring it fresh and have the sense not to monkey with it too much" at this easy-going eatery in Borough Market, run by a wholesaler to restaurants; led by the "exceptional oysters", "the quality of the food makes up for the tight seating", which includes actual shellfish barrels on the sidewalk.

XO *Pan-Asian*

FOOD | DECOR | SERVICE | COST

| 21 | 20 | 19 | £41 |

Hampstead | 29 Belsize Ln., NW3 (Belsize Park) | 020-7433 0888 | fax 7794 3474 | www.rickerrestaurants.com

"From the e&o team", this "modernist" black-and-citron–coloured Pan-Asian is "never going to be as swish and hip as its Notting Hill cousin, but it's still by far the trendiest option in Belsize Park"; "professional" staff offer the chic chow Will Ricker regulars will recognise, including an "out-of-this-world duck, watermelon and cashew salad."

Yakitoria ☒ *Japanese*

| ▽ 17 | 21 | 11 | £37 |

Paddington | 25 Sheldon Sq., W2 (Paddington) | 020-3214 3000 | fax 3214 3001 | www.yakitoria.co.uk

"Good luck finding this one" snarl sushi-seekers sick of scouring the Paddington Basin for this tucked-away Japanese; however, it's worth persevering for the "lovely location looking out onto the canal", "authentic" sushi and yakitori and an extensive sake menu – a bit spoilt by "slightly ropey service."

☒ Yauatcha ◕ *Chinese*

| 26 | 23 | 19 | £43 |

Soho | 15 Broadwick St., W1 (Piccadilly Circus) | 020-7494 8888 | fax 7287 6959

"Welcome to Blofeld's basement" cackle converts to restaurateur Alan Yau's "psychedelic" Soho all-day dim sum diner that offers an "unforgettable experience"; disciples descend the darkened stairs to the "stylish" yet "romantic" dining room where "inventive ingredients such as ostrich and venison" make for "delicious dumplings" and other Chinese treats, accompanied by "sublime", "creative" cocktails; less loved, however, is the staff's sometimes "crude" enforcement of two-hour time limit on the "tight" tables; P.S. fans of "fancy" French pastries and "aromatic" Asian teas "will be in heaven" on the "airy, light" ground-floor cafe.

Ye Olde Cheshire Cheese *British*

| 16 | 23 | 14 | £23 |

Blackfriars | 145 Fleet St., EC4 (Blackfriars) | 020-7353 6170 | fax 7353 0845

It's "a tourist trap" but "we don't care – any place that was rebuilt in 1667 is ok in our book" declare defiant devotees of this Blackfriars boozer, whose "limestone cavelike rooms" have barely changed in centuries; whilst most are here "for the history" (it's hosted the literati from Johnson to Dickens), there's Traditional Brit "comfort food" ("proper steak and kidney pie or roast beast") and "cheap" Samuel Smith beers on offer.

Yming ◕☒ *Chinese*

| ▽ 24 | 15 | 19 | £32 |

Soho | 35-36 Greek St., W1 (Leicester Sq.) | 020-7734 2721 | fax 7437 0292 | www.yminglondon.com

You don't usually hear Chinese eateries described as "inventive", "unusual" and "sophisticated", but this blue-hued Soho site is the exception – a "restaurant that knows exactly what it is doing" as it

	FOOD	DECOR	SERVICE	COST

focuses on fare from northern China; with prix fixe menus, space for groups and a "wonderful" maitre d', Y not give it a try?

YO! Sushi *Japanese*

15	14	13	£24

Bloomsbury | 11-13 Bayley St., WC1 (Tottenham Court Rd.) | 020-7636 0076

Knightsbridge | Harrods 102 | 102-104 Brompton Rd., SW3 (Knightsbridge) | 020-7893 8175

Knightsbridge | Harvey Nichols | 109-125 Knightsbridge, 5th fl., SW1 (Knightsbridge) | 020-7201 8641

Marylebone | Selfridges | 400 Oxford St., W1 (Bond St.) | 020-7318 3944

Soho | 52 Poland St., W1 (Oxford Circus) | 020-7287 0443

Westminster | County Hall | Belvedere Rd., SE1 (Westminster) | 020-7928 8871 | fax 7928 5619

Farringdon | 95 Farringdon Rd., EC1 (Farringdon) | 020-7841 0785 | fax 7841 0798

Fulham | Fulham Broadway Ctr. | Fulham Rd., 1st fl., SW6 (Fulham Broadway) | 020-7385 6077

Bayswater | Whiteleys Shopping Ctr. | 151 Queensway, W2 (Bayswater) | 020-7727 9392 | fax 7727 9390

Paddington | Paddington Station, W2 (Paddington) | 020-7706 8388 www.yosushi.com

Additional locations throughout London

"The kids love it" and it's "great for those in a hurry", but grown-ups growl given that "there are better sushi offerings" out there, "the novelty of this conveyor belt" chain and its drink-delivering robots "has worn off"; many now "only go when the half-price offer is on", because as "the piles of colourful dishes mount, so does the check."

Yoshino ⊠ *Japanese*

23	12	20	£27

Piccadilly | 3 Piccadilly Pl., W1 (Piccadilly Circus) | 020-7287 6622 | fax 7287 1733 | www.yoshino.net

It's well "worth figuring out which alleyway leads to" this "hidden" Piccadilly pearl; true, the digs are "cramped and basic, but the extremely fresh sushi and sashimi make up for it" – as do the "excellent-value" prices; P.S. for a really "great experience, sit at the bar and chat with the sushi master" himself.

Yumenoki *Japanese*

-	-	-	M

Chelsea | 204 Fulham Rd., SW1 (Fulham Broadway/South Kensington) | 020-7351 2777 | fax 7351 4288 | www.yumenoki.co.uk

Got a fancy for fish around Fulham Broadway? find your way to this split-level Japanese that serves sushi standards, plus cooked classics, in a Zen setting; in warmer weather, you could even perch on the outdoor patio and pretend you're closer to Kyoto than the Kings Road.

⊠ Zafferano *Italian*

25	20	23	£62

Belgravia | 15 Lowndes St., SW1 (Knightsbridge) | 020-7235 5800 | fax 7235 1971 | www.zafferanorestaurant.com

"To be so far from Rome" and sample such "sublime pasta", not to mention the seasonal "truffle menu that will transport you to nirvana", or "tiramisu worth the price of an entire three-course meal" moan mavens about this "upscale", slightly "businesslike" "Belgravia institution"; true, "tightly packed" tables mean you may find yourself

| | FOOD | DECOR | SERVICE | COST |

"rubbing elbows" with "Russian oligarchs" – "Abramovich is often there" – and prices tend to be "funereally serious", but "you'd be hard-pressed to find better" in *Italia* itself; P.S. to economise, it's "worth taking the day off and having a super long lunch."

Zaika *Indian*

24 | 23 | 20 | £50

Kensington | 1 Kensington High St., W8 (High St. Kensington) | 020-7795 6533 | fax 7937 8854 | www.zaika-restaurant.co.uk

For "an interpretation of Indian you would not find in Brick Lane", visit this "classy" subcontinental set in a former Kensington bank (now all "exotic silks, rose petals and high ceilings"); its "inventive, intriguing cuisine" ("be sure to save space for the chocolate samosas") is far removed from "your granddad's sludgy curries", and "service is helpful"; if "the cost is a giant step" up as well, advocates agree the experience is "worth every rupee."

Zetter
Restaurant & Rooms *Mediterranean*

17 | 20 | 17 | £42

Clerkenwell | The Zetter | 86-88 Clerkenwell Rd., EC1 (Farringdon) | 020-7324 4455 | fax 7324 4445 | www.thezetter.com

"Not your typical hotel restaurant" note visitors to this "trendy" Clerkenwell kitchen where a "tasty" mod Med menu takes you from AM to PM; design-loving diners laud the geometric decor, "*très chic*" in a "sort of Belgrade 1978" way.

Ziani *Italian*

20 | 17 | 21 | £40

Chelsea | 45 Radnor Walk, SW3 (Sloane Sq.) | 020-7351 5297 | fax 7244 8387 | www.ziani.uk.com

"It can get noisy when busy" (which is often), but "the food and wine are so good you can't help becoming enthusiastic" about this "friendly", "compact" Chelsea Italian; the experience gets even "better if you don't mind sitting in your neighbour's lap."

Zilli Fish ●🅱 *Italian/Seafood*

21 | 14 | 18 | £43

Soho | 36-40 Brewer St., W1 (Piccadilly Circus) | 020-7734 8649 | fax 7434 9807 | www.zillialdo.com

It's "not fancy" at this Soho Italian, but that "shouldn't detract" from the "emphasis on seafood", particularly the signature "spaghetti lobster (may be a cliché but it's delicious)"; "patchy service" displeases dissenters, but its late hours and location make it a perfect "pre/post-theatre" spot.

Zizzi ● *Pizza*

16 | 15 | 16 | £21

Covent Garden | 20 Bow St., WC2 (Covent Garden) | 020-7836 6101
Covent Garden | 73-75 The Strand, WC2 (Charing Cross) | 020-7240 1717
Marylebone | 110-116 Wigmore St., W1 (Bond St.) | 020-7935 2336
Marylebone | 35-38 Paddington St., W1 (Baker St.) | 020-7224 1450
Victoria | Unit 15, Cardinal Walk, SW1 (Victoria) | 020-7821 0402
Fitzrovia | 33-41 Charlotte St., W1 (Goodge St.) | 020-7436 9440
Finchley | 202-208 Regents Park Rd., N3 (Finchley Central) | 020-8371 6777
Highgate | 1-3 Hampstead Ln., N6 (Highgate) | 020-8347 0090
Earl's Court | 194-196 Earl's Court Rd., SW5 (Earl's Ct.) | 020-7370 1999

(continued)

Zizzi

Chiswick | 231 Chiswick High Rd., W4 (Chiswick Park) | 020-8747 9400
www.zizzi.co.uk
Additional locations throughout London

Whilst there's "nothing to love, there's a lot to like" at this "consistent" chain specialising in "lovely" wood-fired pizzas; true, "service is a bit functional" and "it's often full of screaming kids", but "you know what you'll be getting" and "it won't break the bank."

☑ **Zuma** *Japanese*

27 | 24 | 20 | £66

Knightsbridge | 5 Raphael St., SW7 (Knightsbridge) | 020-7584 1010 | fax 7584 5005 | www.zumarestaurant.com

Seven years old and "still packed to the rafters" with a mix of "beautiful people, the famous" and "corporate types", this "luscious"-looking Knightsbridge "icon" of the "achingly hip" has an "extensive menu" of Japanese fare, including a "dynamite" "first come, first served robata grill" and "sushi that'll make you moan with delight", plus a "hopping bar" with 25 types of sake; so, even though prices keep zuma-ing up, and their "numerous-sittings policy makes you feel rushed all the time", "deal with it" – the place is "divine."

INDEXES

LOCATION MAPS

Cuisines

Includes restaurant names, locations and Food ratings. ☑ indicates places with the highest ratings, popularity and importance.

AMERICAN

All Star Lanes	**multi.**	12
Automat	**W1**	18
Big Easy	**SW3**	16
Christopher's	**WC2**	19
Diner, The	**multi.**	18
Eagle Bar Diner	**W1**	17
Ed's Easy Diner	**W1**	17
Hard Rock	**W1**	14
Harlem	**W2**	12
Joe Allen	**WC2**	16
Kobe London	**WC1**	19
Lucky 7	**W2**	21
Maxwell's	**WC2**	18
🆕 maze Grill	**W1**	-
Pizza on the Park	**SW1**	17
PJ's B&G	**multi.**	16
Planet Hollywood	**W1**	10
Rainforest Cafe	**W1**	11
Smollensky's	**multi.**	16
Sophie's Steak	**SW10**	21
Sticky Fingers	**W8**	17
Texas Embassy	**SW1**	14
T.G.I. Friday's	**multi.**	12
Tootsies	**multi.**	13

ARGENTINEAN

Buen Ayre/Santa Maria	**E8**	-
El Gaucho	**multi.**	17
☑ Gaucho Grill	**multi.**	22
Santa Maria del Sur	**SW8**	-

ASIAN FUSION

Aquasia	**SW10**	-
☑ Asia de Cuba	**WC2**	21
Blakes	**SW7**	19
Great Eastern	**EC2**	16
🆕 Pacific Oriental	**EC2**	-

BAKERIES

Baker & Spice	**multi.**	23
La Fromagerie	**W1**	25
Le Pain Quotidien	**multi.**	18
☑ Ottolenghi	**multi.**	25

BARBECUE

Bodeans	**multi.**	18
🆕 Chicago Rib	**SW1**	-

BELGIAN

Belgo	**multi.**	18
Bierodrome	**multi.**	16
Le Pain Quotidien	**multi.**	18

BRAZILIAN

Rodizio Rico	**multi.**	17

BRITISH (MODERN)

Academy	**W1**	-
Acorn House	**WC1**	19
Adam St.	**WC2**	20
Admiral Codrington	**SW3**	18
Alastair Little	**W1**	24
Anchor & Hope	**SE1**	25
Anglesea Arms	**W6**	19
Annie's	**multi.**	21
Axis	**WC2**	19
Balans	**multi.**	16
Barnsbury, The	**N1**	21
Bedford & Strand	**WC2**	18
Belvedere, The	**W8**	20
Bevis Marks	**EC3**	22
🆕 Botanist, The	**SW1**	-
☑ Boxwood Café	**SW1**	23
Bradley's	**NW3**	16
Bumpkin	**W11**	19
🆕 Champagne Bar	**NW1**	14
☑ Chez Bruce	**SW17**	29
Clarke's	**W8**	26
Cow Dining Rm.	**W2**	21
Dorchester/The Grill	**W1**	24
Duke of Cambridge	**N1**	22
1802	**E14**	16
Empress of India	**E9**	21
Engineer	**NW1**	20
Fat Badger	**W10**	15
Fifth Floor Cafe	**SW1**	18
Franklins	**multi.**	-
Frederick's	**N1**	21
☑ Gravetye Manor	**W. Sussex**	28
Great Queen St.	**WC2**	24
Greyhound, The	**SW11**	23
Groucho Club	**W1**	18
Gun, The	**E14**	21
Hand & Flowers	**Bucks**	23
Hartwell House	**Bucks**	-
🆕 Hereford Road	**W2**	24
Home House	**W1**	-

Hush | **W1**	14
Island | **W2**	-
☑ Ivy, The | **WC2**	22
NEW Jimmy's | **SW3**	-
Joe's Rest. Bar | **SW1**	19
Julie's | **W11**	17
Just St. James's | **SW1**	20
Kensington Place | **W8**	19
NEW Kensington Sq. | **W8**	-
Konstam | **WC1**	23
Lamberts | **SW12**	21
Launceston Place | **W8**	-
☑ Le Caprice | **SW1**	24
Medcalf | **EC1**	-
Menier Chocolate | **SE1**	16
Mews of Mayfair | **W1**	19
National Dining Rms. | **WC2**	20
NEW Northbank | **EC4**	-
Palmerston, The | **SE2**	-
NEW Paradise | **W1**	-
Portrait | **WC2**	21
Prism | **EC3**	20
Randall & Aubin | **W1**	21
Ransome's Dock | **SW11**	20
Rhodes W1 Brass. | **W1**	16
Rhodes W1 Rest. | **W1**	23
☑ Richard Corrigan | **W1**	26
Roast | **SE1**	19
R.S.J. | **SE1**	18
Smiths/Dining Rm. | **EC1**	21
Snows on Green | **W6**	21
Soho House | **W1**	19
Sotheby's Cafe | **W1**	20
☑ St. John | **EC1**	27
St. John Bread/Wine | **E1**	23
Tate Britain | **SW1**	19
Thomas Cubitt | **SW1**	21
Tom's Kitchen | **SW3**	22
NEW Tom's Place | **SW3**	18
Tuttons Brass. | **WC2**	19
Union Cafe | **W1**	19
NEW Upper Deck | **WC2**	-
Vineyard/Stockcross | **Stockcross/Berks**	25
NEW Wild Honey | **W1**	23

BRITISH (TRADITIONAL)

Abbeville | **SW4**	-
Albemarle, The | **W1**	22
Albion, The | **N1**	17
Annabel's | **W1**	20
Bentley's | **W1**	24
Bistro 190 | **SW7**	-
Bleeding Heart | **EC1**	22

Boisdale | **multi.**	20
Browns | **multi.**	16
Builders Arms | **SW3**	17
Butcher & Grill, The | **multi.**	18
Butlers Wharf | **SE1**	22
Canteen | **multi.**	18
Chelsea Bun | **SW10**	14
Cliveden House | **Berks**	22
Coach & Horses | **EC1**	-
NEW Devonshire, The | **W4**	22
ffiona's | **W8**	23
Fortnum's Fountain | **W1**	17
Foxtrot Oscar | **SW3**	15
French Horn | **Berks**	21
Frontline | **W2**	-
☑ Goring | **SW1**	25
Green's | **SW1**	23
Grenadier, The | **SW1**	17
Grumbles | **SW1**	-
Guinea Grill | **W1**	21
Hinds Head | **Berks**	22
NEW Hix Oyster | **EC1**	-
Inn The Park | **SW1**	18
Island | **W2**	-
Kew Grill | **TW9**	-
Langan's Bistro | **W1**	19
Langan's Brass. | **W1**	19
Maggie Jones's | **W8**	19
Mark's Club | **W1**	23
Marquess Tavern | **N1**	-
Narrow, The | **E14**	22
Notting Grill | **W11**	21
Odin's | **W1**	20
NEW Only Running Footman | **W1**	18
Paternoster Chop | **EC4**	17
Pig's Ear | **SW3**	18
Porters | **WC2**	18
Quality Chop Hse. | **EC1**	21
Rhodes 24 | **EC2**	24
Rib Room | **SW1**	22
Richoux | **multi.**	16
☑ Ritz, The | **W1**	23
Rivington Grill | **multi.**	21
Rowley's | **SW1**	20
☑ Rules | **WC2**	23
1707 Wine Bar | **W1**	21
Shepherd's | **SW1**	23
Simpson's/Strand | **WC2**	20
Smiths/Top Floor | **EC1**	21
Spencer Arms | **SW15**	-
St. James's | **W1**	20
☑ Sweetings | **EC4**	26
NEW Warrington, The | **W9**	-

Z Wilton's | **SW1**	25
Ye Olde Cheshire | **EC4**	16

BURGERS

Automat | **W1**	18
Diner, The | **multi.**	18
Eagle Bar Diner | **W1**	17
Ed's Easy Diner | **W1**	17
Gourmet Burger | **multi.**	19
Hache | **multi.**	20
Hard Rock | **W1**	14
Lucky 7 | **W2**	21
Maxwell's | **WC2**	18
Planet Hollywood | **W1**	10
Smollensky's | **multi.**	16
Sophie's Steak | **SW10**	21
Sticky Fingers | **W8**	17
T.G.I. Friday's | **multi.**	12
Tootsies | **multi.**	13
Vingt-Quatre | **SW10**	13

BURMESE

Mandalay | **W2**	23

CARIBBEAN

Cottons | **multi.**	19

CHINESE

(* dim sum specialist)

Bar Shu | **W1**	23
NEW Cha Cha Moon | **W1**	-
China Tang* | **W1**	20
Chinese Experience* | **W1**	20
Chuen Cheng Ku* | **W1**	21
dim t* | **multi.**	15
Dragon Castle | **SE17**	-
Eight Over Eight* | **SW3**	22
Four Seasons | **W2**	22
Fung Shing | **WC2**	23
Golden Dragon* | **W1**	20
Goldmine | **W2**	-
Good Earth | **multi.**	21
Green Cottage | **NW3**	18
Gung-Ho | **NW6**	19
Z Hakkasan* | **W1**	25
NEW Haozhan | **W1**	23
Harbour City* | **W1**	18
Z Hunan | **SW1**	27
Imperial China* | **WC2**	21
Imperial City | **EC3**	23
Jade Garden* | **W1**	21
Jenny Lo's Tea | **SW1**	21
Joy King Lau* | **WC2**	18
Kai Mayfair | **W1**	23
Lee Ho Fook* | **W1**	18

Mandarin Kitchen | **W2**	24
Mao Tai* | **SW6**	23
Memories of China | **multi.**	22
Mr. Chow | **SW1**	22
Mr. Kong | **WC2**	21
New Culture Rev. | **multi.**	18
New World* | **W1**	19
Pearl Liang* | **W2**	18
Phoenix Palace* | **NW1**	21
Ping Pong* | **multi.**	19
Princess Garden* | **W1**	22
NEW Red 'n' Hot | **WC2**	-
Royal China* | **multi.**	23
Z Royal China Club* | **multi.**	24
Shanghai Blues* | **WC1**	24
Snazz* | **NW1**	-
Wong Kei | **W1**	17
Z Yauatcha* | **W1**	26
Yming | **W1**	24

CHOPHOUSE

Black & Blue | **multi.**	18
Bountiful Cow | **WC1**	21
Butlers Wharf | **SE1**	22
Christopher's | **WC2**	19
El Gaucho | **multi.**	17
Z Gaucho Grill | **multi.**	22
Greig's | **W1**	17
Guinea Grill | **W1**	21
Z Hawksmoor | **E1**	24
NEW Hix Oyster | **EC1**	-
Kew Grill | **TW9**	-
Z Le Relais/Venise | **W1**	22
NEW maze Grill | **W1**	-
Notting Grill | **W11**	21
Paternoster Chop | **EC4**	17
Popeseye | **multi.**	-
Quality Chop Hse. | **EC1**	21
Rib Room | **SW1**	22
Z Rules | **WC2**	23
Smiths/Dining Rm. | **EC1**	21
Smiths/Top Floor | **EC1**	21
Smollensky's | **multi.**	16
Sophie's Steak | **SW10**	21

CUBAN

Z Asia de Cuba | **WC2**	21
Floridita | **W1**	17

EAST AFRICAN

Kastoori | **SW17**	-

ECLECTIC

Annex 3 | **W1**	-
Archipelago | **W1**	22

Axis	**WC2**	19
Bacchus	**N1**	21
Blakes	**SW7**	19
Books for Cooks	**W11**	23
Brinkley's	**SW10**	14
Brompton Quarter	**SW3**	15
Cantina Vinopolis	**SE1**	18
NEW Cape Town Fish	**W1**	18
Club, The	**W1**	-
Collection	**SW3**	13
Court	**WC1**	18
Dans Le Noir	**EC1**	8
NEW Daylesford	**multi.**	18
Delfina	**SE1**	-
Ebury Wine Bar	**SW1**	18
Electric Brass.	**W11**	17
Elk in the Woods	**N1**	-
Enterprise	**SW3**	17
Giraffe	**multi.**	16
NEW Harrison's	**SW12**	15
Hoxton Apprentice	**N1**	-
Hoxton Grille	**EC2**	15
Kettners	**W1**	15
Light House	**SW19**	-
Z Michael Moore	**W1**	26
Z Mosimann's	**SW1**	25
Motcombs	**SW1**	20
Napket	**multi.**	-
Providores, The	**W1**	22
Ransome's Dock	**SW11**	20
NEW Saf	**EC2**	-
Six13	**W1**	-
Tom's Deli	**W11**	16
Troubadour, The	**SW5**	18
222 Veggie Vegan	**W14**	-
Vingt-Quatre	**SW10**	13
Westbourne, The	**W2**	18
NEW Whole Foods	**W8**	18

EUROPEAN (MODERN)

Abbeville	**SW4**	-
Abingdon, The	**W8**	18
About Thyme	**SW1**	-
Addendum	**EC3**	-
Admiral Codrington	**SW3**	18
Albannach	**WC2**	16
Ambassador, The	**EC1**	-
Andrew Edmunds	**W1**	22
Z Arbutus	**W1**	24
NEW Artisan	**W1**	18
Auberge du Lac	**Herts**	26
Avenue, The	**SW1**	19
Babylon	**W8**	17
Bank Westminster	**SW1**	16

Bluebird	**SW3**	18
Blueprint Café	**SE1**	18
Brackenbury	**W6**	21
NEW Brickhouse, The	**E1**	-
Brown Dog, The	**SW13**	-
NEW Brumus	**SW1**	-
Bull, The	**N6**	-
Bush B&G	**W12**	18
Camden Brass.	**NW1**	20
Chancery, The	**EC4**	17
Chapter Two	**SE3**	23
Charlotte's Place	**W5**	-
Chelsea Brass.	**SW1**	17
City Café	**SW1**	17
Clerkenwell Dining	**EC1**	22
NEW Cruse 9	**N1**	-
Cuckoo Club	**W1**	-
Don, The	**EC4**	22
Dover St.	**W1**	15
Draper's Arms	**N1**	19
Ebury Dining Rm.	**SW1**	16
11 Abingdon Rd.	**W8**	19
Z Fat Duck	**Berks**	27
Fifth Floor	**SW1**	21
Fig	**N1**	22
Flaneur	**EC1**	24
Foliage	**SW1**	25
Forge, The	**WC2**	18
Frederick's	**N1**	21
George	**W1**	22
Glasshouse, The	**TW9**	25
Z Gordon Ramsay/Claridge's	**W1**	26
Greyhound, The	**SW11**	23
Hat & Feathers	**EC1**	-
High Road Brass.	**W4**	19
Home House	**W1**	-
Indigo	**WC2**	21
Inside	**SE10**	25
Z Ivy, The	**WC2**	22
Ladbroke Arms	**W11**	19
La Fromagerie	**W1**	25
NEW Landau, The	**W1**	25
Lansdowne, The	**NW1**	17
Z La Trompette	**W4**	28
NEW L'Autre Pied	**W1**	23
Le Café/Jardin	**WC2**	19
Z Le Caprice	**SW1**	24
Le Deuxième	**WC2**	20
Little Bay	**multi.**	21
Living Rm.	**W1**	17
Magdalen	**SE1**	23
Mu	**SW1**	-
Nicole's	**W1**	21

Notting Hill Brass. | **W11**	25
NEW Number Twelve | **WC1**	-
Odette's | **NW1**	20
Old Bull & Bush | **NW3**	12
1 Lombard Brass. | **EC3**	19
Oriel | **SW1**	15
Z Oxo Tower | **SE1**	21
NEW Pantechnicon Rms. | **SW1**	-
Patterson's | **W1**	24
Petersham, The | **TW10**	-
Petersham Nurseries | **TW10**	24
Pigalle Club | **W1**	15
Quaglino's | **SW1**	18
Refuel | **W1**	-
Royal Exchange | **EC3**	14
Salt Yard | **W1**	21
Sam's Brass. | **W4**	19
Sketch/Gallery | **W1**	17
Z Sketch/Lecture Rm. | **W1**	21
Skylon | **SE1**	19
Sonny's | **SW13**	22
St. Alban | **SW1**	22
Tate Modern | **SE1**	17
NEW Texture | **W1**	21
NEW Tom Ilic | **SW8**	24
Trinity | **SW4**	26
202 | **W11**	18
Union Cafe | **W1**	19
NEW Vanilla | **W1**	-
Vinoteca | **EC1**	-
Vivat Bacchus | **EC4**	20
Wapping Food | **E1**	19
NEW Water House | **N1**	-
Waterway, The | **W9**	15
Wells, The | **NW3**	20
Z Wolseley, The | **W1**	22

FISH 'N' CHIPS

Geales Fish | **W8**	20
Z Golden Hind | **W1**	23
Livebait | **multi.**	19
Nautilus Fish | **NW6**	22
Z North Sea | **WC1**	24
Rock & Sole Plaice | **WC2**	-
Seashell | **NW1**	20
Z Sweetings | **EC4**	26
NEW Tom's Place | **SW3**	18
2 Brothers Fish | **N3**	22

FRENCH (BISTRO)

Aubaine | **multi.**	19
Bedford & Strand | **WC2**	18
Bibendum Oyster | **SW3**	21
Bistrotheque | **E2**	20

Café Rouge | **multi.**	14
Z Comptoir Gascon | **EC1**	23
Ebury Wine Bar | **SW1**	18
French House | **W1**	17
Z Galvin Bistrot | **W1**	23
Grumbles | **SW1**	-
La Bouchée | **SW7**	21
Langan's Coq d'Or | **SW5**	18
La Poule au Pot | **SW1**	21
L'Artiste Muscle | **W1**	20
Le Boudin Blanc | **W1**	22
Le Café/Marché | **EC1**	23
Le Colombier | **SW3**	21
Z Le Vacherin | **W4**	26
Patisserie Valerie | **multi.**	18
Z Racine | **SW3**	23
Truc Vert | **W1**	17

FRENCH (BRASSERIE)

Z NEW Angelus | **W2**	23
Z Bellamy's | **W1**	22
NEW BORD'EAUX | **W1**	-
Brasserie Roux | **SW1**	21
NEW Brass. St. Jacques | **SW1**	-
Brass. St. Quentin | **SW3**	20
Café Boheme | **W1**	18
Z Cheyne Walk | **SW3**	23
Chez Gérard | **multi.**	17
NEW Côte | **multi.**	-
Incognico | **WC2**	21
La Brasserie | **SW3**	18
Langan's Brass. | **W1**	19
NEW Le Café Anglais | **W2**	20
Mon Plaisir | **WC2**	19
Oriel | **SW1**	15
St. Germain | **EC1**	22
Tartine | **SW3**	17
Tuttons Brass. | **WC2**	19
NEW Waterloo Brass. | **SE1**	19

FRENCH (CLASSIC)

Almeida | **N1**	19
Annabel's | **W1**	20
Auberge du Lac | **Herts**	26
Bradley's | **NW3**	16
Chez Kristof | **W6**	20
Cliveden House | **Berks**	22
Coq d'Argent | **EC2**	22
Elena's l'Etoile | **W1**	18
Farm | **SW6**	19
Foliage | **SW1**	25
French Horn | **Berks**	21
Hush | **W1**	14
Ladurée | **SW1**	23

Langan's Bistro | **W1**	19
La Poule au Pot | **SW1**	21
La Trouvaille | **W1**	25
L'Aventure | **NW8**	24
Le Café/Marché | **EC1**	23
☑ Le Gavroche | **W1**	27
Le Pont/Tour | **SE1**	20
☑ Le Relais/Venise | **W1**	22
L'Escargot | **W1**	23
☑ Les Trois Garçons | **E1**	21
Le Suquet | **SW3**	22
L'Oranger | **SW1**	25
Lou Pescadou | **SW5**	-
NEW Marco | **SW6**	-
Mark's Club | **W1**	23
Mon Plaisir | **WC2**	19
Odin's | **W1**	20
☑ Oslo Court | **NW8**	26
Papillon | **SW3**	21
Pigalle Club | **W1**	15
Poissonnerie | **SW3**	21
☑ Ritz, The | **W1**	23
Sauterelle | **EC3**	-
Villandry | **W1**	22
Vineyard/Stockcross | **Stockcross/Berks**	25
Wallace, The | **W1**	18
☑ Waterside Inn | **Berks**	27

FRENCH (NEW)

Admiralty, The | **WC2**	18
☑ **NEW** Alain Ducasse | **W1**	26
Aubergine | **SW10**	25
Belvedere, The | **W8**	20
Bibendum | **SW3**	23
Bleeding Heart | **EC1**	22
Bonds | **EC2**	22
Café des Amis | **WC2**	19
☑ Capital Rest. | **SW3**	26
Cellar Gascon | **EC1**	-
Cliveden House | **Berks**	22
☑ Clos Maggiore | **WC2**	25
☑ Club Gascon | **EC1**	26
Cross Keys, The | **SW3**	-
Galvin/Windows | **W1**	20
☑ Gordon Ramsay/68 Royal | **SW3**	29
☑ Greenhouse, The | **W1**	26
Hand & Flowers | **Bucks**	23
NEW Hibiscus | **W1**	24
Incognico | **WC2**	21
☑ L'Atelier/Robuchon | **WC2**	27
☑ La Trompette | **W4**	28
La Trouvaille | **W1**	25

Le Cercle | **SW1**	23
☑ Ledbury, The | **W11**	28
☑ Le Manoir/Quat | **Oxfordshire**	27
Le Mercury | **N1**	16
Le Palais Du Jardin | **WC2**	21
L'Etranger | **SW7**	23
☑ maze | **W1**	25
☑ Morgan M | **N7**	26
Morton's | **W1**	22
1 Lombard St. | **EC3**	23
One-O-One | **SW1**	23
Orrery | **W1**	24
Pearl | **WC1**	25
☑ Pétrus | **SW1**	28
☑ Pied à Terre | **W1**	27
Pig's Ear | **SW3**	18
Plateau | **E14**	19
☑ Roussillon | **SW1**	26
Spread Eagle | **SE10**	24
☑ Square, The | **W1**	27
Tom Aikens | **SW3**	25
Upstairs | **SW2**	-
☑ Waterside Inn | **Berks**	27

GASTROPUB

Admiral Codrington | British/Euro. | **SW3**	18
Anchor & Hope | British | **SE1**	25
Anglesea Arms | British | **W6**	19
Barnsbury, The | British | **N1**	21
Brown Dog, The | Euro. | **SW13**	-
Builders Arms | British | **SW3**	17
Bull, The | Euro. | **N6**	-
Churchill Arms | Thai | **W8**	20
Coach & Horses | British/Med. | **EC1**	-
Cow Dining Rm. | British | **W2**	21
NEW Devonshire, The | British | **W4**	22
Draper's Arms | Euro. | **N1**	19
Duke of Cambridge | British | **N1**	22
Eagle, The | Med. | **EC1**	23
Ebury Dining Rm. | Euro. | **SW1**	16
Engineer | British | **NW1**	20
Enterprise | Eclectic | **SW3**	17
Farm | French | **SW6**	19
Great Queen St. | British | **WC2**	24
Grenadier, The | British | **SW1**	17
Greyhound, The | British/Euro. | **SW11**	23
Gun, The | British | **E14**	21
Hat & Feathers | Euro. | **EC1**	-
Ladbroke Arms | Euro. | **W11**	19
Lansdowne, The | Euro. | **NW1**	17
Marquess Tavern | British | **N1**	-

Narrow, The | British | **E14**	22
NEW Only Running Footman | British | **W1**	18
Palmerston, The | British | **SE2**	–
NEW Paradise | British | **W1**	–
Pig's Ear | British/French | **SW3**	18
Salusbury Pub | Italian | **NW6**	–
Spencer Arms | British | **SW15**	–
Thomas Cubitt | British | **SW1**	21
NEW Warrington, The | British | **W9**	–
Wells, The | Euro. | **NW3**	20
Westbourne, The | Eclectic | **W2**	18
Ye Olde Cheshire | British | **EC4**	16

GREEK

Costas Grill | **W8**	14
Halepi | **W2**	19
Lemonia | **NW1**	18
Real Greek | **multi.**	16

HUNGARIAN

Gay Hussar | **W1**	19

INDIAN

Z Amaya | **SW1**	26
Atma | **NW3**	–
Benares | **W1**	23
Bengal Clipper | **SE1**	19
Bombay Bicycle | **multi.**	18
Bombay Brass. | **SW7**	22
Café Spice Namasté | **E1**	23
Chor Bizarre | **W1**	19
Chowki | **W1**	17
Chutney Mary | **SW10**	23
Chutney's | **NW1**	23
Z Cinnamon Club | **SW1**	24
Gopal's of Soho | **W1**	20
Hot Stuff | **SW8**	–
Imli | **W1**	19
Indian Zing | **W6**	–
Kastoori | **SW17**	–
Khan's | **W2**	21
Khan's/Kensington | **SW7**	23
La Porte des Indes | **W1**	21
Ma Goa | **SW15**	22
Malabar | **W8**	22
Malabar Junction | **WC1**	23
Masala Zone | **multi.**	19
Mela | **WC2**	21
Mint Leaf | **SW1**	19
Moti Mahal | **WC2**	25
Noor Jahan | **multi.**	22
Painted Heron | **SW1**	23

Quilon | **SW1**	25
Rasa | **multi.**	24
Z Rasoi Vineet Bhatia | **SW3**	27
Red Fort | **W1**	24
Sitaaray | **WC2**	–
Z Star of India | **SW5**	25
Z Tamarind | **W1**	25
NEW Urban Turban | **W2**	17
Vama | **SW10**	25
Veeraswamy | **W1**	23
Zaika | **W8**	24

INDONESIAN

Nancy Lam's Enak | **SW11**	–

IRISH

Z Richard Corrigan | **W1**	26

ITALIAN

Aglio e Olio | **SW10**	21
Al Duca | **SW1**	20
Alloro | **W1**	21
Amici | **SW17**	16
Aperitivo | **W1**	–
NEW Apsleys | **SW1**	–
Ark, The | **W8**	24
Armani Caffé | **SW3**	19
Artigiano | **NW3**	20
Ask Pizza | **multi.**	15
Z Assaggi | **W2**	26
Bertorelli | **multi.**	16
Brunello | **SW7**	23
Buona Sera | **multi.**	18
Caldesi | **multi.**	22
Camerino | **W1**	–
Cantina del Ponte | **SE1**	18
Caraffini | **SW1**	22
Caravaggio | **EC3**	15
Carluccio's Caffè | **multi.**	17
Carpaccio | **SW3**	18
Casale Franco | **N1**	–
Cecconi's | **W1**	21
Cipriani | **W1**	20
Ciro's Pizza | **multi.**	16
Como Lario | **SW1**	21
Da Mario | **SW7**	16
Daphne's | **SW3**	22
NEW Dehesa | **W1**	–
Delfino | **W1**	20
Diverso | **W1**	17
Elena's l'Etoile | **W1**	18
Elistano | **SW3**	22
Enoteca Turi | **SW15**	24
Essenza | **W11**	18

Franco's | **SW1**	19
Frankie's Italian | **multi.**	14
Getti | **multi.**	14
Giardinetto | **W1**	-
Giovanni's | **WC2**	20
NEW Giusto | **W1**	-
Green Olive | **W9**	23
Harry's Bar | **W1**	23
Z Il Bordello | **E1**	23
Il Convivio | **SW1**	22
Il Falconiere | **SW7**	15
Il Portico | **W8**	24
L'Accento Italiano | **W2**	-
La Famiglia | **SW1**	21
La Figa | **E14**	22
La Genova | **W1**	25
NEW L'Anima | **EC2**	-
La Porchetta | **multi.**	18
Latium | **W1**	23
L'Incontro | **SW1**	21
Little Italy | **W1**	16
Z Locanda Locatelli | **W1**	25
Locanda Ottoemezzo | **W8**	24
Luciano | **SW1**	19
Lucio | **SW3**	22
Made in Italy | **SW3**	20
Manicomio | **SW3**	19
Mediterraneo | **W11**	21
Metrogusto | **N1**	-
Mimmo d'Ischia | **SW1**	18
Montpeliano | **SW7**	18
Monza | **SW3**	18
Mosaico | **W1**	-
Z Oliveto | **SW1**	21
Olivo | **SW1**	19
Olivomare | **SW1**	21
Orso | **WC2**	19
Osteria Antica | **SW11**	17
Z Osteria Basilico | **W11**	22
Osteria dell'Arancio | **SW1**	20
NEW Osteria Stecca | **NW8**	-
Pappagallo | **W1**	23
Passione | **W1**	22
Pellicano | **SW3**	22
Z Pizza Express | **multi.**	16
Pizza Metro | **SW11**	-
Pizza on the Park | **SW1**	17
Quadrato | **E14**	-
Quirinale | **SW1**	23
Red Pepper | **W9**	20
Refettorio | **EC4**	22
Riccardo's | **SW3**	20
Rist. Semplice | **W1**	24
Riva | **SW13**	21

Z River Café | **W6**	28
Sale e Pepe | **SW1**	22
Salusbury Pub | **N** | **NW6**	-
San Lorenzo | **multi.**	20
Santa Lucia | **SW10**	-
Santini | **SW1**	21
Sardo | **W1**	21
Sardo Canale | **NW1**	21
Sartoria | **W1**	20
Scalini | **SW3**	23
Signor Sassi | **SW1**	21
Spago | **SW7**	18
Spiga | **W1**	17
Strada | **multi.**	18
Tentazioni | **SE1**	24
NEW Terranostra | **EC4**	-
Theo Randall | **W1**	23
NEW 3 Bridges | **SW8**	-
Timo | **W8**	27
Toto's | **SW3**	23
2 Veneti | **W1**	19
Vasco & Piero's | **W1**	21
Via Condotti | **W1**	19
Z Zafferano | **SW1**	25
Ziani | **SW3**	20
Zilli Fish | **W1**	21
Zizzi | **multi.**	16

JAPANESE

(* sushi specialist)

NEW Aaya | **W1**	-
Abeno | **multi.**	18
Asakusa* | **NW1**	25
Atami | **SW1**	19
Benihana | **multi.**	19
NEW Bincho Yakitori | **multi.**	21
Café Japan* | **NW11**	25
Chisou | **W1**	23
City Miyama* | **EC4**	-
Z Defune* | **W1**	26
Dinings* | **W1**	24
Feng Sushi* | **multi.**	18
Ikeda* | **W1**	26
Inaho* | **W2**	25
itsu* | **multi.**	17
Z Jin Kichi* | **NW3**	27
Kiku* | **W1**	23
Kobe London | **WC1**	19
Koi* | **W8**	21
Kulu Kulu* | **multi.**	19
NEW Kyashi* | **WC2**	-
Matsuri* | **multi.**	23
Mitsukoshi* | **SW1**	19
Miyama* | **W1**	23

Moshi Moshi*	**multi.**	19
Z Nobu Berkeley St*	**W1**	26
Z Nobu London*	**W1**	27
Nozomi	**SW3**	19
Roka*	**W1**	25
NEW Sake no hana*	**SW1**	19
Saki Bar/Food Emp.*	**EC1**	-
Sakura*	**W1**	18
Satsuma	**W1**	19
Shogun*	**W1**	-
Sumosan	**W1**	24
Ten Ten Tei*	**W1**	23
Tokyo Diner	**WC2**	16
Tsunami	**SW4**	26
Z Ubon*	**E14**	26
Z Umu*	**W1**	26
Z Wagamama	**multi.**	19
Yakitoria*	**W2**	17
YO! Sushi*	**multi.**	15
Yoshino*	**W1**	23
Yumenoki*	**SW1**	-
Z Zuma*	**SW7**	27

JEWISH

Bevis Marks	**EC3**	22
Bloom's	**NW11**	17
Gaby's	**WC2**	-
Harry Morgan's	**multi.**	15
Reubens	**W1**	15
Solly's	**NW11**	19

KOREAN

Asadal	**WC1**	-

KOSHER

Bevis Marks	**EC3**	22
Bloom's	**NW11**	17
Met Su Yan	**NW11**	-
Reubens	**W1**	15
Six13	**W1**	-
Solly's	**NW11**	19

LEBANESE

Al Hamra	**W1**	21
Z Al Sultan	**W1**	23
Z Al Waha	**W2**	23
Beiteddine	**SW1**	21
Dish Dash	**multi.**	21
Z Fairuz	**W1**	22
Fakhreldine	**W1**	19
Ishbilia	**SW1**	22
NEW Kenza	**EC2**	-
Levant	**W1**	21

Levantine	**W2**	-
Maroush	**multi.**	22
Noura	**multi.**	20

MALAYSIAN

Awana	**SW3**	22
Champor	**SE1**	20
Nyonya	**W11**	22
Silks & Spice	**NW10**	16
Singapore Garden	**NW6**	19
Suka	**W1**	-

MEDITERRANEAN

About Thyme	**SW1**	-
Aquasia	**SW10**	-
Baker & Spice	**multi.**	23
Bistro 190	**SW7**	-
Cafe Med	**NW8**	17
Cantina Vinopolis	**SE1**	18
Citrus	**W1**	19
Cru	**N1**	-
Eagle, The	**EC1**	23
Fifteen	**N1**	25
Fifth Floor Cafe	**SW1**	18
Franco's	**SW1**	19
Joe's	**SW3**	-
Z NEW La Petite Maison	**W1**	25
Leon	**multi.**	19
Meza	**W1**	13
Z Moro	**EC1**	25
Nicole's	**W1**	21
Z Ottolenghi	**multi.**	25
Z Oxo Tower Brass.	**SE1**	18
Pescatori	**W1**	19
Portal	**EC1**	20
Raoul's	**multi.**	20
Rocket	**multi.**	17
Sarastro	**WC2**	12
Union Cafe	**W1**	19
Zetter	**EC1**	17

MEXICAN

Cafe Pacifico	**WC2**	16
Crazy Homies	**W2**	19
Green & Red Bar	**E1**	19
La Perla	**multi.**	19
Mestizo	**NW1**	23
Taqueria	**W11**	22
Texas Embassy	**SW1**	14
NEW Wahaca	**WC2**	20

MIDDLE EASTERN

Gaby's	**WC2**	-
Solly's	**NW11**	19

MOROCCAN

Aziz	**SW6**	19
Bouga	**N8**	-
🆕 Kenza	**EC2**	-
Original Tagine	**W1**	-
🔽 Pasha	**SW7**	21

NOODLE SHOPS

New Culture Rev.	**multi.**	18

NORTH AFRICAN

Momo	**W1**	19
Souk	**WC2**	17

PAKISTANI

🔽 New Tayyabs	**E1**	28
Original Lahore	**multi.**	25
Salloos	**SW1**	23

PAN-ASIAN

Bam-Bou	**W1**	22
Cicada	**EC1**	21
Cocoon	**W1**	21
dim t	**multi.**	15
e&o	**W11**	22
Eight Over Eight	**SW3**	22
🔽 Gilgamesh	**NW1**	19
Haiku	**W1**	19
Kiasu	**W2**	21
Mao Tai	**SW6**	23
Met Su Yan	**NW11**	-
🔽 Oxo Tower Brass.	**SE1**	18
Park, The	**SW1**	24
🔽 Taman Gang	**W1**	21
Tamarai	**WC2**	20
Uli	**W11**	26
XO	**NW3**	21

PERSIAN

Alounak	**multi.**	22
Dish Dash	**multi.**	21
Kandoo	**W2**	-

PIZZA

Ask Pizza	**multi.**	15
Basilico	**multi.**	20
Buona Sera	**multi.**	18
Cantina del Ponte	**SE1**	18
Casale Franco	**N1**	-
Ciro's Pizza	**multi.**	16
Delfino	**W1**	20
Fire & Stone	**WC2**	18
Firezza	**multi.**	19
🆕 Giusto	**W1**	-

🔽 Il Bordello	**E1**	23
Kettners	**W1**	15
La Porchetta	**multi.**	18
Made in Italy	**SW3**	20
🔽 Oliveto	**SW1**	21
Orso	**WC2**	19
🔽 Osteria Basilico	**W11**	22
🔽 Pizza Express	**multi.**	16
Pizza Metro	**SW11**	-
Pizza on the Park	**SW1**	17
Red Pepper	**W9**	20
Rocket	**multi.**	17
Santa Lucia	**SW10**	-
Spago	**SW7**	18
Spiga	**W1**	17
Strada	**multi.**	18
Zizzi	**multi.**	16

POLISH

Baltic	**SE1**	22
Daquise	**SW7**	15
Wòdka	**W8**	21

PORTUGUESE

Eyre Brothers	**EC2**	22
Nando's	**multi.**	-
Portal	**EC1**	20

RUSSIAN

Potemkin	**EC1**	-

SCOTTISH

Albannach	**WC2**	16
Boisdale	**multi.**	20

SEAFOOD

Belgo	**multi.**	18
Bentley's	**W1**	24
Bibendum Oyster	**SW3**	21
Big Easy	**SW3**	16
🆕 Cape Town Fish	**W1**	18
Cow Dining Rm.	**W2**	21
fish!	**SE1**	19
Fish Club	**SW11**	-
Fish Hook	**W4**	20
Fish Shop	**EC1**	18
FishWorks	**multi.**	19
Geales Fish	**W8**	20
🔽 Golden Hind	**W1**	23
Green's	**SW1**	23
🔽 J. Sheekey	**WC2**	26
Le Pont/Tour	**SE1**	20
Le Suquet	**SW3**	22
Livebait	**multi.**	19

CUISINES

Loch Fyne | **WC2** — 21

Lou Pescadou | **SW5** — -

Nautilus Fish | **NW6** — 22

Z North Sea | **WC1** — 24

Olivomare | **SW1** — 21

One-O-One | **SW1** — 23

Pescatori | **W1** — 19

Poissonnerie | **SW3** — 21

Randall & Aubin | **W1** — 21

Rock & Sole Plaice | **WC2** — -

Z Scott's | **W1** — 24

Seashell | **NW1** — 20

Z Sweetings | **EC4** — 26

NEW Tom's Place | **SW3** — 18

2 Brothers Fish | **N3** — 22

Z Wilton's | **SW1** — 25

Wright Brothers' | **SE1** — -

Zilli Fish | **W1** — 21

SINGAPOREAN

Singapore Garden | **NW6** — 19

Singapura | **multi.** — 20

SMALL PLATES

(See also Spanish tapas specialist)

Z Amaya | Indian | **SW1** — 26

Aperitivo | Italian | **W1** — -

Cellar Gascon | French | **EC1** — -

NEW Champagne Bar | British | **NW1** — 14

Z Club Gascon | French | **EC1** — 26

Dinings | Japanese | **W1** — 24

Dish Dash | Lebanese/Persian | **multi.** — 21

Z Hunan | Chinese | **SW1** — 27

Il Convivio | Italian | **SW1** — 22

Imli | Indian | **W1** — 19

La Perla | Mex. | **multi.** — 19

Z L'Atelier/Robuchon | French | **WC2** — 27

Le Cercle | French | **SW1** — 23

Z maze | French | **W1** — 25

Providores, The | Eclectic | **W1** — 22

Real Greek | Greek | **N1** — 16

Trinity | Euro. | **SW4** — 26

SOUTH AMERICAN

El Rincon Latino | **SW4** — -

Sabor | **N1** — -

SPANISH

(* tapas specialist)

Z Barrafina* | **W1** — 25

Z Cambio de Tercio | **SW5** — 25

Cigala* | **WC1** — 21

NEW Dehesa | **W1** — -

El Blason* | **SW3** — 18

El Faro | **E14** — 23

El Pirata* | **W1** — 20

El Rincon Latino* | **SW4** — -

Eyre Brothers | **EC2** — 22

Z Fino* | **W1** — 25

Galicia* | **W10** — 19

Goya* | **SW1** — 16

La Rueda* | **multi.** — 15

L-Rest. & Bar* | **W8** — -

Meson Don Felipe* | **SE1** — 20

NEW Pinchito Tapas | **EC1** — -

Rebato's* | **SW8** — -

Salt Yard* | **W1** — 21

Tapas Brindisa* | **SE1** — 24

Tendido Cero* | **SW5** — 16

NEW Tendido Cuatro | **SW6** — -

SWEDISH

Garbo's | **W1** — 17

THAI

Bangkok | **SW7** — 25

Benja | **W1** — -

Ben's Thai | **W9** — -

Blue Elephant | **SW6** — 20

Z Busaba Eathai | **multi.** — 22

Chiang Mai | **W1** — 20

Churchill Arms | **W8** — 20

Z Crazy Bear | **W1** — 20

Esarn Kheaw | **W12** — 25

Isarn | **N1** — -

Jim Thompson's | **multi.** — 16

Mango Tree | **SW1** — 21

Z Nahm | **SW1** — 24

Z Patara | **multi.** — 24

Pepper Tree | **SW4** — 20

Silks & Spice | **NW10** — 16

Singapura | **multi.** — 20

Sri Nam | **E14** — 20

Thai Square | **multi.** — 18

TURKISH

Efes | **W1** — -

Gallipoli | **N1** — 18

Haz | **E1** — 22

Ishtar | **W1** — 19

Özer | **W1** — 17

Pasha | **N1** — 19

Sofra | **multi.** — 19

Tas | **multi.** — 20

VEGETARIAN

(* vegan)

Blah! Blah! Blah! | **W12**	-
Chutney's | **NW1**	23
Eat & Two Veg | **W1**	16
Food for Thought | **WC2**	24
⏃ Gate, The | **W6**	25
Kastoori | **SW17**	-
Mildreds* | **W1**	22
⏃ Morgan M | **N7**	26
Rasa | **multi.**	24
⏃ Roussillon | **SW1**	26
NEW Saf* | **EC2**	-
222 Veggie Vegan* | **W14**	-

VIETNAMESE

Cay tre | **EC1**	23
Nam Long-Le Shaker | **SW5**	-
Pho | **multi.**	-
Song Que | **E2**	25
Viet Grill | **E2**	-
Viet Hoa | **E2**	18

CUISINES

Locations

Includes restaurant names, cuisines, Food ratings and, for locations that are mapped, top list and map coordinates (excluding private clubs). ⓩ indicates places with the highest ratings, popularity and importance.

Central London

BELGRAVIA

(See map on page 212)

TOP FOOD

Pétrus	*French*	**A9**	28
Amaya	*Indian*	**B9**	26
Zafferano	*Italian*	**B9**	25
Ottolenghi	*Bakery/Med.*	**B9**	25
Nahm	*Thai*	**C9**	24

LISTING

ⓩ Amaya	*Indian*	26
🆕 Apsleys	*Italian*	-
Baker & Spice	*Bakery/Med.*	23
ⓩ Boxwood Café	*British*	23
Ebury Wine Bar	*Eclectic*	18
Goya	*Spanish*	16
Grenadier, The	*British*	17
Il Convivio	*Italian*	22
Ishbilia	*Lebanese*	22
Jenny Lo's Tea	*Chinese*	21
Memories of China	*Chinese*	22
Mimmo d'Ischia	*Italian*	18
ⓩ Mosimann's	*Eclectic*	25
Motcombs	*Eclectic*	20
ⓩ Nahm	*Thai*	24
ⓩ Oliveto	*Italian*	21
Olivomare	*Italian/Seafood*	21
ⓩ Ottolenghi	*Bakery/Med.*	25
🆕 Pantechnicon Rms.	*Euro.*	-
Patisserie Valerie	*French*	18
ⓩ Pétrus	*French*	28
Pizza on the Park	*Pizza*	17
Rib Room	*British/Chops*	22
Salloos	*Pakistani*	23
Santini	*Italian*	21
Thomas Cubitt	*British*	21
ⓩ Zafferano	*Italian*	25

BLOOMSBURY/ FITZROVIA

Abeno	*Japanese*	18
All Star Lanes	*Amer.*	12
Annex 3	*Eclectic*	-
Archipelago	*Eclectic*	22
Ask Pizza	*Pizza*	15
Bam-Bou	*Pan-Asian*	22
Bertorelli	*Italian*	16
ⓩ Busaba Eathai	*Thai*	22
Camerino	*Italian*	-
Carluccio's Caffè	*Italian*	17
Chez Gérard	*French*	17
Cigala	*Spanish*	21
Court	*Eclectic*	18
ⓩ Crazy Bear	*Thai*	20
dim t	*Chinese*	15
Eagle Bar Diner	*Amer.*	17
Efes	*Turkish*	-
Elena's l'Etoile	*French/Italian*	18
ⓩ Fino	*Spanish*	25
ⓩ Hakkasan	*Chinese*	25
Harry Morgan's	*Deli/Jewish*	15
Kobe London	*Japanese*	19
La Perla	*Mex.*	19
Latium	*Italian*	23
Malabar Junction	*Indian*	23
Nando's	*Portug.*	-
ⓩ North Sea	*Seafood*	24
🆕 Number Twelve	*Euro.*	-
Passione	*Italian*	22
Pescatori	*Med.*	19
Pho	*Viet.*	-
ⓩ Pied à Terre	*French*	27
Ping Pong	*Chinese*	19
Rasa	*Indian*	24
Roka	*Japanese*	25
Salt Yard	*Euro.*	21
Sardo	*Italian*	21
Suka	*Malaysian*	-
Tas	*Turkish*	20
🆕 Vanilla	*Euro.*	-
Villandry	*French*	22
ⓩ Wagamama	*Japanese*	19
YO! Sushi	*Japanese*	15
Zizzi	*Pizza*	16

CHINATOWN

Chinese Experience	*Chinese*	20
Chuen Cheng Ku	*Chinese*	21
Fung Shing	*Chinese*	23
Golden Dragon	*Chinese*	20
🆕 Haozhan	*Chinese*	23
Harbour City	*Chinese*	18
Imperial China	*Chinese*	21
Jade Garden	*Chinese*	21
Joy King Lau	*Chinese*	18

LOCATIONS

Brass. St. Quentin	*French*	20
Brompton Quarter	*Eclectic*	15
Café Rouge	*French*	14
Z Capital Rest.	*French*	26
NEW Chicago Rib	*BBQ*	-
Ciro's Pizza	*Pizza*	16
NEW Daylesford	*Eclectic*	18
Fifth Floor	*Euro.*	21
Fifth Floor Cafe	*British/Med.*	18
Foliage	*Euro./French*	25
Frankie's Italian	*Italian*	14
Good Earth	*Chinese*	21
Harry Morgan's	*Deli/Jewish*	15
Ishbilia	*Lebanese*	22
Joe's Rest. Bar	*British*	19
Ladurée	*French*	23
Maroush	*Lebanese*	22
Montpeliano	*Italian*	18
Monza	*Italian*	18
Mr. Chow	*Chinese*	22
Mu	*Euro.*	-
Noura	*Lebanese*	20
Nozomi	*Japanese*	19
One-O-One	*French/Seafood*	23
Park, The	*Pan-Asian*	24
Z Patara	*Thai*	24
Patisserie Valerie	*French*	18
Z Pizza Express	*Pizza*	16
Z Racine	*French*	23
Richoux	*British*	16
Sale e Pepe	*Italian*	22
San Lorenzo	*Italian*	20
Signor Sassi	*Italian*	21
Z Wagamama	*Japanese*	19
YO! Sushi	*Japanese*	15
Z Zuma	*Japanese*	27

MARYLEBONE

Ask Pizza	*Pizza*	15
Black & Blue	*Chops*	18
Z Busaba Eathai	*Thai*	22
Caldesi	*Italian*	22
Carluccio's Caffè	*Italian*	17
Chutney's	*Indian*	23
Z Defune	*Japanese*	26
Dinings	*Japanese*	24
Eat & Two Veg	*Veg.*	16
Z Fairuz	*Lebanese*	22
FishWorks	*Seafood*	19
Frankie's Italian	*Italian*	14
Z Galvin Bistrot	*French*	23
Garbo's	*Swedish*	17
Getti	*Italian*	14
Giraffe	*Eclectic*	16

NEW Giusto	*Italian*	-
Z Golden Hind	*Seafood*	23
Home House	*British/Euro.*	-
Ishtar	*Turkish*	19
Kandoo	*Persian*	-
La Fromagerie	*Euro.*	25
NEW Landau, The	*Euro.*	25
Langan's Bistro	*British/French*	19
La Porte des Indes	*Indian*	21
NEW L'Autre Pied	*Euro.*	23
Leon	*Med.*	19
Le Pain Quotidien	*Bakery/Belgian*	18
Z Le Relais/Venise	*French*	22
Levant	*Lebanese*	21
Z Locanda Locatelli	*Italian*	25
Mandalay	*Burmese*	23
Maroush	*Lebanese*	22
Z Michael Moore	*Eclectic*	26
Nando's	*Portug.*	-
Odin's	*British/French*	20
Original Tagine	*Moroccan*	-
Orrery	*French*	24
Özer	*Turkish*	17
Patisserie Valerie	*French*	18
Phoenix Palace	*Chinese*	21
Ping Pong	*Chinese*	19
Providores, The	*Eclectic*	22
Real Greek	*Greek*	16
Reubens	*Deli/Jewish*	15
Rhodes W1 Brass.	*British*	16
Rhodes W1 Rest.	*British*	23
Royal China	*Chinese*	23
Z Royal China Club	*Chinese*	24
Seashell	*Seafood*	20
Six13	*Eclectic/Kosher*	-
Sofra	*Turkish*	19
Strada	*Italian*	18
NEW Texture	*Euro.*	21
Tootsies	*Amer.*	13
2 Veneti	*Italian*	19
Union Cafe	*British/Med.*	19
Z Wagamama	*Japanese*	19
Wallace, The	*French*	18
YO! Sushi	*Japanese*	15
Zizzi	*Pizza*	16

MAYFAIR

(See map on page 211)

TOP FOOD

Square, The	*French*	**B4**	27
Le Gavroche	*French*	**B1**	27
Nobu London	*Japanese*	**E2**	27
Alain Ducasse	*French*	**D2**	26
Greenhouse, The	*French*	**D3**	26

LISTING

Z NEW Alain Ducasse	*French*	26
Albemarle, The	*British*	22
Al Hamra	*Lebanese*	21
Alloro	*Italian*	21
Z Al Sultan	*Lebanese*	23
Annabel's	*British/French*	20
NEW Artisan	*Euro.*	18
Ask Pizza	*Pizza*	15
Automat	*Amer.*	18
Z Bellamy's	*French*	22
Benares	*Indian*	23
NEW BORD'EAUX	*French*	–
Browns	*British*	16
Carluccio's Caffè	*Italian*	17
Cecconi's	*Italian*	21
Chez Gérard	*French*	17
China Tang	*Chinese*	20
Chisou	*Japanese*	23
Chor Bizarre	*Indian*	19
Cipriani	*Italian*	20
Delfino	*Italian*	20
Dorchester/The Grill	*British*	24
Dover St.	*Euro.*	15
El Pirata	*Spanish*	20
Galvin/Windows	*French*	20
George	*Euro.*	22
Giardinetto	*Italian*	–
Z Gordon Ramsay/Claridge's	*Euro.*	26
Z Greenhouse, The	*French*	26
Greig's	*British/Chops*	17
Guinea Grill	*British/Chops*	21
Haiku	*Pan-Asian*	19
Harry's Bar	*Italian*	23
NEW Hibiscus	*French*	24
Hush	*British/French*	14
Ikeda	*Japanese*	26
Kai Mayfair	*Chinese*	23
Kiku	*Japanese*	23
La Genova	*Italian*	25
Langan's Brass.	*British/French*	19
Z NEW La Petite Maison	*Med.*	25
L'Artiste Muscle	*French*	20
Le Boudin Blanc	*French*	22
Z Le Gavroche	*French*	27
Mark's Club	*British/French*	23
Z maze	*French*	25
NEW maze Grill	*Chops*	–
Mews of Mayfair	*British*	19
Miyama	*Japanese*	23
Morton's	*French*	22
Mosaico	*Italian*	–
Napket	*Sandwiches*	–
Nicole's	*Euro./Med.*	21
Z Nobu Berkeley St	*Japanese*	26
Z Nobu London	*Japanese*	27
Noura	*Lebanese*	20
NEW Only Running Footman	*British*	18
Pappagallo	*Italian*	23
Z Patara	*Thai*	24
Patterson's	*Euro.*	24
Pescatori	*Med.*	19
Princess Garden	*Chinese*	22
Rasa	*Indian*	24
Richoux	*British*	16
Rist. Semplice	*Italian*	24
Rocket	*Med.*	17
Sakura	*Japanese*	18
Sartoria	*Italian*	20
Z Scott's	*Seafood*	24
Shogun	*Japanese*	–
Sketch/Gallery	*Euro.*	17
Z Sketch/Lecture Rm.	*Euro.*	21
Sofra	*Turkish*	19
Sotheby's Cafe	*British*	20
Z Square, The	*French*	27
Strada	*Italian*	18
Sumosan	*Japanese*	24
Z Taman Gang	*Pan-Asian*	21
Z Tamarind	*Indian*	25
Thai Square	*Thai*	18
Theo Randall	*Italian*	23
Truc Vert	*French*	17
Z Umu	*Japanese*	26
Veeraswamy	*Indian*	23
Via Condotti	*Italian*	19
NEW Wild Honey	*British*	23

PICCADILLY

(See map on page 211)

TOP FOOD

Bentley's	*British/Seafood*	**C5**	24
Yoshino	*Japanese*	**D6**	23
St. Alban	*Euro.*	**D6**	22
Gaucho Grill	*Argent./Chops*	**C5**	22
Wolseley, The	*Euro.*	**D4**	22

LISTING

Academy	*British*	–
Aubaine	*French*	19
Benihana	*Japanese*	19
Bentley's	*British/Seafood*	24
NEW Brumus	*Euro.*	–
Chez Gérard	*French*	17
Chowki	*Indian*	17
Citrus	*Med.*	19

LOCATIONS

Cocoon	*Pan-Asian*	21
Cuckoo Club	*Euro.*	–
Diverso	*Italian*	17
Ed's Easy Diner	*Burgers*	17
Fakhreldine	*Lebanese*	19
FishWorks	*Seafood*	19
Z Gaucho Grill	*Argent./Chops*	22
Hard Rock	*Amer.*	14
Living Rm.	*Euro.*	17
Mitsukoshi	*Japanese*	19
Momo	*African*	19
Napket	*Sandwiches*	–
Noura	*Lebanese*	20
Patisserie Valerie	*French*	18
Pigalle Club	*Euro./French*	15
Planet Hollywood	*Amer.*	10
Rainforest Cafe	*Amer.*	11
Richoux	*British*	16
St. Alban	*Euro.*	22
Z Wolseley, The	*Euro.*	22
Yoshino	*Japanese*	23

SOHO

(See map on page 211)

TOP FOOD

Richard Corrigan	*British/Irish*	**B7**	26
Yauatcha	*Chinese*	**B6**	26
Barrafina	*Spanish*	**B7**	25
Arbutus	*Euro.*	**A7**	24
Alastair Little	*British*	**B7**	24

LISTING

NEW Aaya	*Japanese*	–
Alastair Little	*British*	24
Albannach	*Scottish*	16
Andrew Edmunds	*Euro.*	22
Aperitivo	*Italian*	–
Z Arbutus	*Euro.*	24
Balans	*British*	16
Z Barrafina	*Spanish*	25
Bar Shu	*Chinese*	23
Benja	*Thai*	–
Bertorelli	*Italian*	16
NEW Bincho Yakitori	*Japanese*	21
Bodeans	*BBQ*	18
Z Busaba Eathai	*Thai*	22
Café Boheme	*French*	18
NEW Cape Town Fish	*Eclectic/Seafood*	18
NEW Cha Cha Moon	*Chinese*	–
Chiang Mai	*Thai*	20
Club, The	*Eclectic*	–
NEW Côte	*French*	–
NEW Dehesa	*Italian/Spanish*	–
Diner, The	*Amer.*	18

Ed's Easy Diner	*Burgers*	17
Floridita	*Cuban*	17
French House	*French*	17
Gay Hussar	*Hungarian*	19
Gopal's of Soho	*Indian*	20
Groucho Club	*British*	18
Imli	*Indian*	19
Incognico	*French*	21
itsu	*Japanese*	17
Kettners	*Eclectic*	15
Kulu Kulu	*Japanese*	19
La Trouvaille	*French*	25
Leon	*Med.*	19
Le Pain Quotidien	*Bakery/Belgian*	18
L'Escargot	*French*	23
Little Italy	*Italian*	16
Masala Zone	*Indian*	19
Meza	*Med.*	13
Mildreds	*Veg.*	22
National Dining Rms.	*British*	20
Z Patara	*Thai*	24
Patisserie Valerie	*French*	18
Ping Pong	*Chinese*	19
Z Pizza Express	*Pizza*	16
Portrait	*British*	21
NEW Quo Vadis	*British*	–
Randall & Aubin	*British/Seafood*	21
Red Fort	*Indian*	24
Refuel	*Euro.*	–
Z Richard Corrigan	*British/Irish*	26
Satsuma	*Japanese*	19
Soho House	*British*	19
Souk	*African*	17
Spiga	*Italian*	17
Ten Ten Tei	*Japanese*	23
Thai Square	*Thai*	18
Vasco & Piero's	*Italian*	21
Z Wagamama	*Japanese*	19
Z Yauatcha	*Chinese*	26
Yming	*Chinese*	24
YO! Sushi	*Japanese*	15
Zilli Fish	*Italian/Seafood*	21

ST. JAMES'S

(See map on page 211)

TOP FOOD

L'Oranger	*French*	**E5**	25
Wilton's	*British/Seafood*	**D5**	25
Le Caprice	*British/Euro.*	**D5**	24
Ritz, The	*British/French*	**D4**	23
Matsuri	*Japanese*	**D5**	23

LISTING

| Al Duca | *Italian* | 20 |
| Avenue, The | *Euro.* | 19 |

Brasserie Roux	*French*	21
NEW Brass. St. Jacques	*French*	-
Fortnum's Fountain	*British*	17
Franco's	*Italian/Med.*	19
Getti	*Italian*	14
Green's	*British/Seafood*	23
Inn The Park	*British*	18
Just St. James's	*British*	20
Z Le Caprice	*British/Euro.*	24
L'Oranger	*French*	25
Luciano	*Italian*	19
Matsuri	*Japanese*	23
Mint Leaf	*Indian*	19
Quaglino's	*Euro.*	18
Z Ritz, The	*British/French*	23
Rowley's	*British*	20
NEW Sake no hana	*Japanese*	19
1707 Wine Bar	*British*	21
St. James's	*British*	20
Texas Embassy	*Tex-Mex*	14
Thai Square	*Thai*	18
Z Wilton's	*British/Seafood*	25

VICTORIA

Ask Pizza	*Pizza*	15
Bank Westminster	*Euro.*	16
Boisdale	*British/Scottish*	20
Chez Gérard	*French*	17
dim t	*Chinese*	15
Z Goring	*British*	25
Mango Tree	*Thai*	21
Noura	*Lebanese*	20
Olivo	*Italian*	19
Quilon	*Indian*	25
Zizzi	*Pizza*	16

WESTMINSTER

Atami	*Japanese*	19
Z Cinnamon Club	*Indian*	24
City Café	*Euro.*	17
Quirinale	*Italian*	23
Shepherd's	*British*	23
Tate Britain	*British*	19
YO! Sushi	*Japanese*	15

East/South East London

BLACKFRIARS

Bertorelli	*Italian*	16
NEW Northbank	*British*	-
Z Pizza Express	*Pizza*	16
Refettorio	*Italian*	22
Singapura	*SE Asian*	20
Z Wagamama	*Japanese*	19
Ye Olde Cheshire	*British*	16

BOW/MILE END/ HACKNEY/ BETHNAL GREEN

Bistrotheque	*French*	20
Buen Ayre/Santa Maria	*Argent.*	-
Empress of India	*British*	21
Green & Red Bar	*Mex.*	19
Nando's	*Portug.*	-

CANARY WHARF/ DOCKLANDS

Browns	*British*	16
Café Rouge	*French*	14
Carluccio's Caffè	*Italian*	17
1802	*British*	16
El Faro	*Spanish*	23
Z Gaucho Grill	*Argent./Chops*	22
Gun, The	*British*	21
itsu	*Japanese*	17
La Figa	*Italian*	22
Moshi Moshi	*Japanese*	19
Plateau	*French*	19
Quadrato	*Italian*	-
Royal China	*Chinese*	23
Smollensky's	*Chops*	16
Sri Nam	*Thai*	20
Z Ubon	*Japanese*	26
Wapping Food	*Euro.*	19

CITY

(See map on page 216)

TOP FOOD

Sweetings	*British/Seafood*	**D7**	26
Rhodes 24	*British*	**B8**	24
Café Spice Namasté	*Indian*	**C11**	23
1 Lombard St.	*French*	**C8**	23
Don, The	*Euro.*	**D8**	22
Coq d'Argent	*French*	**C7**	22
Bonds	*French*	**C8**	22
Gaucho Grill	*Argent./Chops*	**A8**	22
Haz	*Turkish*	**B10**	22

LISTING

Bertorelli	*Italian*	16
Bevis Marks	*British/Jewish*	22
Boisdale	*British/Scottish*	20
Bonds	*French*	22
Browns	*British*	16
Café Spice Namasté	*Indian*	23
Caravaggio	*Italian*	15
Chez Gérard	*French*	17
Ciro's Pizza	*Pizza*	16
City Miyama	*Japanese*	-
Coq d'Argent	*French*	22

LOCATIONS

Don, The | *Euro.*	22
🔒 Gaucho Grill | *Argent./Chops*	22
Haz | *Turkish*	22
Imperial City | *Chinese*	23
NEW Kenza | *Lebanese/Moroccan*	-
NEW L'Anima | *Italian*	-
Leon | *Med.*	19
Moshi Moshi | *Japanese*	19
1 Lombard St. | *French*	23
1 Lombard Brass. | *Euro.*	19
NEW Pacific Oriental | *Asian Fusion*	-
Paternoster Chop | *British/Chops*	17
Patisserie Valerie | *French*	18
NEW Pinchito Tapas | *Spanish*	-
Prism | *British*	20
Rhodes 24 | *British*	24
Rocket | *Med.*	17
Royal Exchange | *Euro.*	14
Sauterelle | *French*	-
Singapura | *SE Asian*	20
🔒 Sweetings | *British/Seafood*	26
NEW Terranostra | *Italian*	-
Thai Square | *Thai*	18
Vivat Bacchus | *Euro.*	20
🔒 Wagamama | *Japanese*	19

CLERKENWELL/ SMITHFIELD/ FARRINGDON

Ambassador, The | *Euro.*	-
Bleeding Heart | *British/French*	22
Carluccio's Caffè | *Italian*	17
Cellar Gascon | *French*	-
Cicada | *Pan-Asian*	21
Clerkenwell Dining | *Euro.*	22
🔒 Club Gascon | *French*	26
Coach & Horses | *British*	-
🔒 Comptoir Gascon | *French*	23
Dans Le Noir | *Eclectic*	8
Eagle, The | *Med.*	23
Fish Shop | *Seafood*	18
Flaneur | *Euro.*	24
Hat & Feathers | *Euro.*	-
NEW Hix Oyster | *British*	-
La Porchetta | *Pizza*	18
Le Café/Marché | *French*	23
Little Bay | *Euro.*	21
Medcalf | *British*	-
🔒 Moro | *Med.*	25
Pho | *Viet.*	-
Portal | *Portug.*	20
Potemkin | *Russian*	-
Quality Chop Hse. | *British/Chops*	21

Real Greek | *Greek*	16
Saki Bar/Food Emp. | *Japanese*	-
Smiths/Dining Rm. | *British*	21
Smiths/Top Floor | *British/Chops*	21
St. Germain | *French*	22
🔒 St. John | *British*	27
Strada | *Italian*	18
Tas | *Turkish*	20
Vinoteca | *Euro.*	-
YO! Sushi | *Japanese*	15
Zetter | *Med.*	17

GREENWICH/ BLACKHEATH

Chapter Two | *Euro.*	23
Inside | *Euro.*	25
Nando's | *Portug.*	-
Rivington Grill | *British*	21
Rodizio Rico | *Brazilian*	17
Spread Eagle | *French*	24
Tootsies | *Amer.*	13

SHOREDITCH/ SPITALFIELDS/ HOXTON/WHITECHAPEL

Bacchus | *Eclectic*	21
NEW Brickhouse, The | *Euro.*	-
Canteen | *British*	18
Cay tre | *Viet.*	23
Cru | *Med.*	-
Diner, The | *Amer.*	18
Eyre Brothers | *Portug./Spanish*	22
Fifteen | *Med.*	25
Giraffe | *Eclectic*	16
Great Eastern | *Asian Fusion*	16
🔒 Hawksmoor | *Chops*	24
Hoxton Apprentice | *Eclectic*	-
Hoxton Grille | *British/French*	15
Leon | *Med.*	19
🔒 Les Trois Garçons | *French*	21
🔒 New Tayyabs | *Pakistani*	28
Original Lahore | *Pakistani*	25
Real Greek | *Greek*	16
Rivington Grill | *British*	21
NEW Saf | *Eclectic*	-
Song Que | *Viet.*	25
St. John Bread/Wine | *British*	23
Viet Grill | *Viet.*	-
Viet Hoa | *Viet.*	18
NEW Water House | *Euro.*	-

SOUTH BANK/BOROUGH

NEW Bincho Yakitori | *Japanese*	21
Black & Blue | *Chops*	18

Canteen | *British*	18
Cantina Vinopolis | *Eclectic/Med.*	18
Delfina | *Eclectic*	-
dim t | *Chinese*	15
Feng Sushi | *Japanese*	18
fish! | *Seafood*	19
Leon | *Med.*	19
Le Pain Quotidien | *Bakery/Belgian*	18
Magdalen | *Euro.*	23
Z Oxo Tower | *Euro.*	21
Z Oxo Tower Brass. | *Asian/Med.*	18
Ping Pong | *Chinese*	19
Real Greek | *Greek*	16
Roast | *British*	19
Skylon | *Euro.*	19
Tapas Brindisa | *Spanish*	24
Tas | *Turkish*	20
Tate Modern | *Euro.*	17
Wright Brothers' | *Seafood*	-

TOWER BRIDGE/ LIMEHOUSE/ WAPPING

Addendum | *Euro.*	-
Bengal Clipper | *Indian*	19
Blueprint Café | *Euro.*	18
Browns | *British*	16
Butlers Wharf | *British*	22
Cantina del Ponte | *Italian*	18
Champor | *Malaysian*	20
Z Gaucho Grill | *Argent./Chops*	22
Z Il Bordello | *Italian*	23
Le Pont/Tour | *French/Seafood*	20
Narrow, The | *British*	22
Ping Pong | *Chinese*	19
Tentazioni | *Italian*	24

WATERLOO/ SOUTHWARK/ KENNINGTON

Anchor & Hope | *British*	25
Baltic | *Polish*	22
Chez Gérard | *French*	17
Dragon Castle | *Chinese*	-
Franklins | *British*	-
Giraffe | *Eclectic*	16
Hot Stuff | *Indian*	-
Livebait | *Seafood*	19
Menier Chocolate | *British*	16
Meson Don Felipe | *Spanish*	20
Rebato's | *Spanish*	-
R.S.J. | *British*	18
Tas | *Turkish*	20
NEW Waterloo Brass. | *French*	19

North/North West London

CAMDEN TOWN/ CHALK FARM/ KENTISH TOWN/ PRIMROSE HILL

Asakusa | *Japanese*	25
Belgo | *Belgian*	18
Camden Brass. | *Euro.*	20
Cottons | *Carib.*	19
Engineer | *British*	20
Feng Sushi | *Japanese*	18
FishWorks | *Seafood*	19
Z Gilgamesh | *Pan-Asian*	19
Hache | *Burgers*	20
La Collina | *Italian*	24
Lansdowne, The | *Euro.*	17
Lemonia | *Greek*	18
Masala Zone | *Indian*	19
Mestizo | *Mex.*	23
Nando's | *Portug.*	-
Odette's | *Euro.*	20
Sardo Canale | *Italian*	21
Silks & Spice | *Malaysian/Thai*	16
Z Wagamama | *Japanese*	19

GOLDERS GREEN/ FINCHLEY

Basilico | *Pizza*	20
Bloom's | *Deli/Jewish*	17
Café Japan | *Japanese*	25
Good Earth | *Chinese*	21
Green Cottage | *Chinese*	18
Jim Thompson's | *Thai*	16
Met Su Yan | *Pan-Asian*	-
Solly's | *Mideast.*	19
2 Brothers Fish | *Seafood*	22
Zizzi | *Pizza*	16

HAMPSTEAD/KILBURN/ SWISS COTTAGE

Artigiano | *Italian*	20
Ask Pizza | *Pizza*	15
Atma | *Indian*	-
Baker & Spice | *Bakery/Med.*	23
Benihana | *Japanese*	19
Black & Blue | *Chops*	18
Bombay Bicycle | *Indian*	18
Bradley's | *British/French*	16
dim t | *Chinese*	15
Z Gaucho Grill | *Argent./Chops*	22
Giraffe | *Eclectic*	16
Gourmet Burger | *Burgers*	19

Gung-Ho	*Chinese*	19
🇿 Jin Kichi	*Japanese*	27
Little Bay	*Euro.*	21
Nando's	*Portug.*	-
Nautilus Fish	*Seafood*	22
Old Bull & Bush	*Euro.*	12
NEW Paradise	*British*	-
Ping Pong	*Chinese*	19
Salusbury Pub	*Italian*	-
Singapore Garden	*SE Asian*	19
Tootsies	*Amer.*	13
Wells, The	*Euro.*	20
XO	*Pan-Asian*	21

HIGHGATE/ MUSWELL HILL/ CROUCH END/ TUFNELL PARK

Bouga	*Moroccan*	-
Bull, The	*Euro.*	-
Café Rouge	*French*	14
dim t	*Chinese*	15
Giraffe	*Eclectic*	16
La Porchetta	*Pizza*	18
Original Lahore	*Pakistani*	25
Zizzi	*Pizza*	16

ISLINGTON

Albion, The	*British*	17
Almeida	*French*	19
Barnsbury, The	*British*	21
Basilico	*Pizza*	20
Bierodrome	*Belgian*	16
Browns	*British*	16
Carluccio's Caffè	*Italian*	17
Casale Franco	*Italian*	-
Cottons	*Carib.*	19
NEW Cruse 9	*Euro.*	-
Draper's Arms	*Euro.*	19
Duke of Cambridge	*British*	22
Elk in the Woods	*Eclectic*	-
Fig	*Euro.*	22
Firezza	*Pizza*	19
FishWorks	*Seafood*	19
Frederick's	*British/Euro.*	21
Gallipoli	*Turkish*	18
Giraffe	*Eclectic*	16
Isarn	*Thai*	-
La Porchetta	*Pizza*	18
Le Mercury	*French*	16
Marquess Tavern	*British*	-
Masala Zone	*Indian*	19
Metrogusto	*Italian*	-
🇿 Morgan M	*French*	26
Nando's	*Portug.*	-

New Culture Rev.	*Chinese*	18
🇿 Ottolenghi	*Bakery/Med.*	25
Pasha	*Turkish*	19
Rasa	*Indian*	24
Rodizio Rico	*Brazilian*	17
Sabor	*S Amer.*	-
Strada	*Italian*	18
Thai Square	*Thai*	18
🇿 Wagamama	*Japanese*	19

KING'S CROSS

Acorn House	*British*	19
NEW Champagne Bar	*British*	14
Konstam	*British*	23
Le Pain Quotidien	*Bakery/Belgian*	18
Snazz	*Chinese*	-

ST. JOHN'S WOOD

Baker & Spice	*Bakery/Med.*	23
Ben's Thai	*Thai*	-
Cafe Med	*Med.*	17
Café Rouge	*French*	14
NEW Daylesford	*Eclectic*	18
Green Olive	*Italian*	23
Harry Morgan's	*Deli/Jewish*	15
L'Aventure	*French*	24
🇿 Oslo Court	*French*	26
NEW Osteria Stecca	*Italian*	-
Raoul's	*Med.*	20
Red Pepper	*Italian*	20
Richoux	*British*	16
🇿 Royal China Club	*Chinese*	24
Sofra	*Turkish*	19
NEW Warrington, The	*British*	-
Waterway, The	*Euro.*	15

STOKE NEWINGTON

La Porchetta	*Pizza*	18
Rasa	*Indian*	24

South/South West London

BARNES

Annie's	*British*	21
Barnes Grill	*British*	-
Brown Dog, The	*Euro.*	-
Riva	*Italian*	21
Sonny's	*Euro.*	22

BATTERSEA

Buona Sera	*Italian*	18
Butcher & Grill, The	*British*	18
Firezza	*Pizza*	19
Fish Club	*Seafood*	-

FishWorks | Seafood — 19
Giraffe | Eclectic — 16
Gourmet Burger | Burgers — 19
Greyhound, The | British/Euro. — 23
Little Bay | Euro. — 21
Nancy Lam's Enak | Indonesian — -
Osteria Antica | Italian — 17
Z Pizza Express | Pizza — 16
Pizza Metro | Pizza — -
Ransome's Dock | British/Eclectic — 20
Santa Maria del Sur | Argent. — -
NEW 3 Bridges | Italian — -
NEW Tom Ilic | Euro. — 24

BRIXTON/CLAPHAM

Abbeville | British/Euro. — -
Basilico | Pizza — 20
Bierodrome | Belgian — 16
Bodeans | BBQ — 18
Bombay Bicycle | Indian — 18
Café Rouge | French — 14
El Rincon Latino | S Amer./Spanish — -
La Rueda | Spanish — 15
Nando's | Portug. — -
Pepper Tree | Thai — 20
Strada | Italian — 18
Tootsies | Amer. — 13
Trinity | Euro. — 26
Tsunami | Japanese — 26
Upstairs | French — -

CAMBERWELL/ DULWICH/HERNE HILL

Café Rouge | French — 14
Franklins | British — -
Palmerston, The | British — -

CHELSEA

(See map on page 212)

TOP FOOD

Gordon Ramsay/68 Royal | French | **H7** — 29
Rasoi Vineet Bhatia | Indian | **F8** — 27
Tom Aikens | French | **E6** — 25
Aubergine | French | **H2** — 25
Vama | Indian | **I3** — 25

LISTING

Admiral Codrington | British/Euro. — 18
Aglio e Olio | Italian — 21
Aquasia | Asian/Med. — -
Ask Pizza | Pizza — 15
Aubergine | French — 25
Awana | Malaysian — 22
Baker & Spice | Bakery/Med. — 23

Benihana | Japanese — 19
Big Easy | Amer. — 16
Bluebird | Euro. — 18
NEW Botanist, The | British — -
Brinkley's | Eclectic — 14
Builders Arms | British — 17
Buona Sera | Italian — 18
Caraffini | Italian — 22
Carpaccio | Italian — 18
Chelsea Brass. | Euro. — 17
Chelsea Bun | British — 14
Z Cheyne Walk | French — 23
Chutney Mary | Indian — 23
Cross Keys, The | French — -
Daphne's | Italian — 22
NEW Daylesford | Eclectic — 18
Dish Dash | Lebanese/Persian — 21
Eight Over Eight | Pan-Asian — 22
El Blason | Spanish — 18
El Gaucho | Argent./Chops — 17
Elistano | Italian — 22
Enterprise | Eclectic — 17
Firezza | Pizza — 19
FishWorks | Seafood — 19
Foxtrot Oscar | British — 15
Z Gaucho Grill | Argent./Chops — 22
Z Gordon Ramsay/68 Royal | French — 29
Hache | Burgers — 20
itsu | Japanese — 17
NEW Jimmy's | British — -
La Famiglia | Italian — 21
Le Cercle | French — 23
Le Colombier | French — 21
Le Pain Quotidien | Bakery/Belgian — 18
Le Suquet | French/Seafood — 22
Lucio | Italian — 22
Made in Italy | Italian — 20
Manicomio | Italian — 19
Napket | Sandwiches — -
New Culture Rev. | Chinese — 18
Oriel | Euro. — 15
Osteria dell'Arancio | Italian — 20
Painted Heron | Indian — 23
Patisserie Valerie | French — 18
Pellicano | Italian — 22
Pig's Ear | British/French — 18
Z Pizza Express | Pizza — 16
PJ's B&G | Amer. — 16
Poissonnerie | French/Seafood — 21
Z Rasoi Vineet Bhatia | Indian — 27
Riccardo's | Italian — 20
Santa Lucia | Italian — -
Scalini | Italian — 23

Sophie's Steak | *Amer./Chops*	21
Tartine | *French*	17
Tom Aikens | *French*	25
Tom's Kitchen | *British*	22
NEW Tom's Place | *British/Seafood*	18
Toto's | *Italian*	23
Vama | *Indian*	25
Vingt-Quatre | *Eclectic*	13
Yumenoki | *Japanese*	-
Ziani | *Italian*	20

EARL'S COURT

Balans | *British*	16
Langan's Coq d'Or | *British/French*	18
Lou Pescadou | *French/Seafood*	-
Masala Zone | *Indian*	19
Strada | *Italian*	18
Troubadour, The | *Eclectic*	18
Zizzi | *Pizza*	16

FULHAM

Aziz | *Moroccan*	19
Basilico | *Pizza*	20
Blue Elephant | *Thai*	20
Bodeans | *BBQ*	18
Carluccio's Caffè | *Italian*	17
Farm | *French*	19
Feng Sushi | *Japanese*	18
FishWorks | *Seafood*	19
Gourmet Burger | *Burgers*	19
Jim Thompson's | *Thai*	16
La Rueda | *Spanish*	15
Little Bay | *Euro.*	21
Mao Tai | *Pan-Asian*	23
NEW Marco | *French*	-
Z Pizza Express | *Pizza*	16
Royal China | *Chinese*	23
Strada | *Italian*	18
NEW Tendido Cuatro | *Spanish*	-
T.G.I. Friday's | *Amer.*	12
222 Veggie Vegan | *Veg.*	-
YO! Sushi | *Japanese*	15

PIMLICO

About Thyme | *Euro.*	-
Como Lario | *Italian*	21
NEW Daylesford | *Eclectic*	18
Ebury Dining Rm. | *Euro.*	16
Goya | *Spanish*	16
Grumbles | *British/French*	-
Z Hunan | *Chinese*	27
La Poule au Pot | *French*	21
L'Incontro | *Italian*	21
Z Roussillon | *French*	26

PUTNEY/RICHMOND

Ask Pizza | *Pizza*	15
Basilico | *Pizza*	20
Café Rouge | *French*	14
Carluccio's Caffè | *Italian*	17
Enoteca Turi | *Italian*	24
FishWorks | *Seafood*	19
Frankie's Italian | *Italian*	14
Z Gaucho Grill | *Argent./Chops*	22
Giraffe | *Eclectic*	16
Glasshouse, The | *Euro.*	25
Gourmet Burger | *Burgers*	19
Jim Thompson's | *Thai*	16
Kew Grill | *British*	-
Ma Goa | *Indian*	22
Petersham, The | *Euro.*	-
Petersham Nurseries | *Euro.*	24
Popeseye | *Chops*	-
Real Greek | *Greek*	16
Rocket | *Med.*	17
Spencer Arms | *British*	-
Thai Square | *Thai*	18
Tootsies | *Amer.*	13

SOUTH KENSINGTON

(See map on page 212)

TOP FOOD

Star of India | *Indian* | **F1**	25
Cambio de Tercio | *Spanish* | **F1**	25
Patara | *Thai* | **F4**	24
Bibendum | *French* | **E5**	23
Khan's/Kensington | *Indian* | **D4**	23

LISTING

Ask Pizza | *Pizza*	15
Aubaine | *French*	19
Bangkok | *Thai*	25
Bibendum | *French*	23
Bibendum Oyster | *French/Seafood*	21
Bistro 190 | *British/Med.*	-
Black & Blue | *Chops*	18
Blakes | *Eclectic*	19
Bombay Brass. | *Indian*	22
Z Cambio de Tercio | *Spanish*	25
Collection | *Eclectic*	13
Daquise | *Polish*	15
dim t | *Chinese*	15
El Gaucho | *Argent./Chops*	17
Il Falconiere | *Italian*	15
Joe's | *Med.*	-
Khan's/Kensington | *Indian*	23
Kulu Kulu | *Japanese*	19
La Bouchée | *French*	21
La Brasserie | *French*	18

Le Pain Quotidien	*Bakery/Belgian*	18
L'Etranger	*French*	23
Nam Long-Le Shaker	*Viet.*	-
Noor Jahan	*Indian*	22
Papillon	*French*	21
Z Pasha	*Moroccan*	21
Z Patara	*Thai*	24
Spago	*Italian*	18
Z Star of India	*Indian*	25
Tendido Cero	*Spanish*	16
Thai Square	*Thai*	18

WANDSWORTH/ BALHAM/WIMBLEDON

Amici	*Italian*	16
Butcher & Grill, The	*British*	18
Z Chez Bruce	*British*	29
NEW Côte	*French*	-
Dish Dash	*Lebanese/Persian*	21
Firezza	*Pizza*	19
Gourmet Burger	*Burgers*	19
NEW Harrison's	*Eclectic*	15
Kastoori	*African/Indian*	-
Lamberts	*British*	21
Light House	*Eclectic*	-
San Lorenzo	*Italian*	20
Strada	*Italian*	18
Tootsies	*Amer.*	13

West London

BAYSWATER

All Star Lanes	*Amer.*	12
Z Al Waha	*Lebanese*	23
Z NEW Angelus	*French*	23
Four Seasons	*Chinese*	22
Goldmine	*Chinese*	-
Gourmet Burger	*Burgers*	19
Halepi	*Greek*	19
Inaho	*Japanese*	25
Island	*British*	-
Khan's	*Indian*	21
Kiasu	*Pan-Asian*	21
L'Accento Italiano	*Italian*	-
NEW Le Café Anglais	*French*	20
Mandarin Kitchen	*Chinese*	24
Nando's	*Portug.*	-
Rodizio Rico	*Brazilian*	17
Royal China	*Chinese*	23
YO! Sushi	*Japanese*	15

CHISWICK

Annie's	*British*	21
Balans	*British*	16
Café Rouge	*French*	14

NEW Devonshire, The	*British*	22
Firezza	*Pizza*	19
Fish Hook	*Seafood*	20
FishWorks	*Seafood*	19
Frankie's Italian	*Italian*	14
Giraffe	*Eclectic*	16
Gourmet Burger	*Burgers*	19
High Road Brass.	*Euro.*	19
Z La Trompette	*Euro./French*	28
Z Le Vacherin	*French*	26
Sam's Brass.	*Euro.*	19
Tootsies	*Amer.*	13
Zizzi	*Pizza*	16

EALING

Charlotte's Place	*Euro.*	-

HAMMERSMITH

Brackenbury	*Euro.*	21
Carluccio's Caffè	*Italian*	17
Chez Kristof	*French*	20
Z Gate, The	*Veg.*	25
Indian Zing	*Indian*	-
Z River Café	*Italian*	28
Smollensky's	*Chops*	16

HOLLAND PARK

Alounak	*Persian*	22
Belvedere, The	*British/French*	20
Bombay Bicycle	*Indian*	18
Julie's	*British*	17

KENSINGTON

(See map on page 214)

TOP FOOD

Clarke's	*British*	**G7**	26
Il Portico	*Italian*	**K5**	24
Zaika	*Indian*	**I9**	24
Ark, The	*Italian*	**F7**	24
Locanda Ottoemezzo	Italian	**J9**	24

LISTING

Abingdon, The	*Euro.*	18
Ark, The	*Italian*	24
Babylon	*Euro.*	17
Balans	*British*	16
Black & Blue	*Chops*	18
Brunello	*Italian*	23
Clarke's	*British*	26
Da Mario	*Italian*	16
11 Abingdon Rd.	*Euro.*	19
Feng Sushi	*Japanese*	18
ffiona's	*British*	23
Giraffe	*Eclectic*	16
Il Portico	*Italian*	24

LOCATIONS

Kensington Place | *British* — 19

NEW Kensington Sq. | *British* — -

Koi | *Japanese* — 21

Launceston Place | *British* — -

Le Pain Quotidien | *Bakery/Belgian* — 18

Locanda Ottoemezzo | *Italian* — 24

L-Rest. & Bar | *Spanish* — -

Maggie Jones's | *British* — 19

Memories of China | *Chinese* — 22

Patisserie Valerie | *French* — 18

Z Pizza Express | *Pizza* — 16

Sticky Fingers | *Amer.* — 17

Timo | *Italian* — 27

Z Wagamama | *Japanese* — 19

NEW Whole Foods | *Eclectic* — 18

Wòdka | *Polish* — 21

Zaika | *Indian* — 24

NOTTING HILL

(See map on page 214)

TOP FOOD

Ledbury, The | *French* | **B5** — 28

Assaggi | *Italian* | **D7** — 26

Ottolenghi | *Bakery/Med.* | **C5** — 25

Notting Hill Brass. | *Euro.* | **D4** — 25

Hereford Road | *British* | **D7** — 24

LISTING

Ask Pizza | *Pizza* — 15

Z Assaggi | *Italian* — 26

Bodeans | *BBQ* — 18

Books for Cooks | *Eclectic* — 23

Bumpkin | *British* — 19

Churchill Arms | *Thai* — 20

Costas Grill | *Greek* — 14

Cow Dining Rm. | *British* — 21

Crazy Homies | *Mex.* — 19

e&o | *Pan-Asian* — 22

Electric Brass. | *Eclectic* — 17

Essenza | *Italian* — 18

Fat Badger | *British* — 15

Feng Sushi | *Japanese* — 18

Firezza | *Pizza* — 19

Galicia | *Spanish* — 19

Geales Fish | *Seafood* — 20

Harlem | *Amer.* — 12

NEW Hereford Road | *British* — 24

Ladbroke Arms | *Euro.* — 19

Z Ledbury, The | *French* — 28

Lucky 7 | *Amer./Burgers* — 21

Malabar | *Indian* — 22

Mediterraneo | *Italian* — 21

New Culture Rev. | *Chinese* — 18

Notting Grill | *British/Chops* — 21

Notting Hill Brass. | *Euro.* — 25

Nyonya | *Malaysian* — 22

Z Osteria Basilico | *Italian* — 22

Z Ottolenghi | *Bakery/Med.* — 25

Ping Pong | *Chinese* — 19

Z Pizza Express | *Pizza* — 16

Raoul's | *Med.* — 20

Taqueria | *Mex.* — 22

Tom's Deli | *Eclectic* — 16

Tootsies | *Amer.* — 13

202 | *Euro.* — 18

Uli | *Pan-Asian* — 26

NEW Urban Turban | *Indian* — 17

Westbourne, The | *Eclectic* — 18

OLYMPIA

Alounak | *Persian* — 22

Popeseye | *Chops* — -

PADDINGTON

Frontline | *British* — -

Levantine | *Lebanese* — -

Noor Jahan | *Indian* — 22

Pearl Liang | *Chinese* — 18

Yakitoria | *Japanese* — 17

YO! Sushi | *Japanese* — 15

SHEPHERD'S BUSH

Anglesea Arms | *British* — 19

Blah! Blah! Blah! | *Veg.* — -

Bush B&G | *Euro.* — 18

Café Rouge | *French* — 14

Esarn Kheaw | *Thai* — 25

Snows on Green | *British* — 21

In the Country

Auberge du Lac | *Euro./French* — 26

Caldesi | *Italian* — 22

Cliveden House | *British/French* — 22

Z Fat Duck | *Euro.* — 27

French Horn | *British/French* — 21

Z Gravetye Manor | *British* — 28

Hand & Flowers | *British/French* — 23

Hartwell House | *British* — -

Hinds Head | *British* — 22

Z Le Manoir/Quat | *French* — 27

Vineyard/Stockcross | *British/French* — 25

Z Waterside Inn | *French* — 27

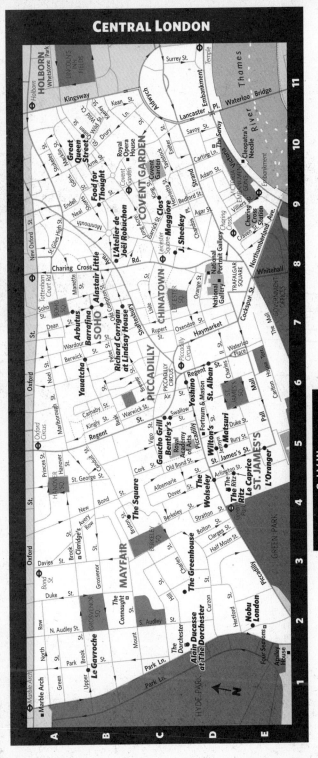

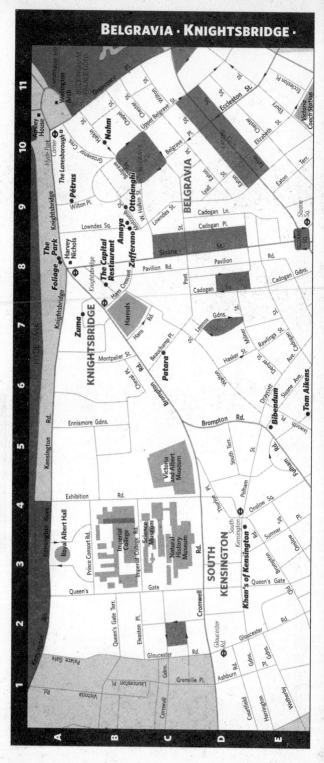

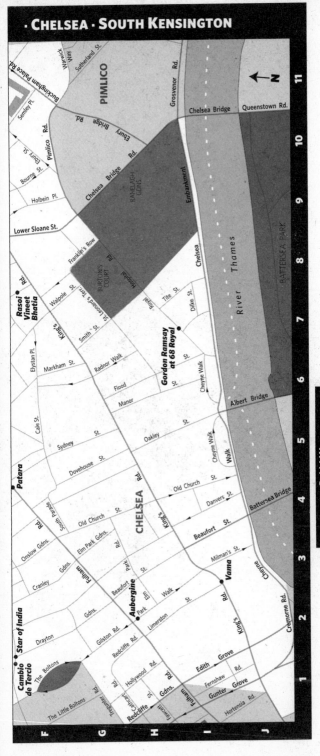

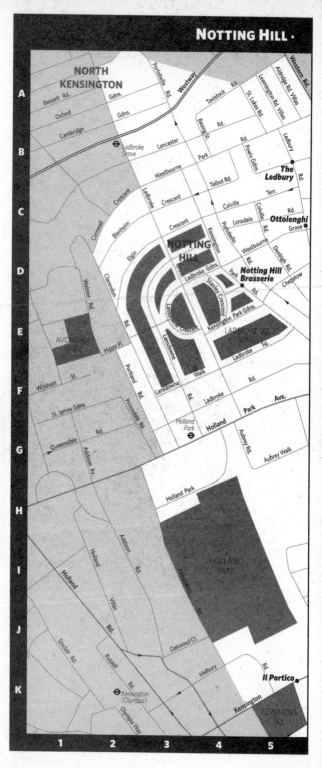

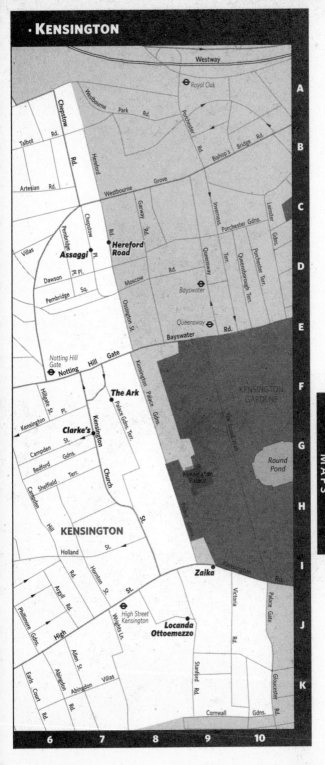

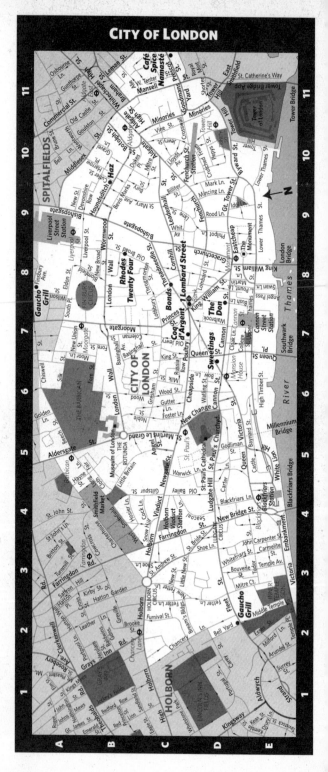

Special Features

Listings cover the best in each category and include names, locations and Food ratings. Multi-location restaurants' features may vary by branch. ☑ indicates places with the highest ratings, popularity and importance.

ALL-DAY DINING

Abeno | **multi.**	18
Acorn House | **WC1**	19
Albannach | **WC2**	16
Albion, The | **N1**	17
Al Hamra | **W1**	21
Alounak | **W14**	22
☑ Al Sultan | **W1**	23
☑ Al Waha | **W2**	23
Anglesea Arms | **W6**	19
Annie's | **multi.**	21
Aperitivo | **W1**	-
Armani Caffé | **SW3**	19
Ask Pizza | **multi.**	15
Aubaine | **multi.**	19
Automat | **W1**	18
Baker & Spice | **multi.**	23
Balans | **multi.**	16
Bar Shu | **W1**	23
Basilico | **multi.**	20
Belgo | **WC2**	18
Bibendum Oyster | **SW3**	21
Big Easy | **SW3**	16
Black & Blue | **multi.**	18
Bloom's | **NW11**	17
NEW BORD'EAUX | **W1**	-
NEW Botanist, The | **SW1**	-
Browns | **multi.**	16
☑ Busaba Eathai | **multi.**	22
Cafe Pacifico | **WC2**	16
Café Rouge | **multi.**	14
Canteen | **multi.**	18
Carluccio's Caffè | **multi.**	17
Cecconi's | **W1**	21
Cellar Gascon | **EC1**	-
Chelsea Brass. | **SW1**	17
Chelsea Bun | **SW10**	14
Chez Gérard | **multi.**	17
Chuen Cheng Ku | **W1**	21
Ciro's Pizza | **EC2**	16
NEW Côte | **multi.**	-
Cross Keys, The | **SW3**	-
Daquise | **SW7**	15
NEW Daylesford | **multi.**	18
NEW Dehesa | **W1**	-
Diner, The | **multi.**	18
Dragon Castle | **SE17**	-
Eat & Two Veg | **W1**	16

Ed's Easy Diner | **W1**	17
Efes | **W1**	-
Feng Sushi | **multi.**	18
Fifth Floor Cafe | **SW1**	18
Firezza | **multi.**	19
FishWorks | **multi.**	19
Flaneur | **EC1**	24
Food for Thought | **WC2**	24
Frankie's Italian | **W1**	14
☑ Gaucho Grill | **multi.**	22
Giraffe | **multi.**	16
Gourmet Burger | **multi.**	19
Grenadier, The | **SW1**	17
Gun, The | **E14**	21
Hache | **NW1**	20
Halepi | **W2**	19
Hard Rock | **W1**	14
Harlem | **W2**	12
NEW Harrison's | **SW12**	15
Harry Morgan's | **multi.**	15
Haz | **E1**	22
High Road Brass. | **W4**	19
Hinds Head | **Berks**	22
Hoxton Apprentice | **N1**	-
Hush | **W1**	14
Imli | **W1**	19
Ishtar | **W1**	19
itsu | **multi.**	17
Jim Thompson's | **SW6**	16
Joe Allen | **WC2**	16
Joe's | **SW3**	-
Julie's | **W11**	17
Kandoo | **W2**	-
NEW Kenza | **EC2**	-
Kettners | **W1**	15
Kiasu | **W2**	21
La Brasserie | **SW3**	18
Ladurée | **SW1**	23
La Fromagerie | **W1**	25
Langan's Brass. | **W1**	19
Langan's Coq d'Or | **SW5**	18
La Porchetta | **multi.**	18
Leon | **multi.**	19
Le Pain Quotidien | **multi.**	18
Le Palais Du Jardin | **WC2**	21
Le Suquet | **SW3**	22
Levantine | **W2**	-
Little Bay | **multi.**	21

Livebait	**multi.**	19
Loch Fyne	**WC2**	21
Lucky 7	**W2**	21
Meson Don Felipe	**SE1**	20
Mildreds	**W1**	22
Mon Plaisir	**WC2**	19
☑ Moro	**EC1**	25
Nando's	**multi.**	-
National Dining Rms.	**WC2**	20
Noura	**multi.**	20
Old Bull & Bush	**NW3**	12
1 Lombard Brass.	**EC3**	19
Oriel	**SW1**	15
Original Lahore	**NW4**	25
Orso	**WC2**	19
☑ Ottolenghi	**multi.**	25
Park, The	**SW1**	24
Pasha	**N1**	19
Patisserie Valerie	**multi.**	18
Pearl Liang	**W2**	18
NEW Pinchito Tapas	**EC1**	-
Ping Pong	**multi.**	19
☑ Pizza Express	**multi.**	16
Pizza Metro	**SW11**	-
PJ's B&G	**multi.**	16
Planet Hollywood	**W1**	10
Porters	**WC2**	18
Portrait	**WC2**	21
Rainforest Cafe	**W1**	11
Randall & Aubin	**W1**	21
Ransome's Dock	**SW11**	20
Raoul's	**multi.**	20
Real Greek	**multi.**	16
Riccardo's	**SW3**	20
Richoux	**multi.**	16
Royal China	**multi.**	23
☑ Royal China Club	**multi.**	24
Royal Exchange	**EC3**	14
☑ Rules	**WC2**	23
Sakura	**W1**	18
Salusbury Pub	**NW6**	-
Sam's Brass.	**W4**	19
Satsuma	**W1**	19
☑ Scott's	**W1**	24
Shanghai Blues	**WC1**	24
Skylon	**SE1**	19
Sofra	**multi.**	19
Solly's	**NW11**	19
Sophie's Steak	**SW10**	21
Sotheby's Cafe	**W1**	20
Spago	**SW7**	18
Sticky Fingers	**W8**	17
St. John Bread/Wine	**E1**	23
Strada	**multi.**	18

Tapas Brindisa	**SE1**	24
Taqueria	**W11**	22
Tartine	**SW3**	17
Tas	**multi.**	20
Texas Embassy	**SW1**	14
T.G.I. Friday's	**multi.**	12
NEW Tom's Place	**SW3**	18
Tootsies	**multi.**	13
Troubadour, The	**SW5**	18
Truc Vert	**W1**	17
202	**W11**	18
Villandry	**W1**	22
Vingt-Quatre	**SW10**	13
☑ Wagamama	**multi.**	19
NEW Wahaca	**WC2**	20
Wallace, The	**W1**	18
NEW Waterloo Brass.	**SE1**	19
☑ Wolseley, The	**W1**	22
Ye Olde Cheshire	**EC4**	16
YO! Sushi	**multi.**	15
Zizzi	**multi.**	16

BREAKFAST

(See also Hotel Dining)

Armani Caffé	**SW3**	19
Aubaine	**multi.**	19
Automat	**W1**	18
Baker & Spice	**multi.**	23
Balans	**multi.**	16
Café Boheme	**W1**	18
Café Rouge	**multi.**	14
Carluccio's Caffè	**multi.**	17
Cecconi's	**W1**	21
☑ Cinnamon Club	**SW1**	24
Coq d'Argent	**EC2**	22
Eat & Two Veg	**W1**	16
Electric Brass.	**W11**	17
Empress of India	**E9**	21
Engineer	**NW1**	20
Fifth Floor Cafe	**SW1**	18
Fortnum's Fountain	**W1**	17
Giraffe	**multi.**	16
Hush	**W1**	14
Inn The Park	**SW1**	18
Joe's	**SW3**	-
Joe's Rest. Bar	**SW1**	19
Julie's	**W11**	17
La Brasserie	**SW3**	18
Ladurée	**SW1**	23
La Fromagerie	**W1**	25
Lucky 7	**W2**	21
Nicole's	**W1**	21
1 Lombard Brass.	**EC3**	19
Oriel	**SW1**	15

Ottolenghi	**multi.**	25
Patisserie Valerie	**multi.**	18
Portrait	**WC2**	21
Providores, The	**W1**	22
Raoul's	**W9**	20
Richoux	**multi.**	16
Rivington Grill	**EC2**	21
Roast	**SE1**	19
Royal Exchange	**EC3**	14
Simpson's/Strand	**WC2**	20
Sotheby's Cafe	**W1**	20
St. John Bread/Wine	**E1**	23
Tate Britain	**SW1**	19
Tom's Deli	**W11**	16
Tom's Kitchen	**SW3**	22
Tootsies	**multi.**	13
Troubadour, The	**SW5**	18
202	**W11**	18
Vingt-Quatre	**SW10**	13
Wolseley, The	**W1**	22

BRUNCH

Abingdon, The	**W8**	18
Admiral Codrington	**SW3**	18
Ambassador, The	**EC1**	-
Annie's	**multi.**	21
Aubaine	**multi.**	19
Automat	**W1**	18
Aziz	**SW6**	19
Bistro 190	**SW7**	-
Blue Elephant	**SW6**	20
Cecconi's	**W1**	21
Christopher's	**WC2**	19
Clarke's	**W8**	26
Cru	**N1**	-
1802	**E14**	16
Fakhreldine	**W1**	19
Fifth Floor Cafe	**SW1**	18
Fish Shop	**EC1**	18
Garbo's	**W1**	17
Giraffe	**multi.**	16
Harlem	**W2**	12
NEW Harrison's	**SW12**	15
Joe Allen	**WC2**	16
Joe's Rest. Bar	**SW1**	19
La Brasserie	**SW3**	18
Le Caprice	**SW1**	24
Lucky 7	**W2**	21
Motcombs	**SW1**	20
PJ's B&G	**multi.**	16
Portrait	**WC2**	21
Providores, The	**W1**	22
Quadrato	**E14**	-
Ransome's Dock	**SW11**	20

Sam's Brass.	**W4**	19
Sophie's Steak	**SW10**	21
St. Germain	**EC1**	22
Tom's Deli	**W11**	16
Tom's Kitchen	**SW3**	22
Troubadour, The	**SW5**	18
202	**W11**	18
Vama	**SW10**	25
Villandry	**W1**	22
Vingt-Quatre	**SW10**	13
Wapping Food	**E1**	19
Zetter	**EC1**	17

BUSINESS DINING

NEW Aaya	**W1**	-
Addendum	**EC3**	-
NEW Alain Ducasse	**W1**	26
Albemarle, The	**W1**	22
Al Duca	**SW1**	20
Alloro	**W1**	21
Almeida	**N1**	19
Amaya	**SW1**	26
NEW Angelus	**W2**	23
NEW Apsleys	**SW1**	-
Arbutus	**W1**	24
NEW Artisan	**W1**	18
Atami	**SW1**	19
Aubergine	**SW10**	25
Avenue, The	**SW1**	19
Awana	**SW3**	22
Axis	**WC2**	19
Bank Westminster	**SW1**	16
Bellamy's	**W1**	22
Belvedere, The	**W8**	20
Benares	**W1**	23
Bentley's	**W1**	24
Bibendum	**SW3**	23
NEW Bincho Yakitori	**SE1**	21
Blakes	**SW7**	19
Bleeding Heart	**EC1**	22
Bluebird	**SW3**	18
Blueprint Café	**SE1**	18
Bonds	**EC2**	22
NEW BORD'EAUX	**W1**	-
NEW Botanist, The	**SW1**	-
Boxwood Café	**SW1**	23
NEW Brass. St. Jacques	**SW1**	-
NEW Brickhouse, The	**E1**	-
Brunello	**SW7**	23
Capital Rest.	**SW3**	26
Cecconi's	**W1**	21
Chez Gérard	**multi.**	17
China Tang	**W1**	20
Christopher's	**WC2**	19

☑ Cinnamon Club | **SW1**	24
Cipriani | **W1**	20
Clarke's | **W8**	26
☑ Club Gascon | **EC1**	26
Dorchester/The Grill | **W1**	24
Elena's l'Etoile | **W1**	18
Fakhreldine | **W1**	19
Fifth Floor | **SW1**	21
☑ Fino | **W1**	25
Foliage | **SW1**	25
Galvin/Windows | **W1**	20
☑ Galvin Bistrot | **W1**	23
☑ Gilgamesh | **NW1**	19
Glasshouse, The | **TW9**	25
☑ Gordon Ramsay/Claridge's | **W1**	26
☑ Gordon Ramsay/68 Royal | **SW3**	29
☑ Goring | **SW1**	25
☑ Gravetye Manor | **W. Sussex**	28
☑ Greenhouse, The | **W1**	26
Green's | **SW1**	23
Haiku | **W1**	19
Hartwell House | **Bucks**	-
NEW Hereford Road | **W2**	24
NEW Hibiscus | **W1**	24
High Road Brass. | **W4**	19
NEW Hix Oyster | **EC1**	-
Il Convivio | **SW1**	22
Imperial City | **EC3**	23
Incognico | **WC2**	21
Indigo | **WC2**	21
☑ Ivy, The | **WC2**	22
NEW Jimmy's | **SW3**	-
☑ J. Sheekey | **WC2**	26
Just St. James's | **SW1**	20
Kai Mayfair | **W1**	23
NEW Kenza | **EC2**	-
NEW Kyashi | **WC2**	-
La Genova | **W1**	25
NEW Landau, The | **W1**	25
Langan's Bistro | **W1**	19
Langan's Brass. | **W1**	19
☑ NEW La Petite Maison | **W1**	25
☑ L'Atelier/Robuchon | **WC2**	27
☑ La Trompette | **W4**	28
Launceston Place | **W8**	-
NEW L'Autre Pied | **W1**	23
NEW Le Café Anglais | **W2**	20
Le Café/Marché | **EC1**	23
☑ Le Caprice | **SW1**	24
Le Cercle | **SW1**	23
☑ Ledbury, The | **W11**	28
☑ Le Gavroche | **W1**	27

☑ Le Manoir/Quat | **Oxfordshire**	27
Le Pont/Tour | **SE1**	20
L'Escargot | **W1**	23
L'Etranger | **SW7**	23
L'Incontro | **SW1**	21
☑ Locanda Locatelli | **W1**	25
L'Oranger | **SW1**	25
Luciano | **SW1**	19
Magdalen | **SE1**	23
NEW Marco | **SW6**	-
Matsuri | **multi.**	23
☑ maze | **W1**	25
NEW maze Grill | **W1**	-
Memories of China | **multi.**	22
Mews of Mayfair | **W1**	19
Mitsukoshi | **SW1**	19
Miyama | **W1**	23
☑ Nahm | **SW1**	24
☑ Nobu Berkeley St | **W1**	26
☑ Nobu London | **W1**	27
NEW Northbank | **EC4**	-
NEW Number Twelve | **WC1**	-
Odin's | **W1**	20
Olivomare | **SW1**	21
One-O-One | **SW1**	23
NEW Only Running Footman | **W1**	18
Orrery | **W1**	24
NEW Osteria Stecca | **NW8**	-
☑ Oxo Tower | **SE1**	21
NEW Pantechnicon Rms. | **SW1**	-
Papillon | **SW3**	21
Park, The | **SW1**	24
Paternoster Chop | **EC4**	17
☑ Pétrus | **SW1**	28
☑ Pied à Terre | **W1**	27
Plateau | **E14**	19
Poissonnerie | **SW3**	21
Princess Garden | **W1**	22
Prism | **EC3**	20
Providores, The | **W1**	22
Quadrato | **E14**	-
Quaglino's | **SW1**	18
Quirinale | **SW1**	23
NEW Quo Vadis | **W1**	-
Rasa | **multi.**	24
☑ Rasoi Vineet Bhatia | **SW3**	27
Red Fort | **W1**	24
Rhodes 24 | **EC2**	24
Rib Room | **SW1**	22
☑ Richard Corrigan | **W1**	26
Rist. Semplice | **W1**	24
☑ Ritz, The | **W1**	23

SPECIAL FEATURES

🔡 Nahm | *David Thompson* | **SW1**	24
Narrow, The | *Gordon Ramsay* | **E14**	22
🔡 Nobu Berkeley St | *Nobu Matsuhisa & Mark Edwards* | **W1**	26
🔡 Nobu London | *Nobu Matsuhisa & Mark Edwards* | **W1**	27
Notting Grill | *Antony Worrall Thompson* | **W11**	21
Pearl | *Jun Tanaka* | **WC1**	25
🔡 Pétrus | *Marcus Wareing* | **SW1**	28
Providores, The | *Peter Gordon* | **W1**	22
Randall & Aubin | *Ed Baines* | **W1**	21
🔡 Rasoi Vineet Bhatia | *Vineet Bhatia* | **SW3**	27
Refettorio | *Giorgio Locatelli* | **EC4**	22
Rhodes 24 | *Gary Rhodes* | **EC2**	24
Rhodes W1 Brass. | *Gary Rhodes* | **W1**	16
Rhodes W1 Rest. | *Gary Rhodes* | **W1**	23
🔡 Richard Corrigan | *Richard Corrigan* | **W1**	26
🔡 River Café | *Rose Gray & Ruth Rodgers* | **W6**	28
Roka | *Rainer Becker* | **W1**	25
Sketch/Gallery | *Pierre Gagnaire* | **W1**	17
🔡 Sketch/Lecture Rm. | *Pierre Gagnaire* | **W1**	21
Smiths/Dining Rm. | *John Torode* | **EC1**	21
Smiths/Top Floor | *John Torode* | **EC1**	21
🔡 Square, The | *Philip Howard* | **W1**	27
🔡 St. John | *Fergus Henderson* | **EC1**	27
St. John Bread/Wine | *Fergus Henderson* | **E1**	23
🔡 Tamarind | *Cyrus Todiwala* | **W1**	25
Theo Randall | *Theo Randall* | **W1**	23
Tom Aikens | *Tom Aikens* | **SW3**	25
Tom's Kitchen | *Tom Aikens* | **SW3**	22
🆕 Tom's Place | *Tom Aikens* | **SW3**	18
Trinity | *Adam Byatt* | **SW4**	26
🔡 Ubon | *Nobu Matsuhisa & Mark Edwards* | **E14**	26
🆕 Urban Turban | *Vineet Bhatia* | **W2**	17
🆕 Wahaca | *Thomasina Miers* | **WC2**	20
🆕 Warrington, The | *Gordon Ramsay* | **W9**	-
🔡 Waterside Inn | *Michel Roux* | **Berks**	27
Zilli Fish | *Aldo Zilli* | **W1**	21
🔡 Zuma | *Rainer Becker* | **SW7**	27

CHEESE BOARDS

🔡 🆕 Alain Ducasse | **W1**	26
Almeida | **N1**	19
Ambassador, The | **EC1**	-
Artigiano | **NW3**	20
🔡 Assaggi | **W2**	26
Aubaine | **W1**	19
Auberge du Lac | **Herts**	26
Aubergine | **SW10**	25
Axis | **WC2**	19
Bank Westminster | **SW1**	16
Bedford & Strand | **WC2**	18
Belvedere, The | **W8**	20
Bibendum | **SW3**	23
Bistro 190 | **SW7**	-
Bistrotheque | **E2**	20
Bleeding Heart | **EC1**	22
Bonds | **EC2**	22
🆕 BORD'EAUX | **W1**	-
Bradley's | **NW3**	16
Brasserie Roux | **SW1**	21
🆕 Brass. St. Jacques | **SW1**	-
Brass. St. Quentin | **SW3**	20
Brunello | **SW7**	23
Caravaggio | **EC3**	15
Cellar Gascon | **EC1**	-
🔡 Cheyne Walk | **SW3**	23
🔡 Chez Bruce | **SW17**	29
Clarke's | **W8**	26
Cliveden House | **Berks**	22
Coq d'Argent | **EC2**	22
Cross Keys, The | **SW3**	-
Cru | **N1**	-
Dorchester/The Grill | **W1**	24
Ebury Dining Rm. | **SW1**	16
1802 | **E14**	16
Elena's l'Etoile | **W1**	18
Enoteca Turi | **SW15**	24
🔡 Fat Duck | **Berks**	27
Fifteen | **N1**	25
Fifth Floor | **SW1**	21
Foliage | **SW1**	25
French Horn | **Berks**	21
Glasshouse, The | **TW9**	25
🔡 Gordon Ramsay/Claridge's | **W1**	26
🔡 Gordon Ramsay/68 Royal | **SW3**	29
🔡 Goring | **SW1**	25
🔡 Gravetye Manor | **W. Sussex**	28

☑ Greenhouse, The | **W1**	26
Green's | **SW1**	23
Greig's | **W1**	17
Greyhound, The | **SW11**	23
Hand & Flowers | **Bucks**	23
High Road Brass. | **W4**	19
Hoxton Grille | **EC2**	15
Hush | **W1**	14
Il Convivio | **SW1**	22
Indigo | **WC2**	21
Julie's | **W11**	17
La Fromagerie | **W1**	25
☑ La Trompette | **W4**	28
La Trouvaille | **W1**	25
Launceston Place | **W8**	-
Le Café/Jardin | **WC2**	19
Le Café/Marché | **EC1**	23
Le Cercle | **SW1**	23
☑ Ledbury, The | **W11**	28
☑ Le Gavroche | **W1**	27
☑ Le Manoir/Quat | **Oxfordshire**	27
Le Pont/Tour | **SE1**	20
L'Escargot | **W1**	23
L'Etranger | **SW7**	23
L'Incontro | **SW1**	21
☑ Locanda Locatelli | **W1**	25
L'Oranger | **SW1**	25
Lou Pescadou | **SW5**	-
Lucio | **SW3**	22
Manicomio | **SW3**	19
Mon Plaisir | **WC2**	19
☑ Morgan M | **N7**	26
Mu | **SW1**	-
One-O-One | **SW1**	23
Orrery | **W1**	24
☑ Oslo Court | **NW8**	26
☑ Osteria Basilico | **W11**	22
Osteria dell'Arancio | **SW1**	20
☑ Oxo Tower | **SE1**	21
☑ Oxo Tower Brass. | **SE1**	18
Paternoster Chop | **EC4**	17
Pearl | **WC1**	25
Pellicano | **SW3**	22
Petersham, The | **TW10**	-
☑ Pétrus | **SW1**	28
☑ Pied à Terre | **W1**	27
Pig's Ear | **SW3**	18
Plateau | **E14**	19
Prism | **EC3**	20
Quality Chop Hse. | **EC1**	21
Refettorio | **EC4**	22
Refuel | **W1**	-
Rhodes 24 | **EC2**	24

Rhodes W1 Rest. | **W1**	23
Rib Room | **SW1**	22
☑ Richard Corrigan | **W1**	26
Rist. Semplice | **W1**	24
☑ Ritz, The | **W1**	23
☑ River Café | **W6**	28
Roast | **SE1**	19
☑ Roussillon | **SW1**	26
Royal Exchange | **EC3**	14
Salt Yard | **W1**	21
Salusbury Pub | **NW6**	-
San Lorenzo | **SW19**	20
Santa Maria del Sur | **SW8**	-
Sarastro | **WC2**	12
Sartoria | **W1**	20
Sauterelle | **EC3**	-
☑ Scott's | **W1**	24
Sketch/Gallery | **W1**	17
☑ Sketch/Lecture Rm. | **W1**	21
Smiths/Dining Rm. | **EC1**	21
Smiths/Top Floor | **EC1**	21
Spread Eagle | **SE10**	24
☑ Square, The | **W1**	27
☑ St. John | **EC1**	27
St. John Bread/Wine | **E1**	23
Tate Britain | **SW1**	19
Tate Modern | **SE1**	17
Tentazioni | **SE1**	24
Thomas Cubitt | **SW1**	21
Tom Aikens | **SW3**	25
NEW Tom Ilic | **SW8**	24
Toto's | **SW3**	23
Truc Vert | **W1**	17
Tuttons Brass. | **WC2**	19
Upstairs | **SW2**	-
Villandry | **W1**	22
Vineyard/Stockcross | **Stockcross/Berks**	25
Vivat Bacchus | **EC4**	20
☑ Waterside Inn | **Berks**	27
Waterway, The | **W9**	15
Wells, The | **NW3**	20
Westbourne, The | **W2**	18
☑ Wilton's | **SW1**	25
☑ Zafferano | **SW1**	25
Zetter | **EC1**	17

CHILD-FRIENDLY

(Besides the normal fast-food
places; * children's menu available)

Abbeville | **SW4**	-
Abingdon, The | **W8**	18
Al Duca | **SW1**	20
Almeida | **N1**	19
Aperitivo | **W1**	-

Restaurant	Rating
Archipelago | **W1**	22
Armani Caffé | **SW3**	19
Ask Pizza* | **multi.**	15
Z Assaggi | **W2**	26
Aubaine | **SW3**	19
Axis* | **WC2**	19
Babylon* | **W8**	17
Baker & Spice | **multi.**	23
Belgo* | **multi.**	18
Benihana | **multi.**	19
Bibendum | **SW3**	23
Bibendum Oyster | **SW3**	21
Big Easy* | **SW3**	16
Black & Blue | **multi.**	18
Bloom's* | **NW11**	17
Bluebird* | **SW3**	18
Blue Elephant | **SW6**	20
Bodeans* | **multi.**	18
Books for Cooks | **W11**	23
Z Boxwood Café* | **SW1**	23
Brasserie Roux* | **SW1**	21
Browns* | **multi.**	16
Buona Sera | **multi.**	18
Z Busaba Eathai | **multi.**	22
Cafe Pacifico* | **WC2**	16
Café Rouge* | **multi.**	14
Café Spice Namasté | **E1**	23
Cantina del Ponte | **SE1**	18
Caraffini | **SW1**	22
Caravaggio | **EC3**	15
Carluccio's Caffè* | **multi.**	17
Carpaccio | **SW3**	18
Casale Franco | **N1**	-
Cecconi's | **W1**	21
Z Cheyne Walk | **SW3**	23
Z Chez Bruce | **SW17**	29
Chez Gérard* | **multi.**	17
Chez Kristof* | **W6**	20
NEW Chicago Rib* | **SW1**	-
Christopher's* | **WC2**	19
Chuen Cheng Ku | **W1**	21
Churchill Arms | **W8**	20
Cigala | **WC1**	21
Z Cinnamon Club | **SW1**	24
Citrus* | **W1**	19
Coach & Horses | **EC1**	-
Daphne's | **SW3**	22
Eagle, The | **EC1**	23
e&o* | **W11**	22
Eat & Two Veg | **W1**	16
Ed's Easy Diner* | **W1**	17
Eight Over Eight | **SW3**	22
Electric Brass. | **W11**	17
Elistano* | **SW3**	22
Fifteen | **N1**	25
Fifth Floor Cafe* | **SW1**	18
Z Fino | **W1**	25
fish!* | **SE1**	19
Fish Shop | **EC1**	18
Fortnum's Fountain* | **W1**	17
Frankie's Italian* | **multi.**	14
Frederick's* | **N1**	21
Z Gaucho Grill | **multi.**	22
Gay Hussar | **W1**	19
Giraffe* | **multi.**	16
Glasshouse, The* | **TW9**	25
Gourmet Burger* | **multi.**	19
Great Eastern | **EC2**	16
Grenadier, The | **SW1**	17
Z Hakkasan | **W1**	25
Hard Rock* | **W1**	14
NEW Harrison's* | **SW12**	15
Indigo* | **WC2**	21
Inn The Park* | **SW1**	18
itsu | **multi.**	17
Jenny Lo's Tea | **SW1**	21
Jim Thompson's* | **multi.**	16
Joe Allen | **WC2**	16
Joe's Rest. Bar | **SW1**	19
Julie's* | **W11**	17
Kensington Place* | **W8**	19
Kettners | **W1**	15
La Brasserie* | **SW3**	18
Ladurée | **SW1**	23
La Famiglia | **SW1**	21
La Fromagerie | **W1**	25
La Porchetta | **multi.**	18
NEW Le Café Anglais | **W2**	20
Z Le Caprice | **SW1**	24
Le Cercle* | **SW1**	23
Z Le Manoir/Quat* | **Oxfordshire**	27
L'Etranger | **SW7**	23
Livebait* | **multi.**	19
Z Locanda Locatelli | **W1**	25
Locanda Ottoemezzo | **W8**	24
Lucio | **SW3**	22
Lucky 7* | **W2**	21
Made in Italy | **SW3**	20
Mango Tree | **SW1**	21
Manicomio | **SW3**	19
Maroush | **multi.**	22
Masala Zone* | **multi.**	19
Mediterraneo | **W11**	21
Mela | **WC2**	21
Mitsukoshi* | **SW1**	19
Nicole's | **W1**	21
Z Nobu Berkeley St | **W1**	26

ⓩ Nobu London | **W1**	27
Noura | **multi.**	20
ⓩ Oliveto | **SW1**	21
Oriel | **SW1**	15
Orso | **WC2**	19
ⓩ Ottolenghi | **multi.**	25
ⓩ Oxo Tower* | **SE1**	21
ⓩ Oxo Tower Brass.* | **SE1**	18
Park, The* | **SW1**	24
ⓩ Patara | **multi.**	24
Patisserie Valerie | **multi.**	18
Pellicano | **SW3**	22
Petersham, The | **TW10**	-
ⓩ Pizza Express* | **multi.**	16
Pizza Metro* | **SW11**	-
Pizza on the Park | **SW1**	17
PJ's B&G* | **multi.**	16
Planet Hollywood* | **W1**	10
Plateau | **E14**	19
Porters* | **WC2**	18
Quadrato* | **E14**	-
Quaglino's* | **SW1**	18
Quality Chop Hse. | **EC1**	21
Quilon | **SW1**	25
Quirinale | **SW1**	23
Rainforest Cafe* | **W1**	11
Randall & Aubin | **W1**	21
Ransome's Dock | **SW11**	20
Raoul's | **multi.**	20
Rasa | **multi.**	24
ⓩ Rasoi Vineet Bhatia | **SW3**	27
Real Greek* | **multi.**	16
Red Pepper | **W9**	20
Reubens* | **W1**	15
Riccardo's | **SW3**	20
Richoux* | **multi.**	16
ⓩ Ritz, The* | **W1**	23
Riva | **SW13**	21
ⓩ River Café | **W6**	28
Rocket* | **multi.**	17
ⓩ Roussillon* | **SW1**	26
Royal China | **multi.**	23
Royal China Club | **NW8**	24
ⓩ Rules | **WC2**	23
Sabor* | **N1**	-
Sale e Pepe | **SW1**	22
San Lorenzo | **SW3**	20
Santini | **SW1**	21
Seashell* | **NW1**	20
Shepherd's | **SW1**	23
Shogun | **W1**	-
Six13* | **W1**	-
Smollensky's* | **multi.**	16
Sofra* | **multi.**	19

Sonny's* | **SW13**	22
Sophie's Steak* | **SW10**	21
Spiga | **W1**	17
Sticky Fingers* | **W8**	17
Strada | **multi.**	18
Tas | **multi.**	20
Texas Embassy* | **SW1**	14
T.G.I. Friday's* | **multi.**	12
Tom's Deli | **W11**	16
Tom's Kitchen | **SW3**	22
NEW Tom's Place* | **SW3**	18
Tootsies* | **multi.**	13
Truc Vert | **W1**	17
2 Brothers Fish* | **N3**	22
202 | **W11**	18
ⓩ Ubon | **E14**	26
Uli | **W11**	26
Vama | **SW10**	25
Villandry* | **W1**	22
Vingt-Quatre | **SW10**	13
ⓩ Wagamama* | **multi.**	19
NEW Wahaca | **WC2**	20
ⓩ Waterside Inn* | **Berks**	27
ⓩ Wolseley, The | **W1**	22
YO! Sushi | **multi.**	15
Yoshino | **W1**	23
ⓩ Zafferano | **SW1**	25
Zetter | **EC1**	17
Zizzi* | **multi.**	16
ⓩ Zuma | **SW7**	27

DELIVERY/TAKEAWAY

(D=delivery, T=takeaway)

Alounak | D, T | **multi.**	22
Baker & Spice | T | **multi.**	23
Beiteddine | D, T | **SW1**	21
Big Easy | T | **SW3**	16
Bloom's | D, T | **NW11**	17
Blue Elephant | D, T | **SW6**	20
Café Spice Namasté | D, T | **E1**	23
Cantina del Ponte | T | **SE1**	18
Carluccio's Caffè | T | **multi.**	17
Chor Bizarre | T | **W1**	19
Chuen Cheng Ku | T | **W1**	21
Churchill Arms | T | **W8**	20
Chutney Mary | T | **SW10**	23
Crazy Homies | T | **W2**	19
NEW Daylesford | T | **multi.**	18
ⓩ Defune | T | **W1**	26
Eat & Two Veg | T | **W1**	16
Ed's Easy Diner | T | **W1**	17
Esarn Kheaw | T | **W12**	25
ⓩ Fairuz | D, T | **W1**	22
Fakhreldine | D, T | **W1**	19

Frankie's Italian | T | **SW3** — 14

Ⓩ Gaucho Grill | T | **multi.** — 22

Giraffe | T | **multi.** — 16

Golden Dragon | T | **W1** — 20

Halepi | T | **W2** — 19

Harbour City | T | **W1** — 18

Harlem | T | **W2** — 12

Ikeda | T | **W1** — 26

Imperial City | T | **EC3** — 23

Inn The Park | T | **SW1** — 18

Ishbilia | D, T | **SW1** — 22

itsu | D, T | **multi.** — 17

Jenny Lo's Tea | D, T | **SW1** — 21

Ⓩ Jin Kichi | T | **NW3** — 27

Khan's | T | **W2** — 21

Khan's/Kensington | D, T | **SW7** — 23

Kiku | T | **W1** — 23

Koi | D, T | **W8** — 21

Kulu Kulu | T | **multi.** — 19

La Fromagerie | D, T | **W1** — 25

La Porchetta | T | **multi.** — 18

La Porte des Indes | T | **W1** — 21

Leon | T | **multi.** — 19

Levant | T | **W1** — 21

Levantine | T | **W2** — -

Lucky 7 | T | **W2** — 21

Ma Goa | T | **SW15** — 22

Mandalay | T | **W2** — 23

Mango Tree | T | **SW1** — 21

Mao Tai | D, T | **SW6** — 23

Masala Zone | T | **multi.** — 19

Matsuri | T | **SW1** — 23

Mela | T | **WC2** — 21

Memories of China | T | **multi.** — 22

Moshi Moshi | D, T | **multi.** — 19

Ⓩ North Sea | T | **WC1** — 24

Noura | D, T | **multi.** — 20

Nyonya | T | **W11** — 22

Ⓩ Oliveto | T | **SW1** — 21

Original Lahore | T | **multi.** — 25

Ⓩ Ottolenghi | T | **multi.** — 25

Özer | T | **W1** — 17

Ⓩ Patara | T | **multi.** — 24

Ⓩ Pizza Express | T | **multi.** — 16

Pizza Metro | T | **SW11** — -

Rasa | T | **multi.** — 24

Red Pepper | T | **W9** — 20

Reubens | T | **W1** — 15

Riccardo's | T | **SW3** — 20

Richoux | T | **multi.** — 16

Royal China | T | **multi.** — 23

Royal China Club | T | **NW8** — 24

Salloos | T | **SW1** — 23

Santa Lucia | T | **SW10** — -

Seashell | T | **NW1** — 20

Singapore Garden | D, T | **NW6** — 19

Singapura | T | **multi.** — 20

Six13 | D, T | **W1** — -

Solly's | T | **NW11** — 19

Spago | T | **SW7** — 18

Spiga | T | **W1** — 17

Ⓩ Star of India | T | **SW5** — 25

Sticky Fingers | T | **W8** — 17

Strada | T | **multi.** — 18

Ⓩ Tamarind | D, T | **W1** — 25

Tas | D, T | **multi.** — 20

Thai Square | T | **multi.** — 18

Tom's Deli | T | **W11** — 16

NEW Tom's Place | T | **SW3** — 18

Truc Vert | D, T | **W1** — 17

2 Brothers Fish | T | **N3** — 22

Ⓩ Ubon | T | **E14** — 26

Vama | D, T | **SW10** — 25

Veeraswamy | T | **W1** — 23

Villandry | T | **W1** — 22

YO! Sushi | D, T | **multi.** — 15

Yoshino | T | **W1** — 23

DINING ALONE

(Other than hotels and places with counter service)

Academy | **W1** — -

Ⓩ Amaya | **SW1** — 26

Armani Caffé | **SW3** — 19

Aubaine | **multi.** — 19

Baker & Spice | **multi.** — 23

Ⓩ Barrafina | **W1** — 25

Bibendum Oyster | **SW3** — 21

Books for Cooks | **W11** — 23

Brompton Quarter | **SW3** — 15

Ⓩ Busaba Eathai | **multi.** — 22

Café Rouge | **multi.** — 14

Carluccio's Caffè | **multi.** — 17

Chowki | **W1** — 17

Chuen Cheng Ku | **W1** — 21

Coach & Horses | **EC1** — -

Ⓩ Comptoir Gascon | **EC1** — 23

NEW Daylesford | **multi.** — 18

Eat & Two Veg | **W1** — 16

Ed's Easy Diner | **W1** — 17

Fifth Floor Cafe | **SW1** — 18

Ⓩ Fino | **W1** — 25

Fortnum's Fountain | **W1** — 17

Ⓩ Hakkasan | **W1** — 25

Inaho | **W2** — 25

Inn The Park | **SW1** — 18

Jenny Lo's Tea | **SW1** — 21

Joe's Rest. Bar | **SW1** — 19

Ladurée | **SW1**	23
La Fromagerie | **W1**	25
Le Colombier | **SW3**	21
Leon | **multi.**	19
Le Pain Quotidien | **multi.**	18
Manicomio | **SW3**	19
Matsuri | **multi.**	23
Mildreds | **W1**	22
Mitsukoshi | **SW1**	19
Mon Plaisir | **WC2**	19
New Culture Rev. | **multi.**	18
Nicole's | **W1**	21
Oriel | **SW1**	15
☑ Ottolenghi | **multi.**	25
Patisserie Valerie | **multi.**	18
Ping Pong | **multi.**	19
Porters | **WC2**	18
Portrait | **WC2**	21
Providores, The | **W1**	22
Randall & Aubin | **W1**	21
Richoux | **multi.**	16
1707 Wine Bar | **W1**	21
Sotheby's Cafe | **W1**	20
St. John Bread/Wine | **E1**	23
Tapas Brindisa | **SE1**	24
Taqueria | **W11**	22
Tate Modern | **SE1**	17
Tom's Deli | **W11**	16
Tom's Kitchen | **SW3**	22
Truc Vert | **W1**	17
Villandry | **W1**	22
☑ Wagamama | **multi.**	19
☑ Wolseley, The | **W1**	22
☑ Yauatcha | **W1**	26
YO! Sushi | **multi.**	15

ENTERTAINMENT

(Call for days and times of performances)

Bengal Clipper | piano | **SE1**	19
Bentley's | piano | **W1**	24
Big Easy | live bands | **SW3**	16
Boisdale | jazz | **SW1**	20
☑ Cheyne Walk | jazz | **SW3**	23
Chutney Mary | jazz | **SW10**	23
Coq d'Argent | jazz | **EC2**	22
Efes | belly dancing | **W1**	-
1802 | DJ | **E14**	16
Floridita | Cuban | **W1**	17
☑ Gilgamesh | DJ | **NW1**	19
☑ Hakkasan | DJ | **W1**	25
Ishbilia | belly dancing | **SW1**	22
Joe Allen | jazz/piano | **WC2**	16
Langan's Brass. | piano | **W1**	19

Le Café/Marché | jazz/piano | **EC1**	23
☑ Le Caprice | piano | **SW1**	24
Le Pont/Tour | piano | **SE1**	20
Levant | belly dancing | **W1**	21
Levantine | belly dancing | **W2**	-
Little Italy | DJ | **W1**	16
Maroush | belly dancing | **multi.**	22
Meson Don Felipe | guitar | **SE1**	20
☑ Oxo Tower Brass. | jazz | **SE1**	18
Pigalle Club | cabaret | **W1**	15
Pizza on the Park | jazz | **SW1**	17
PJ's B&G | jazz | **WC2**	16
Planet Hollywood | DJ | **W1**	10
Quaglino's | jazz | **SW1**	18
Rib Room | piano | **SW1**	22
☑ Ritz, The | piano | **W1**	23
Simpson's/Strand | piano | **WC2**	20
Smollensky's | varies | **multi.**	16
Souk | belly dancing | **WC2**	17
Tas | guitar | **SE1**	20
Thai Square | DJ/karaoke | **SW1**	18
Vineyard/Stockcross | piano | **Stockcross/Berks**	25

FIREPLACES

Abbeville | **SW4**	-
Admiral Codrington | **SW3**	18
Albemarle, The | **W1**	22
Anglesea Arms | **W6**	19
Aubergine | **SW10**	25
Babylon | **W8**	17
Bam-Bou | **W1**	22
Barnsbury, The | **N1**	21
Belgo | **NW1**	18
Belvedere, The | **W8**	20
Ben's Thai | **W9**	-
Bleeding Heart | **EC1**	22
Bouga | **N8**	-
Brackenbury | **W6**	21
Al Hamra | **W1**	21
Brown Dog, The | **SW13**	-
Brunello | **SW7**	23
Builders Arms | **SW3**	17
Bull, The | **N6**	-
☑ Cambio de Tercio | **SW5**	25
☑ Cheyne Walk | **SW3**	23
Christopher's | **WC2**	19
Churchill Arms | **W8**	20
Cicada | **EC1**	21
Clerkenwell Dining | **EC1**	22
Cliveden House | **Berks**	22
☑ Clos Maggiore | **WC2**	25
☑ Crazy Bear | **W1**	20

SPECIAL FEATURES

Fifteen | **N1**	25
Fig | **N1**	22
✚ Fino | **W1**	25
Foliage | **SW1**	25
Forge, The | **WC2**	18
Fortnum's Fountain | **W1**	17
Franklins | **multi.**	-
French Horn | **Berks**	21
Glasshouse, The | **TW9**	25
✚ Gordon Ramsay/Claridge's | **W1**	26
✚ Gordon Ramsay/68 Royal | **SW3**	29
✚ Goring | **SW1**	25
✚ Gravetye Manor | **W. Sussex**	28
Great Queen St. | **WC2**	24
✚ Greenhouse, The | **W1**	26
Green's | **SW1**	23
Grenadier, The | **SW1**	17
Greyhound, The | **SW11**	23
Grumbles | **SW1**	-
Gun, The | **E14**	21
Hand & Flowers | **Bucks**	23
Hartwell House | **Bucks**	-
NEW Hereford Road | **W2**	24
Hinds Head | **Berks**	22
Hoxton Grille | **EC2**	15
✚ Hunan | **SW1**	27
✚ Il Bordello | **E1**	23
Il Portico | **W8**	24
Incognico | **WC2**	21
Inside | **SE10**	25
✚ Ivy, The | **WC2**	22
NEW Jimmy's | **SW3**	-
Joe Allen | **WC2**	16
Julie's | **W11**	17
Just St. James's | **SW1**	20
Kensington Place | **W8**	19
Kew Grill | **TW9**	-
Konstam | **WC1**	23
La Famiglia | **SW1**	21
Lamberts | **SW12**	21
Langan's Bistro | **W1**	19
La Poule au Pot | **SW1**	21
✚ La Trompette | **W4**	28
La Trouvaille | **W1**	25
Launceston Place | **W8**	-
NEW L'Autre Pied | **W1**	23
L'Aventure | **NW8**	24
NEW Le Café Anglais | **W2**	20
✚ Le Caprice | **SW1**	24
Le Cercle | **SW1**	23
Le Colombier | **SW3**	21
✚ Ledbury, The | **W11**	28
✚ Le Gavroche | **W1**	27
✚ Le Manoir/Quat | **Oxfordshire**	27
Le Pont/Tour | **SE1**	20
L'Escargot | **W1**	23
✚ Les Trois Garçons | **E1**	21
L'Etranger | **SW7**	23
✚ Le Vacherin | **W4**	26
✚ Locanda Locatelli | **W1**	25
Lucio | **SW3**	22
✚ Michael Moore | **W1**	26
Mon Plaisir | **WC2**	19
Montpeliano | **SW7**	18
✚ Morgan M | **N7**	26
✚ Moro | **EC1**	25
Mosaico | **W1**	-
NEW Northbank | **EC4**	-
Notting Grill | **W11**	21
Notting Hill Brass. | **W11**	25
NEW Number Twelve | **WC1**	-
Odin's | **W1**	20
Old Bull & Bush | **NW3**	12
Olivo | **SW1**	19
1 Lombard St. | **EC3**	23
Orrery | **W1**	24
✚ Oslo Court | **NW8**	26
Osteria Antica | **SW11**	17
Osteria dell'Arancio | **SW1**	20
✚ Oxo Tower | **SE1**	21
Palmerston, The | **SE2**	-
Papillon | **SW3**	21
Passione | **W1**	22
Paternoster Chop | **EC4**	17
Pearl | **WC1**	25
✚ Pétrus | **SW1**	28
Pig's Ear | **SW3**	18
Prism | **EC3**	20
Providores, The | **W1**	22
Quadrato | **E14**	-
Quaglino's | **SW1**	18
Quirinale | **SW1**	23
✚ Racine | **SW3**	23
Refettorio | **EC4**	22
Rhodes 24 | **EC2**	24
Rhodes W1 Brass. | **W1**	16
Rhodes W1 Rest. | **W1**	23
Rib Room | **SW1**	22
Riccardo's | **SW3**	20
✚ Richard Corrigan | **W1**	26
Rist. Semplice | **W1**	24
✚ Ritz, The | **W1**	23
Riva | **SW13**	21
✚ River Café | **W6**	28
Rivington Grill | **multi.**	21

SPECIAL FEATURES

Roast | SE1	19
Rodizio Rico | multi.	17
Ⓩ Roussillon | SW1	26
Ⓩ Rules | WC2	23
San Lorenzo | multi.	20
Santini | SW1	21
Sardo | W1	21
Sardo Canale | NW1	21
Simpson's/Strand | WC2	20
Sketch/Gallery | W1	17
Ⓩ Sketch/Lecture Rm. | W1	21
Smiths/Dining Rm. | EC1	21
Smiths/Top Floor | EC1	21
Snows on Green | W6	21
Sonny's | SW13	22
Spread Eagle | SE10	24
Ⓩ Square, The | W1	27
St. Alban | SW1	22
Ⓩ Star of India | SW5	25
Ⓩ St. John | EC1	27
St. John Bread/Wine | E1	23
Tate Britain | SW1	19
Tentazioni | SE1	24
Theo Randall | W1	23
Thomas Cubitt | SW1	21
NEW 3 Bridges | SW8	-
Timo | W8	27
Tom Aikens | SW3	25
NEW Tom Ilic | SW8	24
Tom's Kitchen | SW3	22
Trinity | SW4	26
Veeraswamy | W1	23
Villandry | W1	22
Vineyard/Stockcross | Stockcross/Berks	25
Vinoteca | EC1	-
Vivat Bacchus | EC4	20
Wapping Food | E1	19
Ⓩ Waterside Inn | Berks	27
Ⓩ Wilton's | SW1	25
Wòdka | W8	21
Ⓩ Wolseley, The | W1	22
Ⓩ Zafferano | SW1	25
Zaika | W8	24
Ziani | SW3	20

HISTORIC PLACES

(Year opened; * building)

1300 | Hand & Flowers* | Bucks	23
1520 | Just St. James's* | SW1	20
1550 | Fat Duck* | Berks	27
1571 | Royal Exchange* | EC3	14
1598 | Gravetye Manor* | W. Sussex	28
1650 | Spread Eagle* | SE10	24

1662 | Bleeding Heart* | EC1	22
1667 | Ye Olde Cheshire* | EC4	16
1680 | French Horn* | Berks	21
1690 | Hinds Head | Berks	22
1692 | Giovanni's* | WC2	20
1700 | Admiralty, The* | WC2	18
1700 | Bellamy's* | W1	22
1700 | Cru* | N1	-
1700 | Ransome's Dock* | SW11	20
1721 | Old Bull & Bush | NW3	12
1725 | Patisserie Valerie* | WC2	18
1740 | Richard Corrigan* | W1	26
1742 | Grenadier, The* | SW1	17
1742 | Wilton's | SW1	25
1750 | Food for Thought* | WC2	24
1750 | Gun, The* | E14	21
1755 | Randall & Aubin* | W1	21
1760 | Auberge du Lac* | Herts	26
1760 | Sotheby's Cafe* | W1	20
1780 | Andrew Edmunds* | W1	22
1790 | Carluccio's Caffè* | EC1	17
1790 | Chez Gérard* | EC2	17
1790 | Rowley's* | SW1	20
1798 | Don, The* | EC4	22
1798 | Rules | WC2	23
1800 | Anglesea Arms* | W6	19
1800 | Axis* | WC2	19
1800 | Churchill Arms* | W8	20
1800 | Cuckoo Club* | W1	-
1800 | Hoxton Apprentice* | N1	-
1800 | Ladbroke Arms* | W11	19
1800 | Snows on Green* | W6	21
1802 | 1802* | E14	16
1810 | Angelus* | W2	23
1810 | Pig's Ear* | SW3	18
1820 | Builders Arms* | SW3	17
1828 | Simpson's/Strand* | WC2	20
1834 | Albion, The* | N1	17
1837 | Albemarle, The* | W1	22
1849 | Harry Morgan's* | SW1	15
1850 | Coach & Horses* | EC1	-
1850 | El Blason* | SW3	18
1850 | Marquess Tavern* | N1	-
1851 | Scott's* | W1	24
1855 | Baltic* | SE1	22
1857 | Warrington, The* | W9	-
1860 | Pepper Tree* | SW4	20
1865 | Landau, The* | W1	25
1865 | Petersham, The* | TW10	-
1867 | Kettners* | W1	15
1872 | Bistro 190* | SW7	-
1875 | Quality Chop Hse.* | EC1	21
1880 | Bombay Brass.* | SW7	22
1881 | Duke of Cambridge* | N1	22

1888	Da Mario*	SW7	16
1889	Foliage*	SW1	25
1889	Sweetings	EC4	26
1890	Bradley's*	NW3	16
1890	La Fromagerie*	W1	25
1890	Maggie Jones's*	W8	19
1890	Potemkin*	EC1	-
1890	R.S.J.*	SE1	18
1894	Ciro's Pizza*	EC2	16
1896	Elena's l'Etoile*	W1	18
1898	J. Sheekey*	WC2	26
1900	Annie's*	W4	21
1900	Artigiano*	NW3	20
1900	Balans*	SW5	16
1900	Blakes*	SW7	19
1900	Brinkley's*	SW10	14
1900	Frontline*	W2	-
1900	La Famiglia*	SW1	21
1905	Almeida*	N1	19
1906	Ritz, The*	W1	23
1910	Goring*	SW1	25
1911	Bibendum*	SW3	23
1911	Bibendum Oyster*	SW3	21
1913	Bertorelli*	WC2	16
1913	Bertorelli	W1	16
1914	Golden Hind	W1	23
1920	Bloom's	NW11	17
1920	Orso*	WC2	19
1920	Prism*	EC3	20
1920	Tamarind*	W1	25
1921	Wolseley, The*	W1	22
1923	Bluebird*	SW3	18
1926	Patisserie Valerie	W1	18
1926	Quo Vadis	W1	-
1926	Veeraswamy	W1	23
1927	L'Escargot	W1	23
1930	Sonny's*	SW13	22
1931	Dorchester/The Grill	W1	24
1933	Sartoria*	W1	20
1935	Bistrotheque*	E2	20
1935	Lee Ho Fook*	W1	18
1937	Pappagallo	W1	23
1939	Geales Fish	W8	20
1942	French House*	W1	17
1942	Mon Plaisir	WC2	19
1946	Le Caprice	SW1	24
1947	Daquise	SW7	15
1948	Harry Morgan's	NW8	15
1948	Lansdowne, The*	NW1	17
1950	Bush B&G*	W12	18
1950	Fortnum's Fountain	W1	17
1950	Greig's	W1	17
1952	Star of India	SW5	25
1953	Gay Hussar	W1	19
1953	Guinea Grill	W1	21
1954	Troubadour, The	SW5	18
1955	Brass. St. Quentin*	SW3	20
1956	Pescatori	W1	19
1957	Costas Grill	W8	14

HOTEL DINING

Ambassadors Hotel		
NEW Number Twelve	WC1	-
Apex City of London Hotel		
Addendum	EC3	-
Baglioni		
Brunello	SW7	23
Berkeley, The		
Ⓩ Boxwood Café	SW1	23
Ⓩ Pétrus	SW1	28
Blakes Hotel		
Blakes	SW7	19
Brown's Hotel		
Albemarle, The	W1	22
Capital Hotel		
Ⓩ Capital Rest.	SW3	26
City Inn		
City Café	SW1	17
Claridge's Hotel		
Ⓩ Gordon Ramsay	W1	26
Cliveden House Hotel		
Cliveden House	Berks	22
Crowne Plaza		
Refettorio	EC4	22
Crowne Plaza St. James Hotel		
Quilon	SW1	25
Cumberland Hotel		
Rhodes W1 Brass.	W1	16
Rhodes W1 Rest.	W1	23
Dorchester, The		
Ⓩ NEW Alain Ducasse	W1	26
China Tang	W1	20
Dorchester/The Grill	W1	24
Four Seasons Canary Wharf		
Quadrato	E14	-
French Horn Hotel		
French Horn	Berks	21
Gore Hotel		
Bistro 190	SW7	-
Goring Hotel		
Ⓩ Goring	SW1	25
Gravetye Manor		
Ⓩ Gravetye Manor	W. Sussex	28
Grosvenor House		
NEW BORD'EAUX	W1	-
Halkin Hotel		
Ⓩ Nahm	SW1	24

Hartwell House	
Hartwell House | **Bucks**	‿
Haymarket Hotel	
NEW Brumus | **SW1**	‿
Holiday Inn King's Cross	
Rasa | **WC1**	24
Hoxton Hotel	
Hoxton Grille | **EC2**	15
Hyatt Regency - The Churchill	
Z Locanda Locatelli | **W1**	25
InterContinental Park Ln.	
Theo Randall | **W1**	23
Jumeirah Carlton Tower Hotel	
Rib Room | **SW1**	22
Lanesborough, The	
NEW Apsleys | **SW1**	‿
Langham, The	
NEW Landau, The | **W1**	25
Le Manoir aux Quat'Saisons	
Z Le Manoir/Quat | **Oxfordshire**	27
London Hilton on Park Ln.	
Galvin/Windows | **W1**	20
Mandarin Oriental Hyde Park	
Foliage | **SW1**	25
Park, The | **SW1**	24
Metropolitan Hotel	
Z Nobu London | **W1**	27
Millennium Knightsbridge	
Mu | **SW1**	‿
Millennium Mayfair	
Shogun | **W1**	‿
One Aldwych Hotel	
Axis | **WC2**	19
Indigo | **WC2**	21
Park Lane Hotel	
Citrus | **W1**	19
Petersham Hotel	
Petersham, The | **TW10**	‿
Renaissance Chancery Court	
Pearl | **WC1**	25
Ritz Hotel	
Z Ritz, The | **W1**	23
Royal Lancaster Hotel	
Island | **W2**	‿
Sanderson Hotel	
Suka | **W1**	‿
Sheraton Park Tower	
One-O-One | **SW1**	23
Sloane Square Hotel	
Chelsea Brass. | **SW1**	17
Sofitel St. James London	
Brasserie Roux | **SW1**	21

Soho Hotel	
Refuel | **W1**	‿
St. Giles Hotel	
Kobe London | **WC1**	19
St. Martins Lane Hotel	
Z Asia de Cuba | **WC2**	21
The Marriott Grosvenor Sq.	
Z maze | **W1**	25
NEW maze Grill | **W1**	‿
Thistle Hotel	
Chez Gérard | **SW1**	17
Threadneedles Hotel	
Bonds | **EC2**	22
Vineyard at Stockcross	
Vineyard/Stockcross | **Stockcross/Berks**	25
Waterside Inn	
Z Waterside Inn | **Berks**	27
Westbury Hotel	
NEW Artisan | **W1**	18
Wyndham Hotel	
Aquasia | **SW10**	‿
Zetter	
Zetter | **EC1**	17

LATE DINING

(Weekday closing hour)

Alounak | varies | **W14**	22
Z Al Sultan | 12 AM | **W1**	23
Z Amaya | 11:30 PM | **SW1**	26
Annex 3 | 12 AM | **W1**	‿
Z Asia de Cuba | varies | **WC2**	21
Automat | 1 AM | **W1**	18
Avenue, The | 12 AM | **SW1**	19
Balans | varies | **multi.**	16
Basilico | 12 AM | **multi.**	20
Beiteddine | 12 AM | **SW1**	21
Z Boxwood Café | 1 AM | **SW1**	23
Buona Sera | 12 AM | **multi.**	18
Cafe Med | 12 AM | **NW8**	17
Cecconi's | 12 AM | **W1**	21
NEW Chicago Rib | 12 AM | **SW1**	‿
Chuen Cheng Ku | 12 AM | **W1**	21
Ciro's Pizza | varies | **SW3**	16
Cocoon | varies | **W1**	21
Cross Keys, The | 12 AM | **SW3**	‿
Diner, The | varies | **W1**	18
Dover St. | 2 AM | **W1**	15
Efes | 12 AM | **W1**	‿
Electric Brass. | 1 AM | **W11**	17
Fire & Stone | 11:30 PM | **WC2**	18
Floridita | 1 AM | **W1**	17
Forge, The | 12 AM | **WC2**	18
Greig's | 12 AM | **W1**	17
Z Hakkasan | varies | **W1**	25

Halepi | 12 AM | **W2**	19
Hard Rock | 12:30 AM | **W1**	14
Harlem | 1 AM | **W2**	12
Haz | 12 AM | **E1**	22
Hush | 12 AM | **W1**	14
Imperial China | 12 AM | **WC2**	21
Ishbilia | 12 AM | **SW1**	22
Ishtar | 12 AM | **W1**	19
Z Ivy, The | 12 AM | **WC2**	22
Joe Allen | 12:45 AM | **WC2**	16
Z J. Sheekey | 12 AM | **WC2**	26
Julie's | varies | **W11**	17
Kandoo | 12 AM | **W2**	-
Kettners | 1 AM | **W1**	15
La Porchetta | 12 AM | **N10**	18
Z L'Atelier/Robuchon | varies | **WC2**	27
Le Café/Jardin | 12 AM | **WC2**	19
Z Le Caprice | 12 AM | **SW1**	24
Le Deuxième | 12 AM | **WC2**	20
Lee Ho Fook | 12 AM | **W1**	18
Le Mercury | 1 AM | **N1**	16
Le Pain Quotidien | 12 AM | **NW1**	18
Levant | 1 AM | **W1**	21
Little Bay | 12 AM | **multi.**	21
Little Italy | 4 AM | **W1**	16
Living Rm. | 12 AM | **W1**	17
Lou Pescadou | 12 AM | **SW5**	-
Maroush | varies | **multi.**	22
Maxwell's | 12 AM | **WC2**	18
Meza | varies | **W1**	13
Montpeliano | 12 AM | **SW7**	18
Mr. Chow | 12 AM | **SW1**	22
Mr. Kong | 2:45 AM | **WC2**	21
New World | 12 AM | **W1**	19
Noura | varies | **multi.**	20
Original Lahore | 12 AM | **multi.**	25
Orso | 12 AM | **WC2**	19
Özer | 12 AM | **W1**	17
Z Pasha | 12 AM | **SW7**	21
Ping Pong | varies | **multi.**	19
Z Pizza Express | varies | **multi.**	16
PJ's B&G | varies | **WC2**	16
Planet Hollywood | 1 AM | **W1**	10
Quaglino's | 12 AM | **SW1**	18
Rodizio Rico | 12 AM | **SE10**	17
Sabor | varies | **N1**	-
Souk | 12 AM | **WC2**	17
Spago | 12 AM | **SW7**	18
Spencer Arms | 12 AM | **SW15**	-
Spiga | 12 AM | **W1**	17
St. Alban | 12 AM | **SW1**	22
Suka | varies | **W1**	-
T.G.I. Friday's | 1 AM | **W1**	12

Tokyo Diner | 12 AM | **WC2**	16
Tom's Kitchen | 12 AM | **SW3**	22
Toto's | 12 AM | **SW3**	23
Vingt-Quatre | 24 hrs. | **SW10**	13
Z Wolseley, The | 12 AM | **W1**	22
Z Yauatcha | 11:30 PM | **W1**	26

NOTEWORTHY NEWCOMERS

Aaya | **W1**	-
Z Alain Ducasse | **W1**	26
Z Angelus | **W2**	23
Apsleys | **SW1**	-
Artisan | **W1**	18
Bincho Yakitori | **multi.**	21
BORD'EAUX | **W1**	-
Botanist, The | **SW1**	-
Brass. St. Jacques | **SW1**	-
Brickhouse, The | **E1**	-
Brumus | **SW1**	-
Cape Town Fish | **W1**	18
Cha Cha Moon | **W1**	-
Champagne Bar | **NW1**	14
Chicago Rib | **SW1**	-
Côte | **multi.**	-
Cruse 9 | **N1**	-
Daylesford | **multi.**	18
Dehesa | **W1**	-
Devonshire, The | **W4**	22
Giusto | **W1**	-
Haozhan | **W1**	23
Harrison's | **SW12**	15
Hereford Road | **W2**	24
Hibiscus | **W1**	24
Hix Oyster | **EC1**	-
Jimmy's | **SW3**	-
Kensington Sq. | **W8**	-
Kenza | **EC2**	-
Kyashi | **WC2**	-
Landau, The | **W1**	25
L'Anima | **EC2**	-
Z La Petite Maison | **W1**	25
Launceston Place | **W8**	-
L'Autre Pied | **W1**	23
Le Café Anglais | **W2**	20
Marco | **SW6**	-
maze Grill | **W1**	-
Northbank | **EC4**	-
Number Twelve | **WC1**	-
Only Running Footman | **W1**	18
Osteria Stecca | **NW8**	-
Pacific Oriental | **EC2**	-
Pantechnicon Rms. | **SW1**	-
Paradise | **W1**	-

SPECIAL FEATURES

Pinchito Tapas | **EC1**	-
Quo Vadis | **W1**	-
Red 'n' Hot | **WC2**	-
Saf | **EC2**	-
Sake no hana | **SW1**	19
Tendido Cuatro | **SW6**	-
Terranostra | **EC4**	-
Texture | **W1**	21
3 Bridges | **SW8**	-
Tom Ilic | **SW8**	24
Tom's Place | **SW3**	18
Upper Deck | **WC2**	-
Urban Turban | **W2**	17
Vanilla | **W1**	-
Wahaca | **WC2**	20
Warrington, The | **W9**	-
Water House | **N1**	-
Waterloo Brass. | **SE1**	19
Whole Foods | **W8**	18
Wild Honey | **W1**	23

OFFBEAT

Acorn House | **WC1**	19
Albannach | **WC2**	16
All Star Lanes | **WC1**	12
Alounak | **multi.**	22
Annex 3 | **W1**	-
Annie's | **multi.**	21
Aperitivo | **W1**	-
Archipelago | **W1**	22
⊡ Asia de Cuba | **WC2**	21
Baker & Spice | **multi.**	23
Belgo | **multi.**	18
Benihana | **multi.**	19
Bierodrome | **multi.**	16
Blah! Blah! Blah! | **W12**	-
Bloom's | **NW11**	17
Blue Elephant | **SW6**	20
Boisdale | **multi.**	20
Books for Cooks | **W11**	23
⊡ Cambio de Tercio | **SW5**	25
Cellar Gascon | **EC1**	-
Chor Bizarre | **W1**	19
Chowki | **W1**	17
⊡ Club Gascon | **EC1**	26
Cocoon | **W1**	21
Costas Grill | **W8**	14
⊡ Crazy Bear | **W1**	20
Crazy Homies | **W2**	19
Cru | **N1**	-
Dans Le Noir | **EC1**	8
Daquise | **SW7**	15
Dinings | **W1**	24
Dish Dash | **SW12**	21

⊡ Fat Duck | **Berks**	27
ffiona's | **W8**	23
Fifteen | **N1**	25
FishWorks | **W4**	19
Flaneur | **EC1**	24
Food for Thought | **WC2**	24
⊡ Gilgamesh | **NW1**	19
Hoxton Apprentice | **N1**	-
Inaho | **W2**	25
itsu | **multi.**	17
Jenny Lo's Tea | **SW1**	21
Jim Thompson's | **multi.**	16
Kulu Kulu | **multi.**	19
La Fromagerie | **W1**	25
La Porte des Indes | **W1**	21
Le Cercle | **SW1**	23
⊡ Les Trois Garçons | **E1**	21
Levant | **W1**	21
Levantine | **W2**	-
Lucky 7 | **W2**	21
Maggie Jones's | **W8**	19
Menier Chocolate | **SE1**	16
Momo | **W1**	19
⊡ Moro | **EC1**	25
Moshi Moshi | **EC2**	19
Mu | **SW1**	-
⊡ Nahm | **SW1**	24
Nautilus Fish | **NW6**	22
⊡ Ottolenghi | **multi.**	25
Petersham Nurseries | **TW10**	24
Pho | **EC1**	-
Pizza Metro | **SW11**	-
Providores, The | **W1**	22
Quality Chop Hse. | **EC1**	21
Rainforest Cafe | **W1**	11
Randall & Aubin | **W1**	21
Ransome's Dock | **SW11**	20
⊡ Rasoi Vineet Bhatia | **SW3**	27
Real Greek | **EC1**	16
⊡ Richard Corrigan | **W1**	26
Rivington Grill | **EC2**	21
Sabor | **N1**	-
Sale e Pepe | **SW1**	22
Sketch/Gallery | **W1**	17
Solly's | **NW11**	19
Souk | **WC2**	17
⊡ St. John | **EC1**	27
St. John Bread/Wine | **E1**	23
Tapas Brindisa | **SE1**	24
Taqueria | **W11**	22
Tate Britain | **SW1**	19
Tom's Deli | **W11**	16
NEW Tom's Place | **SW3**	18
Troubadour, The | **SW5**	18

OUTDOOR DINING

(G=garden; P=patio; PV=pavement; T=terrace; W=waterside)

PEOPLE-WATCHING

SPECIAL FEATURES

Albemarle, The	**W1**	22
All Star Lanes	**WC1**	12
🆉 Amaya	**SW1**	26
Armani Caffè	**SW3**	19
🆉 Asia de Cuba	**WC2**	21
Aubaine	**multi.**	19
Avenue, The	**SW1**	19
Bam-Bou	**W1**	22
Bangkok	**SW7**	25
🆉 Barrafina	**W1**	25
Bar Shu	**W1**	23
🆉 Bellamy's	**W1**	22
Bibendum	**SW3**	23
Bibendum Oyster	**SW3**	21
Blakes	**SW7**	19
🆉 Boxwood Café	**SW1**	23
Bumpkin	**W11**	19
Caraffini	**SW1**	22
Carpaccio	**SW3**	18
Cecconi's	**W1**	21
NEW Cha Cha Moon	**W1**	-
NEW Champagne Bar	**NW1**	14
China Tang	**W1**	20
Christopher's	**WC2**	19
🆉 Cinnamon Club	**SW1**	24
Cipriani	**W1**	20
Club, The	**W1**	-
🆉 Club Gascon	**EC1**	26
Daphne's	**SW3**	22
NEW Daylesford	**multi.**	18
NEW Dehesa	**W1**	-
e&o	**W11**	22
Eight Over Eight	**SW3**	22
Electric Brass.	**W11**	17
Fifteen	**N1**	25
🆉 Fino	**W1**	25
Frankie's Italian	**multi.**	14
Galvin/Windows	**W1**	20
🆉 Galvin Bistrot	**W1**	23
🆉 Gilgamesh	**NW1**	19
🆉 Gordon Ramsay/Claridge's	**W1**	26
🆉 Gordon Ramsay/68 Royal	**SW3**	29
Great Queen St.	**WC2**	24
🆉 Hakkasan	**W1**	25
NEW Harrison's	**SW12**	15
NEW Hereford Road	**W2**	24
High Road Brass.	**W4**	19
NEW Hix Oyster	**EC1**	-
Hush	**W1**	14
🆉 Ivy, The	**WC2**	22
NEW Jimmy's	**SW3**	-
🆉 J. Sheekey	**WC2**	26
Kensington Place	**W8**	19
NEW Kyashi	**WC2**	-
La Famiglia	**SW1**	21
🆉 NEW La Petite Maison	**W1**	25
🆉 L'Atelier/Robuchon	**WC2**	27
🆉 La Trompette	**W4**	28
NEW Le Café Anglais	**W2**	20
🆉 Le Caprice	**SW1**	24
Le Cercle	**SW1**	23
🆉 Ledbury, The	**W11**	28
🆉 Locanda Locatelli	**W1**	25
Lucio	**SW3**	22
Manicomio	**SW3**	19
🆉 maze	**W1**	25
NEW maze Grill	**W1**	-
Mews of Mayfair	**W1**	19
Momo	**W1**	19
Narrow, The	**E14**	22
Nicole's	**W1**	21
🆉 Nobu Berkeley St	**W1**	26
🆉 Nobu London	**W1**	27
Olivo	**SW1**	19
Olivomare	**SW1**	21
NEW Only Running Footman	**W1**	18
NEW Pantechnicon Rms.	**SW1**	-
Papillon	**SW3**	21
🆉 Pétrus	**SW1**	28
Pigalle Club	**W1**	15
PJ's B&G	**SW3**	16
NEW Quo Vadis	**W1**	-
🆉 Racine	**SW3**	23
Riccardo's	**SW3**	20
Rist. Semplice	**W1**	24
🆉 River Café	**W6**	28
Roka	**W1**	25
NEW Sake no hana	**SW1**	19
San Lorenzo	**SW3**	20
Santini	**SW1**	21
🆉 Scott's	**W1**	24
Sketch/Gallery	**W1**	17
🆉 Sketch/Lecture Rm.	**W1**	21
Sophie's Steak	**SW10**	21
Sotheby's Cafe	**W1**	20
St. Alban	**SW1**	22
Suka	**W1**	-
Sumosan	**W1**	24
Tartine	**SW3**	17
NEW Tendido Cuatro	**SW6**	-
Tom Aikens	**SW3**	25
Tom's Deli	**W11**	16
Tom's Kitchen	**SW3**	22
NEW Tom's Place	**SW3**	18
202	**W11**	18

Z Ubon | **E14** — 26
Vingt-Quatre | **SW10** — 13
NEW Waterloo Brass. | **SE1** — 19
Z Waterside Inn | **Berks** — 27
NEW Wild Honey | **W1** — 23
Z Wilton's | **SW1** — 25
Z Wolseley, The | **W1** — 22
XO | **NW3** — 21
Z Yauatcha | **W1** — 26
Z Zafferano | **SW1** — 25
Zetter | **EC1** — 17
Z Zuma | **SW7** — 27

POWER SCENES

Acorn House | **WC1** — 19
Z NEW Alain Ducasse | **W1** — 26
Albemarle, The | **W1** — 22
Avenue, The | **SW1** — 19
Bentley's | **W1** — 24
Blueprint Café | **SE1** — 18
Z Boxwood Café | **SW1** — 23
Caravaggio | **EC3** — 15
China Tang | **W1** — 20
Z Cinnamon Club | **SW1** — 24
Cipriani | **W1** — 20
Z Club Gascon | **EC1** — 26
Daphne's | **SW3** — 22
Z Gordon Ramsay/Claridge's | **W1** — 26
Z Gordon Ramsay/68 Royal | **SW3** — 29
Z Goring | **SW1** — 25
Z Greenhouse, The | **W1** — 26
Green's | **SW1** — 23
Hat & Feathers | **EC1** — -
NEW Hibiscus | **W1** — 24
Z Ivy, The | **WC2** — 22
Z J. Sheekey | **WC2** — 26
NEW Landau, The | **W1** — 25
Langan's Brass. | **W1** — 19
Z NEW La Petite Maison | **W1** — 25
Z L'Atelier/Robuchon | **WC2** — 27
Launceston Place | **W8** — -
Z Le Caprice | **SW1** — 24
Z Ledbury, The | **W11** — 28
Z Le Gavroche | **W1** — 27
Z Le Manoir/Quat | **Oxfordshire** — 27
Le Pont/Tour | **SE1** — 20
L'Incontro | **SW1** — 21
Z maze | **W1** — 25
NEW maze Grill | **W1** — -
Z Nahm | **SW1** — 24
Z Nobu Berkeley St | **W1** — 26
Z Nobu London | **W1** — 27

1 Lombard St. | **EC3** — 23
Z Pétrus | **SW1** — 28
Prism | **EC3** — 20
Quirinale | **SW1** — 23
NEW Quo Vadis | **W1** — -
Rhodes 24 | **EC2** — 24
Z Ritz, The | **W1** — 23
NEW Sake no hana | **SW1** — 19
San Lorenzo | **SW3** — 20
Shepherd's | **SW1** — 23
Z Sketch/Lecture Rm. | **W1** — 21
Z Square, The | **W1** — 27
St. Alban | **SW1** — 22
St. Germain | **EC1** — 22
Tom Aikens | **SW3** — 25
Z Umu | **W1** — 26
Via Condotti | **W1** — 19
Z Waterside Inn | **Berks** — 27
NEW Wild Honey | **W1** — 23
Z Wilton's | **SW1** — 25
Z Wolseley, The | **W1** — 22
Z Zafferano | **SW1** — 25
Z Zuma | **SW7** — 27

PRE-THEATRE MENUS

(Call for prices and times)
Alastair Little | **W1** — 24
Al Duca | **SW1** — 20
Almeida | **N1** — 19
Z Arbutus | **W1** — 24
Axis | **WC2** — 19
Baltic | **SE1** — 22
Bank Westminster | **SW1** — 16
Benares | **W1** — 23
NEW BORD'EAUX | **W1** — -
Brasserie Roux | **SW1** — 21
Brass. St. Quentin | **SW3** — 20
Christopher's | **WC2** — 19
Z Cinnamon Club | **SW1** — 24
Z Clos Maggiore | **WC2** — 25
NEW Dehesa | **W1** — -
Dorchester/The Grill | **W1** — 24
Z Gordon Ramsay/Claridge's | **W1** — 26
Z Goring | **SW1** — 25
NEW Harrison's | **SW12** — 15
Indigo | **WC2** — 21
Joe Allen | **WC2** — 16
La Bouchée | **SW7** — 21
NEW Landau, The | **W1** — 25
Le Café/Jardin | **WC2** — 19
Le Deuxième | **WC2** — 20
L'Escargot | **W1** — 23
Matsuri | **SW1** — 23
Mint Leaf | **SW1** — 19

Mon Plaisir	**WC2**	19
Orso	**WC2**	19
Z Oxo Tower Brass.	**SE1**	18
Porters	**WC2**	18
Quaglino's	**SW1**	18
NEW Quo Vadis	**W1**	-
Z Racine	**SW3**	23
Red Fort	**W1**	24
Z Richard Corrigan	**W1**	26
Z Ritz, The	**W1**	23
NEW Sake no hana	**SW1**	19
Tom's Kitchen	**SW3**	22
Veeraswamy	**W1**	23
NEW Wild Honey	**W1**	23
Zaika	**W8**	24

PRIVATE ROOMS

(Call for capacity)

Admiral Codrington	**SW3**	18
Admiralty, The	**WC2**	18
Z NEW Alain Ducasse	**W1**	26
Alastair Little	**W1**	24
Albannach	**WC2**	16
Alloro	**W1**	21
All Star Lanes	**WC1**	12
Almeida	**N1**	19
Z Amaya	**SW1**	26
Auberge du Lac	**Herts**	26
Babylon	**W8**	17
Baltic	**SE1**	22
Bam-Bou	**W1**	22
Belgo	**WC2**	18
Benares	**W1**	23
Benihana	**multi.**	19
Bentley's	**W1**	24
Blakes	**SW7**	19
Bombay Bicycle	**SW12**	18
Z Boxwood Café	**SW1**	23
Brunello	**SW7**	23
Z Cambio de Tercio	**SW5**	25
Z Capital Rest.	**SW3**	26
Z Chez Bruce	**SW17**	29
Chez Kristof	**W6**	20
China Tang	**W1**	20
Christopher's	**WC2**	19
Chuen Cheng Ku	**W1**	21
Chutney Mary	**SW10**	23
Chutney's	**NW1**	23
Z Cinnamon Club	**SW1**	24
Cipriani	**W1**	20
Clerkenwell Dining	**EC1**	22
Cocoon	**W1**	21
Cru	**N1**	-
Daphne's	**SW3**	22

NEW Dehesa	**W1**	-
e&o	**W11**	22
Eight Over Eight	**SW3**	22
Z Fairuz	**W1**	22
Floridita	**W1**	17
Franco's	**SW1**	19
French Horn	**Berks**	21
Z Gilgamesh	**NW1**	19
Z Gordon Ramsay/Claridge's	**W1**	26
Z Gravetye Manor	**W. Sussex**	28
Z Greenhouse, The	**W1**	26
Green's	**SW1**	23
Greyhound, The	**SW11**	23
Guinea Grill	**W1**	21
Z Hakkasan	**W1**	25
NEW Harrison's	**SW12**	15
Z Hawksmoor	**E1**	24
NEW Hibiscus	**W1**	24
Hush	**W1**	14
Il Convivio	**SW1**	22
Ishbilia	**SW1**	22
itsu	**SW3**	17
Z Ivy, The	**WC2**	22
Julie's	**W11**	17
Kai Mayfair	**W1**	23
Kensington Place	**W8**	19
NEW Landau, The	**W1**	25
La Porte des Indes	**W1**	21
La Poule au Pot	**SW1**	21
La Trouvaille	**W1**	25
Launceston Place	**W8**	-
NEW Le Café Anglais	**W2**	20
Le Cercle	**SW1**	23
Le Colombier	**SW3**	21
Z Le Manoir/Quat	**Oxfordshire**	27
Le Pont/Tour	**SE1**	20
L'Escargot	**W1**	23
Z Les Trois Garçons	**E1**	21
Le Suquet	**SW3**	22
L'Incontro	**SW1**	21
L'Oranger	**SW1**	25
Manicomio	**SW3**	19
Mao Tai	**SW6**	23
Masala Zone	**multi.**	19
Matsuri	**multi.**	23
Memories of China	**SW1**	22
Metrogusto	**N1**	-
Mimmo d'Ischia	**SW1**	18
Mint Leaf	**SW1**	19
Mitsukoshi	**SW1**	19
Momo	**W1**	19
Mon Plaisir	**WC2**	19

Restaurant	Rating
Ⓩ Morgan M	N7	
Motcombs	SW1	20
Mr. Chow	SW1	22
Ⓩ Nahm	SW1	24
Narrow, The	E14	22
Ⓩ Nobu London	W1	27
Notting Hill Brass.	W11	25
Noura	W1	20
1 Lombard St.	EC3	23
1 Lombard Brass.	EC3	19
One-O-One	SW1	23
Papillon	SW3	21
Ⓩ Pasha	SW7	21
Ⓩ Patara	SW3	24
Patterson's	W1	24
Pearl	WC1	25
Pellicano	SW3	22
Ⓩ Pétrus	SW1	28
Ⓩ Pied à Terre	W1	27
Plateau	E14	19
Poissonnerie	SW3	21
Prism	EC3	20
Quaglino's	SW1	18
NEW Quo Vadis	W1	-
Rainforest Cafe	W1	11
Rasa	multi.	24
Ⓩ Rasoi Vineet Bhatia	SW3	27
Real Greek	multi.	16
Rib Room	SW1	22
Ⓩ Richard Corrigan	W1	26
Ⓩ Ritz, The	W1	23
Rivington Grill	EC2	21
Rocket	multi.	17
Ⓩ Roussillon	SW1	26
Royal China	multi.	23
Royal China Club	NW8	24
Royal Exchange	EC3	14
Ⓩ Rules	WC2	23
NEW Sake no hana	SW1	19
San Lorenzo	SW19	20
Santini	SW1	21
Sartoria	W1	20
Shepherd's	SW1	23
Six13	W1	-
Ⓩ Sketch/Lecture Rm.	W1	21
Smiths/Dining Rm.	EC1	21
Ⓩ Square, The	W1	27
Ⓩ Star of India	SW5	25
Ⓩ St. John	EC1	27
Sumosan	W1	24
Tentazioni	SE1	24
Texas Embassy	SW1	14
Thai Square	multi.	18
Thomas Cubitt	SW1	21
Timo	W8	27
Tom Aikens	SW3	25
Tom's Kitchen	SW3	22
Vasco & Piero's	W1	21
Veeraswamy	W1	23
Villandry	W1	22
Vineyard/Stockcross	Stockcross/Berks	25
Vivat Bacchus	EC4	20
NEW Warrington, The	W9	-
Ⓩ Waterside Inn	Berks	27
Wells, The	NW3	20
Ⓩ Wilton's	SW1	25
Wòdka	W8	21
Ⓩ Wolseley, The	W1	22
Ye Olde Cheshire	EC4	16
Ⓩ Zafferano	SW1	25
Zetter	EC1	17
Ⓩ Zuma	SW7	27

PUDDING SPECIALISTS

Restaurant	Rating
Ⓩ NEW Alain Ducasse	W1	26
Alastair Little	W1	24
Almeida	N1	19
Ⓩ Amaya	SW1	26
Ⓩ Asia de Cuba	WC2	21
Aubaine	multi.	19
Auberge du Lac	Herts	26
Aubergine	SW10	25
Baker & Spice	multi.	23
Belvedere, The	W8	20
Bibendum Oyster	SW3	21
Blakes	SW7	19
Ⓩ Boxwood Café	SW1	23
Ⓩ Capital Rest.	SW3	26
Ⓩ Chez Bruce	SW17	29
Cipriani	W1	20
Clarke's	W8	26
Ⓩ Club Gascon	EC1	26
Ⓩ Fat Duck	Berks	27
Fifth Floor	SW1	21
Foliage	SW1	25
Fortnum's Fountain	W1	17
Galvin/Windows	W1	20
Ⓩ Galvin Bistrot	W1	23
Glasshouse, The	TW9	25
Ⓩ Gordon Ramsay/Claridge's	W1	26
Ⓩ Gordon Ramsay/68 Royal	SW3	29
Ⓩ Greenhouse, The	W1	26
NEW Hibiscus	W1	24
Ladurée	SW1	23
Ⓩ L'Atelier/Robuchon	WC2	27
Ⓩ La Trompette	W4	28

SPECIAL FEATURES

Launceston Place | **W8**	–
NEW Le Café Anglais | **W2**	20
Le Cercle | **SW1**	23
Z Ledbury, The | **W11**	28
Z Le Gavroche | **W1**	27
Z Le Manoir/Quat | **Oxfordshire**	27
Z Locanda Locatelli | **W1**	25
L'Oranger | **SW1**	25
Z maze | **W1**	25
Z Nobu Berkeley St | **W1**	26
Z Nobu London | **W1**	27
Orrery | **W1**	24
Z Ottolenghi | **multi.**	25
Patisserie Valerie | **multi.**	18
Z Pétrus | **SW1**	28
Z Pied à Terre | **W1**	27
Plateau | **E14**	19
Providores, The | **W1**	22
Z Rasoi Vineet Bhatia | **SW3**	27
Rhodes W1 Rest. | **W1**	23
Z Richard Corrigan | **W1**	26
Richoux | **multi.**	16
Rist. Semplice | **W1**	24
Z Ritz, The | **W1**	23
Z River Café | **W6**	28
Sketch/Gallery | **W1**	17
Z Sketch/Lecture Rm. | **W1**	21
Z Square, The | **W1**	27
St. Alban | **SW1**	22
Theo Randall | **W1**	23
Tom Aikens | **SW3**	25
Z Ubon | **E14**	26
Z Waterside Inn | **Berks**	27
Z Wolseley, The | **W1**	22
Z Yauatcha | **W1**	26
Z Zafferano | **SW1**	25
Z Zuma | **SW7**	27

QUIET CONVERSATION

Addendum | **EC3**	–
Z NEW Alain Ducasse | **W1**	26
Z Al Sultan | **W1**	23
NEW Apsleys | **SW1**	–
Z Arbutus | **W1**	24
NEW Artisan | **W1**	18
Aubergine | **SW10**	25
Axis | **WC2**	19
Benares | **W1**	23
Bengal Clipper | **SE1**	19
Benja | **W1**	–
Blakes | **SW7**	19
NEW BORD'EAUX | **W1**	–
NEW Brass. St. Jacques | **SW1**	–

Z Capital Rest. | **SW3**	26
NEW Devonshire, The | **W4**	22
Foliage | **SW1**	25
Z Goring | **SW1**	25
Green's | **SW1**	23
Hartwell House | **Bucks**	–
NEW Hibiscus | **W1**	24
Il Convivio | **SW1**	22
Indigo | **WC2**	21
NEW Jimmy's | **SW3**	–
NEW Kensington Sq. | **W8**	–
La Genova | **W1**	25
NEW Landau, The | **W1**	25
Launceston Place | **W8**	–
NEW L'Autre Pied | **W1**	23
Z Le Gavroche | **W1**	27
Z Le Manoir/Quat | **Oxfordshire**	27
L'Oranger | **SW1**	25
L-Rest. & Bar | **W8**	–
Magdalen | **SE1**	23
Mitsukoshi | **SW1**	19
Mosaico | **W1**	–
Mu | **SW1**	–
Z Nahm | **SW1**	24
NEW Northbank | **EC4**	–
NEW Number Twelve | **WC1**	–
Odin's | **W1**	20
One-O-One | **SW1**	23
Orrery | **W1**	24
NEW Osteria Stecca | **NW8**	–
Park, The | **SW1**	24
Z Pied à Terre | **W1**	27
Quadrato | **E14**	–
Quirinale | **SW1**	23
Z Rasoi Vineet Bhatia | **SW3**	27
Rhodes W1 Brass. | **W1**	16
Rhodes W1 Rest. | **W1**	23
Z Ritz, The | **W1**	23
Z Roussillon | **SW1**	26
Saki Bar/Food Emp. | **EC1**	–
Salloos | **SW1**	23
Z Sketch/Lecture Rm. | **W1**	21
NEW Texture | **W1**	21
Theo Randall | **W1**	23
Via Condotti | **W1**	19
Z Waterside Inn | **Berks**	27
Z Wilton's | **SW1**	25

ROMANTIC PLACES

NEW Aaya | **W1**	–
Z NEW Alain Ducasse | **W1**	26
Albion, The | **N1**	17
Z Amaya | **SW1**	26

Andrew Edmunds	W1	22
Z NEW Angelus	W2	23
Archipelago	W1	22
Babylon	W8	17
Belvedere, The	W8	20
Benja	W1	-
Blakes	SW7	19
Blue Elephant	SW6	20
Z Capital Rest.	SW3	26
Z Cheyne Walk	SW3	23
Z Chez Bruce	SW17	29
Chutney Mary	SW10	23
Cipriani	W1	20
Clarke's	W8	26
Z Club Gascon	EC1	26
Z Crazy Bear	W1	20
Daphne's	SW3	22
Frederick's	N1	21
French Horn	Berks	21
Galvin/Windows	W1	20
Glasshouse, The	TW9	25
Z Gordon Ramsay/Claridge's	W1	26
Z Gordon Ramsay/68 Royal	SW3	29
Z Gravetye Manor	W. Sussex	28
Z Greenhouse, The	W1	26
Z Hakkasan	W1	25
Hartwell House	Bucks	-
Julie's	W11	17
NEW Kyashi	WC2	-
La Poule au Pot	SW1	21
Z L'Atelier/Robuchon	WC2	27
Z La Trompette	W4	28
L'Aventure	NW8	24
Le Café/Marché	EC1	23
Z Le Caprice	SW1	24
Le Cercle	SW1	23
Z Ledbury, The	W11	28
Z Le Gavroche	W1	27
Z Le Manoir/Quat	Oxfordshire	27
Le Pont/Tour	SE1	20
Z Les Trois Garçons	E1	21
Z Locanda Locatelli	W1	25
L'Oranger	SW1	25
Maggie Jones's	W8	19
Momo	W1	19
Z Nobu London	W1	27
NEW Northbank	EC4	-
Odette's	NW1	20
Odin's	W1	20
Orrery	W1	24
NEW Osteria Stecca	NW8	-

Z Pasha	SW7	21
Z Pétrus	SW1	28
Pigalle Club	W1	15
Prism	EC3	20
NEW Quo Vadis	W1	-
Z Rasoi Vineet Bhatia	SW3	27
Rhodes W1 Rest.	W1	23
Z Richard Corrigan	W1	26
Z Ritz, The	W1	23
Z River Café	W6	28
Z Roussillon	SW1	26
San Lorenzo	SW3	20
Sitaaray	WC2	-
Z Sketch/Lecture Rm.	W1	21
Snows on Green	W6	21
Z Square, The	W1	27
Tom Aikens	SW3	25
Toto's	SW3	23
Trinity	SW4	26
Veeraswamy	W1	23
Z Waterside Inn	Berks	27
Z Zafferano	SW1	25
Z Zuma	SW7	27

SENIOR APPEAL

Academy	W1	-
Z NEW Alain Ducasse	W1	26
Albemarle, The	W1	22
Al Duca	SW1	20
Z Amaya	SW1	26
NEW Apsleys	SW1	-
Z Arbutus	W1	24
NEW Artisan	W1	18
Aubaine	multi.	19
Aubergine	SW10	25
Z Bellamy's	W1	22
Belvedere, The	W8	20
Bentley's	W1	24
Bibendum	SW3	23
Bloom's	NW11	17
Bonds	EC2	22
NEW BORD'EAUX	W1	-
Z Boxwood Café	SW1	23
Brasserie Roux	SW1	21
NEW Brass. St. Jacques	SW1	-
Brass. St. Quentin	SW3	20
Z Capital Rest.	SW3	26
Cecconi's	W1	21
Chelsea Brass.	SW1	17
China Tang	W1	20
Cipriani	W1	20
Citrus	W1	19
Cliveden House	Berks	22
NEW Devonshire, The	W4	22

Dorchester/The Grill | **W1**	24
Elena's l'Etoile | **W1**	18
11 Abingdon Rd. | **W8**	19
Foliage | **SW1**	25
Forge, The | **WC2**	18
Fortnum's Fountain | **W1**	17
Foxtrot Oscar | **SW3**	15
Franco's | **SW1**	19
Galvin/Windows | **W1**	20
Z Galvin Bistrot | **W1**	23
Glasshouse, The | **TW9**	25
Z Gordon Ramsay/Claridge's | **W1**	26
Z Gordon Ramsay/68 Royal | **SW3**	29
Z Goring | **SW1**	25
Z Gravetye Manor | **W. Sussex**	28
Z Greenhouse, The | **W1**	26
Green's | **SW1**	23
Hartwell House | **Bucks**	-
NEW Hibiscus | **W1**	24
Z Ivy, The | **WC2**	22
Z J. Sheekey | **WC2**	26
Kai Mayfair | **W1**	23
Ladurée | **SW1**	23
La Genova | **W1**	25
NEW Landau, The | **W1**	25
Langan's Bistro | **W1**	19
La Poule au Pot | **SW1**	21
Z L'Atelier/Robuchon | **WC2**	27
Launceston Place | **W8**	-
NEW L'Autre Pied | **W1**	23
NEW Le Café Anglais | **W2**	20
Z Le Caprice | **SW1**	24
Le Colombier | **SW3**	21
Z Ledbury, The | **W11**	28
Z Le Gavroche | **W1**	27
Z Le Manoir/Quat | **Oxfordshire**	27
Le Suquet | **SW3**	22
L'Etranger | **SW7**	23
L'Incontro | **SW1**	21
Z Locanda Locatelli | **W1**	25
L'Oranger | **SW1**	25
Luciano | **SW1**	19
Magdalen | **SE1**	23
NEW maze Grill | **W1**	-
Mimmo d'Ischia | **SW1**	18
Montpeliano | **SW7**	18
Motcombs | **SW1**	20
Noura | **multi.**	20
Odin's | **W1**	20
Olivomare | **SW1**	21
One-O-One | **SW1**	23

Orrery | **W1**	24
NEW Osteria Stecca | **NW8**	-
NEW Pantechnicon Rms. | **SW1**	-
Papillon | **SW3**	21
Park, The | **SW1**	24
Patisserie Valerie | **multi.**	18
Z Pétrus | **SW1**	28
Poissonnerie | **SW3**	21
Quadrato | **E14**	-
Quirinale | **SW1**	23
NEW Quo Vadis | **W1**	-
Z Racine | **SW3**	23
Red Fort | **W1**	24
Reubens | **W1**	15
Rhodes W1 Rest. | **W1**	23
Rib Room | **SW1**	22
Richoux | **multi.**	16
Rist. Semplice | **W1**	24
Z Ritz, The | **W1**	23
Riva | **SW13**	21
Roast | **SE1**	19
Rowley's | **SW1**	20
Z Rules | **WC2**	23
Santini | **SW1**	21
Sartoria | **W1**	20
Scalini | **SW3**	23
Z Scott's | **W1**	24
Shepherd's | **SW1**	23
Shogun | **W1**	-
Simpson's/Strand | **WC2**	20
Z Sketch/Lecture Rm. | **W1**	21
Sotheby's Cafe | **W1**	20
Z Square, The | **W1**	27
St. Alban | **SW1**	22
St. James's | **W1**	20
Tate Britain | **SW1**	19
Theo Randall | **W1**	23
Tom Aikens | **SW3**	25
Toto's | **SW3**	23
Via Condotti | **W1**	19
Wallace, The | **W1**	18
Z Waterside Inn | **Berks**	27
NEW Wild Honey | **W1**	23
Z Wilton's | **SW1**	25
Z Wolseley, The | **W1**	22
Z Zafferano | **SW1**	25

SET-PRICE MENUS

(Call for prices and times)

Abingdon, The | **W8**	18
Alastair Little | **W1**	24
Al Duca | **SW1**	20
Alloro | **W1**	21
Almeida | **N1**	19

Amaya | **SW1**	26
Arbutus | **W1**	24
Aubergine | **SW10**	25
Avenue, The | **SW1**	19
Axis | **WC2**	19
Baltic | **SE1**	22
Bellamy's | **W1**	22
Benares | **W1**	23
Bengal Clipper | **SE1**	19
Bibendum | **SW3**	23
Blue Elephant | **SW6**	20
Boxwood Café | **SW1**	23
Brasserie Roux | **SW1**	21
Brass. St. Quentin | **SW3**	20
Brunello | **SW7**	23
Butlers Wharf | **SE1**	22
Café Japan | **NW11**	25
Café Spice Namasté | **E1**	23
Capital Rest. | **SW3**	26
Caravaggio | **EC3**	15
Champor | **SE1**	20
Chez Bruce | **SW17**	29
Chez Kristof | **W6**	20
Chor Bizarre | **W1**	19
Christopher's | **WC2**	19
Chutney Mary | **SW10**	23
Cigala | **WC1**	21
Cinnamon Club | **SW1**	24
Ciprianj | **W1**	20
Clerkenwell Dining | **EC1**	22
Clos Maggiore | **WC2**	25
Club Gascon | **EC1**	26
Coq d'Argent | **EC2**	22
Crazy Bear | **W1**	20
Defune | **W1**	26
Dorchester/The Grill | **W1**	24
Eight Over Eight | **SW3**	22
El Pirata | **W1**	20
Enoteca Turi | **SW15**	24
Essenza | **W11**	18
Fakhreldine | **W1**	19
Fat Duck | **Berks**	27
Fifteen | **N1**	25
Foliage | **SW1**	25
Galvin Bistrot | **W1**	23
Glasshouse, The | **TW9**	25
Gordon Ramsay/Claridge's | **W1**	26
Gordon Ramsay/68 Royal | **SW3**	29
Goring | **SW1**	25
Gravetye Manor | **W. Sussex**	28
Greenhouse, The | **W1**	26
NEW Hibiscus | **W1**	24

High Road Brass. | **W4**	19
Hunan | **SW1**	27
Il Convivio | **SW1**	22
Indigo | **WC2**	21
Ivy, The | **WC2**	22
Joy King Lau | **WC2**	18
J. Sheekey | **WC2**	26
Kai Mayfair | **W1**	23
Kensington Place | **W8**	19
Kiku | **W1**	23
Langan's Bistro | **W1**	19
La Poule au Pot | **SW1**	21
L'Atelier/Robuchon | **WC2**	27
Latium | **W1**	23
La Trompette | **W4**	28
Launceston Place | **W8**	-
L'Aventure | **NW8**	24
Le Café/Marché | **EC1**	23
Le Cercle | **SW1**	23
Le Colombier | **SW3**	21
Ledbury, The | **W11**	28
Le Gavroche | **W1**	27
Le Manoir/Quat | **Oxfordshire**	27
L'Escargot | **W1**	23
Les Trois Garçons | **E1**	21
Le Suquet | **SW3**	22
L'Etranger | **SW7**	23
L'Incontro | **SW1**	21
Locanda Ottoemezzo | **W8**	24
L'Oranger | **SW1**	25
Lucio | **SW3**	22
Matsuri | **multi.**	23
maze | **W1**	25
Mela | **WC2**	21
Memories of China | **multi.**	22
Mint Leaf | **SW1**	19
Mitsukoshi | **SW1**	19
Morgan M | **N7**	26
Nobu Berkeley St | **W1**	26
Nobu London | **W1**	27
Noura | **multi.**	20
Olivo | **SW1**	19
1 Lombard St. | **EC3**	23
One-O-One | **SW1**	23
Orrery | **W1**	24
Oslo Court | **NW8**	26
Oxo Tower | **SE1**	21
Özer | **W1**	17
Patara | **multi.**	24
Patterson's | **W1**	24
Pellicano | **SW3**	22
Pétrus | **SW1**	28
Pied à Terre | **W1**	27

Plateau | **E14**	19
Poissonnerie | **SW3**	21
Porters | **WC2**	18
Princess Garden | **W1**	22
Quaglino's | **SW1**	18
Quilon | **SW1**	25
☑ Racine | **SW3**	23
Rasa | **multi.**	24
☑ Rasoi Vineet Bhatia | **SW3**	27
Rib Room | **SW1**	22
☑ Richard Corrigan | **W1**	26
Rist. Semplice | **W1**	24
☑ Ritz, The | **W1**	23
Roka | **W1**	25
☑ Roussillon | **SW1**	26
Royal China | **multi.**	23
Royal China Club | **NW8**	24
Sardo Canale | **NW1**	21
Sartoria | **W1**	20
Shogun | **W1**	-
Six13 | **W1**	-
☑ Sketch/Lecture Rm. | **W1**	21
Snows on Green | **W6**	21
Sonny's | **SW13**	22
Sophie's Steak | **SW10**	21
☑ Square, The | **W1**	27
☑ Taman Gang | **W1**	21
☑ Tamarind | **W1**	25
Tentazioni | **SE1**	24
Tom Aikens | **SW3**	25
Toto's | **SW3**	23
Trinity | **SW4**	26
Vama | **SW10**	25
Vasco & Piero's | **W1**	21
Veeraswamy | **W1**	23
Via Condotti | **W1**	19
Vineyard/Stockcross | **Stockcross/Berks**	25
☑ Waterside Inn | **Berks**	27
Yoshino | **W1**	23
☑ Zafferano | **SW1**	25
Zaika | **W8**	24
Ziani | **SW3**	20

SINGLES SCENES

Admiral Codrington | **SW3**	18
Albannach | **WC2**	16
☑ Amaya | **SW1**	26
Annex 3 | **W1**	-
☑ Asia de Cuba | **WC2**	21
Avenue, The | **SW1**	19
Balans | **multi.**	16
Bank Westminster | **SW1**	16
Belgo | **multi.**	18

Bierodrome | **multi.**	16
Big Easy | **SW3**	16
Bistro 190 | **SW7**	-
Bluebird | **SW3**	18
Bountiful Cow | **WC1**	21
Brinkley's | **SW10**	14
Browns | **multi.**	16
Buona Sera | **SW3**	18
Cafe Pacifico | **WC2**	16
Cecconi's | **W1**	21
Cellar Gascon | **EC1**	-
Christopher's | **WC2**	19
Cocoon | **W1**	21
Collection | **SW3**	13
Dish Dash | **SW12**	21
Draper's Arms | **N1**	19
e&o | **W11**	22
Ebury Wine Bar | **SW1**	18
Eight Over Eight | **SW3**	22
Engineer | **NW1**	20
Enterprise | **SW3**	17
Fifteen | **N1**	25
Fifth Floor Cafe | **SW1**	18
☑ Fino | **W1**	25
Floridita | **W1**	17
☑ Gilgamesh | **NW1**	19
☑ Hakkasan | **W1**	25
Hush | **W1**	14
Just St. James's | **SW1**	20
NEW Kenza | **EC2**	-
Kettners | **W1**	15
La Perla | **WC2**	19
La Rueda | **multi.**	15
Le Cercle | **SW1**	23
Living Rm. | **W1**	17
Maroush | **multi.**	22
☑ maze | **W1**	25
Medcalf | **EC1**	-
Mews of Mayfair | **W1**	19
Momo | **W1**	19
☑ Moro | **EC1**	25
Motcombs | **SW1**	20
Nam Long-Le Shaker | **SW5**	-
☑ Nobu Berkeley St | **W1**	26
☑ Nobu London | **W1**	27
Nozomi | **SW3**	19
Oriel | **SW1**	15
☑ Oxo Tower | **SE1**	21
☑ Oxo Tower Brass. | **SE1**	18
Ping Pong | **multi.**	19
Pizza on the Park | **SW1**	17
PJ's B&G | **SW3**	16
Quaglino's | **SW1**	18
Real Greek | **multi.**	16

Roka | **W1**	25
Sabor | **N1**	-
Sketch/Gallery | **W1**	17
Smiths/Dining Rm. | **EC1**	21
Sophie's Steak | **SW10**	21
Spiga | **W1**	17
Sticky Fingers | **W8**	17
Suka | **W1**	-
Sumosan | **W1**	24
Tartine | **SW3**	17
Texas Embassy | **SW1**	14
Waterway, The | **W9**	15
XO | **NW3**	21
☒ Zuma | **SW7**	27

SLEEPERS

(Good to excellent food,
but little known)

Archipelago | **W1**	22
Asakusa | **NW1**	25
Auberge du Lac | **Herts**	26
Bangkok | **SW7**	25
Bevis Marks | **EC3**	22
Brunello | **SW7**	23
Cay tre | **EC1**	23
Chisou | **W1**	23
Chutney's | **NW1**	23
Clerkenwell Dining | **EC1**	22
El Faro | **E14**	23
Esarn Kheaw | **W12**	25
Fig | **N1**	22
Green Olive | **W9**	23
Greyhound, The | **SW11**	23
Hand & Flowers | **Bucks**	23
Ikeda | **W1**	26
Imperial City | **EC3**	23
Inaho | **W2**	25
Inside | **SE10**	25
Konstam | **WC1**	23
La Collina | **NW1**	24
La Figa | **E14**	22
La Trouvaille | **W1**	25
Mao Tai | **SW6**	23
Mestizo | **NW1**	23
Moti Mahal | **WC2**	25
Nautilus Fish | **NW6**	22
Nyonya | **W11**	22
Pappagallo | **W1**	23
Pellicano | **SW3**	22
Petersham Nurseries | **TW10**	24
Spread Eagle | **SE10**	24
St. Germain | **EC1**	22
Tentazioni | **SE1**	24
Ten Ten Tei | **W1**	23
Timo | **W8**	27

Trinity | **SW4**	26
Tsunami | **SW4**	26
Uli | **W11**	26
Vineyard/Stockcross | **Stockcross/Berks**	25
Yming | **W1**	24

SPECIAL OCCASIONS

☒ **NEW** Alain Ducasse | **W1**	26
Albemarle, The | **W1**	22
Almeida | **N1**	19
☒ Amaya | **SW1**	26
☒ Asia de Cuba | **WC2**	21
Auberge du Lac | **Herts**	26
Aubergine | **SW10**	25
Belvedere, The | **W8**	20
Benja | **W1**	-
Bentley's | **W1**	24
Bibendum | **SW3**	23
Blakes | **SW7**	19
Bluebird | **SW3**	18
Blue Elephant | **SW6**	20
☒ Boxwood Café | **SW1**	23
Brunello | **SW7**	23
☒ Capital Rest. | **SW3**	26
Cecconi's | **W1**	21
☒ Chez Bruce | **SW17**	29
China Tang | **W1**	20
Chutney Mary | **SW10**	23
☒ Cinnamon Club | **SW1**	24
Cipriani | **W1**	20
Clarke's | **W8**	26
☒ Club Gascon | **EC1**	26
☒ Crazy Bear | **W1**	20
Daphne's | **SW3**	22
Dorchester/The Grill | **W1**	24
☒ Fat Duck | **Berks**	27
Fifteen | **N1**	25
☒ Fino | **W1**	25
Floridita | **W1**	17
Foliage | **SW1**	25
French Horn | **Berks**	21
Galvin/Windows | **W1**	20
☒ Galvin Bistrot | **W1**	23
Glasshouse, The | **TW9**	25
☒ Gordon Ramsay/Claridge's | **W1**	26
☒ Gordon Ramsay/68 Royal | **SW3**	29
☒ Goring | **SW1**	25
☒ Gravetye Manor | **W. Sussex**	28
☒ Greenhouse, The | **W1**	26
Haiku | **W1**	19
☒ Hakkasan | **W1**	25
Hartwell House | **Bucks**	-

NEW Hibiscus | **W1**	24
Z Ivy, The | **WC2**	22
Z J. Sheekey | **WC2**	26
NEW Landau, The | **W1**	25
Z NEW La Petite Maison | **W1**	25
Z L'Atelier/Robuchon | **WC2**	27
Z La Trompette | **W4**	28
Launceston Place | **W8**	-
NEW Le Café Anglais | **W2**	20
Z Le Caprice | **SW1**	24
Le Cercle | **SW1**	23
Z Ledbury, The | **W11**	28
Z Le Gavroche | **W1**	27
Z Le Manoir/Quat | **Oxfordshire**	27
Le Pont/Tour | **SE1**	20
Z Locanda Locatelli | **W1**	25
L'Oranger | **SW1**	25
Luciano | **SW1**	19
Z maze | **W1**	25
NEW maze Grill | **W1**	-
Momo | **W1**	19
Z Morgan M | **N7**	26
Z Nahm | **SW1**	24
Z Nobu Berkeley St | **W1**	26
Z Nobu London | **W1**	27
Orrery | **W1**	24
Z Pétrus | **SW1**	28
Z Pied à Terre | **W1**	27
Plateau | **E14**	19
Providores, The | **W1**	22
Quaglino's | **SW1**	18
NEW Quo Vadis | **W1**	-
Z Rasoi Vineet Bhatia | **SW3**	27
Rhodes W1 Rest. | **W1**	23
Z Richard Corrigan | **W1**	26
Rist. Semplice | **W1**	24
Z Ritz, The | **W1**	23
Z River Café | **W6**	28
Roast | **SE1**	19
NEW Sake no hana | **SW1**	19
San Lorenzo | **SW3**	20
Santini | **SW1**	21
Z Scott's | **W1**	24
Z Sketch/Lecture Rm. | **W1**	21
Skylon | **SE1**	19
Smiths/Dining Rm. | **EC1**	21
Smiths/Top Floor | **EC1**	21
Z Square, The | **W1**	27
St. Alban | **SW1**	22
NEW Texture | **W1**	21
Theo Randall | **W1**	23
Tom Aikens | **SW3**	25
Trinity | **SW4**	26

Z Ubon | **E14**	26
Z Umu | **W1**	26
Vineyard/Stockcross | **Stockcross/Berks**	25
Z Waterside Inn | **Berks**	27
Z Wilton's | **SW1**	25
Z Wolseley, The | **W1**	22
Z Zafferano | **SW1**	25
Zaika | **W8**	24
Z Zuma | **SW7**	27

TEA SERVICE

(See also Hotel Dining)	
Academy | **W1**	-
Armani Caffé | **SW3**	19
NEW Botanist, The | **SW1**	-
Chor Bizarre | **W1**	19
Cipriani | **W1**	20
Court | **WC1**	18
NEW Daylesford | **multi.**	18
Empress of India | **E9**	21
Fifth Floor Cafe | **SW1**	18
Food for Thought | **WC2**	24
Fortnum's Fountain | **W1**	17
Frontline | **W2**	-
Inn The Park | **SW1**	18
Joe's Rest. Bar | **SW1**	19
Julie's | **W11**	17
NEW Kensington Sq. | **W8**	-
La Brasserie | **SW3**	18
Ladurée | **SW1**	23
La Fromagerie | **W1**	25
Momo | **W1**	19
National Dining Rms. | **WC2**	20
Nicole's | **W1**	21
NEW Paradise | **W1**	-
Patisserie Valerie | **multi.**	18
Porters | **WC2**	18
Portrait | **WC2**	21
Richoux | **multi.**	16
Roast | **SE1**	19
Sotheby's Cafe | **W1**	20
St. James's | **W1**	20
Tate Britain | **SW1**	19
Tate Modern | **SE1**	17
Truc Vert | **W1**	17
202 | **W11**	18
Wallace, The | **W1**	18
Z Wolseley, The | **W1**	22
Z Yauatcha | **W1**	26

TRENDY

NEW Aaya | **W1**	-
Admiral Codrington | **SW3**	18
Alloro | **W1**	21

Restaurant	Rating
All Star Lanes | **WC1**	12
Z Amaya | **SW1**	26
Anchor & Hope | **SE1**	25
Armani Caffè | **SW3**	19
Z Asia de Cuba | **WC2**	21
Z Assaggi | **W2**	26
Aubaine | **multi.**	19
Automat | **W1**	18
Avenue, The | **SW1**	19
Baker & Spice | **multi.**	23
Bam-Bou | **W1**	22
Z Barrafina | **W1**	25
Bar Shu | **W1**	23
Belvedere, The | **W8**	20
Bibendum Oyster | **SW3**	21
Bierodrome | **multi.**	16
NEW Bincho Yakitori | **multi.**	21
Blakes | **SW7**	19
Z Boxwood Café | **SW1**	23
NEW Brickhouse, The | **E1**	-
Bumpkin | **W11**	19
Z Busaba Eathai | **multi.**	22
Bush B&G | **W12**	18
Canteen | **multi.**	18
Caraffini | **SW1**	22
Carluccio's Caffè | **multi.**	17
Cecconi's | **W1**	21
Cellar Gascon | **EC1**	-
NEW Cha Cha Moon | **W1**	-
Z Cheyne Walk | **SW3**	23
Z Chez Bruce | **SW17**	29
Christopher's | **WC2**	19
Cicada | **EC1**	21
Z Cinnamon Club | **SW1**	24
Cipriani | **W1**	20
Clarke's | **W8**	26
Z Club Gascon | **EC1**	26
Cocoon | **W1**	21
Z Crazy Bear | **W1**	20
Crazy Homies | **W2**	19
Daphne's | **SW3**	22
NEW Daylesford | **multi.**	18
NEW Dehesa | **W1**	-
e&o | **W11**	22
Eight Over Eight | **SW3**	22
Electric Brass. | **W11**	17
Elistano | **SW3**	22
Enterprise | **SW3**	17
Fifteen | **N1**	25
Fifth Floor Cafe | **SW1**	18
Z Fino | **W1**	25
fish! | **SE1**	19
Frankie's Italian | **multi.**	14
Z Galvin Bistrot | **W1**	23
Z Gilgamesh | **NW1**	19
Z Gordon Ramsay/Claridge's | **W1**	26
Z Gordon Ramsay/68 Royal | **SW3**	29
Great Queen St. | **WC2**	24
Green & Red Bar | **E1**	19
Haiku | **W1**	25
Z Hakkasan | **W1**	25
NEW Harrison's | **SW12**	15
Z Hawksmoor | **E1**	24
NEW Hereford Road | **W2**	24
High Road Brass. | **W4**	19
NEW Hix Oyster | **EC1**	-
Hoxton Grille | **EC2**	15
Hush | **W1**	14
itsu | **multi.**	17
Z Ivy, The | **WC2**	22
Z J. Sheekey | **WC2**	26
Kensington Place | **W8**	19
NEW Kenza | **EC2**	-
NEW Kyashi | **WC2**	-
La Fromagerie | **W1**	25
Z NEW La Petite Maison | **W1**	25
Z L'Atelier/Robuchon | **WC2**	27
Z La Trompette | **W4**	28
NEW Le Café Anglais | **W2**	20
Z Le Caprice | **SW1**	24
Le Cercle | **SW1**	23
Le Colombier | **SW3**	21
Z Ledbury, The | **W11**	28
Z Les Trois Garçons | **E1**	21
L'Etranger | **SW7**	23
Z Locanda Locatelli | **W1**	25
Lucio | **SW3**	22
Lucky 7 | **W2**	21
Manicomio | **SW3**	19
Masala Zone | **multi.**	19
Z maze | **W1**	25
NEW maze Grill | **W1**	-
Mews of Mayfair | **W1**	19
Momo | **W1**	19
Z Moro | **EC1**	25
Napket | **multi.**	-
Nicole's | **W1**	21
Z Nobu Berkeley St | **W1**	26
Z Nobu London | **W1**	27
NEW Northbank | **EC4**	-
Nozomi | **SW3**	19
Z Oliveto | **SW1**	21
Olivo | **SW1**	19
Olivomare | **SW1**	21
Orso | **WC2**	19
Z Ottolenghi | **multi.**	25

Oxo Tower | **SE1**	21
Papillon | **SW3**	21
Pasha | **SW7**	21
Ping Pong | **multi.**	19
PJ's B&G | **SW3**	16
Providores, The | **W1**	22
NEW Quo Vadis | **W1**	-
Racine | **SW3**	23
Rasoi Vineet Bhatia | **SW3**	27
Refettorio | **EC4**	22
River Café | **W6**	28
Roka | **W1**	25
NEW Sake no hana | **SW1**	19
Salt Yard | **W1**	21
San Lorenzo | **SW3**	20
Scott's | **W1**	24
Sketch/Gallery | **W1**	17
Smiths/Dining Rm. | **EC1**	21
Sophie's Steak | **SW10**	21
Sotheby's Cafe | **W1**	20
St. Alban | **SW1**	22
St. Germain | **EC1**	22
St. John | **EC1**	27
St. John Bread/Wine | **E1**	23
Suka | **W1**	-
Tamarai | **WC2**	20
Tapas Brindisa | **SE1**	24
Taqueria | **W11**	22
Tartine | **SW3**	17
NEW Tendido Cuatro | **SW6**	-
Thomas Cubitt | **SW1**	21
Tom Aikens | **SW3**	25
Tom's Deli | **W11**	16
Tom's Kitchen | **SW3**	22
NEW Tom's Place | **SW3**	18
Tsunami | **SW4**	26
202 | **W11**	18
Ubon | **E14**	26
NEW Urban Turban | **W2**	17
Vama | **SW10**	25
Vingt-Quatre | **SW10**	13
Wagamama | **multi.**	19
NEW Wahaca | **WC2**	20
Wapping Food | **E1**	19
NEW Warrington, The | **W9**	-
NEW Water House | **N1**	-
NEW Waterloo Brass. | **SE1**	19
Wells, The | **NW3**	20
NEW Whole Foods | **W8**	18
Wolseley, The | **W1**	22
XO | **NW3**	21
Yauatcha | **W1**	26
Zafferano | **SW1**	25
Zetter | **EC1**	17
Ziani | **SW3**	20
Zilli Fish | **W1**	21
Zuma | **SW7**	27

VIEWS

Addendum | **EC3**	-
Amici | **SW17**	16
Aquasia | **SW10**	-
Auberge du Lac | **Herts**	26
Babylon | **W8**	17
Belvedere, The | **W8**	20
NEW Bincho Yakitori | **SE1**	21
Blueprint Café | **SE1**	18
Butler & Grill, The | **SW11**	18
Butlers Wharf | **SE1**	22
Cantina del Ponte | **SE1**	18
NEW Champagne Bar | **NW1**	14
Cheyne Walk | **SW3**	23
Cocoon | **W1**	21
Coq d'Argent | **EC2**	22
dim t | **SE1**	15
1802 | **E14**	16
El Faro | **E14**	23
Fakhreldine | **W1**	19
Fifth Floor | **SW1**	21
Foliage | **SW1**	25
French Horn | **Berks**	21
Galvin/Windows | **W1**	20
Gaucho Grill | **multi.**	22
Gravetye Manor | **W. Sussex**	28
Greenhouse, The | **W1**	26
Gun, The | **E14**	21
Hartwell House | **Bucks**	-
Inn The Park | **SW1**	18
Le Manoir/Quat | **Oxfordshire**	27
Le Pont/Tour | **SE1**	20
maze | **W1**	25
Narrow, The | **E14**	22
Nobu London | **W1**	27
NEW Northbank | **EC4**	-
Orrery | **W1**	24
Oslo Court | **NW8**	26
Oxo Tower | **SE1**	21
Oxo Tower Brass. | **SE1**	18
Park, The | **SW1**	24
Petersham, The | **TW10**	-
Pizza on the Park | **SW1**	17
Plateau | **E14**	19
Portrait | **WC2**	21
Ransome's Dock | **SW11**	20
Rhodes 24 | **EC2**	24
River Café | **W6**	28
Roast | **SE1**	19

Rocket | **SW15**	17
Royal China | **E14**	23
Skylon | **SE1**	19
Smiths/Top Floor | **EC1**	21
Tate Modern | **SE1**	17
Thai Square | **SW1**	18
Tootsies | **SW1**	13
Z Ubon | **E14**	26
NEW Upper Deck | **WC2**	-
NEW Water House | **N1**	-
Z Waterside Inn | **Berks**	27
Waterway, The | **W9**	15
Yakitoria | **W2**	17

VISITORS ON EXPENSE ACCOUNT

NEW Aaya | **W1**	-
Addendum | **EC3**	-
Z NEW Alain Ducasse | **W1**	26
Albemarle, The | **W1**	22
Almeida | **N1**	19
Z Amaya | **SW1**	26
NEW Apsleys | **SW1**	-
Z Arbutus | **W1**	24
Z Asia de Cuba | **WC2**	21
Auberge du Lac | **Herts**	26
Aubergine | **SW10**	25
Bank Westminster | **SW1**	16
Belvedere, The | **W8**	20
Benares | **W1**	23
Bentley's | **W1**	24
Bibendum | **SW3**	23
Blakes | **SW7**	19
Z Boxwood Café | **SW1**	23
NEW Brass. St. Jacques | **SW1**	-
Z Capital Rest. | **SW3**	26
Caravaggio | **EC3**	15
Cecconi's | **W1**	21
Z Chez Bruce | **SW17**	29
China Tang | **W1**	20
Christopher's | **WC2**	19
Chutney Mary | **SW10**	23
Z Cinnamon Club | **SW1**	24
Cipriani | **W1**	20
Clarke's | **W8**	26
Cliveden House | **Berks**	22
Z Club Gascon | **EC1**	26
Coq d'Argent | **EC2**	22
Daphne's | **SW3**	22
Dorchester/The Grill | **W1**	24
Elena's l'Etoile | **W1**	18
Z Fat Duck | **Berks**	27
Fifteen | **N1**	25
Fifth Floor | **SW1**	21

Z Fino | **W1**	25
Foliage | **SW1**	25
Forge, The | **WC2**	18
Galvin/Windows | **W1**	20
Z Galvin Bistrot | **W1**	23
Glasshouse, The | **TW9**	25
Z Gordon Ramsay/Claridge's | **W1**	26
Z Gordon Ramsay/68 Royal | **SW3**	29
Z Gravetye Manor | **W. Sussex**	28
Z Greenhouse, The | **W1**	26
Green's | **SW1**	23
Z Hakkasan | **W1**	25
NEW Hibiscus | **W1**	24
Z Ivy, The | **WC2**	22
NEW Jimmy's | **SW3**	-
Z J. Sheekey | **WC2**	26
Kai Mayfair | **W1**	23
NEW Kyashi | **WC2**	-
NEW Landau, The | **W1**	25
Langan's Brass. | **W1**	19
Z NEW La Petite Maison | **W1**	25
Z L'Atelier/Robuchon | **WC2**	27
Launceston Place | **W8**	-
NEW L'Autre Pied | **W1**	23
NEW Le Café Anglais | **W2**	20
Z Le Caprice | **SW1**	24
Z Ledbury, The | **W11**	28
Z Le Gavroche | **W1**	27
Z Le Manoir/Quat | **Oxfordshire**	27
Le Pont/Tour | **SE1**	20
L'Incontro | **SW1**	21
Z Locanda Locatelli | **W1**	25
L'Oranger | **SW1**	25
Matsuri | **multi.**	23
Z maze | **W1**	25
NEW maze Grill | **W1**	-
Mitsukoshi | **SW1**	19
Z Nahm | **SW1**	24
Z Nobu Berkeley St | **W1**	26
Z Nobu London | **W1**	27
NEW Northbank | **EC4**	-
Odin's | **W1**	20
One-O-One | **SW1**	23
NEW Only Running Footman | **W1**	18
Orrery | **W1**	24
NEW Osteria Stecca | **NW8**	-
Z Oxo Tower | **SE1**	21
NEW Pantechnicon Rms. | **SW1**	-
Z Pétrus | **SW1**	28
Z Pied à Terre | **W1**	27

SPECIAL FEATURES

Wine Vintage Chart

This chart, based on our 0 to 30 scale, is designed to help you select wine. The ratings (by **Howard Stravitz**, a law professor at the University of South Carolina) reflect the vintage quality and the wine's readiness to drink. We exclude the 1991–1993 vintages because they are not that good. A dash indicates the wine is either past its peak or too young to rate. Loire ratings are for dry white wines.

Whites

	88	89	90	94	95	96	97	98	99	00	01	02	03	04	05	06
French:																
Alsace	–	25	25	24	23	23	22	25	23	25	27	25	22	24	25	–
Burgundy	–	23	22	–	28	27	24	22	26	25	24	27	23	27	26	24
Loire Valley	–	–	–	–	–	–	–	–	–	24	25	26	23	24	27	24
Champagne	24	26	29	–	26	27	24	23	24	24	22	26	–	–	–	–
Sauternes	29	25	28	–	21	23	25	23	24	24	28	25	26	21	26	23
California:																
Chardonnay	–	–	–	–	–	–	–	–	24	23	26	26	25	27	29	25
Sauvignon Blanc	–	–	–	–	–	–	–	–	–	–	27	28	26	27	26	27
Austrian:																
Grüner Velt./Riesling	–	–	–	–	25	21	26	26	25	22	23	25	26	25	26	–
German:	25	26	27	24	23	26	25	26	23	21	29	27	24	26	28	–

Reds

	88	89	90	94	95	96	97	98	99	00	01	02	03	04	05	06
French:																
Bordeaux	23	25	29	22	26	25	23	25	24	29	26	24	25	24	27	25
Burgundy	–	24	26	–	26	27	25	22	27	22	24	27	25	25	27	25
Rhône	26	28	28	24	26	22	25	27	26	27	26	–	25	24	25	–
Beaujolais	–	–	–	–	–	–	–	–	–	24	–	23	25	22	28	26
California:																
Cab./Merlot	–	–	28	29	27	25	28	23	26	22	27	26	25	24	24	23
Pinot Noir	–	–	–	–	–	–	24	23	24	23	27	28	26	25	24	–
Zinfandel	–	–	–	–	–	–	–	–	–	–	25	23	27	24	23	–
Oregon:																
Pinot Noir	–	–	–	–	–	–	–	–	–	–	–	27	25	26	27	–
Italian:																
Tuscany	–	–	25	22	24	20	29	24	27	24	27	20	25	25	22	24
Piedmont	–	27	27	–	23	26	27	26	25	28	27	20	24	25	26	–
Spanish:																
Rioja	–	–	–	26	26	24	25	22	25	24	27	20	24	25	26	24
Ribera del Duero/Priorat	–	–	–	26	26	27	25	24	25	24	27	20	24	26	26	24
Australian:																
Shiraz/Cab.	–	–	–	24	26	23	26	28	24	24	27	27	25	26	24	–
Chilean:	–	–	–	–	–	–	24	–	25	23	26	24	25	24	26	–

subscribe to ZAGAT.com

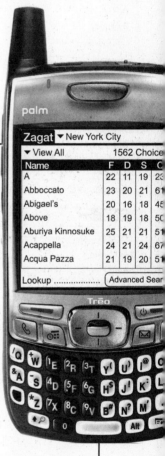

Zagat Products

RESTAURANTS & MAPS

America's Top Restaurants
Atlanta
Beijing
Boston
Brooklyn
California Wine Country
Cape Cod & The Islands
Chicago
Connecticut
Europe's Top Restaurants
Hamptons (incl. wineries)
Hong Kong
Las Vegas
London
Long Island (incl. wineries)
Los Angeles I So. California
(guide & map)
Miami Beach
Miami I So. Florida
Montréal
New Jersey
New Jersey Shore
New Orleans
New York City (guide & map)
Palm Beach
Paris
Philadelphia
San Diego
San Francisco (guide & map)
Seattle
Shanghai
Texas
Tokyo
Toronto
Vancouver
Washington, DC I Baltimore
Westchester I Hudson Valley
World's Top Restaurants

LIFESTYLE GUIDES

America's Top Golf Courses
Movie Guide
Music Guide
NYC Gourmet Shop./Entertaining
NYC Shopping

NIGHTLIFE GUIDES

Los Angeles
New York City
San Francisco

HOTEL & TRAVEL GUIDES

Beijing
Hong Kong
Las Vegas
London
New Orleans
Montréal
Shanghai
Top U.S. Hotels, Resorts & Spas
Toronto
U.S. Family Travel
Vancouver
Walt Disney World Insider's Guide
World's Top Hotels, Resorts & Spas

WEB & WIRELESS SERVICES

ZAGAT TO GO℠ for handhelds
ZAGAT.com℠ • ZAGAT.mobi℠

**Available wherever books are sold or at ZAGAT.com. To customise
Zagat guides as gifts or marketing tools,
call 0800-895-221 (from the U.K.), 800-540-9609 (from the U.S.)
or 1-212-977-6000 (from all other countries)**

ZAGATMAP

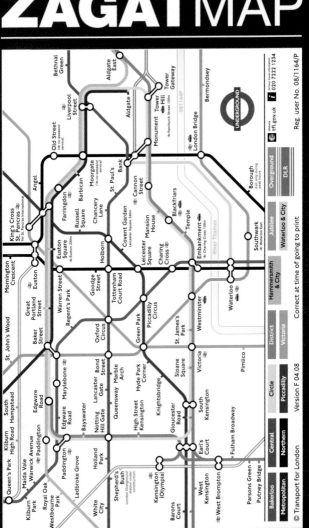

© Transport for London • Version F 04.08 • Correct at time of going to print • Reg. user No. 08/1164/P • tfl.gov.uk • 020 7222 1234

London
Underground
Map

Most Popular Restaurants

Map coordinates follow each name. For chains, only flagship or central locations are plotted. Sections **1-8** lie on the **West London** map (see adjacent). Sections **8-15** lie on the **East London** map (see reverse side of map). Note that section 8 appears on both maps.

1 Wagamama † (C-10)

2 Ivy, The (D-9)

3 J. Sheekey (D-9)

4 Nobu London (E-7)

5 Wolseley, The (D-8)

6 Gordon Ramsay/68 Royal (H-6)

7 Hakkasan (C-9)

8 Gordon Ramsay/Claridge's (D-7)

9 Le Gavroche (D-7)

10 Square, The (D-8)

11 Zuma (F-6)

12 Rules (D-10)

13 Yauatcha* (C-9)

14 Zafferano (F-6)

15 Pétrus (F-7)

16 L'Atelier de Joël Robuchon (D-9)

17 Le Caprice (E-8)

18 Gaucho Grill † (D-8)

19 Locanda Locatelli (C-6)

20 River Café (H-2)

21 Nobu Berkeley St (D-8)

22 Pizza Express † (H-6)

23 Busaba Eathai † (C-9)

24 Chez Bruce* (F-14)

25 maze (D-7)

26 Amaya (F-6)

27 Scott's* (D-7)

28 Tamarind (D-7)

29 Fat Duck (F-13)

30 Capital Rest. (F-6)

31 Asia de Cuba (D-10)

32 Wilton's (D-8)

33 St. John (B-12)

34 Ledbury, The (C-2)

35 Alain Ducasse (E-7)

36 Arbutus (C-9)

37 Cinnamon Club (F-9)

38 Royal China* † (D-3)

39 Boxwood Café (F-7)

40 Pied à Terre* (B-9)

---

* Indicates tie with above   † Indicates multiple branches

CORAM'S FIELD

Calthorpe St.
Phoenix Pl.
Grays
Gough St.
Coley St.
Farringdon
Pine St.
Northampton Rd.
Rosoman St.
Bowling Green
Sans Walk
Aylesbury St.
Goswell Rd.
Compton St.
Ashton
Woodbridge
John St.
Pear Tree
Dallington St.
Northburgh St.
Gt. Sutton St.
Berry
St.
Bastwi

Doughty St.
Mt. Pleasant
Topham
Rd.
Ray St.
Farringdon Ln.
Clerkenwell
Gt. Ormond St.
Rugby St.
Northington
Roger St.
John's Mews
Kings Mews
Clerkenwell
Rd.
Hatton Wall
Saffron Hill
Britton St.
St. John's St.
Rd.
Vic

Great Ormond St.
Orde Hall St.
Emerald St.
Gt. James St.
Raymond Bldgs
Clerkenwell
Portpool Ln.
Leather Ln.
St. Cross St.
Hatton Garden
FARRINGDON
Cowcross St.
33
Charterhouse
Smithfield Market
Cloth
BARBIC
Home

Boswell St.
New N. St.
Theobalds
Red Lion
Bedford Row
Jockey's Fields
Inn
Verulam St.
Baldwins Gdns.
Kirby
Farringdon
Smithfield
West
Hosier Ln.
Little Britain

Drake
Fisher St.
Catton St.
Procter St.
Eagle St.
Sandland St.
High
Holborn
CHANCERY LANE
Brooke
Holborn
Greville
Snow Hill
Holborn
Cock Ln.
Gittspur St.
St. Pa

HOLBORN
Whetstone Park
Furnival St.
St. Andrew St.
New Fetter
New St.
HOLBORN CIRCUS
Viaduct
Holborn Viaduct Station
Newgate St.
An
ST. PAUL

Kingsway
Queen
LINCOLN'S INN FIELDS
Portugal St.
Carey St.
Bell Yard
Bream's Bldgs.
Chancery
Fetter
La.
Little New St.
Shoe Ln.
St. Bride
Old Bailey
Farringdon
Warwick La.
St. Pa
Cathed
St. Paul's Chu.

Wild St.
Russell St.
Kemble St.
Kean St.
Aldwych
Strand
Surrey
St.
Arundel St.
Essex St.
Middle Temple La.
Milford St.
Mitre Ct.
Fleet
Whitefriars
Bouverie
Tudor
St.
St.
Temple Av.
Carmelite St.
John Carpenter St.
New Bridge St.
LUDGATE CIRCUS
Ludgate Hill
Blackfriars Ln.
Carter Ln.
Ludgate Hill
St. Paul's
Queen
Godliman St.
Vic
Baynard

Exeter
Lancaster Pl.
TEMPLE
Temple Pl.
Victoria
Embankment
INNER TEMPLE GDN.
BLACKFRIARS
Blackfriars Station
Castle
White Lion Hill
Baynard
Millennium Bridge

The Savoy (reopens May 2009)

Embankment
Cleopatra's Needle
Waterloo Bridge
Blackfriars Bridge

British Film Institute
Royal National Theatre
Upper
Ground
Broad Wall
Duchy St.
Rennie St.
Hopton St.
Holland St.
Tate Modern
Sumne
SOUT

Royal Festival Hall
SOUTH BANK
Waterloo
Rd.
Stamford
Aquinas St.
Theed St.
Whittlesey St.
Roupell St.
Hatfields
Paris Garden
Meymott St.
Blackfriars
Chancel St.
Bear
Southwark
St
Lavington St.
Great Suffolk St.
Ewer St.
St

Hungerford Bridge
ndon Eye
Belvedere
JUBILEE GDNS
Cornwall
Exton St.
Brad St.
Wootton St.
Joan
Gambia St.
SOUTHWARK
Union St.
Copperfie

York
Chicheley St.
Addington
St.
Leake St.
WATERLOO
Waterloo Station
The
Cut
Mitre Rd.
Ufford St.
Surrey Row
Pocock St.
Great Suffolk St.
Rushworth
Glasshill
Great
Suffolk

nster ge
Westminster Bridge Rd.
Lower Marsh
Frazier St.
Baylis
St.
Station Rd.
Webber St.
Rd.
Webber
Lancaster
Boyfield St.
King James
London
Borough
Rd.

Royal
St.
Centaur
Virgil
Hercules
Carlisle Ln.
Cosser St.
Kennington
Pearman St.
Morley St.
Dodson St.
Peabody Square
Garden Row
St.
Georges Rd.
Keyworth St.
Ontario St.
Rd.
ELEPHANT & CASTLE

Lambeth Palace Rd.
ARCHBISHOPS PARK
LAMBETH NORTH
Westminster
Bridge
Rd.
Lambeth
GERALDINE MARY HARMSWORTH PARK
Imperial War Museum
West
Sq.
Hayles
St.
Elliotts Row
Oswin St.
Elephant & Castle

Lambeth Rd.
Sail St.
Lambeth Walk
Rd.
Brook Dr.